A JEWISH FEMININE

MYSTIQUE?

A JEWISH FEMININE MYSTIQUE?

Jewish Women in Postwar America

EDITED BY
HASIA R. DINER,
SHIRA KOHN,
AND
RACHEL KRANSON

RUTGERS UNIVERSITY PRESS
New Brunswick, New Jersey, and London

Library of Congress Cataloging-in-Publication Data

A Jewish feminine mystique? : Jewish women in postwar America / edited by
Hasia R. Diner, Shira Kohn, and Rachel Kranson.

    p. cm.

  Includes bibliographical references and index.

  ISBN 978-0-8135-4791-6 (hardcover : alk. paper) — ISBN 978-0-8135-4792-3
(pbk. : alk. paper)

    1. Jewish women—United States—History—20th century. 2. Jewish women—United
States—Social conditions—20th century. 3. Jewish women—United States—Intellectual
life—20th century. 4. Feminism—United States—History—20th century.   I. Diner,
Hasia R. II. Kohn, Shira M. III. Kranson, Rachel.

  HQ1172.J49   2010

  305.48′8924073—dc22

                                         2009043155

A British Cataloging-in-Publication record for this book is available from the British Library.

Visit our Web site: http://rutgerspress.rutgers.edu

Manufactured in the United States of America

This book is dedicated to Frances Kohn, Lucille Kranson, Edith Mindlin, and the memory of Esther Schwartzman and Genya Zimmer, women who were young wives and mothers during the postwar years, and whose lives and accomplishments taught us to look beyond the stereotypes.

Contents

Acknowledgments

This volume resulted from our discovering a gaping hole in the scholarship of Jewish women, and our subsequent productive conversations about how to fill it. In the spring of 2005, the three of us came together for a course Hasia taught on Postwar American Jewry. Every week, we discussed and debated the existing literature in this subfield, which included studies on Jewish politics, migrations, religious practices, and consumer patterns. Yet, to our consternation, the syllabus included no work focusing on women and gender, because, as we learned, no such study existed! Rather than be discouraged by this glaring omission in American Jewish scholarship, with Hasia's encouragement we came to see the neglect of this important topic as an opportunity to create new knowledge and further the field.

Because the three of us felt strongly about the need for a study that focused on the lives of Jewish women in postwar America, we decided to send out a call to scholars, both established and emerging, to see if anyone else was thinking about this issue and had undertaken research on it. Happily, we found several individuals working on related topics, and the discussions that the three of us started in a graduate course quickly became a national conversation among practitioners of Jewish studies, women's studies, and American history.

We convened in February 2007 at New York University for a three-day conference which explored the diversity of Jewish women's experiences in the immediate postwar decades. The generous backing of New York University's Skirball Department of Hebrew and Judaic Studies, the Goldstein-Goren Center for American Jewish History, the History Department at New York University, and New York University's Graduate School of Arts and Sciences allowed us to put together the kind of gathering we envisioned. We particularly benefited from the warm support of Dean Catharine Stimpson of the New York University Graduate School of Arts and Sciences, and greatly appreciated her willingness to participate in the conference proceedings. Crucial support for this project also came from outside of New York University. Partnering with the Women's Studies Program at the Jewish Theological Seminary of America allowed us the pleasure of collaborating with Anne Lapidus Lerner and Shuly Rubin Schwartz, two devoted scholars of Jewish women's studies whose insights and advice guided every aspect of the event. The conference also provided us with the opportunity to work with Gail Reimer, Judith Rosenbaum, and Karla Goldman from the Jewish Women's Archive, who put together the creative programs, augmenting the scholarship and allowing the larger community to participate in our conversations. Susan Weidman Schneider and Melanie Weiss of *Lilith* magazine showed their enthusiasm for our project by providing extensive coverage of the conference in their Spring 2007 issue.

We also want to take this opportunity to thank all of the conference participants, from the many scholars who presented papers, to the chairs and commentators who initiated important discussions, and to the audience members who furthered these conversations with their comments and questions. All of their contributions are present in this volume, either directly or indirectly. Their insights convinced us that there was enough work available to make significant conclusions about the lives and choices of American Jewish women of the postwar era.

The warm feedback we received from our colleagues during the conference inspired us to continue our work in postwar Jewish women's history through the creation of an anthology. Transitioning from conference organizers to volume editors has been a wonderful, if at times frustrating, learning process. We know that none of this would have been possible without the tremendous support of several individuals, whom we are proud to acknowledge here. We wish to thank all of the contributors for allowing us to make editing suggestions and working with us so graciously and capably to incorporate them. We always appreciated the contributors' positive attitudes, particularly when we tried their patience and overburdened their already busy schedules with our incessant requests. We also want to thank Marion Kaplan, Joyce Antler, and the members of the History of Women and Gender Working Group at New York University for carefully reading over many of these articles and offering suggestions for improvement. We are appreciative, too, to Beth Kressel, Marlie Wasserman, Allyson Fields, Marilyn Campbell, and Paula Friedman from Rutgers University Press, both for recognizing the importance of this volume and for offering their insight along the way, making it a much better book. Susan Hoffman and Julie Tarshish from the Jewish Historical Society of the Upper Midwest also deserve our thanks for assisting with the striking image on the book cover.

We want to express our sincere gratitude to Shayne Leslie Figueroa, who began her involvement with this project by organizing every detail of the conference, from housing to dining choices. Although she probably wanted (and had every right) to run in the other direction, after the conference she graciously agreed to assist us in the creation of this volume, and helped us by printing out voluminous materials, managing the ever-accumulating pile of paperwork we created, and solving any and all technical issues that arose. She expertly managed these affairs with good nature and forbearance, and we cannot thank her enough for all of her assistance, expertise, and support throughout this process.

We are also pleased to mention those friends and family members who helped and inspired us as we worked on this project. Rachel would like to thank her mother, Annette Kranson, and her mother-in-law, Esther Forrest, who traveled to Brooklyn every week to watch her children and give her the time she needed to do her work; her thanks also go out to her two children, Sasha and Ezra, who have generously shared their mommy with this study of postwar Jewish women since the time they were born; and finally, Rachel thanks Jamie Forrest for his unflagging love, for always believing in her, and for supporting her in every possible way. Shira would like to thank her parents, Karen and William Kohn, for their belief in her potential and for always being just a phone call away; Shira also wishes to express her gratitude to and love for Michael Levy, her confidant and partner in crime, who encouraged her to take this project on and who always provided his support and love throughout. Hasia would like to thank, as always, Steve, Shira, Eli, Matan, and Eugene for supporting her in all her endeavors.

A JEWISH FEMININE
MYSTIQUE?

Introduction

HASIA R. DINER

SHIRA KOHN

RACHEL KRANSON

In her classic 1963 manifesto *The Feminine Mystique*, Betty Friedan railed against a postwar American culture in which women "no longer left their homes, except to shop, chauffeur their children, or attend a social engagement with their husbands."[1] Although she herself grew up in a Jewish home that exerted a powerful impact on her development as an intellectual and an activist, Freidan's portrait of domestic housewives collapsed the experiences of all American women living in this era, regardless of race, ethnicity, religion, or class, and presented the white, middle-class, Christian woman as the norm against which she issued her manifesto for change.[2]

Friedan's formulation has served as the departure point for most scholars of American women's history in the postwar period, scholars who have, by and large, taken her analysis of the "problem that has no name" as an accurate depiction of the ways in which all, or at least most, women experienced the years from the end of World War II through the 1950s and early 1960s.[3] Where scholars have parted company with Friedan and her analysis, they have done so by exposing the racial and class bias of this now firmly fixed way of thinking about American women of the 1950s. These historians have, rightly, noted that many working-class women did not have the luxury of enjoying, let alone hating, life in "comfortable concentration camps," and that women of color often grappled with a different set of gender expectations. Their need to work to support themselves and the families who depended upon them, as well as distinct cultural traditions of work and communal activism, gave them a chance to live, and to be studied, outside the scope of the "mystique."

This book broadens the parameters of the historical writing that takes to task the simple paradigm that in the postwar period American women retreated from the public sector into the private. We train our lens on American Jewish women, and ask how they negotiated postwar pressures to limit their lives to domestic and familial pursuits. Although Jews never constituted more than 4 to 5 percent of the general population, it should not detract from thinking about them as historical actors whose experiences in the postwar period can both shed light on the limitations of the feminine mystique and, at the same time, provide a richer and fuller history of American women in these years. Jewish women functioned within particular communities and distinctive institutions that made their post-war history different from the U.S. norm. We therefore ask, to what degree did the ideology of the feminine mystique apply to them? In what ways did their activities and aspirations conform to or deviate from the model that so dominates thinking about women in America in the years following the end of World War II?

At first blush, Jewish women would seem excellent candidates to embody the era's dominant theme of women living domestic suburban lives, dissociated from the world of work and wages. After all, most American Jewish women enjoyed the comforts of the middle class, and in numbers greater than non-Jews. Surveys from the period demonstrated that 75 to 96 percent of American Jewish men earned their living in nonmanual occupations, while only 38 percent of other American men were similarly employed.[4] The professionalism of Jewish men translated into higher earnings, as well. Even among Jews living in New York, the city in which the majority of working-class Jews resided, a 1951 study found that 12 percent of Jewish households earned yearly salaries of over $10,000, as compared to 5 percent of non-Jewish households, while only 29 percent of Jewish families brought in less than $4,000 a year, as opposed to 49 percent of non-Jews.[5] These numbers reveal the extent to which most Jews in the post-war period had attained middle-class status and show that few remnants of the Jewish working class remained. By and large, those who found themselves still in the ranks of economically marginal industrial laborers and petty shopkeepers represented the older members of the Jewish community, vestiges of the immigrant era.

With their increasing postwar salaries, young, middle-class Jews chose to invest in new housing opportunities that lay outside of their current urban surroundings. They participated enthusiastically, and often disproportionately, in the migration to the suburbs that Friedan had so harshly maligned. While the population of Newton, Massachusetts, a suburb of Boston, increased by 11 percent between 1946 and 1949, the Jewish population doubled in size. And when the overall population of Long Island's Nassau County increased by 220 percent between 1940 and 1960, the Jewish population increased by 1770 percent.[6]

As they moved to the suburbs and began to raise children, significant numbers of Jewish women abandoned the paid labor force. Surveys of the period showed Jewish women to be less likely than other American women to work for wages. Whereas 33.9 percent of American women participated in the labor force in 1950, regional studies of Jewish communities revealed a considerably lower employment rate for Jewish women. In the Pittsburgh area, for instance, 20.2 percent of Jewish women worked for wages in 1953. And in a 1955 survey of Lynn, Massachusetts, a city that, at the time, had attracted a particularly large population of young families, only 13.8 percent of Jewish women worked outside the home.[7] The middle-class salaries earned by Jewish men enabled Jewish families to rely on one income, as the work of wives did not represent the difference between economic survival and ruin.

Middle-class suburban women who did not work for wages have represented the archetypical victim, or exemplar, of the "mystique," and indeed Friedan had them squarely in mind as the subjects of her book. As such, Jewish women, with their significant representation among this group, might actually seem poor candidates by which to interrogate the salience of Friedan's analysis and the subsequent scholarship built on its foundation. Moreover, as members of an ethnic group that had only recently moved into the middle class and, as some have argued, into the privileged racial category of whiteness, Jewish women may have felt even more pressure than other white American women to conform to the dictates of postwar domestic ideals and assume the gender roles associated with their newly gained status.[8]

But as the essays in this volume uncover, Jewish women of the postwar years did not retreat obediently into their trim, suburban homes. They often complicated, and sometimes even rebelled against, the dominant models of middle-class femininity that threatened to circumscribe their lives. Through their roles as workers with or without pay, social justice activists, community builders, artists, and businesswomen, they took on responsibilities and engaged with issues reaching well beyond the confines of their private homes and nuclear families.

As American Jewish women negotiated the constraints of the postwar years, they looked to Jewish cultural traditions, political networks, and religious institutions for opportunities to transcend the boundaries of domesticity. Jewish communal ties and cultural symbols provided postwar women with a launching pad from which to make an impact on the world beyond their homes. Benefiting from their ethnic resources, American Jewish women partook of the period's possibilities and navigated its obstacles in distinctly Jewish ways.

American Jewish women also held certain demographic advantages that enabled them to participate effectively in the public sphere. Jewish women, for instance, attained particularly high levels of education. The postwar years witnessed an overall surge in women's college enrollment, with the number of female collegians increasing from 749,000 to over 2.2 million between 1945 and 1965.[9] At the same time, both male and female American Jews were more likely to attend university than were their non-Jewish peers. One 1953 study showed that that 1 in 6 American Jews graduated from college, whereas only 1 in 20 of the general population attained a bachelor's degree.[10] Benefiting both from American Jews' tendency to pursue a higher education and from the greater educational opportunities becoming available to American women, young Jewish women graduated from college at nearly double the already increased rate of the general female population.[11]

In addition to their significant levels of higher education, postwar Jewish women also tended to have fewer children than did other American women. According to the U.S. Census of 1957, children under the age of fourteen represented 27.7 percent of the Roman Catholic population, 26.7 percent of white Protestants, but only 22.2 percent of the American Jewish populace.[12] American Jewish women also held more positive views of contraception than did non-Jewish women, and embraced contraception as a means by which to limit their childbearing. In a 1958 study of female undergraduates, 85 percent of Jewish women said that they would consider the use of contraceptives, as opposed to only 58 percent of the Protestant, and 18 percent of the Catholic, participants.[13] Thus, as a cadre of women with a particularly high level of education and relatively few children to rear, many American Jewish women of the postwar years had both the time and the skills to pursue activities beyond the home.

Jewish women also drew upon the political commitments that had animated the urban, working-class environments in which they had spent their formative years, even as they moved into their new, middle-class communities. The particular history of the Jewish left and the Jewish labor movement provided crucial contexts for the activities that many Jewish women undertook during the 1950s and early 1960s. Although the combined influences of upward mobility and anti-communist agitation weakened Jewish involvement in the labor movement and radical causes during the years after World War II, the activist ethos and intellectual dynamism of the Jewish left had a fundamental influence on many postwar Jews and led to their leadership on a variety of liberal and sometimes even radical causes.[14] In fact, as Daniel Horowitz has shown in his biography of Betty Friedan, and as he elucidates further in the present volume, Friedan's involvement in the Jewish left exerted a crucial impact on her thinking and development as an activist in the women's movement.

The essays here explore the political and communal endeavors of postwar Jewish women, as well as the images they projected of themselves in the entertainment and business worlds. The broad range of these essays, which draw from a variety of scholarly approaches including social history, historical ethnography, literary analysis, and cultural studies, speak to the wide canvas upon which American Jewish women made their mark in the postwar years. The activities they engaged in, and the variety of sources they left behind, have provided rich fodder for works that draw from many methodological approaches and yet meet the rigorous standards demanded by historical scholarship.

The essays in this volume divide roughly into three main categories. The first group of articles focuses on the many Jewish women who worked as activists to ameliorate pressing societal problems. Not content to confine their passions and talents to the needs of their families, these women engaged with religious institutions, as well as with local, national, and transnational governments, to create change that they believed their country and the world needed. The second section takes as its subject Jewish women who immigrated to the United States in the postwar years, reminding us that not all of the nation's Jewish women inhabited the native-born, middle-class space that made the "feminine mystique" a possibility. The final cluster of articles deals with representations of Jewish women in American postwar culture. These pieces examine the ways in which well-known Jewish women created images that challenged the gender expectations of the postwar years, as well as ways in which everyday Jewish women understood and often defanged images that constricted their dreams and ambitions.

Our first section, on Jewish women activists, begins with a contribution from Raymond Mohl, whose essay shows how Jewish women who grew up in the politically charged, urban neighborhoods of the Northeast often brought the legacy of the Jewish left with them as they relocated to the suburbs or the Sunbelt. Mohl profiles three Miami-based Jewish activists, Matilda "Bobbi" Graff, Shirley Zoloth, and Thalia Stern, who worked tirelessly throughout the postwar period to end segregation in the schools, parent-teacher associations, and businesses of Miami, and, in spite of anticommunist interrogations, protested vigorously against the proliferation and testing of nuclear bombs. The history of these three activists, all of whom became mothers in the postwar years, shows that Jewish women did not always view the advent of motherhood as a mandate to retreat from public life. Rather, for Graff, Zoloth, and Stern— activists shaped as much by the Jewish left as by their position as postwar mothers—the desire to protect their own children from the threat of nuclear war and racial strife provided strong motivation to continue working on behalf of racial equality and peace.

Ironically, as Nancy Sinkoff's essay demonstrates, the Jewish left had a formative influence upon even those Jewish women who adopted far more conservative politics during the postwar years. Sinkoff's discussion of Lucy Dawidowicz uncovers the highly emotional and intellectual journey that led to the political conversion of this Jewish scholar and thinker. Like the male members of the "New York intellectuals," the well-known group of Jewish thinkers who espoused radical Marxism in the 1930s and then largely abandoned their radical principles by the 1950s, Dawidowicz vehemently renounced her former communism and emerged as an uncompromising cold warrior in the postwar years.[15] This change of heart hinged on her fear that the antireligious universalism of Soviet Russia would prove as lethal to Jewish culture as had the genocide perpetuated by the Nazis. Sinkoff's piece adds to our knowledge of the intellectual and political diversity of postwar Jewish women, revealing that not all worked on behalf of leftist or even liberal causes.

For the vast majority of politically active Jews in the postwar years, however, a liberal yet solidly anticommunist commitment to civil rights and civil liberties triumphed over both cold war conservatism and radical leftist attitudes.

The postwar history of Jewish women's organizations reminds us that American Jewish women worked not only as individuals but also collectively to promote this liberal vision of change. In fact, women tended to become involved in these liberal Jewish organizations in greater numbers than men. A 1957–1958 questionnaire distributed among the Jewish residents of a Chicago suburb found that eight out of ten women belonged to at least one Jewish organization that was not a synagogue, while only six out of ten men held similar affiliations.[16]

In this volume, Kathleen Laughlin's study of the National Council of Jewish Women demonstrates that the women in this organization served as leaders in the struggling liberal coalition against racial discrimination, McCarthyism, and other civil rights issues. These women worked in concert with the Jewish organizations run by men, as well as with left-leaning non-Jewish women's groups, and benefited from the resources of both of these powerful coalitions as they actively lobbied the federal government. Although the group did not speak out against the conservative gender ideals of the postwar period, Laughlin argues, the NCJW's effective involvement in national issues presented a de facto challenge to the gendered expectations of the postwar period.

The transnational involvements of American Jews also provided American Jewish women with the opportunity to reach not only beyond the boundaries of their homes, but also beyond America's borders. After World War II, American Jews provided desperately needed aid to the survivors of the European genocide, as well as to the nascent state of Israel that promised to be many survivors' refuge.[17] American Jewish women emerged as leaders in this global relief effort, and Rebecca Boim Wolf's study of Hadassah, the largest Zionist organization in postwar America, traces the two-pronged approach that characterized the group's work in the years after World War II: Hadassah combined its traditional emphasis on philanthropic projects in Israel with greater involvement in educational and antipoverty work in the United States. Positioning themselves as members of a Zionist organization that also engaged extensively in American issues, Hadassah leaders successfully attracted many American Jewish women in the postwar years. The members of Hadassah viewed their allegiance to the Jewish state as complementing, rather than contradicting, their loyalty to the United States. Hadassah's two-pronged approach, unique among U.S. Zionist organizations, allowed the group to retain a dynamic membership even while the constituency of other American Zionist organizations dwindled over the course of the 1950s.

In addition to their involvement in philanthropic and activist organizations, many Jewish women looked toward the religious sphere as a locus for their leadership. In fact, women sustained the many new suburban synagogues built in the postwar years, by acting as unpaid teachers, fundraisers, librarians, and curriculum developers, and they exhibited their commitment to their religious heritage by flocking to adult education programs.[18] Some of these women, emboldened perhaps by their newly acquired Jewish education and by their substantive synagogue involvement, sought change in their religious status as well. As Deborah Waxman's essay reveals, women in the Reconstructionist denomination of Judaism demanded, during the postwar years, the right to participate equally with men in synagogue ritual and practice. This struggle took place in the 1950s, preceding by two decades the advent of the Jewish feminist movement of the 1970s and the first ordination of female rabbis. Although these earlier activist women had no feminist vocabulary to rely upon as they made their demands, they developed a language to serve their purpose, that of changing millennia-old traditions. The women studied by Waxman, for the most part middle-class housewives and mothers, found the religious sphere to be an area where they felt empowered to challenge some of the limitations placed on them because of their gender, and they did so at a time when most non-Jewish venues resisted such innovations.

Our second section of articles focuses on those Jewish women who arrived in America as immigrants in the postwar years. Although most Jews in postwar America, descendents of the 2.5 million Jews who immigrated there between 1870 and 1924, had been born in the United States and enjoyed a comfortable middle-class lifestyle, the studies by Audrey Nasar and Rebecca Kobrin remind us that, in fact, America accepted hundreds of thousands of Jewish immigrants in the postwar years. As immigrants, these women and their families did not enjoy the economic security of those whose parents and grandparents had migrated decades earlier. The new migrants included Jews who survived the European Holocaust, who left Hungary after the 1956 revolution, who fled Cuba in the wake of Castro, and who found themselves unwelcome in many Middle Eastern nations after the emergence of the Jewish state in 1948. Nassar focuses on the struggles and accomplishments of Jewish women who had moved to the United States from Egypt, many of whom had enjoyed a privileged economic status in their native country. These women struggled to perform basic homemaking tasks in America, where they no longer found themselves able to afford outside help. Kobrin's piece concentrates on the plight of female Holocaust survivors who had been trained as doctors in Europe but found their careers stymied in an American climate that discouraged women from working as doctors. Instead of enabling them to reclaim the economic, professional, and social status they had enjoyed in Europe before the war, American norms limited their opportunities. These studies present the unique challenges faced by Jewish women who had not been born in America and who found it more difficult to take part in the economic growth of the postwar years.

The third cluster of essays centers around images of Jewish women in American popular culture, an element in the public sphere that Jewish women helped create during the postwar era. Many of these popular images drew upon the distinctive cultural resources of American Jews, and used them to challenge the expectations and constraints of the feminine mystique. Most American Jewish women of the postwar years had grown up in immigrant, working-class environments that supported a more aggressive and savvy notion of woman- hood than that advanced by middle-class postwar American culture. Giovanna Del Negro's study of Belle Barth, Pearl Williams, and Patsy Abbott profiles three comediennes who used this alternative vision of femininity to shocking, humor- ous effect. These self-proclaimed "bad girls" of Jewish comedy developed a comic style that explicitly addressed bodily functions like sex and excrement in an era that frowned upon women who talked about their bodies. These women spiked their bawdy material with Yiddish words, and folded in references to Jewish and working-class culture. Their comedy played out as a specific reaction to the pressure felt by many upwardly mobile Jews to conform to the gender norms and the social manners of the Protestant middle class.

Judith Smith focuses on Judy Holliday, another Jewish woman whose back- ground in the culture and politics of urban, working-class Jews profoundly shaped her experiences as an artist. Judy Holliday achieved national fame during the postwar years for her portrayal of smart, competent, working-class women in hit films and Broadway plays. Coming from a Jewish immigrant family with strong ties to the labor movement, Holliday began her acting career in collabo- ration with other radical Jewish artists, all of whom tried to use their talents to create social change. Although she depicted rebellious, independent, and intelli- gent women who challenged the social and political status quo, her real-life struggle to combat investigations into her leftist past limited her ability to take on such roles and silenced her personal political voice.

Like these other public figures, Jennie Grossinger used the resources at her disposal as a woman, a mother, and a Jewish immigrant to challenge the bound- aries of the feminine mystique. Hotelier Jennie Grossinger, as Rachel Kranson's essay reveals, became a national celebrity by playing into postwar gender ideals and promoting her own image as a nurturing, maternal figure. Ironically, it was this convincing portrayal of a Jewish mother that transformed her into a wildly successful entrepreneur. At the height of her fame, Grossinger emerged as a kindly, motherly symbol of Jewish upward mobility, domesticating the image of Jewish success in America.

Jewish women not only created images in the popular culture, but they also responded, often in unexpected ways, to the ways that others portrayed them. In his 1955 novel, *Marjorie Morningstar*, Herman Wouk told the story of a young Jewish woman who yearned to pursue a bohemian life in the theater, rebelling against her family's expectations that she marry a young and upwardly mobile Jewish man. Wouk did not allow his heroine's artistic aspirations to triumph, and, by the end of the novel, she had married a lawyer and conformed quite totally to a life of middle-class respectability. Barbara Sicherman's essay shows that real-life Jewish women did not necessarily understand the moral of the novel in the way that Wouk intended. Instead, these readers appreciated the book as a story of sexual and artistic possibility rather than as a cautionary tale.

The surprising autonomy, activism, and leadership of American Jewish women during the age of the feminine mystique had a crucial impact not only on the history of the postwar era but also on the decades that followed. Joyce Antler and Daniel Horowitz have offered two broad essays which explore how the experiences of postwar Jewish women functioned as a harbinger for future developments. Daniel Horowitz, Betty Friedan's biographer, again uses Friedan's life as a starting point from which to comment on the impact of her Jewish background on her activist choices, and to interrogate the radical separation that scholars of Jewish women's history have often wedged between the general and Jewish feminist movements. Joyce Antler's study of four pioneering Jewish activists in the women's liberation movement explores how the seeds of their feminist activism, which flowered in the late 1960s and beyond, grew out of the soil of their postwar, prefeminist upbringing in a Jewish milieu. The essays by Horowitz and Antler represent groundbreaking attempts to systematically analyze the disproportionate involvement of Jewish women in the second wave of the feminist movement, a phenomenon which both authors convincingly argue must be traced back to the postwar years.

Taken together, these essays challenge the standard histories of postwar women that neglected discussions of Jewish difference, as well as studies of postwar American Jews that ignored gender and its effects. Scholars like William Chafe and Eugenia Kaledin first interrogated Friedan's analysis by pointing out the surprising extent of women's postwar economic and political involvement; they demonstrated that women possessed a significant degree of agency when weighing occupational or familial choices.[19] Yet neither of these studies identified Jewish women as distinct participants in these processes. Joanne Meyerowitz built upon these earlier studies in her groundbreaking volume *Not June Cleaver*, which provided nuance to Chafe's and Kaledin's work by probing the ways that class and race informed how American women responded to the supposed gendered confines of the postwar environment.[20] The articles in Meyerowitz's volume underscored the importance of distinguishing between different groups of women, but the studies that mentioned individual Jewish women did not take their Jewish backgrounds into consideration. Thus, although Jewish women figure prominently in academic studies of the postwar period, scholars have seldom analyzed the influence of their distinct background.

Similarly, in Jewish studies, scholars have overlooked the importance of gender when assessing the experiences of American Jews during the postwar years. A cluster of political histories by scholars such as Mark Dollinger, Michael Staub, and Stuart Svonkin discussed the liberal consensus adopted by Jewish organizations in the 1950s and early 1960s, but failed to take into account the ways that Jewish women's organizations such as Hadassah and the National

Council of Jewish Women contributed to communal politics, and how the strategies and positions adopted by these organizations differed from those run by
Jewish men.[21] Studies of Jewish social life in the postwar years have concentrated
on Jewish adaptation to middle-class lifestyles, but have only marginally considered the ways in which gender provided differing possibilities for Jewish men and
for Jewish women.[22] In fact, until the publication of the present volume, the vast
majority of scholarship about Jewish women in the postwar years has concentrated primarily on the 1950s stereotype of the "Jewish Mother" and the impact of
this archetype on the lives of Jewish women.[23] Although this book builds on this
earlier material, it moves beyond a discussion of stereotypes, and focuses instead
on the active choices and self-definitions forged by American Jewish women in
the postwar years. As a result, it offers the first comprehensive study of Jewish
women as actors and agents in the American postwar world.

A Jewish Feminine Mystique? serves as a corrective to crucial gaps in the current
literature and offers scholarship that should open dialogues between practitioners of American history, women's history, and Jewish history through shedding
new light on the many ways in which American women resisted the constraints
of the feminine mystique. The book reveals how American Jewish women
upheld their longstanding activist commitments as they moved into a middle-
class milieu, and used their newfound historical, communal, religious, and cultural background to navigate, and even at times to overcome, the challenges of
postwar America.

ACKNOWLEDGMENTS
We wish to thank Marion Kaplan and the participants of HOWAG, the History of Women
and Gender research group at New York University, who offered us constructive feedback
on earlier drafts of this introduction.

NOTES
1. Betty Friedan, *The Feminine Mystique* (New York: Norton, 1963), 17.

2. On the impact of Friedan's Jewishness, see Kirsten Fermaglich, *American Dreams and
Nazi Nightmares, 1957–1965* (Hanover, NH: University Press of New England, 2006), chap. 2;
Daniel Horowitz, *Betty Friedan and the Making of the Feminine Mystique: The American Left, the
Cold War, and Modern Feminism* (Amherst: University of Massachusetts Press, 1998); and, in
this volume, Daniel Horowitz, "Jewish Women Remaking American Feminism/Women
Remaking American Judaism: Reflections on the Life of Betty Friedan."

3. Elaine Tyler May, *Homeward Bound: American Families in the Cold War Era* (New York:
Basic Books, 1988); Wini Breines, *Young, White, and Miserable: Growing Up Female in the Fifties*
(Boston: Beacon Press, 1992); Benita Eisler, *Private Lives: Men and Women of the 1950s* (New
York: Franklin Watts, 1986); Carol A. B. Warren, *Madwives: Schizophrenic Women in the 1950s*
(New Brunswick, NJ: Rutgers University Press, 1987); Myra Dinnerstein, *Women between Two
Worlds: Midlife Reflections on Work and Family* (Philadelphia: Temple University Press, 1992);
Brett Harvey, *The Fifties: A Women's Oral History* (New York: HarperCollins, 1993).

4. *American Jewish Yearbook* 56 (1955): 26–27, cited in Hasia Diner, *The Jews of the United
States* (Berkeley and Los Angeles: University of California Press, 2004), 285.

5. Nathan Glazer, "The Attainment of Middle-Class Rank," in *The Jews: Social Problems of an American Group*, ed. Marshall Sklare (New York: Free Press, 1951), 141.

6. On Newton, see Albert I. Gordon, Jews in Suburbia (Boston: Beacon Press, 1959), 23, 27. On Nassau County, see Aleisa R. Fishman, "Keeping Up with the Goldbergs: Gender, Consumer Culture, and Jewish Identity in Suburban Nassau County," unpublished dissertation (UMI Dissertation Services no. 3127795, American University, 2004), 27.

7. On occupational patterns of Jewish women, see "Socio-Economic Data: Jewish Population in the United States, 1956," *American Jewish Yearbook* 58 (1957): 70–71; for general occupational patterns of American women, see U.S. Bureau of Labor Statistics, "Changes in Women's Labor Force Participation in the Twentieth Century," http://www.bls.gov/opub/ted/2000/feb/wk3/art03.htm, accessed February 7, 2009.

8. For studies on Jews and whiteness, see Karen Brodkin, *How Jews Became White Folks and What That Says about Race in America* (New Brunswick, NJ: Rutgers University Press, 1998); Matthew Frye Jacobson, *Whiteness of a Different Color: European Immigrants and the Alchemy of Race* (Cambridge, MA: Harvard University Press, 1998), particularly chap. 5; Eric Goldstein, *The Price of Whiteness: Jews, Race, and American Identity* (Princeton, NJ: Princeton University Press, 2006).

9. As cited in table 2.1 in Linda Eisenmann, *Higher Education for Women in Postwar America, 1945–1965* (Baltimore: Johns Hopkins University Press, 2006), 45. Original statistics taken from National Center for Education Statistics, *120 Years of American Education: A Statistical Portrait* (Washington, DC: Office of Education Research and Improvement, 1993). For more on female Jewish collegians, see Diana Turk, "College Students," in *Jewish Women in America: An Historical Encyclopedia*, ed. Paula Hyman and Deborah Dash Moore (New York: Rutledge, 1997), 263.

10. *American Jewish Yearbook* 56 (1955): 26–27, cited in Hasia Diner, *The Jews of the United States*, 285.

11. Erich Rosenthal, "Jewish Fertility in the United States," *American Jewish Yearbook* 62 (1961): 17, table 11. Other regional studies bolster Rosenthal's findings. Sidney Goldstein and Calvin Goldscheider's 1962 study of Jews in the Providence, RI, area found that Jewish men completed only .03 more years of education than did Jewish women: *Jewish Americans: Three Generations in a Jewish Community* (Englewood Cliffs, NJ: Prentice-Hall, 1968), 69, as cited in Riv-Ellen Prell, *Fighting to Become Americans: Assimilation and the Trouble between Jewish Women and Jewish Men* (Boston: Beacon Press, 1999), 173. Similarly, Marshall Sklare's study of Jews in suburban Chicago, based on information taken in 1957–1958, found that 82 percent of Sklare's Jewish female respondents had at that time completed at least some college, as opposed to 89 percent of Jewish men; see Marshall Sklare and Joseph Greenbaum, *Jewish Identity on the Suburban Frontier* (New York: Basic Books, 1967), 27. For the prewar period, Ruth Markowitz has detailed the gendered dimensions of Jewish college attendance, in Ruth Jacknow Markowitz, *My Daughter, the Teacher: Jewish Teachers in the New York City Public Schools* (New Brunswick, NJ: Rutgers University Press, 1993), 18–21.

12. Erich Rosenthal, "Jewish Fertility in the United States": 4.

13. Victor A. Christopherson and James Walters, "Responses of Protestants, Catholics, and Jews Concerning Marriage and Family Life," *Sociology and Social Research* (September–October 1958): 21, cited in Erich Rosenthal, "Jewish Fertility in the United States": 24.

14. On the Jewish left and Jewish involvement in labor movements, see Tony Michels, *A Fire in Their Hearts: Yiddish Socialists in New York* (Cambridge, MA: Harvard University Press, 2005); Gerald Sorin, *The Prophetic Minority: American Jewish Immigrant Radicals, 1880–1920* (Bloomington: Indiana University Press, 1985); Melech Epstein, *Jewish Labor in the U.S.A., 1882–1952* (Jerusalem: KTAV Publishing House, 1969); Hadassa Kossak, *Cultures of Opposition: Jewish Immigrant Workers, New York City, 1881–1905* (Albany: State University of New York

Press, 2000). For the specific involvement of Jewish women, see Annelise Orleck, *Common Sense and a Little Fire: Women and Working-Class Politics in the United States, 1900–1965* (Chapel Hill: University of North Carolina Press, 1995); Susan Glenn, *Daughters of the Shtetl: Life and Labor in the Immigrant Generation* (Ithaca, NY: Cornell University Press, 1990); Alice Kessler-Harris, "Organizing the Unorganizable: Three Jewish Women and Their Union," *Labor History* 17 (Winter 1976): 5–23.

15. On the New York Intellectuals, see Alexander Bloom, *Prodigal Sons: The New York Intellectuals and Their World* (New York: Oxford University Press, 1986).

16. Marshall Sklare, *Jewish Identity on the Suburban Frontier*, 255–256. Sklare's study was based on interviews conducted in 1957 and 1958.

17. Studies of Jewish philanthropy include Yehuda Bauer, *My Brother's Keeper: A History of the American Jewish Joint Distribution Committee* (Philadelphia: Jewish Publication Society of America, 1974); Abraham J. Karp, *To Give Life: the UJA in the Shaping of the American Jewish Community* (New York: Schocken Books, 1981); Marc Lee Raphael, *A History of the United Jewish Appeal* (Chicago: Scholar's Press, 1982). Also see Hasia Diner, *The Jews of the United States*, 219–220, 323; Edward Shapiro, *A Time for Healing: American Jewry since World War II*, Jewish People in America 5 (Baltimore: Johns Hopkins University Press, 1992), 62–63.

18. Diner, *The Jews of the United States*, 301–303.

19. William Chafe, *The American Woman: Her Changing Social, Economic, and Political Roles, 1920–1970* (New York: Oxford University Press, 1972), chap. 20; Eugenia Kaledin, *Mothers and More: American Women in the 1950s* (Boston: Twayne, 1984).

20. Joanne Meyerowitz, *Not June Cleaver: Women and Gender in Postwar America, 1945–1960* (Philadelphia: Temple University Press, 1994). Other studies have concentrated on politically progressive, radical, and feminist women active during the postwar period; these studies include Susan Lynn's *Progressive Women in Conservative Times: Racial Justice, Peace, and Feminism, 1945 to the 1960s* (New Brunswick, NJ: Rutgers University Press, 1992); Sylvie Murray, *The Progressive Housewife: Community Activism in Suburban Queens* (Philadelphia: University of Pennsylvania Press, 2003); Leila Rupp, *Survival in the Doldrums: The American Woman's Rights Movement, 1945 to the 1960s* (New York: Oxford University Press, 1987); Amy Swerdlow, *Women Strike for Peace: Traditional Motherhood and Radical Politics in the 1960s* (Chicago: University of Chicago Press, 1993); Kate Weigand, *Red Feminism: American Communism and the Making of Women's Liberation* (Baltimore: Johns Hopkins University Press, 2001).

21. Marc Dollinger, *Quest for Inclusion: Jews and Liberalism in Modern America* (Princeton, NJ: Princeton University Press, 2000); Stuart Svonkin, *Jews against Prejudice: American Jews and the Fight for Civil Liberties* (New York: Columbia University Press, 1999); Michael Staub, *Torn at the Roots: The Crisis of Jewish Liberalism in Postwar America* (New York: Columbia University Press, 2004).

22. Eitan Diamond, *I Will Dwell in Their Midst: Orthodox Jews in Suburbia* (Chapel Hill: University of North Carolina Press, 2000); Deborah Dash Moore, *To the Golden Cities: Pursuing the American Jewish Dream in Miami and Los Angeles* (Cambridge, MA: Harvard University Press, 1996).

23. Studies that focus primarily on the Jewish mother stereotype include Paula Hyman, Charlotte Baum, and Sonya Michel, *The Jewish Woman in America* (New York: The Dial Press, 1976), 235–261; Joyce Antler, *You Never Call! You Never Write! A History of the Jewish Mother* (Oxford: Oxford University Press, 2008); Joyce Antler, *The Journey Home: How Jewish Women Shaped Modern America* (New York: Schocken Books, 1997), 233–255; Riv-Ellen Prell, *Fighting to Become Americans*, 142–176.

1

"Some of Us Were There before Betty"

JEWISH WOMEN AND POLITICAL
ACTIVISM IN POSTWAR MIAMI

RAYMOND A. MOHL

In the early 1960s, Betty Friedan's *The Feminine Mystique* argued that postwar American culture promoted a repressive form of domesticity that trapped middle-class women in the home, subordinated them to the demands of marriage and family, and denied them the opportunity for personal or career fulfillment. Friedan articulated the unspoken concerns of millions of American women, who endured what she called "the problem that had no name." The book has been credited with initiating the modern feminist movement. Recent historical scholarship, however, has suggested that Freidan overstated her case and that not all American women experienced the postwar era domesticity trap. The women depicted in 1950s television programs or portrayed in popular magazine fiction only partially reflected reality. Working-class women and women of color, by necessity, had always worked outside the home. Similarly, large numbers of college educated, middle-class women built professional careers as teachers, nurses, social workers, union leaders, politicians, and business persons. Among those who may not have worked for wages outside the home yet did not languish in domesticity were those who became local political activists, working for peace, civil rights, and social justice.[1]

The narratives of three Jewish women who never felt trapped by the "feminine mystique," but pursued multiple roles as wives and mothers and as relentless activists for social and political change in postwar Miami, Florida, offer a way to explore the experiences of this last category. These women's activist careers in the postwar era reflect the fact that Jews participated actively in reshaping metropolitan Miami's political and cultural landscape in the years after 1945.

In the midst of cold war tensions and McCarthyite political turmoil, Miami's Jewish activists, especially Jewish women activists, became deeply engaged in an emerging civil rights movement and in building a local peace campaign. Working with local and national civil rights organizations, they challenged racially segregated schools, Jim Crow public accommodations, and the exclusionary political practices typical of most southern cities and states. They also provided the leadership and energy for a peace movement that rejected nuclear testing, promoted nonviolence and mutual disarmament, and opposed American militarism abroad. Mostly recent migrants from northern cities, and reflecting the wide spectrum of the American political left, politically progressive Jews, men and women, changed postwar Miami.

Jewish men and women did not, however, participate in the city's postwar challenges in the same ways. For Miami's Jewish women activists, an important sense of maternalism provided an additional stimulus to movement work. Scholars have debated the use of the term *maternalism*, but it is employed here to identify the motivations of social activists driven not only by ideals of social justice but also by a desire to protect their own children from the effects of anti-Semitism, racism, and cold war militarism. In seeking to change Miami and the larger national political culture, these Jewish activists hoped as well to make a better, safer world for their children and families.[2]

Postwar Miami

Miami in the early postwar period seemed an unlikely place to sprout energetic movements for peace, civil rights, and social justice. In 1950, Miami emerged as the top tourist destination in the nation. It also functioned, in regard to race relations, as a very southern place, deeply segregated in all aspects of life. Jobs, housing, schooling, recreation, transportation, restaurants, and theaters all remained completely segregated, even as late as 1960. The segregated water fountains and rest rooms common to Mississippi and Alabama could also be found in downtown Miami, much to the shock of newcomers and tourists from northern climes.

Anti-Semitism also ran deep in the local culture, and Jews experienced exclusion from many Miami area hotels, country clubs, and neighborhoods. Miami's Ku Klux Klan roared back to life after maintaining a low profile during World War II, targeting blacks and Jews and promoting racial hatred and religious bigotry. The Klan used intimidation and harassment, as well as bombs and arson, to maintain white political power and housing segregation. After the 1954 U.S. Supreme Court decision on school integration, Miami's White Citizens Council, a new organization not unlike the Klan but without robes and masks, resisted school desegregation and generally stirred racial hatred and anti-Semitism. In 1951 and again in 1958, in response to perceived Jewish support for civil rights and school integration, segregationists bombed Miami synagogues and Jewish schools. In the early postwar years, Miami's national tourist image competed with its Deep South reality.[3]

Moreover, the cold war and the politics of anticommunism reverberated locally. Beginning in the late 1940s, the Miami newspapers, primarily the *Miami Daily News*, launched a campaign linking local political activists with domestic subversion. During these years, the U.S. House Un-American Activities Committee (HUAC) and the U.S. Senate Subcommittee on Internal Security both held widely publicized hearings in Miami, searching for evidence of communist infiltration of local institutions. In the mid-1950s, the state of Florida established its own little HUAC, the Florida Legislative Investigation Committee, which focused especially on black and white civil rights activists in Miami. In 1954, pursuing a parallel track, local district attorney George Brautigam embarked on a crusade against Miami's left-wing activists. Labeled "Miami's Little McCarthy" by the left-wing press, Brautigam subpoenaed dozens of Miamians, all but three of them Jewish, mostly activists fighting segregation and militarism. Denounced as "reds," harassed by the FBI, and pilloried in the local press, several dozen activists spent time in jail for contempt after refusing to reveal their political beliefs and associations, while others sought refuge in Canada or Mexico. The political climate fostered in Miami during this period merged anticommunism, anti-Semitism, and white supremacy. This brew created a distinctive atmosphere that made the work of Jewish civil rights and peace activists particularly difficult and dangerous.[4]

Reactionaries and segregationists dominated Miami's political culture in early postwar years, but the city also experienced dramatic changes. Millions of dollars of federal military spending and infrastructure development during World War II set the stage for a postwar economic boom in Miami. The revival of tourism and real estate development led the way, supported by air travel and air conditioning. Home air-conditioning units, monthly social security checks, and an expanding economy attracted retirees and new residents, who poured into south Florida's mushrooming condominiums and subdivisions in unprecedented numbers. Metropolitan Miami's population grew by an astonishing 250 percent between 1940 and 1960—rising from 267,000 to more than 935,000. Massive migration provided the great bulk of the population increase, especially working-class Jews and Italians from New York and other northern cities. Metropolitan Miami had 8,000 Jews in 1940 but about 140,000 in 1960 and 230,000 by 1970. These demographic changes bore important implications for progressive social movements in the city.[5]

Over time, the Jewish migration made Miami more liberal, less southern, and, eventually, more open to racial change. Blacks had been struggling for civil rights in south Florida since the early twentieth century, but few white people had been involved in any of those activities.[6] Migration from the north brought white people, primarily Jews, into the local civil rights movement for the first time. It also provided the base for an emerging peace movement, initially focused on disarmament and defusing cold war tensions, as well as on opposition to the Korean War and atomic testing.

In particular, three Jewish women—Matilda "Bobbi" Graff, Shirley Zoloth, and Thalia Stern—supplied energy and direction for Miami's civil rights and peace movements. Themselves part of the postwar migration to Miami, these Jewish activists shared a distinct perspective on their world and community, one that advanced social justice and racial equality as valuable human aspirations. Motherhood, among other factors, motivated these women, as they sought to protect their children from racism, violence, war, and atomic weapons. Hundreds of Miami's Jewish women became activists for these causes; Graff, Zoloth, and Stern simply exemplified the commitment of a larger community of women who shared progressive goals in a postwar age shaped by tension and danger.

Matilda "Bobbi" Graff

Bobbi Graff and her husband Emanuel joined the early postwar migration to Miami in 1946. Originally from the Brownsville section of Brooklyn, they had moved to Detroit in 1941, after their marriage. Both came from left-wing, immigrant Jewish families active in socialist, Zionist, and trade union circles. Bobbi's socialist training began early, in an after-school Yiddish program in Brownsville. As a high school student in Brooklyn in the mid-1930s, she took a leading role in the left-wing American Student Union and in her school's peace council. In Detroit, Emanuel worked in a General Motors auto plant producing engines for the war effort, while Bobbi worked as a secretary. Maintaining their political activism, the Graffs joined the Young Progressives, the Michigan Civil Rights Congress, and other left-wing groups. By 1942 the FBI began tracking their associations and political activities.[7]

Because of their child's health problems, the Graffs moved after World War II to Miami, where Bobbi's parents had already settled in retirement. Soon the Graffs acquired an interracial circle of friends, primarily left-wing Jews and blacks, most of whom participated in some form of activism—progressive politics, civil liberties, civil rights, world peace, or labor organizing. They joined a vibrant political left that had already emerged among Jews in postwar Miami and Miami Beach and that reflected a large Jewish migration that had included socialists, communists, and assorted left-wingers as well as mainstream liberals. Miami's Jewish radicals, including the Graffs, gathered at the secular Jewish Cultural Center on Miami Beach for concerts, lectures, political discussion groups, Yiddish language and literature classes, and other activities, all heavily political. By 1948, as the cold war political climate heated up, left-wing programs at the Jewish Cultural Center came under attack in the Miami press. By that time, the Graffs had joined the Communist Party.[8]

Over the next several years, Bobbi Graff emerged as an organizer and leading activist of the Miami left. As she had during her years in Michigan, Graff pursued parallel avenues for peace and civil rights, one with the Florida Progressive Party (FPP) and another with the Miami branch of the Civil Rights Congress (CRC). In 1948, when Henry A. Wallace's campaign for the presidency energized the American left, Miami's Jewish activists gravitated to the Progressive Party, abandoning President Harry Truman and rejecting the Democratic Party's moderate stand on civil rights and its hard line on the cold war and domestic communism.

Headed by Pensacola civil liberties attorney John M. Coe, the FPP held positions that strongly attracted Graff, who had worked with the Progressives in Michigan and became an enthusiastic campaigner for Wallace in Florida. With another FPP activist, Gail Gropper, Graff spoke to black and white church groups, held interracial political meetings, organized leftist students at the University of Miami, passed out leaflets on downtown Miami streets, canvassed voters, and organized political rallies, including one event that brought out twelve thousand people for a Wallace speech in Miami's Bayfront Park. Graff and her colleagues emphasized Wallace's support for African American rights, his advocacy of world peace, and his rejection of cold war militarism. Florida Progressives hoped to appeal to black voters, and they took strong positions on antilynching, anti–poll tax, and anti-Klan legislation, issues that the Democratic Party avoided. Bobbi Graff never held an official position within the FPP, but she played a central role in the party's political work, as did her husband. Emanuel Graff, at this time a house painter and union activist, sought to integrate the building trades unions in Miami, as part of the FPP appeal to black voters. Wallace lost decisively, but Miami's Progressives persisted into the 1950s, pushing for housing reform in black Miami, publishing a newspaper, and running a few candidates, unsuccessfully, for local office in Miami and Miami Beach. The FPP's stand on racial justice posed a challenge to segregation and white power in Miami, and its leftist political stance led to charges of communism, to police harassment, and to Klan threats. For Graff, the Progressive campaign demonstrated the hard realities facing the political left in a southern state dominated by segregationist and anticommunist ideologies.[9]

In the aftermath of the Wallace defeat, Graff took a more active role in the Civil Rights Congress (CRC), a group she had worked with in Michigan. Organized in Detroit in 1946 and labeled a communist front group by the U.S. Department of Justice, the CRC selected as its national leader William L. Patterson, a black labor lawyer and one of the nation's top communists. Committed to racial justice and civil liberties, the CRC advocated "mass action" such as public rallies and picketing to draw attention to a cause, combined with legal action in defense of civil liberties. Radicals at the Jewish Cultural Center in Miami Beach established the Miami CRC in 1948 after an early civil liberties battle that centered around the visit to Miami of Elizabeth Gurley Flynn, another American communist leader. When the conservative Miami press attacked Flynn and the Jewish Cultural Center, Miami's left-wing Jews mobilized politically.[10]

As the FPP gradually faded away in the early 1950s, Miami radicals increasingly focused on the CRC as an instrument for change. Graff became the unofficial coordinator of the Miami CRC in 1949, following the basic strategy outlined by William Patterson, a strategy including mass action, public rallies, picketing, public exposure to draw attention to a cause, and subsequent legal action. Miami CRC pursued these methods in exposing police brutality, in organizing black and white airline and airport workers, and in building alliances with local black churches. Through leafleting, public rallies, and newspaper articles, Graff and the CRC publicized the racial injustice of the Groveland case in central Florida, a case in which a white woman's false accusation of four young black men of rape was followed by a white vigilante attack on the rural black community of Groveland. The CRC also took on the Ku Klux Klan, lobbying Florida governor Fuller Warren and holding interracial rallies condemning Klan violence. Graff even proposed that Miami CRC picket the Klan's office in Orlando, although that demonstration never took place. By midcentury, Miami CRC had become the Klan's most vigorous and outspoken opponent in Florida.[11]

But the early postwar period did not prove a good time for a political leftist, a Jewish communist leftist at that, to be challenging the anticommunist orthodoxy or advocating racial change in Deep South Miami. The FBI investigated Graff and her colleagues in Miami CRC, followed them, and bugged their telephones. The Miami police harassed them by breaking up interracial gatherings and pushing them around during downtown leafleting. The Klan threatened them, and the local newspapers attacked them. Under these multiple pressures, Miami CRC officially disbanded in the early 1950s. Graff then joined the Miami NAACP, where she worked on voter registration campaigns and other issues, such as integrating the local parent-teacher association.[12]

The PTA provided a particularly fitting place for Graff to engage in political work. Throughout her decade in Miami, as she would write in her memoir, her political activism for peace, civil rights, and civil liberties was motivated by "dreams for a beautiful world in which our children could grow up unafraid of the future." As she looked back on her involvement with the Wallace campaign and the period as a whole, Bobbi recalled, "We believed we owed it to our children and to our country to work for a better America." Her passion and her dream turned to nightmare, however, in 1954. District attorney Brautigam, in the course of his witch hunt of that year, served a subpoena on Graff and her husband, ordering them to testify about their political beliefs and activities. Bobbi received hers while lying in a hospital bed after delivering her third child. Terrified by these scare tactics, she fled to Canada by train with her children, eventually returning to Detroit. Emanuel spent several weeks in jail before the Florida Supreme Court ordered him and other CRC detainees freed. Other CRC radicals went into exile in Mexico, some staying for decades. Miami's hostile racial politics and anticommunist fervor cut short the CRC's early civil rights challenge to racial segregation.[13]

Graff left the Communist Party in the late 1950s, but she never gave up her political activism. She worked with numerous peace and civil rights organizations, including the Congress of Racial Equality, the National Committee for a Sane Nuclear Policy, Women Strike for Peace, and many others, in the late 1950s and in the 1960s. She also earned two degrees from Wayne State University, built a career as an administrator at the Wayne State Medical School, and in 1990 retired back to Florida. Needless to say, she is still, as of this writing, actively promoting peace, racial justice, and environmental reform.[14]

Shirley Zoloth

In 1954, around the time the Graffs were being driven out of Miami, Shirley and Milton Zoloth arrived in the city from Philadelphia. Milton came from a socialist labor background and had joined the Young People's Socialist League. A photograph of Karl Marx hung on the wall of his parents' home. Shirley's parents were more liberal than radical, members of mainstream Jewish groups such as the American Jewish Congress. Shirley moved to the left of her parents, joining the Women's International League for Peace and Freedom (WILPF) in Philadelphia and becoming active in other left-liberal groups. At the same time, she participated actively in the work of Hadassah, the Women's Zionist Organization of America. Like the Graffs, Shirley and Milton worked in Henry Wallace's Progressive Party presidential campaign in 1948. They supported civil rights causes and participated in interracial activities. They had been outraged by a 1953 HUAC hearing in Philadelphia and a subsequent anticommunist investigation of that city's school system, which had led to the firing of several dozen teachers, most Jewish. Shirley's parents had already migrated to Miami, and the Zoloths followed. There, although trained at Drexel University as an electrical engineer, Milton went to work in the real estate firm established by Shirley's father.[15]

Within a week of moving to Miami in September 1954, Shirley Zoloth connected with progressives in the WILPF and plunged into the local activist arena. Miami WILPF had many Jewish members, including Bobbi Graff's sister and mother, Mildred Kaminsky and Fannie Soller, and others previously involved in the Progressive Party and Miami CRC. The FBI had already infiltrated Miami WILPF, investigating some of its members; the Brautigam grand jury subpoenaed a few others. In the early 1950s, Miami WILPF focused primarily on peace issues, supporting the United Nations, promoting world disarmament, and opposing participation in the Korean War. Reacting to the still recent U.S. Supreme Court decision in the *Brown* case, Miami WILPF also began pushing into the area of civil rights and school desegregation. In interviews, the Zoloths recalled their deep concern about the Jim Crow racial practices they encountered in Miami; they expressed special outrage over the fact that the Dade County school board did nothing to implement the *Brown* decision. Shirley Zoloth took up this cause, through the WILPF and in other forums. Within three years of her arrival in Miami, she had become WILPF's vice president, attending school board meetings, publicly challenging what she termed the board's delaying tactics, and engaging in community relations work to achieve peaceful school integration.[16]

Zoloth's activist energy took a new turn in 1958, when she helped in the reelection campaign of Miami state legislator John B. "Jack" Orr. White, Protestant, and from a well-known Miami family, Orr's father had been mayor of Miami in the early 1940s. A trial lawyer, the younger Orr believed strongly in civil liberties. During the early 1950s, he had defended black clients in racial justice cases and provided legal representation for Miami CRC, Miami WILPF, and Jewish activists jailed in the Brautigam investigation. Risking his reputation and career, he had challenged Miami's communist registration ordinance on behalf of a Jewish Progressive Party activist, Al Rosenberg. Elected to the state legislature in 1954, Orr had been a lonely voice in Tallahassee, during 1956 legislative debates, urging school integration. In 1958, his membership in the Miami NAACP damaged his reelection prospects at a time when Florida's "little HUAC" targeted that organization for its alleged communist affiliations. Miami's left-liberal Jews turned out in force for Orr, but he lost the Democratic primary election to a segregationist.[17]

The Orr campaign helped forge a strong sense of community among a younger generation of Miami's Jewish activists. Shirley Zoloth quickly connected with Jack and Barbara Gordon and with Barbara's sister, Thalia Stern. They shared a progressive political stance, as well as a passionate commitment to social action. As Zoloth put it in an interview, "The Orr campaign introduced a lot of people and they moved into other activities together."[18]

Progressive Jews from the North admired Orr's stand on school desegregation. After Orr's defeat, Zoloth, Gordon, and Stern met to plan what to do next about the Dade County schools. The school board had implemented many delaying tactics, such as the pupil assignment law common in other southern states. Under pressure to act, in the fall of 1958 the school board announced an experimental plan to integrate a few black students into the white Orchard Villa Elementary School, with complete desegregation of the school by the beginning of the next academic year, the fall of 1959. Orchard Villa was a racially changing neighborhood, from which whites had already begun to flee, and its exodus intensified after the school board announcement. Within ten days of Orr's primary election defeat, the three women contacted the national office of the Congress of Racial Equality (CORE). Zoloth had read a CORE pamphlet about the school desegregation crisis in Nashville, where interracial teams of CORE people escorted black children to white schools integrated under court order. Zoloth and her new friends believed that a similar program in Miami might ease racial tensions, prevent white flight from transitional neighborhoods, and maintain integrated enrollments. They requested CORE literature, but, more important, they asked that a CORE field agent be sent to Miami to help them organize. CORE responded quickly, sending field agents Gordon Carey and James McClain to Miami, leading to the creation of Miami CORE in February 1959. A few weeks later, Carey reported back to national CORE secretary James Robinson: "Thalia Stern and Shirley Zoloth are a couple of fireballs. Never have I seen so much energy and enthusiasm." Robinson responded enthusiastically, urging "with fireballs like Mrs. Stern and Mrs. Zoloth, you have to give them action in a hurry."[19]

The action came quickly. Zoloth and her friends initially hoped that the new organization would focus on desegregating Dade County schools, but black members recruited to CORE wanted to eliminate the daily indignities suffered in segregated downtown lunch counters, restaurants, and other public accommodations. Thus, in March 1959, Miami CORE began several months of interracial sit-ins at downtown eating establishments and department stores, a civil rights campaign that began almost a year before the more celebrated 1960 student sit-ins in Greensboro, North Carolina. Miami CORE's direct action plan drew many from the Jewish left, including several dozen elderly Jewish women from the left-wing Emma Lazarus Federation. On more than one occasion, Zoloth and her friends recruited black men from bars, poolrooms, barber shops, and street corners in Miami's nearby black community, called Overtown. The sit-ins grabbed the media spotlight, with almost daily television reportage locally and even nationally. Downtown business persons and store owners rebuffed demonstrators' demands for negotiations, but local political leaders worried that bad publicity would damage Miami's national image as a tourist playground. After a new round of sit-ins in the spring and summer of 1960, back-room negotiations involving CORE, black preachers, and political and business leaders finally desegregated Miami's downtown lunch counters.[20]

From the beginning, Shirley Zoloth served as the unofficial chairperson of Miami CORE. Another CORE leader, John O. Brown, a black physician, represented the organization and its goals to the press and the public, but Zoloth ran the meetings, wrote the reports, organized the sit-ins, handled all correspondence, and negotiated with business persons to desegregate their lunch counters. She was the engine that kept the organization moving toward its goals.[21]

Zoloth did not forget her interest in school desegregation, either. A vibrant organizer, she ran Jack Gordon's successful campaign in 1960 for a seat on the Dade County school board, hoping to influence school politics from the inside rather than the outside. A decade later, Zoloth managed Gordon's campaign for a seat in the Florida state senate, where he was to have a distinguished twenty-year career advocating for progressive causes. In the late 1960s, Zoloth spent five years working as deputy director of Miami's antipoverty agency, Equal Opportunity Program, Inc. (EOPI), making effective use of her organizational skills and community connections. Within two years of its establishment in 1965, EOPI managed almost two dozen different programs and community centers, had 850 employees and a weekly payroll of over $100,000, and regularly served 85,000 Dade County citizens. Many of CORE's Jewish civil rights activists also took important positions with EOPI. Jack Gordon sat on EOPI's board of directors, attorney Howard Dixon headed EOPI's legal services, and Barbara Gordon and Thalia Stern worked with the Head Start program run by EOPI. According to Zoloth and the others, working in the War on Poverty provided a way of continuing the civil rights work they had started with CORE in the late 1950s.[22]

While involved in the postwar years with WILPF and CORE, Zoloth actively engaged also in the work of such organizations as SANE, the Florida ACLU, the National Council of Jewish Women, the Women's Division of the American Jewish Congress, and the Florida Mobilization Committee to End the War in Vietnam (Florida MOBE). At a memorial service after Zoloth's death in 1999, Jack Gordon noted what everyone knew about her: "If there was any kind of progressive action in Miami, she was there—it was a given."[23]

For Shirley Zoloth, as for Bobbi Graff, activism for social justice and civil rights represented a means of achieving a better, more harmonious world for her children. Before moving to Miami, she had enrolled her children in an interracial nursery school in Philadelphia, hoping that "they would learn about race" in an unthreatening intercultural atmosphere. She was outraged by segregated schools in Miami and doubly concerned that the Florida legislature would carry out its threats in the late 1950s to close all Florida public schools to prevent desegregation. Writing to Miami state legislator W. C. Herrell in 1959, she challenged his segregationist stance on schooling and asked, "Would you care to explain the morality of this to my children for me?" Learning about race in a different context, Shirley's teenage daughter Barbara often accompanied her mother during civil rights sit-ins and other direct action protests. Both racial justice and maternalism, that is, drove Zoloth's postwar activism.[24]

Thalia Stern

Thalia Stern grew up in the Washington, D.C., suburb of Bethesda, Maryland, where her mother imbued her children with social justice ideals. In the mid-1940s, along with her sister Barbara, Thalia attended the University of Wisconsin, a place where progressive politics persisted through much of the twentieth century and where, in the midst of World War II, her peace activism began. After her freshman year at Wisconsin, Thalia traveled to Berkeley, California, where she worked as a waitress for six months, and then traveled to Mexico, where she had relatives. Her parents moved to Miami after the war, and there her father, an attorney, established a retail lighting business. Thalia joined them in 1946 and transferred to the University of Miami. She soon married Philip Stern, a Miami dentist, and in the late 1940s began a family. Her career as an activist began in the early 1950s, when she joined the WILPF and headed its world disarmament committee. The WILPF had not been known for direct action, but Stern nevertheless organized pacifist demonstrations in the mid-1950s. Many WILPF members were caught up in the Brautigam investigation, but Stern somehow escaped attention, possibly because she had no direct leftist associations.

Stern, along with the small group of Jewish activists, worked in Jack Orr's 1958 legislative campaign and helped to establish Miami CORE in 1959. Outraged over mandatory Bible reading in the Dade County schools, the Sterns joined two other couples in a 1960 lawsuit. Led by the American Jewish Congress, the effort successfully challenged the constitutionality of school prayer and Bible reading. By 1960, Thalia Stern had achieved a wide local reputation in Miami as a dedicated political activist. Her opponents on the right also labeled her a communist and an atheist.[25]

Stern espoused a deep passion for peace and pacifism. Much of her direct action work in the late 1950s focused on antiwar and anti-nuclear-testing activities. At the time, scientists reported that nuclear fallout, especially the dangerous radioactive isotope strontium-90, had potentially serious effects on children. As a dentist, Philip Stern knew the dangers of radiation and began using lead shields on his patients and himself when taking x-rays long before this became standard procedure. As Thalia Stern recalled, Philip "talked about the perils of radiation and I listened."[26]

Actually, she did more than listen. She brought her activist energy to a local SANE campaign against nuclear testing. Drawing on the Jewish activist network of CORE, WILPF, and other groups, Stern and a few others organized the Greater Miami Committee for a Sane Nuclear Policy, or Miami SANE, undertaking work that coincided with the CORE sit-ins and the school desegregation fight. Katherine Palmer, a retired teacher, a Protestant pacifist, and Miami SANE's chair in the late 1950s, reported to SANE executive secretary Donald Keys in New York that "if it had not been for the Jews on the Beach, [and] some members of the WIL, . . . nothing would have been accomplished." Palmer worried that heavy Jewish participation in Miami SANE would stimulate anti-Semitism, but she admitted a few months later that "the only reason there has been any success at all is because the Jews took over, as one might say, and did the 'leg work.'"[27]

Nationally, SANE emphasized public education on nuclear issues, but in Miami Stern turned SANE into a confrontational direct action group, one that made the more conservative national SANE leaders a bit nervous. In addition to orchestrating a public information campaign, Miami SANE periodically organized street demonstrations and picket lines promoting pacifist and antinuclear positions. The group regularly demonstrated on Hiroshima Day and protested the futility of civil defense measures. Playing to maternal instincts, Stern promoted a local plan to collect baby teeth and have them tested for strontium-90, following an earlier baby tooth study in St. Louis. When a Hialeah businessman sought to promote bomb shelters with a publicity scheme to send a honeymooning couple into a backyard bomb shelter for a two-week trial demonstration, Miami SANE responded. They disrupted the wedding and made pacifist speeches. They picketed the bomb shelter site for a week, carrying homemade signs reading "No Defense against the H-Bomb" and "You Can't Hide from Death, Invest in Peace." The newspapers reported that a placard on the Stern's home in Miami Beach read: "This house has no fallout shelter. Peace is our only security." For Thalia Stern, picketing for peace was a family affair, involving her mother, her husband, her sister, and her own children.[28]

The conservative political climate in cold war Miami made the work of SANE activists difficult. A relatively small, mostly Jewish, left-liberal group, Miami SANE had little support in the community at large. Palmer complained about "the indifference of the general public" and the opposition of the local newspapers. Prominent Miamians who privately supported SANE refused to take public positions because, as one stated, he was "afraid of becoming involved in an FBI investigation of communist infiltration." In the heat of the cold war and persisting Florida anticommunism, Miami activists found it difficult to overcome the public perception that the SANE movement ought to be considered "extremist."[29] These same perceptions and tensions existed at the national level, as SANE came under attack from the anticommunist right. SANE's national leader, editor Norman Cousins, purged suspected or former communists from the organization's leadership positions, but the move undermined SANE's stature and influence in the national peace and antinuclear movements.[30]

As SANE lost direction nationally, Miami SANE's activists began cooperating on peace projects with local Quakers from the American Friends Service Committee (AFSC). In September 1962, Thalia Stern and Thyrza Jacocks, a Quaker who had recently moved to Miami from Philadelphia, worked together to establish the Miami Peace Center, initially in Coral Gables and later relocated to downtown Miami. Then, as the Vietnam War heated up in the mid-1960s, the Peace Center took the lead in local antiwar activity. Activists and pacifists at the center conducted draft counseling, distributed antiwar and pacifist literature, and sponsored antiwar lectures and films. They conducted weekly silent vigils in downtown Miami and on Miami Beach. The activists also organized mass protests, such as the Miami demonstration that drew 350 people in opposition to a public address by New York's Francis Cardinal Spellman, who headed the U.S. Catholic lobby in support of the Vietnam War. Most of the Jewish activists involved in CORE and SANE participated in Peace Center activities.[31]

The Miami Peace Center had a number of challenges. Imitating the 1950s tactics of Senator Joseph McCarthy, opponents red-baited the organization, claiming to know of "forty-six known Communists working out of the Peace Center"; such Peace Center critics never could or did name names, however. The arrival after 1959 of several hundred thousand hardcore anticommunist, anti-Castro Cubans inflamed and perpetuated the cold war tensions of the late 1940s and early 1950s. Miami's Cuban exile newspapers and Spanish-language talk-radio programs, according to local peace activist Heather C. Moir, consistently expressed "inflammatory and hostile views" toward the Peace Center. After much harassment and several bomb threats, an actual bombing in May 1967 destroyed the center's building, forcing the peace activists to relocate to nearby Coconut Grove.[32]

Further, internal issues divided the Peace Center's Quakers and Jews. Jacocks and Stern disagreed on the use of direct action and civil disobedience, and the pro-Palestinian stance of the Quaker pacifists offended the pro-Israeli Jewish activists. Nevertheless, Jacocks and Stern remained close throughout the 1960s, and SANE and AFSC worked together effectively, if at times warily, during the early years of the Vietnam War. As *Miami Herald* writer Lee Winfrey noted, the Peace Center avoided "detailed policy statements so that adherents can unite in simple opposition to the Bomb."[33]

Miami SANE and the Miami Peace Center persisted through the 1960s, but new peace groups sprouted up, as well, with Thalia Stern at the center of the action. One such organization, Women Strike for Peace (WSP), began in 1961 when a handful of women in Washington, D.C., called for a nationwide women's peace demonstration. A mere five weeks later, on November 1, 1961, an estimated fifty thousand women in sixty cities left their jobs or household work and marched against nuclear testing. In Miami, Stern and her activist friends responded, conducting a WSP peace march in downtown Miami, many pushing baby carriages or carrying homemade peace signs. One speaker, Gertrude Leiner, imaginatively condemned the arms race as "immoral, un-Christian, and un-Jewish." In 1963, Stern and two friends traveled to Washington for another major WSP antinuclear demonstration; while there, they also lobbied Florida congresspersons and senators to ratify the test-ban treaty with the Soviet Union. Over the next few years, using the "rhetoric of motherhood," autonomous local WSP groups engaged in spontaneous direct action challenging bomb testing, U.S. militarism, the cold war, and, after 1965, the war in Vietnam. With no structure or hierarchy, no officers or dues, WSP provided the perfect peace group for Miami's Jewish activists, who tended to act autonomously and spontaneously and often resisted the leadership demands of a structured organization. By the mid-1960s, Miami WSP activities merged into the work of the Miami Peace Center.[34]

Stern also served as the Miami point person for the Committee for Non-Violent Action (CNVA), organized in 1957 as a loose network of radical pacifists, including A. J. Muste and David Dellinger. Dedicated to civil disobedience and direct action, CNVA acted primarily through symbolic protest projects against nuclear testing and nuclear war. In 1963, a handful of CNVA activists began a peace walk from Quebec to Miami en route to Guantanamo, Cuba, an eventful year-long effort that reached Miami in the summer of 1964. Once in Miami, the peace walkers orchestrated antiwar demonstrations, gave radical speeches, and confronted hard-line Cuban exiles. Miami activists supported the CNVA peace walkers, fed them, found them housing, provided cars, and hosted fund-raising parties. When, inevitably, the police arrested some walkers, the Miami activists found lawyers and raised bail for those arrested. When the walkers purchased a boat to get to Cuba, they docked their vessel in the canal behind Stern's home.[35]

Stern's activism for peace and racial justice, like that of Graff and Zoloth, stemmed in part from her concern about raising children in an environment marked by the cold war and racial segregation. Nuclear testing and radiation fallout threatened children everywhere—thus her support for the baby tooth study. Her three daughters often participated with their mother in picketing for peace. Women Strike for Peace, described by historian Amy Swerdlow as "women who fought like lions for their children's welfare," clearly reflected the maternalist ethic in Miami.[36]

In the early 1970s, Thalia and Philip Stern divorced, and she moved with her children to Berkeley, California, where she worked on a graduate degree in music. She remembered Berkeley fondly from her college days, and its activist environment was also an obvious attraction. She still lives in Berkeley and remains committed to the social justice ideals that motivated her Miami activities in the postwar era.

Commonalities and Conclusions

These three Jewish women, dedicated activists and mothers, shared many commonalities. All three moved to Miami from northern cities—Graff from New York by way of Detroit, Zoloth from Philadelphia, and Stern from Washington, D.C. In all three cases, the women's parents had already moved to Miami for business or retirement. Each of the women came from East European immigrant families in which Jewish conceptions of social justice pervaded the atmosphere. Each had been born in the 1920s, and, during their activist years, all three women combined their political lives with their roles as wives and mothers with young children at home. Maternalist instincts helped motivate all three to push for integrated schooling, racial justice, civil liberties, and an end to nuclear testing. At various times, too, during the 1950s and 1960s, as their children grew older, all three women worked at full-time or part-time jobs, Graff as a secretary, Zoloth as a legal secretary and then as an antipoverty administrator, and Stern as a Head Start music teacher in Miami's black Overtown community. And all three also took college courses at one time or another during these years. Thus, each juggled the multiple roles of wife, mother, homemaker, jobholder, college student, and sometimes caretaker of aging parents, along with simultaneous activist work in many civil rights and peace organizations. Each had a husband who supported her work and often participated with her in direct action sit-ins, picketing, and demonstrations. They all attended a lot of meetings, but often held the meetings in their own homes.

The three women had all read Betty Friedan's *The Feminine Mystique* soon after its publication, but they did not think it applied to them. They saw themselves as already liberated. When asked recently about Friedan's book, Bobbi Graff gave an instant reply, "Some of us were there before Betty," suggesting that she and her cohort had already confronted and dealt with the contradictions between the demands of the domestic sphere and public activism.[37] All three women expressed sympathy with the goals of the National Organization of Women, but did not consider themselves feminists. Many of the organizations they started or joined—CRC, CORE, SANE, CNVA, and the others—attracted both women and men. Graff, Zoloth, and Stern took leading roles in these groups as organizers, activists, instigators, motivators, and managers. They did so as politically progressive Jews committed to the ideals of peace, civil rights, and social justice, but also as mothers concerned about the world their children would inherit.

NOTES

1. Betty Friedan, *The Feminine Mystique* (New York: W. W. Norton, 1963); Daniel Horowitz, *Betty Friedan and the Making of the Feminine Mystique: The American Left, the Cold War, and Modern Feminism* (Amherst: University of Massachusetts Press, 1998); Susan Oliver, *Betty Friedan: The Personal Is Political* (New York: Pearson Longman, 2008); Susan Lynn, "Gender and Post World War II Progressive Politics: A Bridge to Social Activism in the 1960s," *Gender and History* 4 (Summer 1992): 215–239; Joanne Meyerowitz, "Beyond the Feminine Mystique: A Reassessment of Postwar Mass Culture, 1946–1958," *Journal of American History* 79 (March 1993): 1455–1482; Joanne Meyerowitz, ed., *Not June Cleaver: Women and Gender in Postwar America, 1945–1960* (Philadelphia: Temple University Press, 1994); Kate Weigand, *Red Feminism: American Communism and the Making of Women's Liberation* (Baltimore: Johns Hopkins University Press, 2001).

2. Lynn Y. Weiner, "Maternalism as a Paradigm: Defining the Issues," *Journal of Women's History* 5 (Fall 1993): 96–98; Molly Ladd-Taylor, "Toward Defining Maternalism in U.S. History," *Journal of Women's History* 5 (Fall 1993): 110–113.

3. Stetson Kennedy, "Miami: Anteroom to Fascism," *The Nation* 173 (December 22, 1951): 546–547; Joe Alex Morris, "The Truth about the Florida Race Troubles," *Saturday Evening Post* (June 21, 1952): 24–25, 50, 55–58; Nathan Perlmutter, "Bombing in Miami: Anti-Semitism and the Segregationists," *Commentary* 25 (June 1958): 498–503; Raymond A. Mohl, "The Pattern of Race Relations in Miami since the 1920s," in *The African-American Heritage of Florida*, ed. David R. Colburn and Jane L. Landers (Gainesville: University Press of Florida, 1995), 326–365.

4. "Miami's Little McCarthy Rouses Storm," *Daily Worker*, August 3, 1954; Leslie B. Bain, "Red Hunt in Miami: Who Formed the Posse?" *The Nation* 179 (August 7, 1954): 110–112; Louis Harap, "Nightmare in Miami," *Jewish Life* 9 (December 1954): 4–8; Frank Donner, "The Miami Formula: An Exposé of Grass-Roots McCarthyism," *The Nation* 180 (January 22, 1955): 65–71; Gregory W. Bush, "'We Must Picture an Octopus': Anticommunism, Desegregation, and Local News in Miami, 1945–1960," *Tequesta: Journal of the Historical Association of Southern Florida* 65 (2005): 48–63; Steven F. Lawson, "The Florida Legislative Investigation Committee and the Constitutional Readjustment of Race Relations, 1956–1963," in *An Uncertain Tradition: Constitutionalism and the History of the South*, ed. Kermit L. Hall and James E. Ely (Athens: University of Georgia Press, 1989), 296–325.

5. Raymond A. Mohl, "Miami: The Ethnic Cauldron," in *Sunbelt Cities: Politics and Growth since World War II*, ed. Richard M. Bernard and Bradley R. Rice (Austin: University of Texas Press, 1983), 58–99; Deborah Dash Moore, "Jewish Migration to the Sunbelt," in *Shades of the Sunbelt: Essays on Ethnicity, Race, and the Urban South*, ed. Randall M. Miller and George E. Pozzetta (Westport, CT: Greenwood Press, 1988), 41–52.

6. Mohl, "The Pattern of Race Relations in Miami"; Marvin Dunn, *Black Miami in the Twentieth Century* (Gainesville: University Press of Florida, 1997), 171–223; Chanelle Rose, "The 'Jewel' of the South? Miami, Florida, and the NAACP's Struggle for Civil Rights in America's Vacation Paradise," *Florida Historical Quarterly* 86 (Summer 2007): 39–69.

7. Matilda "Bobbi" Graff, interviews by the author, May 18, 1992, September 30, 1992, January 29, 1993; Raymond A. Mohl, *South of the South: Jewish Activists and the Civil Rights Movement in Miami, 1945–1960* (Gainesville: University Press of Florida, 2004), 36, 75–77.

8. Graff interviews, May 18, 1992, September 30, 1992, January 29, 1993; Mohl, *South of the South*, 37–39; 77–80, 101–103; Sandi Wisenberg, "Left on the Beach," *Miami Herald, Tropic Magazine* (July 21, 1985); Dan Froomkin, "Old Age Steals Jewish Center's Fire," *Miami Herald*, March 17, 1989.

9. Mohl, *South of the South*, 39–40, 81–83; [Florida] Peoples Progressive Party, Minutes of State Executive Committee, June 27, 1948, John M. Coe Papers, Box 1, Folder 49, Special Collections, Robert W. Woodruff Library, Emory University, Atlanta, Georgia; Gail Gropper to John M. Coe, April 16, 1949, Coe Papers, Box 2, Folder 7; Gropper to Miriam Arons, June 22, 1949, Coe Papers, Box 2, Folder 6; Al Rosenberg, "This Thing Called Fear," *Florida Progressive* 1 (January 1950): 3–4; Sarah Hart Brown, "Pensacola Progressive: John Moreno Coe and the Campaign of 1948," *Florida Historical Quarterly* 68 (July 1989): 1–26. On the racial and political context of Miami labor organizing during this period, see Eric Tscheschlok, "'So Goes the Negro': Race and Labor in Miami, 1940–1963," *Florida Historical Quarterly* 76 (Summer 1997): 42–67; Alex Lichtenstein, "Putting Labor's House in Order: The Transport Workers Union and Labor Anti-Communism in Miami during the 1940s," *Labor History* 39 (February 1998): 7–23.

10. Gerald Horne, *Communist Front? The Civil Rights Congress, 1946–1956* (Rutherford, NJ: Fairleigh Dickinson University Press, 1988); William L. Patterson, *The Man Who Cried Genocide* (New York: International Publishers, 1971); Bush, "'We Must Picture an Octopus,'" 52–53; Sarah Hart Brown, *Standing Against Dragons: Three Southern Lawyers in an Era of Fear* (Baton Rouge: Louisiana State University Press, 1998), 69–71.

11. Graff interviews, May 18, 1992, September 30, 1992, January 29, 1993; Matilda Graff, "What's Behind the Anti-Negro Terror?" *National Guardian*, August 29, 1949; Mohl, *South of the South*, 38–42, 87–95. For Graff's extensive correspondence with William L. Patterson and other national CRC leaders, see Papers of the Civil Rights Congress, microfilm edition, Part 2, Reel 24, Schomburg Library, New York, New York.

12. Mohl, *South of the South*, 42–47, 87–95, 103–105, 108–112; Matilda Graff's FBI file, copy in Graff's possession, documenting FBI investigation and harassment of Graff, from 1942 to 1972, in almost five hundred typed pages; Matilda Graff, voter registration files, early 1950s, copy in author's possession.

13. Matilda Graff, "A Child Is Born in Fear," *National Guardian*, September 27, 1954; Mohl, *South of the South*, 73–76, 82, 112–118. On Miami radicals in exile in Mexico, see Diana Anhalt, *A Gathering of Fugitives: American Political Expatriates in Mexico, 1946–1965* (Santa Maria, CA: Archer Books, 2001).

14. Graff interviews, May 18, 1992, December 19, 2000.

15. Shirley Zoloth, interviews with author, August 23, 1991, December 14, 1992; Milton Zoloth, telephone interview with author, December 15, 2000. On the witch hunt in the Philadelphia schools, see "Philadelphia Fights Back against Witch-hunters in Its Schools," *National Guardian* (April 19, 1954): 7; Philip Jenkins, *The Cold War at Home: The Red Scare in Pennsylvania, 1945–1960* (Chapel Hill: University of North Carolina Press, 1999), 118–141.

16. Zoloth interviews, August 23, 1991, December 14, 1992; Shirley Zoloth to Bernice Ullrich, September 24, 1954, Desegregation Folder, Jack D. Gordon Papers, Box 10, University Archives, Florida International University, Miami, Florida; Bernice Ullrich, "Civil Rights Being Violated," *Miami Herald*, October 11, 1954; Shirley Zoloth to [Dade County] Board of Public Instruction, September 18, 1957, Desegregation Folder, Gordon Papers, Box 10; Shirley Zoloth, clipping scrapbook, 1957–1959, in author's possession; Mohl, *South of the South*, 47–48, 125–126. On FBI infiltration of Miami WILPF, see FBI Report from Miami, November 14, 1952, June 24, 1953, FBI Investigation and Surveillance Records, Women's International League for Peace and Freedom Files, Box 2, Archives, Marquette University Library, Milwaukee, Wisconsin; Robbie Lieberman, *The Strangest Dream: Communism,*

Anticommunism, and the U.S. Peace Movement, 1945–1963 (Syracuse, NY: Syracuse University Press, 2000), 128–129.

17. Hampton Dunn, "Miami's Jack Orr First Dixie Politician to Support Openly Integration Move," *Tampa Daily Times*, July 28, 1956; Ed Seney, "John B. Orr—The Man Who Shocked the State," *The Miamian Magazine* (December 1956): 20–21; Wilma Dykeman and James Stokely, *Neither Black Nor White* (New York: Rinehart, 1957), 357–359.

18. Zoloth interviews, August 23, 1991, December 14, 1992; Jack D. Gordon, telephone interviews with author, October 25, December 4, December 6, 2001; Thalia Stern Broudy, telephone interview with author, July 30, 2002.

19. Zoloth interviews, August 23, 1991, October 2, 1992; Gordon interviews, October 25, 2001, December 6, 2001; Anna Holden, *A First Step toward School Integration* (New York: Congress of Racial Equality, 1958); Thalia Stern to James R. Robinson, October 10, 1958, Congress of Racial Equality Papers (hereafter cited as CORE Papers), microfilm edition, Reel 19, Wisconsin State Historical Society, Madison, Wisconsin; Gordon Carey to Robinson, March 3, 1959, CORE Papers, Reel 19; James R. Robinson to Gordon Carey, March 5, 1959, CORE Papers, Reel 19; August Meier and Elliott Rudwick, *CORE: A Study in the Civil Rights Movement* (New York: Oxford University Press, 1973), 90–91. On the Orchard Villa school plan, see Ed Cony, "Miami Race Plan," *Wall Street Journal*, December 9, 1958; Shirley Zoloth, "Miami Integration: Silence Causes Failure," *Southern Patriot* 17 (December 1959): 1–3.

20. Zoloth interviews, August 23, 1991, December 15, 1992; Gordon interview, December 6, 2001; Shirley Zoloth, "Miami CORE Reports and Minutes," in Mohl, *South of the South*, 147–191; Shirley Zoloth, "The Miami CORE Story," *CORE-lator*, no. 27 (Summer 1959): 2.

21. Zoloth interview, December 15, 1992; Fletcher Knebel and Ben Kovicar, "The Negro in Florida: One Man's Progress and the Road Ahead," *Look* 23 (April 14, 1959): 34–37.

22. Zoloth interviews, August 23, 1991, December 14, 1992; Gordon interviews, October 25, 2001, December 4, 2001; Broudy, telephone interview, July 30, 2002; Mohl, *South of the South*, 128–130.

23. Anabelle deGale, "Shirley Zoloth, Played Role in Desegregation," *Miami Herald*, October 21, 2001.

24. Zoloth interview, August 23, 1991; Shirley Zoloth to W. C. Herrell, April 3, 1959, copy in Mohl, *South of the South*, 148–149; Barbara Zoloth, e-mail message to author, June 9, 2003.

25. Broudy interviews, July 30, 2002, February 17, 2003; Thalia Stern Broudy to author, June 19, 2004, in author's possession.

26. Broudy interviews, July 30, 2002, February 17, 2003; Broudy to Mohl, June 19, 2004; Walter Schnier, "Strontium-90 in U.S. Children," *The Nation* 188 (April 25, 1959): 355–357; Paul Boyer, *Fallout: A Historian Reflects on America's Half-Century Weapons* (Columbus: Ohio State University Press, 1998), 61–86. On the late 1950s fallout fears, see Linus Pauling, *No More War* (New York: Dodd, Mead, 1958); Jack Schubert and Ralph E. Lapp, *Radiation: What It Is and How It Affects You* (New York: Viking Press, 1957); John M. Fowler, ed., *Fallout: A Study of Superbombs, Strontium 90, and Survival* (New York: Basic Books, 1960). For historical studies, see Robert A. Divine, *Blowing on the Wind: The Nuclear Test Ban Debate, 1954–1960* (New York: Oxford University Press, 1978); Milton M. Katz, *Ban the Bomb: A History of SANE, the Committee for a Sane Nuclear Policy, 1957–1985* (Westport, CT: Greenwood Press, 1986); Lawrence Wittner, *Resisting the Bomb: A History of the World Nuclear Disarmament Movement, 1954–1970* (Stanford, CA: Stanford University Press, 1997).

27. Katherine B. Palmer to Alfred Williams, July 26, 1958, SANE Records, 1957–1987, Series B, Box 3/10, Swarthmore College Peace Collection, Swarthmore, PA; Palmer to Donald Keys, December 12, December 14, 1958, SANE Records, Series B, Box 3/10; Palmer to Keys, January 1, 1959, November 16, 1959, SANE Records, Series B, Box 4/22.

28. Greater Miami Committee for a Sane Nuclear Policy, "Informal Report on Plans and Problems," June 28, 1958, SANE File, Gordon Papers, Box 5; Palmer to Keys, July 10, August 18, October 10, November 16, 1959, SANE Records, Series B, Box 4/22; Thalia Stern to Keys, July 15, 1959, SANE Records, Series B, Box 4/22; Keys to Stern, September 22, 1959, SANE Records, Series B, Box 4/22; William K. Wyant, "50,000 Baby Teeth: Strontium-90 in St. Louis," *The Nation* 188 (June 13, 1959): 535–537; Gene Miller, "Just Like Atom, Eve: Trouble's Overhead," *Miami Herald*, July 13, 1959.

29. Katherine B. Palmer to Norman Cousins, April 15, 1958, SANE Records, Series B, Box 3/10; Palmer to Williams, July 26, 1958, SANE Records, Series B, Box 3/10; Katherine B. Palmer to Walter J. Lear, August 5, 1958, SANE Records, Series B, Box 3/10; Palmer to Keys, December 4, 1958; Keys to Palmer, December 5, 1958, SANE Records, Series B, Box 3/10.

30. James Tracy, *Direct Action: Radical Pacifism from the Union Eight to the Chicago Seven* (Chicago: University of Chicago Press, 1996), 114–115. On SANE's decline, see also Arthur Mitzman, "Not SANE Enough," *Liberation* 4 (October 1959): 16–18; A. J. Muste, "The Crisis in SANE," *Liberation* 5 (July–August 1960): 10–13; Barbara Deming, "The Ordeal of SANE," *The Nation* 192 (March 11, 1961): 200–205; Nathan Glazer, "The Peace Movement in America—1961," *Commentary* 29 (April 1961): 288–296.

31. Broudy to author, June 19, 2004; Broudy interviews, July 30, 2002, February 17, 2003, February 23, 2007; Thyrza Jaccoks, interview with author, November 17, 2005, Sarasota, FL; Phyllis Resnick, interview with author, June 15, 2007, Aventura, FL; Jack Oswald, "Peace Lovers Have a Place for Palavaer," *Miami News*, November 18, 1962; Lee Winfrey, "What Miami's Peaceseekers Try to Do," *Miami Herald*, April 28, 1963; Maurice LaBelle, "A Center for Peace and Agitation," *Coral Gables Times*, April 7, 1966.

32. Charles Whited, untitled column, *Miami Herald*, n.d. [c. 1966], Thalia Stern Broudy, clipping file, copy in author's possession; Maurice LaBelle, "Ties That Bind at Peace Center," *Coral Gables Times*, April 21, 1966; "Bomb Explosion Forces Peace Center Relocation," *Miami News*, May 29, 1967; Heather C. Moir to A. Gandero (Channel 10 News Coordinator), June 16, 1967, copy in Broudy, clipping file.

33. Broudy interviews, July 30, 2002, February 17, 2003, February 23, 2007; Jacocks interview, November 17, 2005; Heather Moir, telephone interview with author, December 13, 2005; Winfrey, "What Miami's Peaceseekers Try to Do."

34. Broudy interviews, July 30, 2002, February 17, 2003; Resnick interview, June 15, 2007; Miami Women Strike for Peace, demonstration flyer, November 1, 1961, Broudy, clipping file; "Life March," *Miami Herald*, November 2, 1961; Midge Decter, "The Peace Ladies," *Harper's* 226 (March 1963): 48–53; Jeanne Bellamy, "Peace-Pushers Going Bigtime," *Miami Herald*, April 12, 1963; "Anti-War Pickets Here Join Nationwide Protest," *Miami News*, March 27, 1966; Amy Swerdlow, *Women Strike for Peace: Traditional Motherhood and Radical Politics in the 1960s* (Chicago: University of Chicago Press, 1993).

35. Broudy interviews, July 30, 2002, February 17, 2003; Broudy to Mohl, June 19, 2004; Jerry Lehrmann, "Report on CNVA Demonstration before the Cuban Revolutionary Council in Miami on February 21, 1963," CNVA News Sheet, March 3, 1963, in Broudy, clipping file; "Confrontation in Miami," *Liberation* 9 (March 1963): 3–5; Dave Dellinger, "Ten Days with the Cuba Walk," *Liberation* 8 (January 1964): 5–31.

36. Swerdlow, *Women Strike for Peace*, 23.

37. Graff interview, July 24, 2006.

2

The Polishness of Lucy S. Dawidowicz's Postwar Jewish Cold War

NANCY SINKOFF

Lucy S. Dawidowicz (1915–1990), the American Jewish historian known for her work on East European Jewry and its destruction, was a fierce political animal in the postwar years. Her interests included the history of Jewish politics and the role of the leaders of the formal Jewish community as stewards of Jewish communal life. Late in life, while working on a history of American Jews, she wrote to historian Robert Dallek: "For some years now I've been engaged in research for a broad-gauged history of Jews in America. Politics is one of the many aspects of Jewish life I want to write about—Jews in politics, as office holders, and in relation to men in power."[1] Although her youthful political education had begun on the left, by the 1970s Dawidowicz had firmly entrenched herself in the emergent neoconservative camp, a vocal critic of the New Left and of the social movements associated with 1960s radicalism. Like that of many other Jewish neoconservatives, Dawidowicz's politics were fueled by an unrelenting anticommunism. Already in the 1950s, when she wrote several major articles on communism for liberal anticommunist popular journals like *Commentary* and *The New Leader*, Dawidowicz had begun to develop a public persona as a cold warrior.

Although passionate ideological feuding informed the anticommunism of the group of primarily male intellectuals associated with *Partisan Review* and *Commentary*, later dubbed the "New York intellectuals" by Irving Howe in his *Commentary* article of 1968, "The New York Intellectuals: A Chronicle and a Critique," Dawidowicz's rejection of communism was also based in her life-long involvement with modern Yiddish culture.[2] Educated in the interwar years in the Sholem Aleichem Folk Institute schools, Dawidowicz (then Schildkret) went to Vilna, Poland, in 1938 as a graduate fellow (*aspirant*) of the YIVO Institute. During the war years, she worked for New York YIVO's director Max Weinreich, returning to Europe in 1946 as an employee of the American Jewish Joint Distribution Committee's educational department to focus on the educational needs of Jewish refugees. In 1948 she married Szymon Dawidowicz, a Warsaw Bundist, and the marriage solidified her intimate connection to Yiddish and to

Poland. Balancing her Yiddishist and American selves, Dawidowicz's journey to becoming a New York intellectual and a cold warrior coursed through the brutal torrents of the European twentieth century that destroyed and dislocated the heartland of East European Jewry. Her connection to her experiences in Europe before and after the war, as much as the broad social, economic, and intellectual changes informing postwar American Jews, shaped Dawidowicz's life and career.

The historiography on postwar American Jews has emphasized their distance from their European origins. Increasingly "at home in America," the children and grandchildren of European Jewish immigrants are characterized as having moved out of densely populated urban neighborhoods, embraced a suburban lifestyle and the expectations of separate gendered spheres, discarded Yiddish, and created an Americanized Judaism.[3] Yet Dawidowicz's life challenges this complacent image of postwar Americanized Jews.[4] Always living within the municipal boundaries of New York City, working for pay outside the home, and remaining connected to Yiddishist circles, Dawidowicz brought a European persona and perspective to her politics and her attitudes toward American society. Although she lived and wrote in New York City, prewar Poland, particularly the city of Vilna, was always on her mind.

Like Irving Kristol, Nathan Glazer, Daniel Bell, and Irving Howe, Lucy Schildkret hailed from an immigrant home in New York City, attended a public school, and went on to one of the city's free public colleges. In contrast to these men, however, she also went to a supplementary Yiddish afternoon school, a *shule*, and to a Yiddish summer camp, Camp Boiberik, through her high school years.[5] At Hunter College, the women's college equivalent to the more famous City College of New York, incubator of the "New York intellectuals," Schildkret took classmates and faculty by storm. Majoring in English, she contributed to Hunter's literary magazine, *Echo*, becoming editor in 1935, and joined the school's chapter of the Young Communist League (YCL). Soon thereafter, the Seventh Congress of the Communist Party initiated the Popular Front, an international campaign of cooperation with noncommunists, including members of bourgeois and socialist parties. From 1935 to 1939, the Communist Party actively cultivated ethnic and national cultures, formerly considered suspicious bourgeois expressions of parochialism.[6] In her memoir and in supporting archival material, Dawidowicz reported that the Popular Front line tested her politics and personality. The Hunter College YCL rejected both the rapprochement with bourgeois parties and the autocratic demand for compliance demanded by the Comintern; nevertheless, the latter order spurred Schildkret's exit from the YCL.[7] After college, she found herself marginally employed and personally adrift. To fill her time, she immersed herself in secular Yiddish culture through the Sholem Aleichem Yungt Gezelshaft (SAYG), the youth organization affiliated with her earlier Yiddish school movement. Although SAYG tended to lean to the left, its political autonomy reflected the beginning of Schildkret's own political independence.

As Adolf Hitler consolidated power in Germany in the 1930s, Yiddish-speaking American Jews became acutely aware of the looming crisis in Europe, and in Poland in particular. In 1935, Roman Dmowski replaced the deceased Józef Piłsudski as president of the Republic of Poland, auguring a shift in that nation's political climate that turned open anti-Semitism into government policy.[8] As literary scholar Anita Norich has shown, interwar American Yiddish writers, while inhabiting the same space as their Anglo-Jewish peers, differed from them in cultural outlook. The former still looked to Europe, and created works that presupposed a transnational secular Jewish cultural world. They expected to be read on both sides of the Atlantic.[9] Youth in the Yiddishist world engaged equally with Europe and America. Lucy Schildkret wrote for and edited *Shrift* (Writing), the organ of the SAYG, which devoted regular columns to developments in Europe. A 1937 editorial, "You Will Not Drive Them Out," saluted the efforts of a Jewish deputy to the Polish *Sejm*, Emil Sommerstein (1883–1957), who rejected the call for Jewish emigration from Poland. *Shrift*'s pages cried out: "The Jews of the world stand with you to build a free and renewed Poland. For us American Jews, there is only one way—unity in our support for Polish Jews. The Jewish Congress should continue to lead American Jewry in huge demonstrations and protest cries against the murderers who are attacking our brothers in Poland. We will not let you drive the Jews out of Poland!"[10]

Urged by her *shule* history teacher Jacob Shatzky to continue her study of modern Yiddish at the YIVO institute in Vilna, Schildkret set off for Poland in the summer of 1938. At the Vilna YIVO, she met and befriended the luminaries of modern secular Yiddish culture: Elias Tcherikower, Chaim Grade, Avrom Sutzkever, Zalman Reisen, Zelig Kalmanovich, and Max Weinreich.[11] These relationships proved to be not only personal for Schildkret, but also represented to her the vitality, diversity, and resilience of Polish Jewish culture, and these aspects of that culture would later inform her historical and public writings. Paradoxically, though, Schildkret's ambivalence toward secular Yiddish culture began in Vilna, the imagined urban apotheosis of Jewish secularism.[12] Her Vilna year also proved decisive in extinguishing any positive feelings toward communism that she had had.

Schildkret's deep connection to Riva and Zelig Kalmanovich, the latter of whom had fled Bolshevik Russia in 1921, permanently shaped her hostility to communism. Zelig Kalmanovich, a Diaspora nationalist and a Yiddishist, became a member of the Jewish Socialist Workers Party, which advocated Jewish cultural autonomy within the future socialist Russian state, and wrote for the party's journal, *Di folksshtime* (The People's Voice). After World War I, he ended up in the Soviet Union, where he witnessed the radicalization of Yiddish culture in war-roiled Ukraine. Soon recoiling from Bolshevik ideological constraints on Yiddish culture, he fled, his hatred of the Bolsheviks severing any kind of socialist leanings from his Yiddishism.[13] His 1931 Yiddish essay, "Perspectives for Yiddish Culture in the Soviet Union," argued against the possibility of a Yiddish future in the Soviet Union since the proletarian goals of the Yevsektsiya, the Jewish section of the Communist Party, reduced Yiddish to a utilitarian means of inculcating Bolshevism among Jews; Yiddish as an autonomous expression of modern Jewish culture was considered dispensable.[14] By 1934, Kalmanovich had settled in Vilna, becoming central to the operation of the YIVO, which he believed offered the best hope for bolstering secular Jewish culture and the Yiddish language in the new independent nation states that had emerged after World War I. His mistrust of any kind of political litmus test for Yiddish culture was to have a lifelong effect on Schildkret.

Riva Kalmanovich, aware that Schildkret possessed an American passport that would allow her safe passage back to the United States, insisted that the young woman leave Poland in late August 1939. After about a year in Albany, Schildkret joined Max Weinreich, who had managed to leave Europe, at the New York branch of the YIVO, located on the Lower East Side. Throughout the war years, Schildkret worked at this skeletal branch, the only remnant of its Vilna forebear. She and Weinreich would be among the few YIVO employees who had known the Vilna institution. In these years, the war in Europe was never far from their minds, and her memoir details the agony of watching it unfold at a distance.

The Hitler-Stalin pact initially spared Vilna's Jews from Nazi brutality, as the city fell to the Soviets in September 1939. At the end of that October, Lithuania wrested itself from Soviet rule, but this respite proved short-lived; by mid-June 1940, the Soviets again occupied Lithuania. Quickly, the YIVO became Sovietized, a process that transformed once ideologically varied and independent Jewish schools into state-run Marxist Yiddish institutions.[15] Moyshe Lerer, a YIVO staff member with Bolshevik leanings, now ran the institute; Zalman Reisen and his son, Saul, had been earlier arrested, and many suspected they had been killed; and the YIVO began to offer courses in Marxism. According to Dawidowicz's memory, "Kalmanovich, who had never concealed his dislike for communism and Communists, had been dismissed, along with other staff members."[16]

A continuous encounter with refugees from war-torn Europe solidified Schildkret's pessimistic views of the future of Jews and Yiddish culture across the Atlantic. In 1940, a small group of Polish Jewish refugees, including Raphael Mahler, Elias Tcherikower, Yudel Mark, Jacob Lestchinsky, and Shmuel Zygielbaum, who had sojourned in New York before returning to Europe, received political visas for the United States and made their way to the YIVO.[17] Daily contact with East European Jews who spoke Yiddish, along with reading the Yiddish press, gave Yiddishists like Schildkret access, before other Americans, to developments in Europe regarding the Jews. By June 1941, they knew that the worst had transpired: abrogating the Hitler-Stalin pact, the Nazis had invaded Soviet-occupied Poland and begun the brutalization of its Jewish population.

The news of deportations, ghettoization, and murder flowed through the Yiddish press throughout 1942 and 1943. Schildkret and the others found particularly shocking the revelation that two leaders of the Bund, Henryk Erlich and Viktor Alter, whom William Green, head of the American Federation of Labor, had been reassured were still alive in 1942, had in fact been murdered by the Soviets. On March 30, 1943, Schildkret attended a protest meeting organized by David Dubinsky and the International Ladies' Garment Workers Union.[18] The event was hotly contested by many in the American labor movement because of the Soviet alliance with the United States, but, for Schildkret, Jewish oppression under the Soviet sickle was beginning to seem like Jewish oppression under the Nazi boot.[19] In April of that year, reports about Auschwitz-Birkenau and of the Warsaw Ghetto uprising appeared. The leveling of the Jewish ghetto in Warsaw struck deeply at many of YIVO's employees. As Dawidowicz wrote, "The people I knew had lost children, wives, parents, their dearest friends."[20] An article in October 1943 from the Jewish Telegraphic Agency reported that the remaining Jews of Vilna had been murdered, news that shook the YIVO world to its core. Knowledge of the fate of Zelig and Riva Kalmanovich came later. Dawidowicz devoted pages 271–273 in her memoir to a lament for her beloved Vilna friends; this was her own personal elegy. The world and people she had known in 1938 had been completely destroyed.

Although the Red Army aided in the defeat of Hitler, Soviet reentry into Vilna did not assure the safety of the Jewish cultural treasures hidden during the war by YIVO activists, who were known as the *papir brigade* (Paper Brigade).[21] Avrom Sutzkever and Szmerke Kaczerginski, who survived the war on Soviet territory, found upon their return that the YIVO building had been demolished and many, but not all, of their secret hiding places completely destroyed.[22] Working with the Ministry of Culture of the Lithuanian Soviet Socialist Republic, Sutzkever and Kaczerginski believed they could reconstitute some kind of institution devoted to Jewish culture in the city now called Vilnius. But by mid-1945 they lost hope, and Sutzkever started to mail materials to New York; Kaczerginski, who had been an ardent communist, also aided in the smuggling. Kaczerginski later recalled, "We, the group of museum activists, had a bizarre realization—we must save our treasures *again*, and get them out of here."[23] Both he and Sutzkever fled Lithuania, leaving behind many of YIVO's holdings.

Schildkret herself returned to Europe after the war to work with Jewish refugees, the so-called displaced persons, in the American and British zones of occupied Germany. Hired in July 1946 as an education officer of the American Jewish Joint Distribution Committee (AJJDC), she helped salvage those remnants of YIVO's library that had been pillaged by the Nazis and later stored at the Offenbach Archive Depot (OAD).[24] By July 1947, the books arrived in New York. Schildkret later described her role in transporting YIVO's library to New York as a symbolic response "to the obsessive fantasies of rescue which had tormented me for years."[25]

Although the transfer of YIVO's books to the United States closed Schildkret's work relationship with the YIVO, her professional, political, and personal life remained bound to Polish Jewry. Hired in January 1949 as a researcher at the American Jewish Committee (AJC), the now-married Schildkret, or Lucy Dawidowicz, worked at this oldest Jewish defense organization in the United States for almost twenty years and was one of the few women on its permanent staff. The AJC position gave her an important institutional home from which to express her research interests and politics. She covered, among other topics, communism, Soviet anti-Semitism, the influence of the Soviet Union in the Middle East, and the role of religion in American politics.[26] Already in her post–Popular Front years, she began to articulate fervent support for the American government. Her anticommunist writings, which dominated her work in the 1950s, through their concomitant fealty to the American state and its governmental agencies reflected Dawidowicz's embrace of a longstanding trend within Diaspora Jewish politics, the imperatives to uphold the law of the gentile hosts, a principle known colloquially by the rabbinic principle *dina dimalkhuta dina*, and to align the Jewish community with the highest authority within the gentile state.[27] In her anticommunist writings, Dawidowicz strove to convince the American Jewish public that dissociating Jews from the socialist left in general and from communism in particular lay in the Jewish community's best interests. Supporting the American state's system of electoral politics, rather than aspiring to a revolutionary politics that rejected the authority of those in power, Dawidowicz believed, best served Jewish communal life in America.[28]

Although raised in the socialist zeitgeist of modern secular Yiddish culture, Dawidowicz had become a Roosevelt Democrat before the war.[29] The victory of the Allies over the Nazis under Franklin D. Roosevelt's stewardship only confirmed her loyalty, and, despite her political shifts toward the right in her later years, she staunchly and consistently defended Roosevelt's behavior during the war, throughout her life.[30] This attachment to Roosevelt, which characterized the sentiments of many American Jews, became another element in her anticommunism.[31] Not only had the American government defeated the Nazis, but her American passport had enabled her to leave Europe on the eve of the war, and the United States had accepted the Polish-Jewish refugees who came to YIVO in 1940. Moreover, the American army and the federal Library of Congress expedited the transfer of the YIVO's library from Offenbach. Indeed, when describing her work in the OAD, in a manuscript draft of her memoir, Dawidowicz typed, "And so, in a strange turn of fate, the books which Avrom Sutzkever and his colleagues had sorted under the Germans went through my hands," adding in pen, "under the protection of the American Army."[32] All of these factors represented many of the tangled roots of Dawidowicz's insistent anticommunism during the cold war.

Smitten with communism's allure as a young woman, Dawidowicz well knew about the Jewish romance with the left.[33] Yet her prewar experience in Vilna, friendship with Zelig Kalmanovich, awareness of the Nazi use of the canard associating Jews with Bolshevism, and knowledge of Stalin's purges in the

1930s made Dawidowicz acutely sensitive to the ways communist universalism imperiled Jewish life and to how Jewish radicalism could awaken conservative, anti-Semitic forces in society. Moreover, as someone intimately tied to the European stage in the immediate postwar period, Dawidowicz focused upon the volatility of the Jewish association with communism in the postwar Soviet bloc. After the war, many individuals of Jewish origin became prominent in the new bureaucracies in Hungary, East Germany, Czechoslovakia, and Poland.[34] Indigenous non-Jewish populations, resentful of the imposition of Soviet rule, projected their animosity upon those members of these new bureaucracies who were of Jewish origin. Further, as Joseph Stalin realized that Soviet control of the satellite states required local support, not merely obedience, he replaced loyal communists of Jewish background with communists born to the majority culture. Many of these new bureaucrats used anti-Jewish sentiment as a tool to gain political cal power, often exploiting new eruptions of the local urban violence that had characterized anti-Jewish sentiment before the war. In the postwar period, Jewish survivors returning to Poland, for example, felt vulnerable and powerless— particularly after the pogroms in Kraków in 1945 and Kielce in 1946 that claimed roughly one hundred Jewish lives—while the native Polish population saw them as privileged beneficiaries of Soviet patronage.[35] Official Soviet anti-Semitism expressed itself in the notorious 1953 "Doctors Plot," when Stalin mounted a campaign to purge officials of Jewish origin from the Soviet bureaucracy—a scheme to discredit and destroy Soviet Jewry stayed only by Stalin's death.[36] These events on distant shores did not seem so distant for someone like Dawidowicz who so thoroughly identified with the suffering of East European Jewry.

In the United States, meanwhile, political conformity provided the watchword of the increasingly suburban and middle-class Jewish community in the postwar period.[37] Eager to assert the loyalty of the Jewish community to the American government, during this time of cold war, Jewish defense organizations, such as the American Jewish Committee, the Anti-Defamation League, and the American Jewish Congress, cooperated to varying degrees with McCarthyist demands to expel communists and their sympathizers.[38] As historian Michael Staub has argued, the cold war brought about an "analogy shift" among the Jewish defense organizations. In the 1930s, systemic expressions of American racism, such as Jim Crow legislation, were compared by Jewish organizations to Nazi racial legislation, most notably to the Nuremberg Laws, yet, during the cold war, this analogy diminished, replaced by an analogy between Stalinist and Nazi totalitarianism.[39] In fact, the American Jewish Committee's research wing, strongly oriented toward the social sciences, published *The Authoritarian Personality* in 1950, eliding the distinction between Nazi and Soviet authoritarianism. In the tense environment of the 1950s, the liberal Jewish defense organizations defined their missions as working against the forces in society that could lead to an embrace of authoritarianism, whether originating on the left or on the right.[40]

The AJC's Library of Jewish Information (LJI) generated and fostered the committee's liberal campaign against communism in the late 1940s and early 1950s.[41] The LJI provided the research by which the Domestic Affairs Committee of the AJC and the AJC leadership justified their purge of communists from Jewish communal life, focusing in particular on the Jewish People's Fraternal Order (JPFO), the 50,000-member Jewish branch of the International Workers Order (IWO).[42] On June 27, 1950, the Domestic Affairs Committee adopted a policy toward communist-affiliated and communist-led organizations, characterized as upholding an ideology "so inimical to the welfare of the American community and to Jewish needs and problems to make impossible any collaboration in the solution of those problems or the filling of those needs." The Communist Party, the memo continued, sought the establishment of a political dictatorship and an authoritarian society; the memo posited this totalitarianism as analogous to that of the "Fascist Right" and utterly incompatible with "the security and free development of Jewish life no less than the survival of democratic civilization." The memo concluded that, in the future, "membership in Jewish communal institutions should be denied to any organization which, despite its apparent purpose or functions, is demonstrably Communist-affiliated or Communist-led."[43] This meant ousting the JPFO from Jewish community councils nationwide, as well as disaffiliating Jewish organizations from the Social Services Employees Union, a procommunist union that the CIO had expelled in 1950.[44] The LJI also sought to unmask the anti-Semitism of the Soviet Union, with the hope of ending any attraction communism might have to American Jews and to disassociate from the American public's mind any connection between the Jewish community and communist politics—even though, as committee members conceded, public opinion in the 1950s did not necessarily assume such a connection.[45]

Cooperating with McCarthyism had its perils, however. Demagoguery could foment latent anti-Semitic forces within American society. As Stuart Svonkin has shown, the battle against communism compromised the civil liberties commitments of the AJC and of the Anti-Defamation League, as well as, to a lesser degree, of the American Jewish Congress.[46]

For Dawidowicz, who played a central role as a researcher for the LJI's studies exposing communist activities, the authoritarian illiberalism of communism and Soviet anti-Semitism trumped the threat, in McCarthyism, to civil liberties, as well as the fear of stimulating anti-Semitism on American shores. She became secretary of the LJI's Staff Committee on Communism in December 1950, and later a full-fledged member of the committee. Her knowledge of Yiddish and of the Yiddish left proved assets for the committee; so too did her expertise in the press.[47] She quickly became the point person for research into the JPFO, the Jewish Fraternalists (the Jewish youth associate of the JPFO), the Yiddish communist newspaper, *Frayhayt*, and *Frayhayt*'s English-language magazine, *Jewish Life*.[48] By this time, Dawidowicz equated Stalinist and Nazi totalitarianism, even if the former subordinated its anti-Jewish aims to broader political goals while the latter had, from its very origins, as she insisted, singled out the Jews for destruction. In October 1950, she authored a research memo, "The National Jewish Youth Conference (NJYC): Example of Communist United-Front Policy in Action," examining the efforts of the Jewish Fraternalists to circumvent the expulsion of the JPFO from the major Jewish organizations by working from within the NJYC, an umbrella organization of Jewish youth movements under the auspices of the mainstream Jewish Welfare Board (JWB).[49] Relying on an article in *Political Affairs*, a communist journal, "For a United Front Policy among the Jewish People—Sharpen the Struggle against Bourgeois Nationalism," which called for communist work within the NJYC, Dawidowicz's memo drew a line between the Jewish Fraternalists and other left-oriented Jewish youth movements. For Dawidowicz, the Fraternalists' views, in particular their opposition to the Marshall Plan, their support for Soviet-directed Yiddish culture, and their criticism of Zionism and Judaism in the Soviet bloc, derived not from an autonomous evaluation of the political issues but from rigid subservience to the Soviet line, thus delegitimizing the group.

Dawidowicz's memos continued to focus on exposing communist tactics. The memo "Communist Approach to Jews: A Study of Communist Periodicals of July to October, 1950, Relating to Jews" bore Dawidowicz's initials, examining and then seeking to debunk five ways in which the communists shaped their rhetoric to appeal to the Jewish community. These included the assertion that Jews, special victims of hatred during World War, had an "especial" desire for peace; the assertion that the Soviet Union had a historically positive attitude toward Jews; the claim that only fascist regimes produced anti-Semitism; the charge that Western Germany harbored anti-Semitism and, supported by the British, French, and U.S. governments, presented a danger to peace; and, last, the argument that although the State of Israel needed peace, Ben-Gurion's government courted disaster by its alliance with the United States.[50] A November 1950 memo, "The National Committee of the Communist Party of the U.S.A. on Work among the Jews," emphasized that the Communist Party, recognizing the decline of official Yiddish communism in the United States, had decided to turn to the English-language communist Jewish press to attract Jews; *Jewish Life*, edited by Morris Schappes, who had recently been dismissed from City College due to his communist membership, had become, she noted, the party's semi-official Jewish organ.[51] In "Communist Propaganda on Germany," Dawidowicz tackled the thorny problem of the West's leniency with regard to German war criminals reentering West Germany society, and attempted to show that war criminals had also made their home in East Germany, concluding that "pacifists and others who for legitimate reasons are opposed to some of the activities of the American government in reference to Germany, Korea, etc., must be careful to avoid exploitation by those whose purpose is to further Communist ambitions."[52]

Dawidowicz found particularly galling the way in which communist rhetoric depicted its opponents as Nazis, a point she stressed in her October 1950 memo. There, she cited a July 24, 1950, editorial from *Frayhayt* urging support of the Stockholm Peace Conference, depicted as the only hope to rescue Jews from "the terror of the Maidaneks, Buchenwalds, and Oswiecims, which were the fearful price Jews paid in the Second World War."[53] The piece characterized the West as *pogromchiks*, perpetrators of violence against Jews in Poland and Russia, which they rhymed with *atomchiks*, supporters of atomic war. She also cited an October 10, 1950, *Frayhayt* editorial that exhorted: "Jews must be the first to fight against the war-mongers, against the crusaders for a war against the Soviet Union. They have paid with six million sacrifices in the second world war, and the lives of all remaining Jews are in jeopardy in case of a third world war."[54] In the black-and-white world of Jewish cold war polemics, both the communist and anticommunist sides used the Holocaust to anathematize their opponents.[55]

The Rosenberg trial, perhaps more than any other event, gave full expression to the exploitation of the Holocaust analogy among American Jews in the postwar years. As Deborah Dash Moore has astutely argued, because Jews constituted all the parties involved with the case, including the defendants, the prosecution, and the defense, the Rosenberg case "became a definitional ceremony in which opposing versions of American Jewish identity competed for ascendancy."[56] Dawidowicz stood at the forefront of exposing what she believed to be the hypocrisy of communist support for the Rosenbergs at the same time that Rudolf Slansky and other Czechoslovak communists had been driven out of the communist world because of their Jewish origins. Besides writing internal memos for the LJI, Dawidowicz went public with her views, publishing anticommunist articles in *Commentary, The New Leader,* and *The Reconstructionist.*[57] Dedicated to exposing communism's danger to Jews, Dawidowicz argued that communist atheistic authoritarianism could not tolerate any kind of ethnic or religious distinctiveness; communist universalism needed to be seen as, at its very root, inimical to Jewish particularism. In its efforts to win adherents among Jews, communist strategy had, she wrote, occasionally allowed for expressions of Jewish culture, as during the Popular Front and after June 1941 when allied with the United States against the Nazis, but this utilitarian use of Jewishness should not be confused with real freedom for Jewish expression. The defense of the Rosenbergs on Jewish grounds, which claimed that anti-Semitism had inspired the charges against them, should be seen as a crass appeal to postwar Jewish fears, she added; the Jewish communist press manipulated terms like *Judenrat* and *pogroms* to depict the actions of the American state.[58] In the *Commentary* article, she condemned the tactics of the National Committee to Secure Justice in the Rosenberg Case for its assertion that the Rosenbergs' Jewish origins led to their death sentence. She directly accused the communist defenders of the Rosenbergs of fomenting anti-Semitism, rather than combating it, by their insistence that the

PROTEST THE AMERICAN DREYFUSS CASE

STOP the *electrocution* *of the* *Rosenbergs*

A young American Jewish couple, Julius and Ethel Rosenberg, parents of two small children, have been sentenced by a Judge of the Federal District Court in New York, to die in the Electric chair—the first Americans in history to receive the Death penalty for alleged treason. The framed-up charge against the Rosenbergs is that they allegedly gave information to the Russians during World War II—at a time when the Russians were our allies!

They were convicted on the most flimsy type of hearsay evidence. The case is now pending on appeal—and the Sentence can still be reversed if you come to the Protest Meeting—

WEDNESDAY, FEBRUARY 6-8 P.M.
TEMPLE JUDEA, 1227 INDEPENDENCE BLVD.

──────────── ★ ★ H E A R ★ ★ ────────────

WILLIAM A. REUBEN, *Correspondent of the National Guardian*

RABBI SAMUEL TEITELBAUM, *of the Hillel Foundation*

REVEREND DOROTHY BRANCH, *Douglas Park Community Forum*

SIDNEY L. ORDOWER, *Chicago Council of Labor Unity*

ATTORNEY MICHAEL F. TUOMEY, *Chairman of the evening*

Also: Timely, Stirring Dramatization—"The **13th JUROR"** | *Admission Free*

Auspices: 6th Congressional District, PROGRESSIVE PARTY, 166 W. Washington St.

Figure 2.1 Flyer comparing the Rosenberg case to the Dreyfus affair, featuring the communist journalist William A. Reuben, founder of the Committee to Secure Justice in the Rosenberg Case. Dawidowicz condemned the language and tactics used by the committee.
Courtesy of the Tamiment Library at the Robert F. Wagner Labor Archives, William A. Reuben Collection Folder 47, Box 12, Tamiment 289, New York University.

sentence against the Rosenbergs was because of their Jewishness, thus heightening the association of anti-American radicalism with the Jewish community. To Dawidowicz, this was tantamount to assigning Jewish collective guilt for the couple's deeds: "It is well to be on guard; we have seen how similar campaigns of identification and accusation have strengthened the hands of anti-Semitic forces elsewhere."[59]

The use of the concept of guilt by association, according to Dawidowicz, not only amounted to a dangerous anti-Semitic ploy, but, in the context of the almost simultaneous show trials in the Soviet satellite of Czechoslovakia, also constituted a blatantly hypocritical and calculated act of political deflection and manipulation. On April 30, 1953, Dawidowicz prepared the memo "The Reaction of American Communists to Soviet Antisemitism" on the Slansky case. She detailed the initial denial of the Jewish origins of the defendants and the acceptance of their guilt in the pages of the *Daily Worker, Frayhayt,* and *Jewish Life,* and the party's later admission of the trial's anti-Jewish tenor, evidence of its political zigzagging.[60] In her published essay on the Slansky case, Dawidowicz drew an explicit comparison between the anti-Semitism of Hitler and that of the Soviet Union and its satellites:

> Thus a whole generation of Jews was on trial because of their origin, because they or their parents were merchants or artisans or self-employed workers, because they were doomed by their origin and early training to be "enemies of the working class." . . . *Jews* were on trial in Prague and their crime was that they were born Jews. . . . Slansky and his ten Jewish co-defendants had no vestige of all Jewishness, either secular or religious, nationalist or internationalist. Yet, the fact that they were born Jews was the most serious charge against them. . . . Hitler believed in the *racial* impurity of some people because they were born Jews. The result was that six million Jews were murdered by the Germans. For some years now Stalin has been trying to establish the *political* impurity of some people because they were born Jews. The result is that Jews in the Soviet Union have been removed from positions of leadership in the Communist Party, in the government, in the arts. The "homeless cosmopolitans," against whom a ruthless campaign continues to be waged, are merely Jews under a transparent disguise.[61]

In Dawidowicz's political consciousness, which always took Polish Jewry and its tragic fate as its point of reference, the anti-Semitism of the Soviet Union and its bloc equaled that of the Nazis. For Dawidowicz, there could be no "ordinary Communists," individuals of goodwill who saw the party as a legitimate expression of American or Jewish radicalism. To Dawidowicz, American communism could not be detached from the Soviet Union, whose postwar incarnation of state-sanctioned anti-Semitism she believed analogous to Nazism—and as dangerous, because it dissembled as a utopian ideology devoted to universalism.

Communism's universalism had attracted Jews since the Bolshevik revolution, and the peril was proven by the murders of Jewish leftists, even stalwart Stalinists, in the Soviet Union in the interwar years and beyond. A responsible Jewish communal leadership therefore had to expose Soviet anti-Semitism and disabuse Jews of the attractiveness of all universalist ideologies.

Dawidowicz held onto the Soviet–Nazi analogy to the end of her life. She concluded her memoir's preface, written in the period of the cold war's final thaw: "When the Soviets first occupied Vilna in 1940, they Sovietized it, destroying its historic identity and its Jewish particularity. The Germans who followed destroyed Vilna altogether, murdering nearly all of its 60,000 Jews—men, women, and children. . . . Hardly anything has remained of its buildings. . . . What little the Nazis had left standing, the Soviets, who returned after the war, erased."[62] Although invoking the destruction of the European Jewry she loved most, Dawidowicz composed these words to warn her American audience of the danger of left-wing forms of universalism, which she believed inevitably led to communal assimilation.[63] She now identified as a neoconservative, favored religious over secular forms of identity, and argued that Jewish communal interests were best served by allegiance to the highest gentile authority generally, and to the American state in particular, even as it shifted rightward politically.

This political move was out of step with the mainstream American Jewish community's liberal political orientation, but in keeping with Dawidowicz's singularity. In contrast to most postwar American Jewish women, Dawidowicz had already, by the 1950s, pursued a public career, had remained in an urban environment, and had worked tirelessly to remind American Jews of their historical and cultural roots in Eastern Europe. Yet, ironically, even as she positioned herself in political opposition to her liberal peers, she shared with them the anxieties about the authenticity and assimilation of postwar American Jewish culture.[64]

NOTES

1. Lucy S. Dawidowicz to Robert Dallek (author of *Franklin D. Roosevelt and American Foreign Policy, 1932–1945,* 1979), February 26, 1984, in papers of Lucy S. Dawidowicz, P-675, Box 8, folder 3, collection of the American Jewish Historical Society, Newton Centre, Massachusetts and New York. Hereafter, papers in the collection will be noted as AJHS.

2. Ethan Goffman, ed., "The New York Intellectuals and Beyond," *Shofar* 21 (Spring 2003).

3. Arthur A. Goren, "A 'Golden Decade' for American Jews: 1945–1955," in *Studies in Contemporary Jewry: A New Jewry? America since the Second World War,* vol. 8, ed. Peter Y. Medding (New York: Oxford University Press, 1992), 3–20; Lloyd Gartner, "The Midpassage of American Jewry," in *The American Jewish Experience,* ed. Jonathan D. Sarna (New York: Holmes and Meier, 1986), 224–233.

4. For a recent interpretation of the 1950s that challenges its image of contentment, see Hasia Diner, *The Jews of the United States* (Berkeley and Los Angeles: University of California Press, 2004), 260–302.

5. As a boy, Nathan Glazer attended a Talmud Torah, not a Yiddish *shule,* in East Harlem; neither Norman Podhoretz nor Irving Kristol had formal Yiddish instruction; Irving Howe

relates in his autobiography that his father forbade his going to the Workmen's Circle *shule* in his East Bronx neighborhood. In Glazer, e-mail correspondence with author, October 8, 2008; Podhoretz, e-mail correspondence with author, October 8, 2008; Kristol, e-mail correspondence with author, October 13, 2008; Irving Howe, *Margin of Hope: An Intellectual Autobiography* (New York: Harcourt Brace Jovanovich, Publishers, 1982), 3.

6. The Popular Front allowed Yiddish communists to embrace openly Jewish culture and history, and American communists to root their political activism in explicitly American terms and narratives. See Mark Naison, *Communists in Harlem during the Depression* (Urbana: University of Illinois Press, 1983); Paul Buhle, "Jews and American Communism: The Cultural Question," *Radical History Review* 3 (Spring 1980): 9–33; Nancy Sinkoff, "Yiddish Schools," in *The Encyclopedia of the American Left* (New York: Garland Publishing, 1990), 868–870. For a critique of New Left historians' reappropriation of the Popular Front as an expression of genuine American radicalism, see Theodore H. Draper, "The Popular Front Revisited," *New York Review of Books* 32, no. 9 (May 30, 1985).

7. In Lucy S. Dawidowicz, *From That Place and Time: A Memoir, 1938–1947* (1990; rpt. New Brunswick, NJ: Rutgers University Press, 2008), 18–19, Dawidowicz writes that her friend Evelyn Konoff, who had remained in the YCL, later told her that she had been expelled, while Dawidowicz's letter to Konoff only mentions her resignation from *Echo*, which was then under the wing of the Communist National Student League (Lucy Schildkret to Evelyn Konoff, February 1936 [?]. Dawidowicz Papers, Box 54, folder 5, AJHS).

8. Ezra Mendelsohn, *The Jews of East Central Europe between the World Wars* (Bloomington: Indiana University Press, 1983), 68–74.

9. Anita Norich, *Discovering Exile: Yiddish and Jewish American Culture during the Holocaust* (Stanford, CA: Stanford University Press, 2007).

10. *Shrift* 1, no. 8–9 (June–July 1937): xx.

11. Dawidowicz, *From That Place and Time*.

12. Nancy Sinkoff, "*Yidishkayt* and the Making of Lucy S. Dawidowicz," introduction to Dawidowicz, *From That Place and Time*.

13. Joshua Michael Karlip, "The Center That Could Not Hold: *Afn Sheydveg* and the Crisis of Diaspora Nationalism," Ph.D. diss., Jewish Theological Seminary of America, 2007; Gennady Estraikh, *In Harness: Yiddish Writers' Romance with Communism* (Syracuse, NY: Syracuse University Press, 2005).

14. Karlip, "The Center That Could Not Hold," 325.

15. Dov Levin, "The Jews of Vilna under Soviet Rule, 19 September–28 October, 1939," *Polin* 9 (1996): 107–137; Cecile Esther Kuznitz, "The Origins of Yiddish Scholarship and the YIVO Institute for Jewish Research," Ph.D. diss., Stanford University, 2000, 270–272.

16. Dawidowicz, *From That Place and Time*, 207.

17. Szymon Dawidowicz, who had left behind a family in Warsaw, was one of these refugees.

18. *New York Times*, March 31, 1943.

19. Lucy S. Dawidowicz, "Two of Stalin's Victims: Review of *Henryk Ehrlich un Viktor Alter*," *Commentary* 12 (1951): 614–616, and Dawidowicz, *From That Place and Time*, 239–240.

20. In the typically restrained style of the memoir, Dawidowicz hesitated to mention that two of the murdered were her husband's children, to whom she dedicated *The War against the Jews*. See Dawidowicz, *From That Place and Time*, 243–244, and Lucy S. Dawidowicz, *The War against the Jews, 1933–1945* (New York: Bantam Books, 1975).

21. David E. Fishman, *Embers Plucked from the Fire: The Rescue of Jewish Cultural Treasures in Vilna* (New York: YIVO Institute for Jewish Research, 1996).

22. Ibid., 11.

23. Cited in ibid., 13. Emphasis in the original.

24. Seymour Pomrenze [Shalom Pomerantz], "'Operation Offenbach': Saving Jewish Cultural Treasures in Germany," *YIVO bleter* 29, no. 2 (Summer 1947): 282–285, and Dawidowicz, *From That Place and Time*, chap. 13.

25. Dawidowicz, *From That Place and Time*, 326.

26. Dawidowicz published regularly on political issues in *The American Jewish Yearbook* from 1953 to 1968; the titles of her articles included: "American Reaction to Soviet Anti-Semitism," "The United States and Israel," "German Collective Indemnity to Israel and the Conference on Jewish Material Claims against Germany," "Civil Rights and Intergroup Tensions," and "Church and State."

27. Richard I. Cohen, "Jews and the State: The Historical Context," ed. Ezra Mendelsohn, *Studies in Contemporary Jewry: Dangerous Alliances and the Perils of Privilege* 19 (New York: Oxford University Press, 2003): 3–16.

28. For a synthetic study of modern East European Jewish politics, see Ezra Mendelsohn, *On Modern Jewish Politics* (Oxford: Oxford University Press, 1993).

29. In her "State of World Jewry Address, 1984," given at New York's 92nd Street YWHA–YMHA on December 2, 1984, Dawidowicz said, "It was Franklin Delano Roosevelt who turned Jews into Democratic fanatics." Her research notes on the Jewish community's attitude toward Roosevelt can be found in Box 8, folders 1–5 and 11 (among others), Dawidowicz Papers, AJHS.

30. Lucy S. Dawidowicz, "Indicting American Jews," *Commentary* 75, no. 6 (June 1983): 36–44, and Lucy S. Dawidowicz, "Could America Have Rescued Europe's Jews?" in *What Is the Use of Jewish History?* ed. Neal Kozodoy (New York: Schocken, 1992), 157–178.

31. Henry Feingold, "Crisis and Response: American Jewish Leadership during the Roosevelt Years," *Modern Judaism* 8, no. 2 (May 1988): 101–118.

32. Box 52, folder 6, Dawidowicz Papers, AJHS.

33. Vivian Gornick, *The Romance of American Communism* (New York: Basic Books, 1977).

34. *Dark Times, Dire Decisions: Jews and Communism, Studies in Contemporary Jewry: An Annual*, vol. 20, ed. Dan Diner (New York: Oxford University Press, 2005); Jerry Z. Muller, "Communism, Anti-Semitism, and the Jews," *Commentary* 86 (August 1988): 28–39.

35. Natalia Aleksiun, "The Vicious Circle: Jews in Communist Poland, 1944–1956," *Studies in Contemporary Jewry: An Annual* 19 (New York: Oxford University Press, 2003): 157–180.

36. Jonathan Brent and Vladimir P. Naumov, *Stalin's Last Crime: The Plot against the Jewish Doctors, 1948–1953* (London: HarperCollins, 2003).

37. Goren, "A 'Golden Decade' for American Jews," 9.

38. Stuart Svonkin, *Jews against Prejudice: American Jews and the Fight for Civil Liberties* (New York: Columbia University Press, 1997), and Marc Dollinger, *Quest for Inclusion: Jews and Liberalism in Modern America* (Princeton, NJ: Princeton University Press, 2000).

39. Michael E. Staub, *Torn at the Roots: The Crisis of Jewish Liberalism in Postwar America* (New York: Columbia University Press, 2002), 19–44.

40. Murray Friedman, *The Neoconservative Revolution: Jewish Intellectuals and the Shaping of Public Policy* (Cambridge: Cambridge University Press, 2005), 19–20.

41. Svonkin, *Jews against Prejudice*, 113–134.

42. Ibid., 166. Minutes of the American Jewish Committee Staff Committee on the Communist Problem, December 7, 1950, p. 1.

43. American Jewish Committee memo, "Statement of Policy toward Communist-Affiliated and Communist-Led Organizations," June 27, 1950.

44. Svonkin, *Jews against Prejudice*, 166–167.

45. Ibid., 116. The Jewish liberal defense organizations were also aware that demagogic McCarthyism had the potential to foment anti-Semitism in postwar American politics.

46. Svonkin, *Jews against Prejudice*, 125.

47. Schildkret wrote her Aspirantur thesis on the Yiddish press in nineteenth-century England and later wrote a master's thesis on a Yiddish newspaper in New York City. Lucy S. Dawidowicz, "Louis Marshall's Yiddish Newspaper: *The Jewish World*: A Study in Contrasts," *Jewish Social Studies* 25, no. 2 (April 1963): 102–132.

48. Dawidowicz's archives contain a two-paged typed list of her anticommunist materials, prepared by Helen Ritter, an AJC archivist. The list, below, is verbatim.

American Federation of Polish Jews (see also Landsmanshaften)
Antisemitism: CP Position
Bick, Abraham
Communism and Assimilation
Communists and Civil Rights
Communist Party
Communist Party—18th National Convention
DPOW (District 65)
Emergency Civil Liberties Committee
Emma Lazarus Federation [See also JFFO]
International Workers Order (IWO) [See also JFFO]
Israel: CP Position
Jewish Community—CP Position
Jewish Life
Jewish Music Alliance
Jewish People's Fraternal order (JPFO) (See also IWO)
JPFO Schools
Jewish Young Fraternalists (See also JPFO)
Jews and Investigations
Jews Against Communism
Kinderland Camp (See also JPFO)
Labor and CP
Landsmanshaften (Communist Dominated) (See also American Federation of Polish
    Jews)
Novick, Paul
"Peace"—Organizations and Activities
Schappes, Morris
Sobell Case
Social Service Employees Union
Soviet antisemitism—CP Position
Soviet Union Death Penalty for Economic Offenses
Yiddish Kultur Farband (YKUF)

Box 8, folder 11. Dawidowicz Papers, AJHS. See, too, The American Jewish Committee, Library of Jewish Information, "Jewish People's Fraternal Order of the International Worker's Order," November 27, 1950, in Box 8, folder 12, Dawidowicz Papers, AJHS. Dawidowicz's initials are at the end of the memo and her full name is handwritten on the front cover.

49. Library of Jewish Information, American Jewish Committee, Staff Committee on Communism, October 12, 1950. Dawidowicz's authorship of this memo can, as with many, be affirmed by her initials, LSD, on the last page.

50. L[ucy]S[.]D[awidowicz], "Communist Approach to Jews: A Study of Communist Periodicals of July to October, 1950, Relating to Jews," October 20, 1950, American Jewish Committee, Library of Jewish Information.

51. L[ucy]S[.]D[awidowicz], "The National Committee of the Communist Party of the U.S.A. on Work among Jews," November 16, 1950, American Jewish Committee, Library of Jewish Information.

52. L[ucy]S[.]D[awidowicz], "Communist Propaganda on Germany," April 12, 1951: 4, American Jewish Committee, Library of Jewish Information.

53. L[ucy]S[.]D[awidowicz], "Communist Approach to Jews: A Study of Communist Periodicals of July to October, 1950, Relating to Jews," October 20, 1950: 5, American Jewish Committee, Library of Jewish Information.

54. Ibid.

55. Staub, *Torn at the Roots*, 19–44.

56. I would add to Moore's interpretation: the trial especially brought to the fore American Jewry's *political* identities. Deborah Dash Moore, "Reconsidering the Rosenbergs: Symbol and Substance in Second-Generation American Jewish Consciousness," *Journal of American Ethnic History* 8, no. 1 (Fall 1988): 21. In 1988, when Moore's article appeared, the bitter polemics between Jewish cold warriors and Jewish New Left historians (and those perceived as New Left historians) still raged and directly implicated Dawidowicz's writing about the Committee to Secure Justice in the Rosenberg Case. See Box 44, Folder 8, Dawidowicz Papers, AJHS; see also Nathan Glazer's letter to the editor and Moore's response, in *Journal of American Ethnic History* 8, no. 2 (Spring 1989): 192–194. On the Jewish elements in the Rosenberg case, see Svonkin, *Jews against Prejudice*; Staub, *Torn at the Roots*; and Jeffrey M. Marker, "The Jewish Community and the Case of Ethel and Julius Rosenberg," *Maryland Historian* 3 (Fall 1972): 105–121.

57. Lucy S. Dawidowicz, "'Anti-Semitism' and the Rosenberg Case: The Latest Communist Propaganda Trap," *Commentary* 14 (July 1952): 41–25; Lucy S. Dawidowicz, "The Communists and the Rosenberg Case," *New Leader* 35, no. 36 (September 8, 1952): 15; Lucy S. Dawidowicz, "The Rosenberg Case: 'Hate-America' Weapon," *New Leader* 35, no. 51 (December 22, 1952): 13; Lucy S. Dawidowicz, "The Crime of Being a Jew," *Reconstructionist* 18, no. 18 (January 9, 1953): 8–12; Lucy S. Dawidowicz, "False Friends and Dangerous Defenders," *Reconstructionist* 19, no. 6 (May 1, 1953): 9–15. Her byline for the last article read, "Lucy S. Dawidowicz is a student of Communist tactics and strategy and has written on this subject for *Commentary* and *The New Leader*."

58. For the use of East European show trials to construct fear in the postwar period, see Melissa Feinberg, "Die Durchsetzungeiner neuen Welt, Politische Prozesse in Osteuropa, 1948–1954," in *Angst im Kalten Krieg*, ed. Bernd Greiner, Christian Th. Müller, and Dierk Walter (Hamburg: Hamburger Edition, 2009), 190–219.

59. Dawidowicz, "'Anti-Semitism' and the Rosenberg Case": 45.

60. L[ucy]S[.]D[awidowicz], "The Reaction of American Communists to Soviet Anti-Semitism," April 23, 1953, American Jewish Committee, Library of Jewish Information.

61. Dawidowicz, "The Crime of Being a Jew": 11. Emphasis in the original.

62. Dawidowicz, *From That Place and Time*, xiii.

63. Reviewing Daniel Aaron's *Writers on the Left: Episodes in American Literary Communism*, Dawidowicz wrote: "The Yiddish Jews of the Communist Party were not Jewishly nationalist. *They were attracted to a world view in which differences would disappear.*" Emphasis is mine. Lucy S. Dawidowicz, "Review of Nathan Glazer, *The Social Basis of American Communism*, and Daniel Aaron, "Writers on the Left: Episodes in American Literary Communism," *American Jewish Historical Quarterly* 53, no. 2 (December 1963): 192.

64. Lucy S. Dawidowicz, "Middle-Class Judaism: A Case Study," *Commentary: A Jewish Review* 60: 29 (June 1960): 492–503; Riv-Ellen Prell, "Community and the Discourse of Elegy: The Postwar Suburban Debate," in *Imagining the American Jewish Community*, ed. Jack Wertheimer (Waltham, MA: Brandeis University Press, 2007), 67–90.

3   "Our Defense against Despair"

THE PROGRESSIVE POLITICS OF THE
NATIONAL COUNCIL OF JEWISH
WOMEN AFTER WORLD WAR II

KATHLEEN A. LAUGHLIN

In a reflective mood at the conclusion of her 1954 report to the national board of directors, Elsie Elfenbein, executive director of the National Council of Jewish Women (NCJW), placed the organization in the context of the perils of the atomic age. Referring with alarm to a test of the H-bomb, which "scattered particles of death to far corners," she proclaimed that the NCJW's program of social action was "our defense against despair."[1] After the horror of World War II and the escalating global tensions in its aftermath, the NCJW made an unprecedented commitment to mainstream politics. The triumph of New Deal liberalism, the redefinition of citizenship and of the role of women during World War II, and the changing orientation of many Jewish organizations in response to the Holocaust, as well as the participation of Jews in suburban culture, required a very different civic commitment after 1945. The rise of fascist governments in the 1930s and 1940s was a grim lesson that politics and policy could either protect or persecute a nation's most vulnerable citizens, and in postwar America Jewish organizations often united in a common cause to more consistently and militantly oppose anti-Semitism. Efforts to safeguard and promote pluralism evolved from philanthropic endeavors to assist Jewish immigrants in the late nineteenth century to various forms of social justice advocacy by the mid-twentieth century. World War II and the politics of the cold war era transformed the NCJW from an organization primarily concerned with social welfare and immigrant aid into an effective political interest group.

Programs and resources during and after World War II embraced civic feminism—a stage of public activism between the social welfare orientation of domestic feminism of the Progressive era and gender-conscious feminism as it developed in the 1960s and 1970s. In its early history, the NCJW practiced *domestic feminism*, a commitment to social activism contained within the boundaries of traditional womanhood; its primary mission in the late nineteenth and early twentieth centuries was to maintain Jewish identity in America by promoting

Jewish education and elevating motherhood.[2] As civic feminists, NCJW members felt no obligation to justify political pursuits by invoking motherhood, as previous generations of activists were compelled to do, but they did not critique traditional gender relations. Younger NCJW members were volunteers, not career women, but their efforts included participation in social justice discourse. The NCJW found legitimacy as a participant in organized responses to the ascendancy of right-wing politics in the 1950s, recasting a commitment to Jewish identity and community as a public promotion of Jewish interests as a group.

Active civic engagement by women in the 1940s and 1950s was legitimized in the context of modern statism, since government agencies and local communities depended on an effective volunteer corps to promote and implement policies. Thus the federal government's reliance on community involvement to execute policies and services during World War II contributed to revitalizing the moribund NCJW. A tremendous increase in membership during the war reflected a renewed commitment to public service among Jewish women, as well as the creation of new sections (state and local branches) in response to population shifts caused by wartime dislocation. In one year, 1944–1945, membership grew by five thousand members.[3] Sections actively promoted cooperation with the Office of Price Administration and worked with the Office of Public Relations of the War Department. A report from the newly formed California Peninsula Section epitomized the NCJW's collaboration with the federal government: "The women have been very much absorbed in war activities and have taken a great deal of responsibility either on a paid or full-time volunteer basis with war agencies."[4] In Santa Barbara, membership growth was attributed to a meaningful mission: "The Section has maintained the interest of its members through a variety of the usual war activities. It has cooperated with many community and war agencies and has established a reputation for good work."[5] Mrs. I. Lee Levy (some women preferred the practice, standard at the time, of using their husband's names), national chairperson of the NCJW's Committee on Social Legislation, believed that World War II led to profound changes in the status of women, changes that required a new civic obligation:

> In order to equip ourselves to meet our obligations as citizens, we must study and we must act. Our membership must be awakened to a more active participation in our legislative program. This is a must . . . we must make clear to American women that they have a personal stake in all of this. During the war, we realized that our voluntary services not only contributed to victory for the nation, but also to our own personal welfare. . . . We can no longer think as our husbands do, or always vote as they do. We must assume our share of responsibility for what happens in the world to be.[6]

An association with the federal government was institutionalized in 1944 when the NCJW hired its first professional lobbyist, Olya Margolin, to work in

Washington, D.C. Margolin began her tenure with no clear job description, but her first task after securing office space in the Jewish Welfare Board building was to contact "key people in various governmental departments and agencies and also private organizations."[7] From the beginning, Margolin sought to maintain and nurture the council's Washington connections, which she believed would raise the organization's stature. During this period, NCJW's national committees made programmatic adjustments to accommodate the policy goals of government agencies. The International Relations Committee worked closely with the Women's Interests Section of the Bureau of Public Relations of the War Department, and it was not unusual for professional staff and volunteer national committee chairs to attend briefings at the State Department and the War Department.

The practice of collaboration between federal agencies and women's organizations was resumed in the context of post–World War II internationalism. The Women's Interest Section of the War Department's Bureau of Public Relations, an agency created to involve women in the war effort, continued to convene regional meetings throughout the country, to which the NCJW sent several representatives.[8] The State Department enlisted the support of voluntary associations in its effort to draft and promote a charter for the incipient United Nations. Former Secretary of State Edward Stettinius, who would later become the first U.S. ambassador to the United Nations, met with representatives from one hundred groups to discuss proposals for the projected organization. According to Mrs. Maxwell Ehrlich, chairperson of the NCJW's Committee on International Relations and Peace, the meeting was an unprecedented engagement with U.S. foreign policy: "This meeting marked a milestone in that it was the first time the State Department had held such a meeting and invited criticism, discussion and suggestions on foreign policy."[9] The NCJW's Fanny Brin, a vice-chair of the Women's Action Committee for Victory and Lasting Peace, remained a consultant with the State Department along with representatives of forty-two other women's organizations.[10] The Committee on International Relations and Peace used these mandates to involve section presidents and section international relations chairpersons in a grassroots effort to urge the U.S. Senate to ratify the charter of the United Nations, signed by fifty nations in San Francisco on June 26, 1945.[11]

The NCJW's close involvement with the State Department ensured its participation as an observer to U.N. deliberations on Palestine in 1947. Historically, the NCJW had eschewed Zionism, preferring to emphasize the acculturation of immigrants in the United States. The Holocaust changed the group's position, and the NCJW used its relationship with the State Department and alliances with women's organizations to advocate for the creation of a Jewish state. Still, after 1948, support for the State of Israel was modest, confined to contributing to educational institutions, as the primary mission of the organization, to represent the interests of Jewish women in the United States, remained unchanged.[12]

Volunteer leaders and staff believed that a broader program and deeper interest in world affairs could achieve a more inclusive membership. When the NCJW
was founded in 1893, by acculturated German Jewish immigrants, the early membership tended to support Reform Judaism, a religious adaptation to reconcile
Jewish religious identity with American culture. Despite efforts to assiduously
avoid sectarian divisions and sidestep controversial doctrinal and political issues,
the NCJW remained, in the 1940s, a group of middle- and upper-middle-class
women involved with Reform congregations. The Section Service chair during
the war years, Viola Hoffman Hymes, emphasized the importance of expanding
NCJW membership to include women from other denominations, writing that
"great membership potentialities lie in an intensive effort to enroll Jewish women
of all phases of Judaism in our cause, to the end that we may be more truly a cross
section of American Jewish women."[13] The organization continued to draw new
members through, in part, Hymes's leadership and plan of outreach. In 1946,
12,177 women joined, creating a paid membership base of 65,743, with 196 sections; the national office set an ambitious goal of 100,000 members for the next
club year.[14]

This reconstituted membership base of civic-minded younger women and
the organization's internal growing pains demanded a critical reevaluation of
its longstanding functions and procedures. The large number of disparate, active
women's clubs in postwar America reflected a desire, among women who made
varied commitments to responsible citizenship during the war emergency, to
join organizations affiliated with local, state, and national politics; the National
Council of Jewish Women was no exception. After World War II, the NCJW
became a more complex bureaucratic organization, with an expanding staff and
a Washington representative to support its proliferating sections. Dues paid by
active sections subsidized an ambitious national program organized by professional lobbyists and public relations personnel, who, in turn, trained Jewish
women in how to be effective community leaders. To adjust to these changes,
a survey committee was formed in 1946 under the direction of Mrs. Harold E.
Beckman, who placed the reassessment of NCJW functions in the context of the
challenges of the postwar world: "The chaos of our times stresses this need, for
Council can contribute to American life only if there is full assurance of where
we are going, why and how. . . . Only through an evaluation of our program and
by the reshaping of it shall we be able to play our part."[15] The survey considered
all aspects of the group's operations, including staff assignments, committee
structures, activities, and publications. Several national committees, including
International Relations and Peace, Social Legislation, and Contemporary Jewish
Affairs, were subsumed by a new committee, Education and Social Action, and
more staff was hired to support the social action initiative.[16]

For the NCJW, organizational reform focused on streamlining activities to
participate more effectively in the emerging coalitions of Jewish organizations

formed to combat social discrimination. Steven Windmueller describes the evolution of Jewish identity and political activism in the United States after World
War II as centering on five principles:

> The security and welfare of Jews, both in the U.S. and worldwide; the case
> for separation of church and state, as symbolic of the Jewish community's
> commitment to and support of America's democratic institutions and social
> values; a commitment to civil rights, economic opportunity, and social jus-
> tice concerns, developed in part through promoting intergroup relationships
> and coalitions; the case for religious tolerance and understanding; a commitment
> to strengthening Israel's political standing and public affairs image.[17]

According to Windmueller, B'nai B'rith, the American Jewish Committee, the
American Jewish Congress, and other Jewish organizations tried to implement
these principles by functioning as political interest groups, jointly lobbying for
legislation and using the courts to challenge exclusionary policies in both the
public and private sectors. The NCJW followed a similar agenda, in collaboration
with a dense network of well-established women's groups, Jewish political and
charitable organizations, state governments, and the federal government. The
NCJW historian, Faith Rogow, explains how World War II and the Holocaust
altered its purpose: "Council's most notable change following World War II was
an increasing sophistication in legislative work. The Holocaust underscored the
importance of legal protection for minorities, leading NCJW to pay closer attention to the processes of government."[18] Despite Jewish upward mobility, NCJW
and other Jewish organizations defined Jewish Americans as a minority group.
Mrs. Edmond M. Lazard, national chairperson of the Committee on Social
Legislation, emphasized this fact to section committee chairpersons, "Discrimination
in employment on both state and national levels is another of the wartime problems we face as one of the minority groups."[19]

NCJW's stellar record of Jewish community involvement over a period of fifty
years made it an important ally in progressive causes. Several umbrella bodies
were formed after World War II to address Jewish issues and to ensure that the
federal government remained committed to equal justice. The election of NCJW's
executive director Elsie Elfenbein as director of the National Council for a
Permanent Fair Employment Practices Commission established Council's role as a
political player. Elfenbein also served on the executive committees of two coalition
groups organized to reform immigration policy and combat anti-Semitism: the
Citizens' Committee for Displaced Persons, which the NCJW was instrumental
in forming in 1947, and the National Community Advisory Relations Council, an
umbrella organization of several Jewish organizations that included the American
Jewish Committee, the American Jewish Congress, and the Anti-Defamation League
of B'nai B'rith.[20] Professional staff from NCJW headquarters in New York City
urged local sections to stimulate interest in the displaced persons problem within

Figure 3.1 Group (National Council of Jewish Women members) with John F. Kennedy and Lyndon B. Johnson, Commission on the Status of Women, Washington, D.C., 1963.
Courtesy of the Minnesota Historical Society, Box 62, Collection no. 142.G.3.1B-1, Viola Hoffman Hymes Papers.

local communities to create a groundswell of support for adjusting immigration quotas; instructions were sent to sections on how to organize community meetings that could establish local citizens committees on displaced persons.[21]

Meanwhile, the anticommunist crusade was initiating assaults on civil liberties that required a vigilant defense of the pluralist ideal. President Harry S. Truman in 1947 issued Executive Order No. 9835, a measure designed to create an investigative mechanism to evaluate the loyalty of federal employees; he did this in part to prove that he was not "soft on Communism."[22] He also approved initiatives to deport foreign radicals. Other measures that sacrificed civil liberties for national security followed. Still, Truman opposed the Internal Security Act of 1950 (known as the McCarran Act after its chief sponsor, Senator Pat McCarran, D-Nevada), a measure requiring the registration of communists and the creation of a Subversive Activities Control Board, which passed over his veto.[23] The election of Republican Dwight D. Eisenhower in 1952 contributed to the ascendancy of right-wing politics. Hardly an anticommunist ideologue, and no friend of the Republican senator from Wisconsin and notorious red-baiter Joseph P. McCarthy, Eisenhower nevertheless promoted an ambitious legislative program designed to ensure internal security, and continued Truman's policy to deport subversives.[24]

The entrenchment of conservatism and the emergence of a suburban culture during the 1950s posed unique challenges for the NCJW. By the 1950s, the national staff tried to balance attention to domestic and foreign policy with the insularity of the suburbs. The unrelenting pressure on women, after World War II, to leave the labor market and relinquish positions of public authority in order to resume domestic duties, and the fact of a rising number of white women retreating to the suburbs, required women's clubs to forge a vision of gendered citizenship. Local civic projects to improve community educational and recreational facilities appealed to stay-at-home mothers attuned to the needs of children. The chair of the NCJW's Public Affairs Committee explained why a focus on the local community captured members' attention:

> Active movement to the suburbs is prevalent everywhere. In those areas we find a lag in public utilities, schools, shopping areas, etc. . . . Needs in these communities for housing and other facilities are such that funds for these purposes take a priority over other community needs. There is a 'rash' of building new synagogues and temples, new centers and such public facilities as libraries and roads.[25]

Women's door-to-door citizenship reflected, too, the increasing importance of local politics in the burgeoning suburbs. Scholars are beginning to assess women's public activism in the postwar period, seeing it as inseparable from a particular political culture emerging in the suburbs during the 1950s, one that emphasized the importance of good citizenship that included both community involvement and awareness of the larger world. Loan programs provided by the GI Bill of Rights enabled 42 percent of World War II veterans (primarily white and male) to become homeowners; thus the suburban population increased 43 percent between 1947 and 1953.[26] The implications of suburban growth were far-reaching: suburbs led to a sharper segmentation of American society by race and class, and changed the nature of political activism and discourses. In socioeconomic enclaves, historian Lizabeth Cohen writes, "suburbanites' conception of the public good narrowed" so that they "linked local government to democracy" and became suspicious of centralized authority.[27]

However, parochial concerns did not necessarily prevent progressive politics from taking root. Sylvie Murray's case study of political activism in Queens, New York, shows that the ideals of civic responsibility and the quest for the good life stimulated, rather than stymied, progressive agendas.[28] NCJW activities tended to fuse community concerns and progressive politics. Cooperative community activities determined the direction of section programs in the early 1950s, with 70 percent of sections reporting active engagement with PTA groups, civil and welfare groups, the League of Women Voters, school boards, and interfaith groups on community betterment projects. At the same time, the NCJW's national efforts to promote action on state legislation also yielded satisfactory

outcomes, as 57 percent of sections reported action on pending bills on state leg-
islatures. Interest in civil liberties and communism helped the national office convince sections to remain involved in national affairs; all sections reported either
creating a study group or holding a general meeting on the topic.[29]

Members of the national board of directors were acutely aware that the
future of the organization depended on suburban women. Longstanding commitments to charity work in urban areas, where the NCJW often functioned
as a voluntary social service agency, were abandoned to support organized civic
engagement in suburban communities as well as informed citizenship. A system
of regional conferences to stimulate legislative action was one of many efforts to
develop leadership in the suburbs.[30] In 1956, the National Membership Committee
was charged by the NCJW board to "give high priority to organizing sections in
the suburban areas around large urban areas," and was given two months to sub-
mit a recruitment plan and budget "for such an intensive campaign."[31] The following year, the national office commissioned a report on operations, to find
new ways to recruit younger members; the report concluded that the NCJW
needed "more emotional appeal" and had to find ways to "adapt our program
and organizational structure to the changing age-level and changing socioeconomic composition of our membership" so as to compete with Hadassah for
membership in the suburbs.[32] Executive Director Elfenbein, in clever terms,
described this approach as "bifocal vision,"[33] with the national office functioning
as the service provider for grassroots work in the suburbs. But Elfenbein was
painfully aware of the "gap between the programs we so painstakingly develop in
our national office and its implementation on the local scene."[34]

To close that gap, the Future Planning Committee, reporting to the national
board of directors in 1956, suggested that the basis of the NCJW's entire program
should be citizen participation:

> Current trends in Jewish life pointed up to the desire of Jewish women to be
> identified with the Jewish community but also to participate more actively in
> the life of the total community. The thought was expressed that NCJW is a
> bridge that enables Jewish women to be identified as a part of the Jewish com-
> munity through their membership in a Jewish organization and, through that
> organization, to accept the role of citizen in relation to the total community.[35]

Citizen training included study groups on public and world affairs, institutes on
lobbying and other means of political work, and leadership training. In 1956, the
national office initiated a two-year pilot project in leadership training for members. The centerpiece of the project was a seminar at national headquarters that
promised to provide extensive training in the "principles and practices of community organization, social planning, understanding human personality, and
group interaction," which would be "applied against a backdrop of Council's
purpose and program."[36]

In spite of the influence of suburban culture, women's clubs and organizations were not uniform in their adjustments to the imperatives of the cold war, and differences in missions, goals, and political ideologies at times fractured potential coalitions around the promotion of national policies on women's issues. Racial, ethnic, class, and ideological differences contributed to rifts within the post–World War II women's movement. The NCJW's commitment to pluralism required the implementation of a progressive agenda not shared by larger national white women's organizations such as the League of Women Voters, the American Association of University Women, the Business and Professional Women's Clubs (BPW), and the General Federation of Women's Clubs. The General Federation of Women's Clubs committed resources to national security and were fiercely anticommunist, while the BPW made no secret of its animosity toward labor unions. Although most national women's organizations were publicly nonpartisan (even sectarian groups such as the National Council of Catholic Women and the NCJW professed inclusion), in practice organizations tended to be in sympathy either with the Republican Party or with the Democratic Party. White, ethnic women with ties to an immigrant past, and African American women had progressive leanings and were far more likely than other U.S. women to view anticommunism as a threat to civil liberties.[37] NCJW alliances with some women's organizations were no longer automatic in the 1950s. Although it was a common practice for sections to have associate membership in local women's clubs affiliated with the with the General Federation of Women's Clubs, in the 1950s the NCJW revisited its ongoing partnership with an organization that was drifting to the right on national security issues.[38] Specifically, the NCJW refused to join the Clearinghouse of Women's Organizations for National Security because that group endorsed an array of policies and programs that could potentially subvert civil liberties in the name of national security.[39] Differences over the efficacy of the Equal Rights Amendment also continued to fuel acrimony in the 1950s. Clubs in the urban ethnic coalition believed that the ERA would erode protective legislation regulating working conditions and establishing minimum and maximum hours for working women; conversely, BPW members believed that the ERA was the only way to address persistent inequalities between the sexes and publicly bemoaned the political clout of organized labor.[40]

What is notable about the NCJW legislative program, compared with that of other national women's organizations in the 1950s (with the exception of the National Council of Negro Women), was a bold advocacy of economic planning in the United States and an agenda that emphasized civil liberties and civil rights at home and a strong commitment to human rights abroad. Like most national women's organizations in postwar America, the NCJW passed resolutions on national issues, creating a platform to guide local study groups, committee projects, and political activism. Resolutions passed during national conventions in the 1950s revealed an active interest in foreign affairs—a commitment stimulated by agencies of the federal government in the 1940s—and a program pledging time and resources to domestic concerns from consumer affairs to government reform. Resolutions passed during the triennial convention in 1953, regarding civil rights and civil liberties, not only promoted a broad advocacy of equal justice, calling for instance for "opportunities for free expression and to safeguard the rights and freedom for all," but also promoted very specific calls to action such as "to work for the strengthening of state and local laws against lynching, and support legislation which will make participation in lynching a federal felony."[41]

Throughout the late 1940s and the 1950s, the national office repeatedly built upon the 1946 internal survey to stimulate leadership and political activism in states and local communities, seeking to accomplish more than simply recommending policies in the form of resolutions. In 1948, the New York headquarters hired a full-time staff member, Sylvia Bushell, to coordinate efforts to pass state legislation. By 1954 each state section was required to pay a "legislative tax" to fund ongoing campaigns to pass state legislation. A year later, funds were allocated to publish a legislative bulletin to keep members informed about political developments in their states.[42] The national Public Affairs Committee's 1954 report to the board of directors attributed structural changes on the national level to increased political activism among the rank and file:

> In 1948, the value of state legislation program was deemed sufficiently great so that a special professional staff member was engaged whose sole responsibility was the stimulation and servicing of state legislation activities. During the five-year period that the state legislation program was served by a staff member, the number of state chairman serving multiplied many times and the effectiveness increased to a marked extent.[43]

State politics became even more significant in the early 1950s, because federal policies focused almost exclusively on national security during the Korean War. A conservative Congress and the focus on national security accentuated the role of the states in ensuring social equality.[44]

Indeed, in the cold war era, Elfenbein's framework of "bifocal vision," a combination of work in local communities and a presence in national affairs, became even more vital with the erosion of civil liberties in the name of national security. A report by Olya Margolin to Helen Raebeck, NCJW's executive director, about a meeting Margolin attended with the postmaster general, Arthur E. Summerfield, related that he wanted to enlist women's organizations in a campaign against obscene material. Margolin expressed incredulity, suspecting that Harden, the former president of the General Federation of Women's Clubs and former state legislator from Indiana who had been appointed assistant postmaster general by President Eisenhower, lay behind this effort to involve women's organizations. Margolin noted that most of the people present at the meeting came from either

from government agencies or Republican organizations. Her sardonic analysis of
the meeting dramatically demonstrates a concern with the eroding of civil liberties and the persecution of liberal groups under the guise of protecting national
security:

> The purpose of the meeting was to present the problems in such a way as to
> arouse the women of the country to some action. However, it occurred to me
> that the real purpose was to encourage the organizations to appear before the
> Post Office and Civil Service subcommittee of the House and present the kind
> of testimony which will produce much stronger legislation than now on the
> statute books. . . . The chief inspector also tried to persuade me and the other
> listeners that the distribution of obscene material is a threat to national secu-
> rity in that dictators use this method of engaging in subversive activities . . .
> my impression is that the chief objective is to arouse public opinion against
> the liberal decisions of the courts. . . . After the speakers "aroused" us about
> the danger to our youth and the national security we were taken to a room,
> kept under lock and key, to be shown an exhibit of some of the pictorial mate-
> rial, which is presumably designed to destroy the country.[45]

The exhibit included copies of *Playboy*, which left Margolin unconvinced that the
nation was threatened. But she did see a threat in the implication that the courts
impeded national security, and in the politicization of the federal bureaucracy.
She contacted the American Library Association (ALA) about the meeting and
wisely ensured that an ALA representative was able to attend. She also informed
the National Clearinghouse on Civil Liberties of the postmaster general's meeting with women's groups.

In addition to being an active participant in the National Clearinghouse for
Civil Liberties, a group that included the American Civil Liberties Union, the
American Library Association, the National Council of Negro Women, the AFL-
CIO, and two major Jewish groups, the American Jewish Committee and the
American Jewish Congress, the NCJW organized national women's organiza-
tions into a separate interest group called National Organizations on Civil
Liberties (NOCL). The National Council of Negro Women, United Church
Women, and the YWCA sent representatives to NOCL meetings at NCJW head-
quarters, but the League of Women Voters and the American Association of
University Women declined invitations to join. Margolin volunteered to contact
the National Council of Catholic Women; there is no record that she approached
the Republican-dominated Business and Professional Women's Clubs or the
General Federation of Women's Clubs.[46] In keeping with the community-focused
orientation of women's clubs during this period, this coalition group of progressive women's organizations promoted several community-based projects promoting civil liberties. The most successful and notable project was the Freedom
to Read campaign, which, in association with the American Library Association,

featured "banned books" displays at local libraries, events covered by the national media. In another community-based project, NCJW members would encourage voluntary associations to develop "freedom codes."[47] One action activity involved encouraging local theater managers to show the Columbia Pictures film *Storm Center,* starring Bette Davis as an embattled librarian. NOCL's executive director, Frances Cahn, urged sections to sponsor a premier of the film, purchase blocks of tickets, and to set up a banned book exhibit in the theater lobby. Cahn's description of the film to section presidents barely disguises a reference to Senator Joseph McCarthy: "It tells the story of what happens to a librarian who refuses to remove an acknowledged communist book from her library shelves. It shows how an unscrupulous politician seizes upon this principled action to denounce her as a communist in order to advance his own career."[48]

The NCJW looked askance at federal policy making that coincided with the ascendancy of right-wing politics, and monitored federal legislation and executive policies designed to expand presidential authority. As the NCJW representative to the National Clearinghouse on Civil Liberties monthly meetings, Margolin reported on several bills that could potentially erode civil liberties in the nation. Margolin, Raebeck, and NCJW's national president, Katherine Engel, were particularly troubled by the use of executive orders and by regulations changes within the federal government put into place without public scrutiny.[49] In addition to new restrictions limiting access to government information, the Internal Revenue Bureau and the Treasury Department were beginning a campaign to deny organizations tax-exempt status, and Margolin believed that "the regulations of the Internal Revenue Bureau are being revised with a view of denying tax exemption to organizations which educate on controversial issues."[50] She reported to the national office that the National Committee against Discrimination in Housing was a target.

When congressional hearings were convened on civil liberties, Margolin actively lobbied Eleanor Bontecou, consultant on loyalty and security to the Subcommittee on Constitutional Rights of the Senate Committee on the Judiciary, to include the NCJW among the list of witnesses. Margolin circulated subcommittee materials to each state and local section to not only stimulate interest in the topic but to gather information about threats to civil liberties in local communities, an approach consistent with the new mission to focus on civic engagement.[51]

The NCJW's commitment to progressive politics was equally apparent in efforts to pass federal civil rights legislation. Olya Margolin in particular was active in coalition groups to promote civil rights. As in the case of immigration reform and support for the United Nations, the NCJW was part of an extensive network of coalition bodies organized, during the cold war era, to promote progressive public policies. Margolin was active on the Leadership Conference on Civil Rights, which included several unions and many national Jewish organizations, such as the American Jewish Congress, the American Jewish Committee, the Jewish Labor Committee, Jewish War Veterans, and United Hebrew Trades; she was also active on the National Council of Negro Women, the YWCA, and the National Women's Committee on Civil Rights, which was organized under the auspices of the Women's Bureau, U.S. Department of Labor; indeed, Margolin's primary focus from the mid-1950s and into the early 1960s was to pass meaningful federal civil rights legislation.[52] After a decade of representing the NCJW as its Washington representative, Margolin was a Washington insider; in 1956 she joined thirty-five organizational representatives in a strategy session convened by Representative James Roosevelt (D-CA) to spur action on a discharge petition on a civil rights bill considered by the House Judiciary Committee. Roosevelt asked each representative to target fifteen members of Congress. However, Margolin contacted Representative Emmanuel Celler (D-NY), chairman of the House Judiciary Committee, instead, to determine if Roosevelt's action had his approval. It did not, and Margolin set out to make sure that the two Democrats worked together.[53] Clearly, she knew how to further the NCJW's political agenda in Washington.

White southerners' resistance to grassroots bus boycotts on the heels of the 1954 *Brown v. Board of Education* decision placed southern NCJW sections uncomfortably at the crossroads of civil rights activism. Alliances with coalition groups drew the NCJW into local activism in both North and South. To support nascent mass-based activism challenging segregation in the South, the National Leadership Conference on Civil Rights sponsored rallies in major cities throughout the country to press Congress to act on civil rights. Bill of Rights Day, planned for December 15, 1955, was the beginning of a national mobilization that would culminate in the March on Washington in 1963. National chair of NCJW's National Committee on Public Affairs, Beatrice Parsonnet, urged section presidents in designated cities to commit time and resources to support the effort.[54] The committee and the national office also presented southern sections with a plan of action to facilitate implementation of the *Brown v. Board of Education* decision. Suggestions ranged from organizing with other groups to plan local approaches, to making public statements endorsing desegregation. A few sections, citing fear of violence and economic vulnerability, did not actively promote desegregation or plan Bill of Rights Day events, however. NCJW president and former NOCL executive director Frances Cahn, a native of New Orleans, attempted to explain to the national board why liberals, in particular Jewish liberals, could not always lead against injustice: "The growth of the White Citizens Councils, some of them with attitudes colored by anti-Semitism, is alarming. The fight-to-the-ditch attitude toward desegregation by so many Southerners, including the governing authorities, has made it difficult for Southern moderates and liberals to find a sympathetic platform for their views in the South."[55]

A study of section independence in implementing national legislative goals reveals the difficulties in assessing the political commitments of NCJW members. Women's clubs and organizations active in postwar America have been described by historians as largely ineffective because they failed to develop and employ a critique of traditional gender relations and did not make significant inroads into mainstream politics. Such analytic myopia accounts for the inattention to the progressive agenda incubating within the National Council of Jewish Women during the postwar years. Because the NCJW's advocacy of civil rights and civil liberties during the cold war era occurred unevenly, on the local level, and within extensive networks with other organizations, and because it was balanced with more prosaic concerns, the organizaton's progressivism has been largely ignored. Yet, as I have here made clear, the programs and policies of the NCJW evolved in postwar America within the context of a progressive response to anticommunism and right-wing politics, and consequently did not represent an unstinting and unchanging commitment to traditional values.

NOTES

1. Addendum to Executive Director Report to the National Board of Directors, April 6–9, 1954, 8, Part I: Administrative Files, Folder: National Board 1954, Box 19, National Office Records of the National Council of Jewish Women, Library of Congress, Washington, D.C. (hereafter cited as NCJW National Office Records).

2. Faith Rogow, *Gone to Another Meeting: The National Council of Jewish Women, 1983–1993* (Tuscaloosa: University of Alabama Press, 1993), 9.

3. Report to the National Board from the Membership Committee, September 20, 1945, Part I: Administrative Files, Folder: National Board 1945, Box 12, NCJW National Office Records.

4. Section Reports, Part I: Administrative Files, Folder: National Board 1945, Box 12, NCJW National Office Records.

5. Ibid.

6. Recommendations to the National Board of Directors, Mrs. I. Lee Levy, Vice Chairman National Committee on Social Legislation, Part I: Administrative Files, Folder: National Board 1945, Box 12, NCJW National Office Records.

7. Report of Washington Representative to the National Board of Directors, October 17–23, 1945, Part I: Administrative Files, Folder: National Board 1945, Box 12, NCJW National Office Records.

8. Report of the Executive Director to the Executive Committee of the National Board of Directors, March 15, 1945, Part I: Administrative Files, Folder: National Board 1945, Box 12, NCJW National Office Records.

9. Report on the National Committee on International Relations and Peace, 1944–45, to the National Board of Directors [no date], Part I: Administrative Files, Folder: National Board 1945, Box 12, NCJW National Office Records.

10. Report of the Executive Director to the Executive Committee of the National Board of Directors, Thursday, April 19, 1945, Part I: Administrative Files, Folder: National Board 1945, Box 12, NCJW National Office Records.

11. Report of the Executive Director to the Executive Committee of the National Board of Directors, July 18, 1945, Part I: Administrative Files, Folder: National Board 1945, Box 12, NCJW National Office Records.

12. Faith Rogow, *Gone to Another Meeting,* 167–203.

13. Report of the Section Service Committee to the National Board of Directors, October 17–23, 1945, Part I: Administrative Files, Folder: Administrative Files 1945, Box 12, NCJW National Office Records.

14. Report of the National Committee on Membership to the National Board of Directors, October 12–17, 1947, Part I: Administrative Files, Folder: National Board 1947, Box 14, NCJW National Office Records.

15. Survey Report Delivered by Mrs. Harold E. Beckman, Chairman, Survey Committee at the Board of Directors, February 14, 1946, Part I: Administrative Files, Folder: Executive Committee 1946, Box 12, NCJW National Office Records.

16. Ibid.

17. Steven Windmueller, "'Defenders': National Jewish Community Relations Agencies," in *Jewish Polity and American Civil Society: Communal Agencies and Religious Movements in the American Public Square*, ed. Alan Mittleman, Jonathan D. Sarna, and Robert Licht (New York: Rowman and Littlefield, 2002), 15. See also *We Are Many: Reflections on American Jewish History and Identity* (Syracuse, NY: Syracuse University Press, 2005); Naomi W. Cohen, *Not Free to Desist: The American Jewish Committee, 1906–1966* (Philadelphia: Jewish Publication Society of America, 1971).

18. Rogow, *Gone to Another Meeting*, 184.

19. Report of the National Committee on Social Legislation, 1944–45, to the National Board of Directors, Part I: Administration Files, Folder: National Board 1945, Box 12, NCJW National Office Records.

20. Report of the Executive Director to the National Board of Directors, November 7–12, 1948, Part I: Administrative Files, Folder: National Board 1947, Box 14, NCJW National Office Records. For the discussion of the Jewish community relations movement, see Michael C. Kotzin "Local Community Relations Councils and their National Body," in *Jewish Polity and American Civil Society*, 68–69.

21. Report of the National Committee on Education and Social Action to the National Board of Directors, October 12–17, 1947, Part I: Administration Files, Folder: National Board 1947, Box 14, NCJW National Office Records.

22. Jeff Broadwater, *Eisenhower and the Anti-Communist Crusade* (Chapel Hill: University of North Carolina Press, 1992), 8–9.

23. M. J. Heale, *American AntiCommunism: Combating the Enemy Within, 1830–1970* (Baltimore: Johns Hopkins University Press, 1990), 156. For perceptions of the communist threat in the 1940s and early 1950s see Ellen Schrecker, *Many Are the Crimes: McCarthyism in America* (Princeton, NJ: Princeton University Press, 1998), 119–153.

24. Broadwater, *Eisenhower and the Anti-Communist Crusade*, 167–188.

25. Report of the National Committee on Public Affairs to the National Board of Directors, October 4–7, 1955, Part I: Administrative Files, Folder: National Board 1955, Box 20, NCJW National Office Records.

26. Lizabeth Cohen, *Consumers' Republic: The Politics of Mass Consumption in Postwar America* (New York: Knopf, 2003), 141.

27. Ibid., 228–229.

28. Sylvie Murray, *The Progressive Housewife: Community Activism in Queens* (Philadelphia: University of Pennsylvania Press, 2003).

29. Report on 1950–1951 Education Questionnaires to Sections [no date], Part I: Administrative Files, Folder: National Board, 1951, Box 17, NCJW National Office Records. There were 140 sections, 60 percent of the total, that returned questionnaires, an improvement from the 1950 response rate of 36 percent of sections.

30. Report of the National Committee on Regional Conferences to the National Board of Directors, October 28–November 2, 1951, Part I: Administrative Files, Folder: National Board 1951, Box 17, NCJW National Office Records.

31. Highlights of the National Board Meeting, October 2–5, 1956, Part I: Administrative Files, Folder National Board 1956, Box 21, NCJW National Office Records.

32. Report of the Executive Director to the National Board of Directors, October 22–25, 1957, Part I: Administrative Files, Folder: National Board 1957, Box 23, NCJW National Office Records.

33. Statement of the Executive Director to the National Board of Directors, October 28–November 2, 1951, Part I: Administrative Files, Folder: National Board 1951, Box 17, NCJW National Office Records.

34. Ibid.

35. Addendum to Report of the National President to the Board of Directors, October 2–5, 1956, Part I: Administrative Files, Folder: National Board 1956, Box 21, NCJW National Office Records.

36. Highlights of the National Board Meeting, October 2–4, 1956, Part I: Administrative Files, Folder: National Board 1956, Box 21, NCJW National Office Records.

37. Although recent scholarship stresses continuity of feminist activism from the post-suffrage victory to the rise of the modern women's movement, several analyses of women's organizing during the postwar years consider divisions over identity and ideology. For studies of working-class feminism during the postwar period, see Nancy Gabin, *Feminism in the Labor Movement: Women in the United Auto Workers Union, 1935–1975* (Ithaca, NY: Cornell University Press, 1990); Dorothy Sue Cobble, "Recapturing Working-Class Feminism: Union Women in the Postwar Era," 57–83, in *Not June Cleaver: Women and Gender in Postwar America, 1945–1960*, ed. Joanne Meyerowitz (Philadelphia: Temple University Press, 1994); and Dennis A. Deslippe, *Rights Not Roses: Unions and the Rise of Working-Class Feminism, 1945–1980* (Urbana: University of Illinois Press, 2000). The following books focus on women's organizations with specific missions and goals: Leila Rupp and Verta Taylor, *Survival in the Doldrums: The American Women's Movement in America, 1945 to the 1960s* (New York: Oxford University Press, 1987); Susan A. Levine, *Degrees of Equality: The American Association of University Women and the Challenge of American Feminism* (Philadelphia: Temple University Press, 1995); Susan Lynn, *Progressive Women in Conservative Times: Racial Justice, Peace, and Feminism, 1945 to the 1960s* (New Brunswick, NJ: Rutgers University Press, 1993). Susan Ware's work on the League of Women Voters recasts voluntarism as political activism, but that activism, as we have seen, did not generally include involvement in progressive coalitions related to civil liberties and civil rights. See "American Women in the 1950s: Nonpartisan Politics and Women's Politicalization," in *Women, Politics and Change*, ed. Louise A. Tilly and Patricia Gurin, 2nd ed. (New York: Russell Sage Foundation, 1992), 281–299. Cynthia Harrison considers how the divisive politics related to the Equal Rights Amendment compromised broader policy networks among women's organizations, in *On Account of Sex: Public Policies on Women's Issues, 1945–1970* (Berkeley and Los Angeles: University of California Press, 1989). Anna L. Harvey, *Votes without Leverage: Women in American Electoral Politics, 1920–1970* (New York: Cambridge University Press, 1998), argues that women's organizations failed to come together to influence electoral politics until the 1970s. Carol M. Mueller makes a similar argument in "The Empowerment of Women: Polling and the Women's Voting Bloc," in *The Politics of the Gender Gap: The Social Construction of Political Influence*, ed. Carol M. Mueller (Beverly Hills, CA: Sage Publications, 1988), 16–36.

38. Report of the Committee Affiliation of the NCJW with the GFWC to the Meeting of National Board of Directors, October 19–23, 1953, Part I: Administrative Files, Folder: National Board 1953, Box 18, NCJW National Office Records.

39. Report of the Liaison on Civil Defense to the National Board of Directors, October 28–November 2, 1951, Part I: Administrative Files, Folder: National Board, Box 17, NCJW National Office Records.

40. Kathleen A. Laughlin examines how a progressive coalition of the National Council of Jewish Women, the National Council of Negro Women, Church Women United, the Young Women's Christian Association (YWCA), and the National Council of Catholic Women worked with the Women's Bureau of the U.S. Department of Labor on civil rights and equal rights legislation, but opposed the Equal Rights Amendment, in *Women's Work and Public Policy: A History of the Women's Bureau, U.S. Department of Labor, 1945–1970* (Boston: Northeastern University Press, 2000). The National Federation of Business and Professional Women's Clubs blamed organized labor for the failure to pass an equal rights amendment; see Kathleen A. Laughlin, "Civic Feminism: The Business and Professional Women's Clubs and Policy Formation, 1945–1965," unpublished article.

41. National Council of Jewish Women, Inc., Resolutions, Adopted or Reaffirmed at the Twentieth Triennial Convention, Cleveland, Ohio, March, 1953, Part I: Administrative Files, Folder: National Board 1954, Box 20, NCJW National Office Records.

42. Report of the National Committee on Public Affairs to the National Board of Directors, October 4–7, 1955, Part I: Administrative Files, Folder: National Board, 1955, Box 20, NCJW National Office Records.

43. Report of the National Committee on Pubic Affairs to the National Board of the Directors, April 6–9, 1954, Part I: Administrative Files, Folder: National Board 1954, Box 20, NCJW National Office Records.

44. Report of the National Committee on Education and Social Action to the National Board of Directors, October 28–November 2, 1951, Part I: Administrative Files, Folder: National Board 1951, Box 17, NCJW National Office Records. At that time, NCJW volunteers and staff believed that the most effective sites for progressive politics were in the states.

45. Memo from Olya Margolin to Helen Raebeck, Executive Director, May 13, 1956, Part I: Subject Files, Folder: Censorship, Box 72, NCJW National Office Records.

46. Memo from Olya Margolin to Elsie Elfenbein, July 31, 1953, Part I: Subject Files, Folder: Censorship, Box 72, NCJW National Office Records. In the memo, Margolin writes "the League of Women Voters does not work in this area" (civil liberties).

47. Report of the National Committee on Public Affairs to the National Board of Directors, April 6–8, 1954, Part I: Administrative Files, Folder: National Board 1954, Box 20, NCJW National Office Records.

48. Memo to Section Presidents from Frances Cahn, Executive Director, August 3, 1956, Part I: Subject Files, Folder: Civil Liberties, Box 72, NCJW National Office Records.

49. Memo from Olya Margolin to Helen Raebeck, June 29, 1956, Part I: Subject Files, Folder: Civil Liberties, Box 72, NCJW National Office Records.

50. Memo from Olya Margolin to Helen Raebeck, November 18, 1955, Part I: Subject Files, Folder: Civil Liberties, Box 72, NCJW National Office Records.

51. Memo from Olya Margolin to Helen Raebeck, November 18, 1955, Part I: Subject Files, Folder: Civil Liberties, Box 72, NCJW National Office Records.

52. Laughlin, *Women's Work and Public Policy*, 91, 97.

53. Memo from Olya Margolin to Helen Raeback, April 12, 1956, Part I: Subject Files, Folder: Civil Rights, 1945–63, Box 73, NCJW National Office Records.

54. Letter to Section Presidents from Beatrice Parsonnet, November 28, 1955, Part I: Subject Files, File: Civil Rights, 1945–63, Box 73, NCJW National Office Records.

55. Statement Re: Desegregation to the National Board of Directors, October 22–25, 1957, Part I: Administrative Files, Folder: National Board 1957, Box 23, NCJW National Office Records.

4

"It's Good Americanism to Join Hadassah"

SELLING HADASSAH IN THE POSTWAR ERA

REBECCA BOIM WOLF

With the creation of the State of Israel and its subsequent victory over the Arab armies of the surrounding countries in 1949, the future of the Jewish home seemed secure. Lacking the urgency of the 1930s and 1940s, the 1950s presented Hadassah, the Women's Zionist Organization of America, with a dilemma it had not faced since the 1920s: it had to struggle with the issue of how to attract new members. The 1950s and 1960s seemed to represent years of limited growth for the organization. Hadassah reported only slight gains in membership, going from 270,000 in 1950 to 295,000 in 1969, a gain of only 25,000 in twenty years.[1]

In contrast, in the decades that witnessed Hitler's rise to power, World War II, and Israel's independence and early struggle for survival, American Jewish women had flocked to Hadassah's membership rolls. Created in 1912 "to promote Jewish institutions and enterprises in Palestine, and to foster Zionist ideals in America,"[2] Hadassah succeeded in creating a network of health clinics, hospitals, school lunch programs, and vocational training facilities throughout Israel. In America, Hadassah initiated educational programs to teach American Jewish women about Israel, Zionism, Jewish history, and the responsibilities inherent in American citizenship. In the urgency of the 1930s and 1940s, Hadassah's Zionist mission and its goals appealed to many American Jewish women, who needed little convincing to join and donate to the organization. Even though Hadassah leaders rarely worried about attracting new members in those years, the organization maintained an energetic recruitment policy. Hadassah produced brochures and placed advertisements in local and national newspapers to tout its work on behalf of rescuing European Jewish youth, building medical facilities in Israel, and contributing to the war effort at home through selling war bonds. In addition, local Hadassah chapters hosted teas, luncheons, education seminars, and intense one-day membership drives in an effort to draw women to the organization. From the close of World War I through the establishment of Israel in 1948, Hadassah multiplied its membership, from almost 24,000 in 1933 to almost 243,000 in 1948.

Thus, compared to the vigorous growth of the 1930s and 1940s, the measured growth of the post-1948 years might lend the impression that Hadassah stagnated during the 1950s and 1960s.

However, the seemingly sluggish statistics of the post-1948 years do not reveal the whole story. A 1964 *Hadassah Magazine* survey of its readers concluded that 50 percent of current members had joined the organization since 1950.[3] In view of the fact that membership totaled 270,000 in 1950 and 275,000 in 1964, the new members acquired from 1950 through 1964 had in actuality replaced members who had dropped from the Hadassah rolls. That is, although Hadassah lost half its members between 1950 and 1964, the organization managed to replace those who left. In view of the fact that other Zionist organizations lost members during those years,[4] Hadassah's ability to replace members with new ones, augment its membership slightly in some years, and increase its fundraising from $9 million in 1950 to over $15 million in 1967 pointed to its overall health and vibrancy in the years following the establishment of Israel.[5]

Between 1948 and 1967, Hadassah managed to adjust to a new era in the history of American Jews and American women, and therefore met success in its drive to replace the women who departed, add more members, and increase its fundraising. Hadassah leaders in the post-1948 years recognized that the rapid growth of the past had come to an end and saw how the organization had lost members whose interest had waned as the crisis abated, or who moved from one city to another (or out to the suburbs) and did not re-enroll; leadership then worked hard to address this issue of attrition. Through a new emphasis on Hadassah's work in the United States, through vigorous membership drives, and through innovative fundraising techniques, Hadassah leaders and members maintained their organization and in fact expanded its activities.

At first, Hadassah developed a recruitment message that emphasized the need for steady work, in the process dismissing the idea of membership as a response only to exigency. In March 1949, less than a year after the establishment of Israel, Hadassah leaders prepared material for recruiters who consistently faced the question from prospective members, "Why should I join Hadassah now? Israel is a state, and the whole world recognizes it. What do you need me for?" Hadassah leaders provided recruiters with an answer that it believed could work in the more normal, postwar, post-State moment: "Hadassah is not an emergency organization. For thirty-seven years we have worked for this moment." The recruiter would, as instructed, continue by explaining Hadassah's need to help Israel absorb the immigrants pouring into the country, and conclude with, "Can you, a Jew who supported the fight for the Jewish State, withdraw now?"[6]

Despite these appeals, women only flocked to Hadassah when Israel faced danger. For instance, when Israel retaliated against Egypt in the Sinai Peninsula, following Egypt's nationalization of the Suez Canal, Hadassah gained over 17,000 new members. The 1957 annual report testified that many women called the

Hadassah national office and asked to enroll in an "act of faith" in Israel.[7] Similarly, during the Six Day War, Hadassah's membership increased by 10,000, and the organization raised $1.3 million as part of a special emergency campaign. However, as soon as the crisis of the moment passed, many of these new members dropped out: Hadassah's 1957–1958 membership numbers revealed a net loss of over 20,000 persons. After the rush of excitement over Israel's victory in 1967, Hadassah's membership department reported a serious challenge in retaining the women who had joined in the heat of the crisis.[8] As such, Hadassah proved able to easily recruit vast numbers of new members only when Israel faced threats; in other years, the organization had to work far harder.

A 1950 article in *Hadassah Headlines*, an internal house publication, "How to Turn a 'No' into a 'Yes,'" posed the argument of a potential Hadassah deserter who asserted, "I am simply no longer interested in Hadassah." The article urged recruiters to respond with the following:

> Surely you understand this: That Hadassah is not just another organization to be joined today and left tomorrow. A woman who signs her name to a membership blank signs this pledge: "So that I may live creatively as a Jew in America, and aid the people of Israel to protect and foster their new birth of freedom through practical projects of healing, teaching and research, I hereby enroll in Hadassah." Are you revoking such a solemn pledge? Your honor, your pride as an American Jew are at stake if you are. Membership Involves a Solemn Pledge.[9]

According to the article, the recruiter ought to answer first with an appeal to enriching the woman's own life in America, and only then move on to the work she can do for Israel. That is, instead of focusing primarily on its work on behalf of, and in, Israel, as in the past, Hadassah appealed to new members by emphasizing its expanded American affairs program: Hadassah's domestic work and its activities at the United Nations in support of equal rights, strong democracy, aiding poor persons and underprivileged children, and building coalitions of likeminded organizations.

Although initiated in 1941 to aid in the war effort and "to strengthen and safeguard the ideals and principles of American democracy,"[10] Hadassah's American Affairs Department remained in place after World War II as a vehicle for chapters "to play a decisive role . . . in helping to shape the national policies of this country."[11] To that end, the organization promoted peace in the Middle East and elsewhere, international human rights, children's health and welfare, civil liberties and civil rights, desegregation, immigration rights, and general social welfare through legislation, community action, and education.

In the area of human rights, Hadassah repeatedly pressured Congress through resolutions, letters, and face-to-face meetings on Capitol Hill to liberalize United States immigration laws to assist Jews and "large numbers of peoples of all faiths"[12] in Displaced Persons camps, to pass the World Health Bill signaling the United States' ratification of the World Health Organization's constitution,[13] to ratify the Convention against Genocide,[14] to appropriate sufficient funds for the Point Four Program calling for economic aid to poor countries,[15] to ban nuclear tests, and to support foreign aid. In keeping with Hadassah's traditional focus on children and youth in need, the organization sent a delegation to the 1959 White House Convention on Children and Youth and resolved to support more federal aid to education. In the 1960s, Hadassah fully endorsed Head Start, a federal project undertaken as part of the War on Poverty, and urged members to contact persons directing Head Start programs in their local communities and to sign up as volunteers.[16]

On civil rights, Hadassah sponsored interfaith and communal panels to discuss discrimination, urged members to write to their congresspersons endorsing specific civil rights legislation, invited politicians and speakers to discuss the issue at national conventions, and published articles in the organization's magazine advocating improved civil rights in the United States. Hadassah supported the Supreme Court's decision in *Brown v. Board of Education*, urging members to comply with the law of the land. National Hadassah's plea even reached some southern communities. Even though West Virginia experienced turmoil over school segregation, the Wheeling-Belmont County (West Virginia) chapter of Hadassah held an open meeting, Operation Freedom '55, that focused on integration. There, facilitated by a rabbi, a three-person panel that included an African American panelist discussed integration. In the 1956 annual Hadassah report, the American Affairs Department reported that, "without entering into the bitter struggle now going on in some of the Southern States with regard to integration, Hadassah has held that the Supreme Court represents the law of the land."[17] In addition to entering the fray on desegregation, Hadassah passed resolutions favoring civil rights for all in 1956 and 1957, and Hadassah supported President John F. Kennedy's and later President Lyndon B. Johnson's Civil Rights Acts.[18]

On the local level, the American affairs program encouraged grassroots activism and cooperation with community organizations. As the December 1948 *Hadassah Headlines* pointed out, "American Affairs can be a good-will wedge which aids better Hadassah community status."[19] More than simply endorsing legislation and promoting the work of the United Nations, local American affairs programs administered local charity through participation in TB Seal campaigns, March of Dimes drives, Red Cross blood drives, and sponsorship of cultural programs to benefit orphaned and underprivileged children. In addition, local American affairs leaders built coalitions and worked to create goodwill within the community. Through such actions as local blood drives, Jewish book fairs at local libraries, participation in the YMCA's "round-the-world-supper," sponsoring a Hadassah float for a local parade, or cohosting a panel to discuss tolerance, local Hadassah chapters succeeded in drawing the support of other community organizations. This support paid dividends when Hadassah sought to enlist help from others to implement its American affairs agenda or garner support for Israel.

A third piece of the American affairs program engaged Hadassah members in projects to educate neighbors and potential new members about democracy, equality, coexistence, and Israel. Even while Hadassah's American affairs programs sought to strengthen democracy, enhance civil rights, and aid the poor and underprivileged within the United States, the good will garnered through intracommunal activities and interfaith programs helped secure sympathetic audiences when Hadassah highlighted its activities in Israel. For example, the January 1955 issue of *Hadassah Headlines* cited the Portsmouth, Virginia, chapter for its education initiatives. The chapter had invited speakers to talk about Israel and Zionism before local groups, including the Optimist Club, Rotary, Kiwanis, Jewish Community Council, and Business and Professional Women's Club. The chapter had created similar programs for high school students, reached out to local newspapers, and provided information on the city's two radio stations. According to the chapter, the successful program encouraged town members to discuss and deliberate about Israel as well as on other current issues. In another example, the New Orleans chapter showed the film *A New Morning*, about Hadassah's vocational schools in Israel, to a local vocational high school. The chapter reported that the principle of the school, a pioneer for vocational education in the city, had been moved by the film and spoke to her students at its conclusion. The newsletter quoted her at length: "Those of us who started with me went through similar situations as presented in this picture. And the women of Hadassah are to be congratulated for starting from the ground up and having faith that this country can grow. Here is a nation that has based its hopes on the abilities developed by its youth. The attention with which this picture was received was a tribute to the work you women of Hadassah are doing. God grant that this work will be carried forward."[20]

Hadassah leaders assessed the impact of these activities; they believed that the American affairs work on the local level played a role in attracting women to the Zionist organization. According to their calculations, when a Hadassah member wanted to see the fruits of her labor, she would in the past have had to travel to Israel. Now, however, she could easily witness the passage of a bill in Congress, the increase in donations to a local blood drive, or the reorientation of neighbors toward supporting civil rights or Israel, all goals her local chapter helped bring about. This fit neatly with the emerging sociological consensus about postwar American Jews; a 1957 survey, for instance, by sociologist Marshall Sklare of Chicago Jews revealed that Jews ranked "to promote civic betterment and improvement in the community" third in a list of essentials of being a "good Jew." Those whom Sklare interviewed believed that such work ranked above belonging to a synagogue, attending religious services, or marrying a Jew.[21] Hadassah recognized this ethos, and the American affairs program provided a way for many Jewish women to call themselves "good Jews" since they both supported Israel through fundraising and advocacy, and expended energy on work in America as citizens trying to improve their country and communities.

At the highest levels of leadership, Hadassah officials acknowledged the centrality of such activities to the health of the organization. Indeed, national American affairs chairperson Bertha Hamerman asserted in 1951 that Hadassah attracted more and more Jewish women because of its American affairs program. She advised chapters to "exploit this interest," because "participation in American Affairs can be the open sesame to active and staunch Hadassah Membership."[22]

Therefore, Hadassah began to target potential members through an emphasis on civic duty. The 1951–1952 annual membership report explained that "American Jewish women as American citizens are asked to serve democracy by joining Hadassah, because our program on the American front aims to strengthen democratic processes here, as well as to buttress the young democracy that is Israel."[23] In 1953, Hadassah formalized this new strategy at its midwinter conference. During a conversation on the problems of recruiting new members and of raising funds, delegates decided to devote more time and emphasis to the American affairs program, through publishing an American affairs article in each issue of the *Hadassah Newsletter* (*Hadassah Magazine* after 1961) and through the preparation of special papers on individual subjects, more discussion groups about American affairs at meetings, provision of better information on the work of the United Nations, and more cooperation among the American Affairs, Education, and Public Relations departments.[24] Hadassah leaders hoped this shift would attract and retain American Jewish women to the organization. But if the focus on American affairs sought to lure women in the door, the goal was to inculcate an affinity for Zionism in the new recruits. Once new members were ensconced in a chapter, the next step for local leaders was to draw the connections between Hadassah's work in the United States and its activities in Israel.

In response to the new mandate from the Mid-Winter Conference, in 1953, the writers and editors of the *Hadassah Newsletter* immediately began to incorporate articles relating to Hadassah's work in America into the newsletter. The May 1953 issue featured an article, "Investigation versus Education," detailing how public schools in America taught children.[25] The November 1953 issue included an article about democracy in America that urged readers not to succumb to "bigots and racists" and the communist hysteria gripping the nation.[26] Along the same lines, the next issue quoted national American affairs chairperson Judith Epstein, who stressed, "Only an alert and informed citizenry can be truly free."[27]

Local Hadassah chapters quickly followed the national office's lead and reinvigorated their American affairs programs. Many conjoined local activism with members' education, complying with the goals of the American affairs program. The September–October 1954 issue of *Hadassah Headlines* cited the San Francisco chapter for its outstanding American affairs program, which incorporated public service work with education of the local community about Hadassah's work in Israel and America.[28] *Hadassah Headlines* also highlighted Boston's successful American affairs program, noting that it sponsored monthly American affairs information sessions, that its American affairs and education chairpersons led study groups together, and that each board meeting featured an American affairs speaker. The chapter, the newsletter added, offered courses to members, including one on Red Cross home nursing and one on public speaking, and sponsored an annual All-Day Boston Education Institute, where hundreds of women would gather to hear speakers and discuss political questions, Zionism, and Jewish education.[29]

To inscribe the new importance of its American affairs program into its constitution, Hadassah's 1955 convention adopted a constitutional change to include as an aim: "to help strengthen American democracy through a program of study and information."[30] This ascendance of Hadassah's American affairs program seemed to reach new heights in 1962, when the American Affairs Report moved to the front of the Hadassah Annual Report; in previous years Israel activities had dominated the first half of the report.

This move to the front of the annual report did not, however, signal a change in priorities for Hadassah. Rather, the move proved logistical. Hadassah, after all, did not abandon its work in Israel. To the contrary, between 1951 and 1952 the organization raised over $10 million in Israeli bonds for the new state, Hadassah and Hebrew University opened a dental school, and fundraising began for a new medical center at Ein Kerem.[31] In 1961, the Hadassah Medical Organization (HMO), with a staff of 1,431 people in clinics, hospitals, and training facilities throughout Israel, reported that it treated over 16,000 inpatients annually and that 50 percent of babies born in Jerusalem had been delivered in Hadassah Hospital. The report also listed the more than sixty institutions and programs under the HMO, including hospitals in Jerusalem, Beersheba, and Safed, community health services throughout Jerusalem, family health clinics, mobile anti-trachoma units in villages (including Arab villages), fellowship programs, and medical research and training. The report concluded by announcing that the new Hadassah–Hebrew University Medical Center at Ein Kerem, dedicated in 1961, would house the Rothschild Hadassah University Hospital, Rosensohn Clinic, Hebrew University–Hadassah Medical School, a Mother-Child Pavilion for maternity and infant care, and the Henrietta Szold School of Nursing.[32] In addition, Hadassah trained young adults in numerous vocational schools throughout the country to work as mechanics, printers, and hotel managers, and in agriculture.[33] Hadassah also expanded its Youth Aliyah programs, begun in Germany in the 1930s, that placed orphans from abroad and Israeli youths from depressed neighborhoods into absorption centers, usually agriculture settlements. By 1957, that program included more than 14,000 youths in 248 absorption centers.[34]

Despite its extensive work in Israel, Hadassah chose to emphasize, in its annual report, publicity materials, and recruitment brochures, not primarily its

Israel work, as in previous decades, but instead its American-oriented projects. In 1950, a member who signed her membership card to enroll or reenroll pledged first to "live creatively as a Jew in America," and second to "aid the people of Israel to protect and foster their new birth of freedom through practical projects of healing, teaching and research."[35] A publicity shopping bag from the 1950s, adorned with the words "Keep the Wheels of Progress Going," depicted two wheels, the top one to represent Hadassah's work in America and the bottom one to represent Hadassah's work in Israel. The wheel on the top right of the bag enclosed an image of a woman and young girl with an American flag in the background. In the bottom left circled image stands a nurse, a doctor, and a girl holding a shovel, with an Israeli flag in the background.[36] In both these examples, Hadassah's work in Israel stood below and after its work in America.

This new positioning of Israel activities appears most obvious in Hadassah's recruitment brochures of the 1950s and 1960s. The brochures discussed the group's support and work for the United Nations, for an International Criminal Court, in favor of human rights, and in support of immigration reform. One recruitment brochure, created in 1957, urged women to join Hadassah through the claim that "It's Good AMERICANISM to Join HADASSAH."[37] The card then listed three reasons to join: "1. Foster democracy and educate yourself for creative Jewish living in the U.S.A.; 2. Guide American Jewish youth; 3. Serve Israel through projects of healing, teaching and research." Again, as in many subsequent recruitment materials of the 1950s and 1960s, Israel took a back seat to domestic activities.

Whereas pictures of women nurses administering to the sick in clinics in Palestine, maps of Palestine, and pictures of *halutzim* working the land had adorned the covers of 1930s and 1940s brochures, most 1950s materials displayed fashionably dressed American women, suitably bejeweled with pearls and gold earrings. That is, in addition to relegating Israel activities to the inside pages, the brochures through these pictures made a direct appeal to 1950s married Jewish women, few of whom worked at outside jobs and most of whom instead dedicated themselves to "women's domestic nature and role."[38] Woman's "domestic role" in the 1950s and 1960s included taking care of her home, children, and husband, often (in this vision of the "upper-middle-class" wife) with the help of a housekeeper, through providing home-cooked meals, clean and neat houses, emotional support, and (at least in the case of observant Jewish women) religious instruction through example. Suburban Jewish women in the post–World War II era, according to historian Deborah Dash Moore, "possessed sufficient leisure time to be Jewish," and therefore, "women and their home domain . . . occupied a crucial, central place in American Judaism."[39] Rabbis, husbands, and Jewish educators placed the onus on mothers to nurture Judaism within the home through lighting Sabbath candles, preparing Sabbath meals, celebrating Jewish holidays, and educating their children to lead meaningful Jewish lives. As Jews flocked to the suburbs in the 1950s, husbands, commuting daily to work in the city, spent less time at home while wives became "the modern matriarch(s) of Jewish suburbia,"[40] responsible for an efficient, modern, safe, clean, enriching environment for children and husband.

Hadassah recognized the emergence of this reality and utilized it to appeal to potential recruits. A middle-class Jewish woman living in suburbia in 1952 might see herself reflected on the covers of Hadassah brochures. One 1950s brochure quoted the poem "Eshet Chayil" ("Woman of Valor"), traditionally recited by Jewish husbands at the onset of the Sabbath to thank their wives for the toil and work performed every day to keep the household running. The brochure claimed that, as a woman, "your responsibility to youth is also basic for a fully rewarding way of life."[41] Other brochures and membership materials appealed to women's desires to maintain their looks and sense of style, through depictions of fashionable women accompanied by enticements such as "Introducing . . . The Hadassah Look" and "Keep Up-to-Date with Hadassah."[42]

The brochures, while on the surface reinforcing 1950s notions of domesticity, including the mother taking impeccable care of children, husband, home, and self, at the same time reflected a different aspect of life for the new Jewish suburban woman. For, although convention dictated that a suburban woman's primary obligation lay in her home or "domestic sphere," in fact Jewish women were enlarging that sphere and, increasingly, as noted by the historian Joyce Antler, "played a vital and growing role in [their] synagogue and in the larger community."[43] Rather than toiling at home over a hot stove, a Jewish suburban woman would more likely, if able, be out taking classes at the local synagogue, organizing rallies, or attending meetings.[44] Hadassah appealed to such Jewish women, who yearned for Jewish learning and meaningful community activism. Inside the brochures, Hadassah leaders placed copy that discussed the multifaceted work of Hadassah in the United States and in Israel.

One 1953 brochure featured a woman with a wide-brimmed hat adorned with American and Israeli flags, farming equipment, and a book on top; the text extolled the jumble of objects, "On You It's Becoming!" Inside, the booklet asked, "Who Is the Attractive, Vital, Intelligent, Proud, and Clearly Happy Woman on the Cover? It's You! When you join Hadassah." This woman presented not only a fashionable image, but also intelligence and pride. The brochure continued to probe its targets: "Ask yourself, what do I want out of my life? As a woman? An American? A Jew? You answer: I want security for my children and Jewish youth. I want to be a better citizen of my community and nation. I want to defend democracy here and abroad . . . I want to help Israel grow and perfect its democracy."[45]

What, according to these brochures, did American Jewish women want? They aspired to be good mothers for their own children and to all Jewish children, but also to be good American citizens and Jews through advocacy, public policy, and education. "There was a Little Woman who had a Big Dream . . ."

Figure 4.1 "On You It's Becoming!" Hadassah Membership Packet, 1953.
Courtesy of Hadassah, the Women's Zionist Organization of America, Inc.

began another brochure, referring to Henrietta Szold, founder of Hadassah. Rather than describe a "little" woman, however, the brochure extolled Szold's enormous accomplishments and those of the organization she founded, and concluded with the call: "To all who wish to aid Israel, to all those who seek through deeds to deepen the meaning of their lives, to those who take pride in the community of man's effort, we say: Hadassah's dream is still a big dream. Help us to continue making it a reality."[46] The women in these brochures, then, while disguised as "little women" and "traditional housewives," projected the idea that their fulfillment would come not only in caretaking, but in taking action in the public arena in America and on behalf of Israel.

The portrait that Hadassah drew of the devoted wife and mother, adorned with pearls and designer dresses, proudly hosting a Hadassah tea or luncheon, achieved a degree of notoriety in 1955 when Herman Wouk's *Marjorie Morningstar* appeared on the literary scene. Herman Wouk himself winked at his own carica-ture of the American Jewish suburban housewife when he addressed Hadassah's 1955 convention:

> It is perfectly obvious before this very serious program proceeds that we are going to have to clear up the question of a very old girl friend of mine, namely Mrs. Marjorie Schwartz, whom I knew long ago as Marjorie Morningstar. I understand there has been a bit of talk about her at this con-vention over the weekend. I haven't any idea what has been said about her but I want you to know that it's not true. I want you to know that she is really a very fine person. That she is happily married, and in fact, my latest infor-mation is that she is going to run in the spring for President of her local chap-ter of Hadassah.[47]

Wouk's joke caused the women at the convention to erupt in laughter, but his words certainly rang true to those assembled. The pinnacle of success for middle-class Jewish suburban wives and mothers, like Marjorie Schwartz, involved their election to the presidency of a local Hadassah chapter. For these women, home and family did not suffice. They aspired to be not only those attractive women on the covers of the Hadassah brochures, but also the signifi-cant women on the inside of the brochures, the ones doing "serious" work, as Wouk pointed out. By dressing the part and fulfilling their obligations as wives and mothers, Hadassah women could extend the meaning of "home" so as to work outside their homes on behalf of their organization, without challenging 1950s notions of domesticity. Even though the presidents of some large Hadassah chapters occupied positions "worthy of $15,000-a-year executives, to put it mildly," they maintained their primary roles as mothers and wives.[48]

Josselyn Shore, husband of Irene Shore, Hadassah's liaison officer with the United Nations, wrote an article for the *Hadassah Newsletter*, "My Career as a Hadassah Husband." Before praising Hadassah for granting his wife the "oppor-tunity to grow in stature and to share fully in the developments of her time," he made sure to attest to his wife's "normal, wholesome woman's interest in fash-ions, dancing and the theater, and . . . a mother's intense devotion to her home."[49] Although proud of his wife and her work for Hadassah, Shore felt com-pelled to prove his wife's normality as a wife and mother. Likewise, Hadassah's membership brochures and publicity materials utilized images of "normal" women interested in fashion, the arts, and their homes to illustrate that Hadassah women reflected "typical" 1950s women and did not deviate. Although Hadassah leaders realized that these depictions led to "a stereotype of the Hadassah woman that has grown up in this country," they sought to show that the stereotype "is a good one."[50] Thus, although the covers of recruitment brochures utilized the "stereotype of the Hadassah woman" always ready to host a membership tea, the brochures also served to up-end that stereotype with details about the significant work performed by these "ladies who lunch."[51]

Hadassah leaders believed, as did Shore, that their organization granted women the opportunity to "grow in stature." Membership in Hadassah, according to the national membership chair, Sue Glassberg, granted a woman the "privilege of molding a tomorrow—for herself, as an alert and mature American Jewish mother, and for our people in Israel, who depend upon Hadassah."[52] A few years later, Fannie Cohen, then the national membership chair, echoed her predecessor when she asserted that Hadassah offers "an over-all framework in which women engage in meaningful activities, which, in turn, brings enrichment to their own lives."[53] Another Hadassah leader, Judith Epstein, explained why Hadassah women dedicated their time, money, and energy to the organization and to Israel, "something thousands of miles away which they may never see in their lifetime":

> These intelligent young women are aware of the shrinking world in which we live; they are deeply concerned w/ the state of America of which they are a part and into which their children must grow and prosper. They realize that Israel's position in the Middle East . . . can be a bridge between developed and undeveloped areas, raising social awareness in that part of the world. . . . But in addition they are deeply and consciously Jewish. They are seeking a deeper significance for their Jewishness. . . . Lastly, they are women, and women through the centuries have been trained to meet the practical realities of home building. They, therefore, know that the health of the people must be cared for if there is to be strong citizenry.[54]

Glassberg, Cohen, and Epstein wrote and spoke about the ways Hadassah offered enrichment and self-fulfillment for intelligent women through their work to improve the health and well-being of citizens in America and Israel. In addition to appeals to women as "home-builders" and mothers, Hadassah leaders promised a "deeper significance for their Jewishness" and their lives.

Hadassah's publicity and membership departments echoed these appeals not only in brochures but in other marketing campaigns. For example, at Hadassah's 1959 convention, a skit highlighting a new member scenario spoke to the "typical" Hadassah mother and wife who yearned for something more, even if she did not know this. The skit opened with a busy housewife feeding her baby, preparing her two older children for school, and driving her husband to the station to catch the 8:26 train. When she returned home, her well-dressed mother walked in, boasting that she bought her dress from Loehmann's with a Nieman Marcus label, and tried to convince her daughter to join her at a Hadassah meeting or at least help out with the Hadassah rummage sale. The daughter protested that her family responsibilities did not leave her free time, but reluctantly agreed to design posters for the sale—and soon ended up involved in Hadassah. She quickly, according to this script, realized that she had been selfish in caring only for her family's well-being and not about other Jewish and needy children. As a result, she chided her husband for belittling her Hadassah work, asserting "I wish you wouldn't be so condescending. There's a lot more to Hadassah than rummage sales and bridge parties. This afternoon I heard a wonderful talk on our foreign policy in the Middle East. What do you know about the Middle East?"[55] The skit illustrated that Hadassah could bring meaning and fulfillment for housewives by broadening their knowledge and showing them how to help those outside their families.

In addition to dramatic presentations and recruitment brochures, Hadassah initiated other programs and incentives to swell its ranks and increase its fundraising. Local Hadassah chapters pored over lists from local branches of B'nai B'rith, Council of Jewish Women, ORT, parent-teacher groups, Jewish federations, and synagogue sisterhoods, checking them against Hadassah membership roles. Any women not on Hadassah's list was a candidate for recruitment.[56] To recruit new members and reenroll existing members, Hadassah chapters used print media, radio, film, mailings, person-to-person appeals, and the offering of awards.

Hadassah Headlines offered prototypes of newspaper advertisements, posters, and billboards that chapters could copy or refine for their particular communities. In the late 1940s and early 1950s, most of these ads and posters featured Hadassah's work in Israel, as a way to pull at heartstrings. For example, the February 1949 issue featured a prototype advertisement, "Help Hadassah Build the First Hospital in the Negev," and urged chapters to place it in local newspapers. The advertisement provided testimonials to Hadassah's work, including a pianist wounded in the 1948 war who cried, "My hands live again because of Hadassah." The bottom of the ad contained a cut-out section instructing readers to clip and mail it with their name and address, and to attach a check. *Hadassah Headlines* told its readers, the potential recruiters, not to be disappointed if the ad failed to bring in too much money because such ads typically did not generate many donations. They were valuable, however, simply for publicizing Hadassah's work: "An ad can be a door-opener in canvassing, a springboard for soliciting contributions by mail, a 'gimmick' for emphasizing invitations to donors. It means that for every phase of your chapter's work, a softening barrage is laid in advance throughout your community."[57]

Chapters followed the advice of the national office and placed advertisements, put up posters, and created billboards to solicit funds, gain members, and publicize the organization's work. The Detroit chapter placed an advertisement in the *Detroit Jewish News*, "Now that the dream is a reality . . . Hadassah's part in the new Jewish state is bigger than ever."[58] In the fall of 1949 the Los Angeles chapter placed twenty billboards around the city proclaiming "JOIN HADASSAH AND SUPPORT ISRAEL!"[59] In New York City, Hadassah placed ads in the subways and on buses.

However, as American affairs took a more central role in the organization, posters and advertisements based on Hadassah's work in America started to appear. In 1959, the group introduced the poster "Hadassah Gives You a Design for Living." The copy underneath the headline listed Hadassah activities in America and was placed well above its activities in Israel. The words "Defend democracy, enrich Jewish life in the USA" appeared above "support healing teaching and research in Israel."[60] Another poster, offered to chapters in 1960, also put America before Israel. The poster depicted a giant key chain and read "Join Hadassah. Your Key to a Richer, Fuller, Life." Inside the key chain, under the command to "Join Hadassah," the copy read "Help Defend Democracy, Live a Vital Jewish Life in the United States, Support Healing, Teaching and Research in Israel."[61] Even though Hadassah's publicity department produced these posters placing America first, it also continued to create posters portraying Hadassah's work in Israel. The same issue of *Hadassah Headlines* that featured the "Design for Living" poster also featured a poster, showing a nurse holding a baby, "Donor of Good Health for Israel."[62] Clearly, Hadassah utilized everything in its arsenal to attract members.

Thus, in addition to print media, radio and film were among Hadassah's weaponry to publicize its work and entice new members and funds. Hadassah opened a radio department in March 1949, and by June 1949, the department reported its first success, "Doctors of Destiny," a dramatization of an Israeli soldier who became one of the first students at Hadassah's medical school. The radio show aired on over forty stations across the United States. In addition to developing such radio dramas, Hadassah also participated in radio interviews and sponsored radio shows to inform listeners about its work. In 1952, Hadassah took over a children's radio show, "Storyteller's Playhouse," on WNBC. The one-night special told a children's story and then included a brief message about Hadassah. The station and Hadassah received many letters from fans praising the show and, when fans requested scripts, the Hadassah office added literature about the organization to the script packet.[63]

Hadassah's film department produced many movies in the post-1948 era that dramatized the group's work in Israel. At Hadassah's 1950 midwinter conference, Judith Epstein explained that Hadassah's films aimed to communicate Israel's accomplishments. Although she lamented that Hadassah had not found a substitute for the drama of the war years and the struggle for independence, she asserted that "what is being done in Israel today is even more dramatic than war and is fraught with social, economic, and political significance."[64] Movies including *Tomorrow's a Wonderful Day, Naomi Says "Yes," This Is the Hour, Shulamith Finds Tomorrow, Passport to Life*, and *Hannah Means Grace* dramatized Hadassah's Youth Aliyah programs, the Hadassah Medical Organization, and other Hadassah programs in Israel. Hadassah aired these movies on television and in movie theaters, and loaned or sold copies to local chapters to use in public relations, membership, and fundraising campaigns. A Hadassah member from New Jersey attested to the success of *Tomorrow's a Wonderful Day* just after the movie aired on ABC. As she solicited a local businessman, he said, "For years you've been pestering me for ads, and telling me what a wonderful job Hadassah does. Last night I saw your movie. Now I know. Here is my check for twenty-five dollars and it's a pleasure to give it to you."[65] *Shulamith Finds Tomorrow*, a Youth Aliyah film, won the Education Filmstrip class at the Golden Reel Film Festival, sponsored by the American Film Assembly, in 1955, and the United States chose *Hannah Means Grace* as one of twenty nontheatrical films to send to the 1959 Venice Film Festival and as one of twenty-three to send to the 1959 Edinburgh Film Festival.[66]

Although Hadassah employed print media, radio, and film to reach large audiences, Jews and non-Jews alike, Hadassah chapters used a more personal, aggressive approach to reach potential members. Through postcards, Rosh Hashanah cards, personal invitations, direct-mail letters, phone calls, small luncheons, intimate teas, and door-to-door canvassing, Hadassah recruiters set out to attract new members to the organization's rolls.[67] Molly Jacobs, membership chair from Bensonhurst, took her reenrollment of sick members very seriously and personally when she delivered a challah to each of them on every Friday.[68] Both national Hadassah and local chapters offered gifts and awards to new members. Chapters gave away gifts such as lipstick with the slogan "Put Hadassah on Every Woman's Lips," promotional pens ("You belong in Hadassah. Sign up today"), key chains to remind new members that joining "linked" them to Hadassah, and coasters in the shape of records ("Hadassah, Record-Making Organization").[69] National Hadassah sponsored membership contests, with prizes such as pins, books, bracelet charms, and free trips to Israel, for the chapters or individuals who brought in the most new members or reenrolled the most current members.[70] In 1949, Hadassah introduced lifetime membership in Hadassah on a national scale, offering such membership for a one-time fee of $100.[71] *Hadassah Headlines* instructed membership chairs to "make the life member feel that she has joined an elite group to which it is a real honor to belong."[72] Lifetime members served to maintain Hadassah's membership numbers, increasing from 4,000 in 1955 to over 28,000 in 1963.[73]

Hadassah chapters utilized these strategies and techniques as an integrated program of recruitment and fundraising. A chapter might place an advertisement in the local Jewish newspaper, follow up with postcards to prospective members, initiate telephone squads to set up appointments with prospective members, and finally invite these prospects to a tea or meeting. Hadassah's membership drives, although an all-year activity, culminated in annual "Hadassah-Day" or "H-Day" campaigns in every chapter. H-Day drives constituted all-day marathons during which Hadassah members canvassed their respective cities and towns in search of new members or to reenroll existing members. Through phone banks, door-to-door canvassing, rallies at the local Jewish Community Center, advertisements in local newspapers, posters in subways and storefronts, and even booths at local banks, post offices, or other public buildings, staffed by Hadassah members wearing nurses' uniforms, the chapters sought to draw in members.

Hadassah's marketing campaigns, membership appeals, and publicity materials succeeded. As previously noted, the organization replaced women who left its ranks with new members, and increased its fundraising, year after year in the 1950s and 1960s.

Of course, one could point to Hadassah's net gain, from 1950 to 1969, of only 25,000 members, as a failure or at least as indicative of trouble. Hadassah leaders reflected these two images of the organization in their discussions. Some rang alarm bells about the difficulty in retaining members and in raising money, and about the perception of their organization. The membership chair, Sue Glassberg, challenged the national board at Hadassah's 1953 midwinter conference by offering a choice: "Either we accept the figures as they exist and glow with pride because we have more or less maintained the status quo, or we analyze the figures and groan because, in light of our membership possibilities in these United States, we have barely scratched the surface."[74] Six years later, in 1959, Hadassah leaders faced the same dilemma, and the group's's president, Miriam Freund, in her report to the national board, warned that, although Hadassah might demonstrate a successful year in terms of membership and fundraising,

> The Board would be derelict in its duties if it did not begin seriously regarding one major problem—namely, membership growth. When the membership figures are examined, we find that although approximately 16,000 new members are enrolled annually, the closing figure remains almost status quo from year to year. Membership is the heart of our organization, and if Hadassah does not continue to increase total membership, it will be in the position of big business that did not advance and suddenly found it was no longer "big business."[75]

This anxiety led Hadassah leaders to overstate their membership numbers in the 1950s and 1960s. With the group no longer growing at the same pace as in the 1940s, the leaders felt compelled to such exaggeration, even to their own members. In 1956, Miriam Fierst, the national membership chair, announced to Hadassah chapters that she was tired of reporting 300,000 Hadassah members every year, and encouraged the organization to aim for 350,000 over the coming year,[76] yet, in fact, membership figures ranged from 273,339 in 1950 to 287,854 in

1956.[77] Bernice Salpeter, in her address to the National Board Meeting preceding Hadassah's 1967 convention, admitted that, although "membership figures have fluctuated throughout our history. . . . We never actually attained the 300,000 of which we speak. We have never gone beyond the figure of 287, 854 achieved in 1956–1957."[78]

Hadassah leaders might have exaggerated their numbers or projected pessimism about the future of their organization because they had expected the group to grow more rapidly as American Jews migrated to the suburbs. However, Hadassah treasurer Fannie Cohen compared population increases in various U.S. cities with Hadassah membership rolls and concluded that membership did not always rise with a rise in population.[79] The 1950s represented the decade of Jewish (and general American) flight to the suburbs. Between 1950 and 1960, the suburban Jewish population more than doubled, and women who might have worked at paid employment during the war years returned to the home, with many settling into suburbia.[80] Thus it would seem logical that Hadassah's ranks would swell with these newly suburban women, and that new chapters would emerge in suburban neighborhoods. However, although Hadassah formed new chapters and groups in many expanding suburbs, including some in northern New Jersey, Long Island, Texas, and California, population shifts often resulted in the disbanding of older chapters or groups and in the merging of others.[81] That is, women who moved in the 1950s and 1960s simply switched their Hadassah memberships from one city or town to another, without adding to the group's ranks. Hadassah worked hard to retain women who moved, encouraging chapters to distribute transfer forms to assist members in their transition, but this strategy often fell short: the 1956 annual report revealed that the organization lost 523 members through death and 2,000 through the women's moving.[82]

Conservative synagogue sisterhoods proved more successful in attracting new members. The Women's League for Conservative Judaism (WLCJ) comprised a membership of 80,000 in 1950; the organization boasted 200,000 members by 1968, a gain of 120,000 during a period when Hadassah gained a mere 25,000 members.[83] What explains this surge in WLCJ ranks may be, as Will Herberg asserted in *Protestant—Catholic—Jew*, that the 1950s signaled the acceptance in America of religious differences, but obscured other differences, such as nationality.[84] Therefore, some suburban Jews expressed their Jewishness through synagogue membership rather than through Zionist affiliation, and the synagogues most often chosen represented Conservative Judaism. Between 1945 and 1965, the Conservative movement increased the number of its synagogues across the United States by 450, more than the number of new Orthodox and Reform synagogues combined.[85] Further, although Jews felt comfortable expressing religious affiliation in the suburbs, they did not wish to appear too distinct from their non-Jewish neighbors; they "wanted very much both to be accepted and not hide their Jewishness, although hardly to live it with much specificity."[86] Conservative

Judaism presented their best option for retaining Judaism while not moving "too far" to the right or to the left.

Although some overlap between Hadassah and sisterhoods certainly existed, Hadassah recruiters wanted every sisterhood member to join Hadassah; they had a ready answer for any who might ask, "I am a sisterhood member, so why do I need both memberships?" The recruiter would answer that the potential recruit needed both because, whereas sisterhood concerns itself with the synagogue and religious education, "Hadassah concerns itself primarily with helping to build up the Jewish State through its health and welfare projects there, and education, American affairs and Zionist public relations in America. One organization complements the other; there is no conflict between them."[87]

Hadassah leaders who worried about the growth of their organization might point to the growth of synagogue sisterhoods as a counterpoint to their own perceived stagnation; however, optimists among Hadassah leaders boasted that Hadassah was "the best fund-raising body in the country and . . . its techniques have been copied by almost every other organization."[88] Hadassah's treasurer reported a net gain of only 1,176 members in 1962, but put a positive spin on this number: "In an era when most organizations are barely holding to the status quo, [this increase] is a great tribute to Hadassah and to the leadership across the country."[89] (She might have been referring to the Zionist Organization of America, Pioneer Women, or Mizrachi Women of America, all of whom lost members or barely maintained the status quo in the 1950s and 1960s.)

In terms of sheer membership numbers and fundraising capabilities and results, then, Hadassah more than held its own in this era as a powerful women's organization. Hadassah managed to maintain its size and status in the 1950s and 1960s through extensive marketing, public relations campaigns, membership drives, and the utilization of suburban women's growing interest in community affairs and search for "self-fulfillment."

NOTES

1. Membership Numbers, Folder: Membership, Box: Subjects, RG23, Hadassah Archives (hereafter Hadassah), New York.

2. Report of Proceedings of First Hadassah Convention, June 29–30, 1914, 7, Folder 1, Box 1, RG3, Hadassah Annual Conventions Series, Hadassah.

3. Report from Esther Gottesman, Editor, *Hadassah Magazine*, at the 50th Annual Hadassah Convention, 1964, 6, Folder3, Box 24,RG3, Hadassah Annual Conventions Series, Hadassah.

4. The membership of the Zionist Organization of America dropped to 106,000 in 1956, a decline of almost 150,000 after 1948; Pioneer Women failed to grow at all in the 1960s and in fact lost 3,000 members. See Naomi Cohen, *American Jews and the Zionist Idea* (New York: Ktav, 1975). Author interview with Judith Sokolow at Naamat USA, December 2, 2004.

5. "Hadassah Raised $9,000,000, Convention Told Here," press release, August 21, 1950, 11, Folder 1, Box 15, RG3, Hadassah Annual Convention Series, Hadassah; *Hadassah News: Special 1967 Convention Issue*, 11, Folder 1, Box 27, RG3, Hadassah Annual Convention Series, Hadassah.

6. *Hadassah Headlines*, March 1949, 2, RG17: Publications, Hadassah.

7. Hadassah Annual Project Reports 1956–1957, 50, Folder 7, Box 19, RG3, Hadassah Annual Convention Series, Hadassah.

8. Hadassah Annual Report 1968–1969, 23, Folder 2, Box 28, RG3, Hadassah Annual Convention Series, Hadassah.

9. *Hadassah Headlines*, December 1950, 3, RG17: Publications, Hadassah.

10. *Hadassah Chapter Instructions*, November–December 1941, 11, RG17: Publications, Hadassah; Resolution on American Affairs Adopted by the 27th Annual Hadassah Convention, 1941, Folder 12, Box 10, RG3, Hadassah Annual Conventions Series, Hadassah.

11. *Hadassah Headlines*, April 1951, 8, RG17: Publications, Hadassah.

12. Resolution on American Immigration Laws Adopted by the 32nd Annual Hadassah Convention, 1946, 10, Folder 4, Box 13, RG3, Hadassah Annual Conventions Series, Hadassah.

13. The World Health Organization (WHO), an arm of the United Nations, formally adopted its constitution on March 7, 1948, when the twenty-sixth nation ratified it. The U.S. Congress allowed the World Health Bill, authorizing U.S. ratification of the WHO's constitution, to sit in committee as the United Nations General Assembly formally adopted it. Congress sent the bill to President Truman in June 1948, and he signed it on June 14, 1948.

14. The Convention on the Prevention and Punishment of the Crime of Genocide was ratified by the United Nations General Assembly on December 9, 1948. The United States did not ratify the convention until 1988.

15. President Harry Truman announced the Point Four Program (so named because it was mentioned fourth in his list of foreign policy objectives) in his 1949 inaugural address. He called for a "bold new program" for making the benefits of American scientific advances and industrial progress available to "underdeveloped nations." See David McCullough, *Truman* (New York: Simon and Schuster, 1992), 730.

16. *Hadassah Headlines*, April–May 1965, 5, RG17: Publications, Hadassah. Started in 1965 as part of President Lyndon Johnson's War on Poverty, Head Start aimed to provide comprehensive child development programs to low-income children.

17. Hadassah Annual Project Reports, 1955–1956, 35, Folder 3, Box 19, RG3, Hadassah Annual Conventions Series, Hadassah.

18. Civil Liberties Resolution Adopted by the 42nd Annual Hadassah Convention, 1956, 3, Folder 3, Box 19, RG3, Hadassah Annual Conventions Series, Hadassah; Resolution on Civil Rights Adopted by the 43rd Annual Hadassah Convention, 1957, 3, Folder 7, Box 19, RG3, Hadassah Annual Conventions Series, Hadassah; *Hadassah Headlines*, September–October 1963, 2, RG17: Publications, Hadassah; Resolution on Civil Rights Adopted by the 49th Annual Hadassah Convention, 1963, 2, Folder 11, Box 23, RG3, Hadassah Annual Conventions Series, Hadassah; Resolution on the Civil Rights Act of 1966 Adopted by the 52nd Annual Hadassah Convention, 1966, 2, Folder 5, Box 26, RG3, Hadassah Annual Conventions Series, Hadassah.

19. *Hadassah Headlines*, December 1948, 6, RG17: Publications, Hadassah.

20. *Hadassah Headlines*, November 1954, 6, RG17: Publications, Hadassah.

21. Riv-Ellen Prell, *Fighting to Become Americans: Assimilation and the Trouble between Jewish Women and Jewish Men* (Boston: Beacon Press, 1999), 159–160.

22. *Hadassah Headlines*, November 1951, 2, RG17: Publications, Hadassah.

23. Hadassah Annual Reports, 1951–1952, Folder 1, Box 17, RG3, Hadassah Annual Conventions Series, Hadassah.

24. *Hadassah Headlines*, May 1953, 1; June 1953, 4, both RG17: Publications, Hadassah.

25. *Hadassah Newsletter*, May 1953, 2, RG17: Publications, Hadassah.

26. *Hadassah Newsletter,* November 1953, RG17: Publications, Hadassah.

27. *Hadassah Newsletter,* December 1953, 2, RG17: Publications, Hadassah.

28. *Hadassah Headlines,* September–October 1954, RG17: Publications, Hadassah.

29. *Hadassah Headlines,* June 1954, 6, RG17: Publications, Hadassah.

30. *Hadassah Headlines,* November 1955, 2, RG17: Publications, Hadassah.

31. Press release, October 30, 1952, 3, Folder 4, Box 17, RG3, Hadassah Annual Convention Series, Hadassah.

32. "Factually Speaking about Hadassah Medical Organization and Medical Center," November 1961, RG15: Program Materials, Hadassah.

33. "Factually Speaking on Vocational Training," November 1957, RG15: Program Materials, Hadassah.

34. "Factually Speaking on Youth Aliyah," September 1957, RG15: Program Materials, Hadassah.

35. *Hadassah Headlines,* December 1950, 3, RG17: Publications, Hadassah.

36. *Hadassah Headlines,* September–October 1955, 6, RG17: Publications, Hadassah.

37. "Join Hadassah for Goodness Sake!" 4, Folder 2, Box 2, RG15: Membership/Guides and Services, Publications, and Circulated Materials, Hadassah.

38. Deborah Dash Moore, *To the Golden Cities: Pursuing the American Jewish Dream in Miami and L.A.* (Cambridge, MA: Harvard University Press, 1994), 103.

39. Ibid, 151.

40. Rabbi Albert Gordon, *Jews in Suburbia* (Boston: Beacon Press, 1959), 59, cited in Joyce Antler, *You Never Call! You Never Write! A History of the Jewish Mother* (New York: Oxford University Press, 2007), 104.

41. "This Is Your Life in Hadassah," September 1954, Box 10 RG17: Membership Pamphlets, Hadassah.

42. "Introducing . . . the Hadassah Look," May 1958, Box10, RG17: Membership Pamphlets; *Hadassah Headlines,* August–September 1960, 2, RG17: Publications, Hadassah.

43. Antler, *You Never Call! You Never Write,* 105.

44. Ibid., 118.

45. "On You It's Becoming," May 1953, Box 10, RG17: Membership Pamphlets, Hadassah.

46. "Once upon a time 39 years ago . . ." November 1950, Box10, RG17: Membership Pamphlets, Hadassah.

47. Herman Wouk's Address to the 41st Annual Hadassah Convention, November 2, 1955, 1, Folder 14, Box 18, RG3, Hadassah Annual Conventions Series, Hadassah.

48. *Hadassah Newsletter,* January 1954, 6, RG17: Publications, Hadassah.

49. *Hadassah Newsletter,* September 1953, 7, RG17: Publications, Hadassah.

50. National Board Minutes, Midwinter Conference, February 14, 1961, 4, Hadassah.

51. "Ladies who lunch" refers to wealthy, well-dressed women who often met for lunch during the week for social reasons or to raise money for charity. Stephen Sondheim popularized the expression in his 1970 play *Company,* which featured the song "Ladies Who Lunch."

52. *Hadassah Headlines,* September–October 1953, 2, RG17: Publications, Hadassah.

53. *Hadassah Headlines,* August–September 1959, 3, RG17: Publications, Hadassah.

54. Speech by Judith Epstein at the 47th Annual Hadassah Convention, August 22, 1961, 1–2, Folder 3, Box 23, RG3, Hadassah Annual Conventions Series, Hadassah.

55. Report of Proceedings of 45th Annual Hadassah Convention, September 13–16, 1959, Folder 8, Box 20, RG3, Hadassah Annual Convention Series, Hadassah.

56. *Hadassah Headlines*, March 1948, 4; December 1948, 8; both RG17: Publications, Hadassah.

57. *Hadassah Headlines*, February 1949, 1–2, RG17: Publications, Hadassah.

58. *Hadassah Headlines*, January 1948, 6, RG17: Publications, Hadassah.

59. *Hadassah Headlines*, October 1949, 3, RG17: Publications, Hadassah.

60. *Hadassah Headlines*, August–September 1959, 3, RG17: Publications, Hadassah.

61. *Hadassah Headlines*, August–September 1960, 2, RG17: Publications, Hadassah.

62. *Hadassah Headlines*, August–September 1959, 5, RG17: Publications, Hadassah.

63. *Hadassah Headlines*, June 1949, 8; September 1949, 8; October 1949, 3; all RG17: Publications, Hadassah. Also, Hadassah National Board Minutes, 1950 Midwinter Conference, Vol. 2, Set 1, 52, Hadassah.

64. Hadassah National Board Minutes, 1950 Midwinter Conference, Vol. 2, Set 1, 61, Hadassah.

65. *Hadassah Headlines*, March 1949, 5 and 7, RG17: Publications, Hadassah.

66. *Hadassah Headlines*, June 1955, 1; June–July 1959, 5; both RG17: Publications, Hadassah.

67. See *Hadassah Headlines*, January 1926, 8; March 1948, 1; December 1948, 8; January 1949, 8; May 1949, 8; June 1949, 6; July–August 1953, 5; September–October 1953, 2; July–August 1954, 3; June–July 1959, 1; August–September 1959, 1 and 8; August–September 1960, 1; July–August 1961, 1 and 8; all RG17: Publications, Hadassah.

68. *Hadassah Headlines*, February 1949, 3, RG17: Publications, Hadassah.

69. Hadassah Progress Report: Projects and Activities, 1954–1955, 47, Folder 9, Box 18, RG3, Hadassah Annual Convention Series, Hadassah; Hadassah Annual Project Reports, 1957–1958, 50, Folder 11, Box 19, RG3: Hadassah Annual Conventions Series, Hadassah; *Hadassah Headlines*, June–July 1960, 3 RG17: Publications, Hadassah; *Hadassah Headlines*, June 1964, 3, RG17: Publications, Hadassah.

70. Hadassah Annual Report, 1954–1955, 47, Folder 9, Box 18, RG3, Hadassah Annual Convention Series, Hadassah; Hadassah Annual Project Reports, 1959–1960, 58, Folder 6, Box 21, RG3, Hadassah Annual Conventions Series, Hadassah; *Hadassah Headlines*, January 1952, 1, RG17: Publications, Hadassah.

71. Hadassah Annual Report, 1948–1949, 9, Folder 1, Box 15, RG3, Hadassah Annual Conventions Series, Hadassah.

72. *Hadassah Headlines*, July–August 1949, 3, RG17: Publications, Hadassah.

73. Hadassah Progress Report, 1954–1955, 46, Folder 9, Box 18, RG3, Hadassah Annual Conventions Series, Hadassah; Hadassah Annual Report, 1962–1963, 44, Folder 10, Box 23, RG3, Hadassah Annual Conventions Series, Hadassah.

74. *Hadassah Newsletter*, April 1953, 6, RG17: Publications, Hadassah.

75. National Board Minutes, September 10, 1959, Preconvention Meeting, 2, Hadassah.

76. *Hadassah Headlines*, January 1956, 3, RG17: Publications, Hadassah.

77. Membership Numbers, Folder: Membership, Box: Subjects, RG23, Hadassah.

78. National Board Minutes, September 14, 1967 (afternoon), Preconvention, 7, Hadassah.

79. National Board Minutes, February 14, 1961, Midwinter Conference, 1, Hadassah.

80. Sidney Goldstein and Calvin Goldscheider, *Jewish Americans: Three Generations in a Jewish Community* (Englewood Cliffs, NJ: Prentice-Hall, 1968), 49, cited in Prell, *Fighting to Become Americans*, 157.

81. Hadassah Annual Report, 1954–1955, 50, Folder 9, Box 18, RG3, Hadassah Annual Convention Series, Hadassah.

82. Hadassah Annual Project Reports, 1955–1956, 44, Folder 3, Box 19, RG3, Hadassah Annual Convention Series; *Hadassah Headlines*, February 1962, 6, RG17: Publications, Hadassah.

83. Shelley Buxbaum, *75 Years of Vision and Volunteerism* (New York: Women's League for Conservative Judaism, 1992), 22–23, 43.

84. Will Herberg, *Protestant—Catholic—Jew* (Chicago: University of Chicago Press, 1955), 27–31, 56–60.

85. Jonathan Sarna, *American Judaism* (New Haven, CT: Yale University Press, 2004), 284.

86. Prell, *Fighting to Become Americans*, 160.

87. *Hadassah Headlines*, December 1950, 3, RG17: Publications, Hadassah.

88. Hadassah National Board Minutes, 1950, Vol, 2, Set 1, 44, Hadassah.

89. National Board Minutes, September 13, 1962, Preconvention Meetings, 4, Hadassah.

5   "A Lady Sometimes Blows the Shofar"

WOMEN'S RELIGIOUS EQUALITY IN
THE POSTWAR RECONSTRUCTIONIST
MOVEMENT

DEBORAH WAXMAN

In 1922, Judith Kaplan, daughter of Reconstructionist ideologue Mordecai Kaplan, became the first girl to celebrate a bat mitzvah at the Society for the Advancement of Judaism (SAJ), the flagship synagogue of Reconstructionist Judaism. Although the creation of a solo coming-of-age ceremony for a girl introduced into Jewish religious life a degree of unprecedented gender parity, the content of Judith Kaplan's ceremony differed from a boy's bar mitzvah, and her postceremony status as an adult female remained distinctly more limited than her male counterparts'. In 1945, a full generation later, the adolescent girls of the SAJ initiated a campaign for greater religious recognition. They lobbied first to carry the Torah on Jewish holidays and then to be called to the Torah for honors on occasions other than the day of becoming bat mitzvah. In 1950, their efforts culminated in the granting of full religious equality for women within the congregation, through the democratic vote of the membership.

In the years following World War II, women affiliated with the Reconstructionist movement—an approach to Judaism developed in the 1920s and 1930s and designed to address the aspirations and preoccupations of first- and second-generation American Jews—in many ways inhabited the domestic realm prescribed for American women by the dominant ideology. Largely middle-class and college educated, many of them stayed at home to raise children. In the synagogues they attended and frequently helped to found, they focused on education and occupied roles conventionally held by women, such as hostessing *kiddushes* (literally, a blessing over wine, but in this usage referring to the refreshments served after a synagogue service), raising funds, and maintaining ritual objects. Yet in critical ways women within the Reconstructionist movement engaged in religious activities that veered sharply from that postwar domestic ideology articulated in *The Feminine Mystique*. Reconstructionist ideology promoted full religious equality for women, and women within the movement took forceful steps to translate this principle into their lives, taking on religious practices traditionally performed only by men—most notably, receiving *aliyot* (Torah honors) and being counted in a *minyan* (prayer quorum).

From a traditional Jewish perspective, and from an American social perspective, the equal status achieved by Reconstructionist women during the postwar years proved unusually progressive. The Reconstructionist movement's ideological and practical changes in this area both anticipated and seeded the movement toward feminist Judaism that emerged in the late 1960s and early 1970s, and the fact of the movement's efforts in the 1940s and 1950s suggests a need to reexamine the periodization that locates the emergence of feminist Judaism entirely in later decades. Reconstructionist consideration of gender equality in the postwar period included the ordination of women as rabbis but, in a manner distinct from, and more comprehensive than, other religious approaches of the era, sought to completely redress the status of women within traditional conceptions of Judaism.

The Reconstructionist approach to women's religious equality emerged directly out of Reconstructionist philosophy, developed primarily by Mordecai M. Kaplan in the middle third of the twentieth century. A Conservative rabbi with graduate training in sociology and anthropology, Kaplan sought to revitalize Judaism in response to the impact of modernity on Jewish life and Jewish self-understanding, and in response to an unprecedented openness—the openness that American society presented to the masses of Jews who had emigrated from Eastern Europe in the decades around the turn of the twentieth century.[1] Since the early nineteenth century, modernity and the prospect of social integration had created both opportunity and crisis for Jews living in democratic societies, and no religious, political, or social movement had been able to stem the resulting fragmentation of the Jewish community and of Jewish self-understanding. In Reconstructionism, Kaplan strove for a positive, modern explication of Judaism that would be compelling to American-born Jews and would help to reestablish a premodern sense of "Jewish unity."[2]

Reconstructionist ideology centered around the definition of Judaism as the evolving religious civilization of the Jewish people. It posited that modern Jews in America lived in two civilizations, the Jewish one and the American one, and that these civilizations could mutually and beneficially influence one another. "Civilization" spanned the full spectrum of Jewish life—religion, arts, culture, philosophy, food, language, ethics, and more—and therefore provided multiple entry points for Jews.[3] Through this model, religion played a central but not singular role in defining Jewish identity; Kaplan prioritized finding ways to legitimate ethnic expressions of Jewish peoplehood and to draw in marginalized or disempowered populations, including women.[4] A commitment to democracy constituted the foremost attribute that Reconstructionism took from American civilization. Reconstructionist leaders sought to introduce democracy throughout Jewish life, lobbying for democratically elected and representative community organizations in place of oligarchic leadership, and empowering laypeople to participate in religious decision making along with rabbis; these leaders also worked to bolster a commitment to democracy across the breadth of American life.[5]

Kaplan functioned primarily as a polemicist, critiquing to the left and the right and sparking intense reaction from all sides.[6] He consistently advanced Reconstructionism as a school of thought designed to influence and unite the American Jewish community.[7] His disciples, however, divided between either following Kaplan's limited ideological approach or acting more assertively to establish a separate denomination. In the postwar years, many American Jews within the Conservative and Reform movements accepted Reconstructionist ideas and principles without much awareness or acknowledgment, while a much smaller segment began to organize expressly Reconstructionist institutions as a fourth denomination.[8] In this period, the increasing equality in the religious status of women emerged as one key marker of an expressly Reconstructionist synagogue.

Although the majority of Mordecai Kaplan's extensive ideological writings did not focus on women, his oft-reprinted "The Status of the Jewish Woman," first published in the biweekly journal *The Reconstructionist* in 1936 and reprinted in his influential 1948 book *The Future of the American Jew*,[9] issued a scathing critique of the status quo of gender relations and put forward a call to action.

> Few aspects of Jewish thought and life illustrate so strikingly the need for reconstructing Jewish law as the traditional status of the Jewish woman. In Jewish tradition, her status is unquestionably that of inferiority to the man. . . . She must attain in Jewish law and practice a position of religious, civic and juridical equality with the man, and this attainment must come about through her own efforts and initiative. Whatever liberal minded men may do in her behalf is bound to remain but a futile and meaningless gesture. The Jewish woman must demand the equality due her as a right to which she is fully entitled.[10]

Shaped by Progressive-era thinking, and drawn to democratic practices, Kaplan saw the challenge provided by Western, modern culture as a positive goad to Judaism's recalcitrance concerning women. He also considered the situation urgent. Without redress, he feared, Jewish women would feel so much more valued in secular culture than in the Jewish world that they would abandon Judaism entirely.[11]

Kaplan argued that the Reconstructionist approach would yield the most satisfactory results in achieving gender equality. Embracing Judaism as a civilization would enable Jews to find modes of communal adjudication other than the traditional rabbinic laws (halakhah), which contained little indigenous impulse toward gender egalitarianism. He asserted that "social justice, rather than immutable precedent," must be the foundation for, and the overarching guide of, Jewish civic and juridical life in the Diaspora.[12] Kaplan closed his argument with a stirring call for Jewish women "to inaugurate a movement that will aim to remove the religious, civic and juridical disabilities which traditional Jewish law imposes on them and that will win for them the status of equality."[13]

Kaplan's repudiation of Jewish law on the issue of women's equality separated Reconstructionism from other Jewish religious approaches of the era. Orthodoxy insisted on the binding nature of halakhah, and preserved the separation of women into a private realm with a restricted range of obligations and opportunities. The Conservative movement shared this view, even as its members sought means of bringing halakhic Judaism into greater conformity with modernity. Indeed, the status of women proved one of the thorniest challenges for Conservative rabbis in the period before and after World War II, especially around the issue of *agunot*, women denied religious divorces by their husbands.[14] Reform Judaism liberated itself entirely from a legal approach and instead prioritized individual autonomy over specifically Jewish governing norms (that is, Jewish law). In Kaplan's estimation, Reform went too far in this regard and risked disassociating Judaism from Jewish particularism and thus driving Jews away from identification with the Jewish people;[15] for example, Kaplan noted, the Reform movement's solution to the problem of women's disempowerment in Jewish divorce urged the setting aside of Jewish divorce practices entirely in favor of civil proceedings.[16] Kaplan's change agent of social justice emerged, then, not out of a liberal, individualistic, rights-oriented impulse, but rather out of a communally mediated value that he hoped and expected would be widely recognized and embraced as a higher good. In the matter of Jewish women's equality, as in others, Kaplan tried to locate or generate deeply Jewish practices and idioms that would strip away or move beyond the crippling and outdated strictures of Jewish law yet would, through their compelling nature, nonetheless unify the modern Jewish community.

Occasionally, *The Reconstructionist*, organized in 1935 by disciples of Kaplan to explicate his ideas, addressed the issue of women's status. The journal editors frequently used the phrase "men and women" when announcing or describing Reconstructionist forums or gatherings,[17] an indication that they considered women important actors in the Reconstructionist movement. They directly addressed the status of women when Christian denominations took steps toward women's ordination; for instance, in June 1946, the editors noted that the General Assembly of the Presbyterian Church had approved the ordination of women. The editors had an agenda, though, that was more modest in its ends, yet more daring in its means. They felt that the matter of ordination was premature, assessing that Jewish organizations were not ready for such a step. But they acknowledged that Jewish women were educated and were serving widely as educators. They advocated that women at least be granted aliyot, and urged women to "lead a revolt demanding the recognition of their equal religious status with men."[18] In a 1947 item reporting on the United Church of Canada's decision to ordain married women, *The Reconstructionist* again focused on general legal status rather than on ordination. In Protestant practice, the editors observed, women enjoyed equal status in all other matters; thus, though highly charged, ordination represented simply the last issue separating the status of men and women in liberal denominations of Christianity. However, for religious Jews who maintained any relationship to traditional conceptions of authority, inequality was more deeply ensconced—embedded into the fabric of Jewish understanding and practice. The editors thus argued that Jews, as a minority population in the Diaspora, would be unlikely to take the lead among all religions in a controversial matter like the ordination of women, but they could readily address Judaism's own internal organization and combat the inequalities inherent in Jewish law.[19] In the mid-1950s, as the Presbyterians, Episcopalians, and Methodists approved ordination of women, and as Reform Judaism began to reconsider the matter, the editors of *The Reconstructionist* began to signal that it was time to press for women's ordination.[20]

However, the postwar treatment of women's status in *The Reconstructionist* functioned primarily as a two-fold litmus test, applied first as a measure of the inadequacies of the halakhic process, and second as an illustration of how Reconstructionism consciously planned the evolution of Judaism.[21] Responding to a general question about the limits of ritual innovation, Kaplan explained: "To reconstruct does not mean to destroy. It means to reaffirm, re-achieve, re-establish." He then elaborated his point by discussing the prohibition of granting women honors during the Torah reading. In the premodern Jewish past, calling women to the Torah was unthinkable, because "women had no share in public life"; at that time, such exclusion was "no derogation" either to them or to the ritual of aliyah. "But in our day, to exclude half of the congregation from participating in this ritual observance because of their sex definitely detracts from [the ritual's] importance. . . . The departure from traditional usage [that is, the affirmative act of granting women the honor] tends to strengthen rather than weaken a traditional value, that of reverence for the Torah."[22] Lay voices joined Kaplan in this call for innovation and in his frustration with the slow process through which Conservative Judaism was approaching the issue, due to halakhic constraints. In "Stoop Down to Your Wife," attorney Benjamin William Mehlman argued for equalizing the role of men and women in synagogue ritual, and insisted that lay initiation should be considered sufficient authority: "We of the Reconstructionist movement surely understand that only great leaders and a militant laity can prevent Judaism in this country from becoming sterile. We have learned the futility of waiting for action by alleged authoritative bodies."[23]

The status of women also served to illustrate Reconstructionism's vanguard practice in the conscious planning of Judaism's evolution. True to his Conservative training, Kaplan embraced historical consciousness and mistrusted the tendency to "arbitrarily [read] into an ancient tradition whatever we happen to think true or just."[24] Kaplan was willing to break with tradition in the intentional pursuit of truth and justice. He thought it dishonest to assume that the traditional halakhah intended equality for women; therefore, "if [Reconstructionists] believe in the equality of the sexes," they should introduce the "necessary changes" as "a conscious and deliberate amendment." This would be "a planned reconstruction in Jewish law and Jewish life," in the service of equality.[25]

In the translation from theory to the living realities of postwar Jewish communities, the progressive Reconstructionist attitude toward women's equality intersected awkwardly with conservative postwar gender ideals in shaping the day-to-day practice of Jewish women within the Reconstructionist movement. Movement leaders expressly identified women's status as a vanguard issue for Jewish reconstruction, and women increasingly took on such practices as ascending to the Torah for honors and being counted in a minyan; however, in social roles separate from the religious service, women in Reconstructionist synagogues tended to conform to mainstream social norms, serving as hostesses and managing the domestic side of congregational life. The Reconstructionist embrace of gender equality affected only one area. It catalyzed radical changes in Jewish ritual practice but did not change the social realities of Reconstructionist women, who continued to be constrained by postwar domestic ideals.[26] Nonetheless, the religious changes anticipated activism by the Jewish feminist movement that would emerge more than twenty years later as part of Second Wave feminism.

At the Society for the Advancement of Judaism, founded in 1922 as the first Reconstructionist synagogue, the period immediately after World War II marked the beginning of a renegotiation of women's religious roles and a more consistent application of Reconstructionist principles. At some point in the years after Judith Kaplan's 1922 bat mitzvah, the ceremony had come to more fully mirror a boy's bar mitzvah, with girls themselves rather than their fathers being called to the Torah in their own right. But for girls who participated in the ritual before 1950, their bat mitzvah would represent not only the first but also the last time that they would be called to the Torah. The aliyah was granted to girls on this one occasion only, whereas post–bar mitzvah males could receive it on any occasion.[27]

In February 1945, the SAJ's board of trustees began an extended consideration of women's participation in religious rituals; the study was sparked in part by the girls of the congregation. Writing in 1953, Ira Eisenstein, who was the SAJ's rabbi at the time,[28] remembered:

> The demand for greater recognition came from the *bat mitzvah* girls themselves. They asked for the right to carry the Torah during the *hakafot* on Simchat Torah.[29] They were strong enough, they thought, certainly as strong as some of "those old men" who are allowed to march around with the scrolls. They won this round without a struggle. Finally, they insisted upon being called up for *aliyot*, even when they were . . . through the *bat mitzvah* ceremony. What was the use, they said, of learning to chant the *berakhot* [blessings] and the Torah text if they were going to use them only once in

their lives. If they were "equal enough" to come up once, they are "equal enough" to be called from time to time.[30]

After extensive discussion on the inherent inequity in practice, the board finally decided to place the topic on the agenda for the annual May membership meeting. They framed the question to consider whether "girls who have been Bat Mitzvah or Confirmed . . . [should] be considered qualified to accept an Aliyah on the Sabbath or Festivals?"[31] The leaders of the congregation deemed education crucial; they did not entertain the possibility of calling to the Torah women who had not undertaken intensive religious study.[32]

The membership meeting of May 28, 1945, proceeded with an organized debate regarding the pros and cons of calling girls up after their original coming-of-age ceremony. Proponents of women's equality argued that Reconstructionism's ideological commitment to equality, as spelled out by Mordecai Kaplan in "The Status of the Jewish Woman," should be realized in day-to-day (or shabbat-to-shabbat) congregational life. They also implied that greater participation by girls in the service was a positive development. For them, the traditional Jewish notion of the religious sphere of synagogue life as an exclusively male public realm had been set aside, possibly in response to the broader range of activities undertaken by women during World War II, or possibly due to the influence of the ideology of Reform Judaism. Partisans of the full-participation position, worried about the increased rates of alienation from Judaism, sought engagement with any and all Jewish youth. They also linked the issue of aliyot for women to a larger goal of Reconstructionist Judaism, the democratization of all realms of Jewish life; egalitarianism represented one plank in this much larger platform.

In contrast, those who opposed changes that would grant women aliyot did not directly address the issue under discussion or even raise traditional arguments against women's participation.[33] They focused on avoiding any "violent, revolutionary" break with tradition and on averting potential ridicule by other congregations. Opponents urged finding alternate ways to engage girls in the religious life of the congregation, and also expressed dismay that the SAJ rabbinic leadership refrained from providing more authoritative guidance, indicating discomfort with the responsibility that democratic participation thrust upon them as lay Jews. Collectively, their arguments opposed innovation in Jewish practice as a general principle.

Mordecai Kaplan heeded the congregants' request for guidance, indicating that "changes are justified when they make for a more intensive Judaism." He emphasized lay empowerment and the democratization of Judaism, urging the women of the SAJ to initiate the desired change and insisting that the decision was not a rabbinic one. If everyone would participate in this change wholeheartedly, it "would definitely be worthwhile." In the end, the debate did not result in a final decision, and no further discussion occurred on a community-wide level for several more years.[34]

In subsequent years, the rabbinic leadership at the SAJ did take a few steps toward promoting women's equality. At Simchat Torah services, celebrating the completion of the yearly cycle of reading the Torah, the rabbis called women to the Torah en masse for an aliyah;[35] also, on those festive holidays when *megilot* (e.g., the Book of Esther on Purim) were read, the Hebrew school children—girls as well as boys—chanted from them during services and offered explanations and interpretations.[36] In the meantime, the rabbis waited for lay initiation, for which they had been calling, before taking further action toward women's equality.

Such lay initiation emerged in 1950 out of a study group on Judaism as a Civilization conducted by Rabbi Jack Cohen. In an oral history interview, Cohen remembered that "the group raised the question, 'Why shouldn't women be given *aliyot?*' And I said, 'Why not, indeed?' So we had a congregational meeting [in May 1950] where it was agreed popularly by the majority that women should have *aliyot.*"[37] Because Ira Eisenstein, the SAJ's official rabbi, was on sabbatical, Cohen did not feel comfortable bringing the issue to a final decision, however, and the vote was not considered binding.[38] Upon his return from sabbatical, Eisenstein convened another membership meeting to discuss the issue "Equality of Women,"[39] and, at the second meeting, the congregation surpassed the boundaries of previous conversations on the topic and decided to grant women full religious equality, voting to call women to the Torah on all occasions regardless of the women's level of education and to count them in the religious quorum.[40]

The women of the SAJ expressed both excitement and fear over the new rights. An anonymous poem, "Thoughts of a Housewife on a Friday Morning," lyrically articulated these conflicting emotions.

> As I work in my modern white kitchen
> With touches of red (fleishig) and blue (milchig),[41]
> I think of the morrow's *aliyah*
> And strive for the long long view.
>
> The pike and the whitefish are chopped now,
> And cooking in Grandmother's pot. . . .
> Was I right to vote for this Freedom,
> Or was I not?
>
> There's the wine and the *chalah* to get now,
> And the ancestral silver to polish. . . .
> When I think of myself on the *bima*[42]
> I *cholish.*[43]
>
> We're told some traditions enrich us,
> But other traditions are chains;
> Is it Women's Dilemma that rends us
> Or Reconstructionist growing pains?

Oh, anthropological angels
Fast becloud the sweet Sabbath creed
When you look at *licht*-benching[44] under the aspect
Of Karen Horney and Margaret Mead.

The dominant male of our culture
Can hug to himself this solace;
He's no longer supreme on the *bima*,
But only he wears the *talis*.[45]

What my fears and my doubts come down to
When all is done and said
Is: Do *schuls*[46] rush in where angels
Fear to tread?

This poem articulated a transitional moment. The author presented herself as a classic homemaker in a kitchen full of modern appliances, consistent with the membership roles of Reconstructionist women throughout the SAJ's existence, and with the 1950s domestic ideal. In the poem, inhabiting the role of traditional Jewish wife preparing for the Sabbath, she felt in close communion with her ancestors. But she is also revealed as a quintessential Reconstructionist, conversant with contemporary social scientific views on gender, speaking in the Reconstructionist adoption of American "freedoms," and expressing some of Kaplan's concerns regarding the fragile nature of Jewish unity. The poem also anticipated future changes that a growing commitment to egalitarianism within the Reconstructionist movement and the emergence of the women's movement would generate, including ever-expanding roles for women and the adoption by women of such traditionally male practices as wearing a prayer shawl.

Eisenstein's 1953 retrospection, "Sex Equality in the Synagogue," provides additional information on the proceedings. Eisenstein reported that particularly compelling testimony came from a young mother who described her heartbreak at her five-year-old daughter's recognition of the degree of women's inferiority in the synagogue. Although the mother had initially opposed the proposal to include women more fully in synagogue practice, her daughter's unhappiness convinced her of the need for the innovation.[47]

In his diary, on December 2, 1950, Kaplan reflected on the congregation's hesitation to embrace equality for women, noting that he or Eisenstein could have imposed the practice earlier, but that Eisenstein had instead coaxed the membership to the point that they endorsed it nearly universally in a democratic vote. Kaplan also reported on the congregation's communal inauguration of this new practice. At a shabbat morning Torah service shortly after the vote, women, Kaplan's eldest daughter Judith and his wife Lena among them, received four of the eight aliyot. The service included remarks by Eisenstein on the impact of the

Figure 5.1 Women involved in the Reconstructionist movement fought for and received religious equality in the postwar years as an expression of Reconstructionist ideology, but, in the social realm, they largely conformed to the dominant domestic ideology. This undated photograph is of members of the Women's Division of the Society for the Advancement of Judaism. Lena Rubin Kaplan (wife of Mordecai M. Kaplan) is seated in the light-colored jacket. Judith Kaplan Eisenstein is standing on the far right. Hadassah Kaplan Musher stands fourth from the right.
Courtesy of the Eisenstein Reconstructionist Archives of the Reconstructionist Rabbinical College.

innovation, a sermon by Rabbi Harold Weisberg on "the meaning of femininity and masculinity from a historical point of view in general and in Jewish life," and music and prayers "in keeping with the [innovative] spirit of the service which many found to be inspiring." Kaplan reported that many worshippers filled the sanctuary, speculating that "the introduction of the innovation must have brought the people."

In the first few years after this radical restructuring of Jewish religious practice, the membership of the SAJ largely equated religious equality with aliyot. Calling women to the Torah was beyond the pale within the Conservative movement with which the SAJ was formally, if uncomfortably, affiliated, and the membership and leadership together apparently viewed this act as sufficiently and satisfyingly symbolic of equality. Eisenstein's 1953 article concluded with a slightly sardonic discussion of women and aliyot, poking those opponents who worried that expanded roles for women would lead to disempowerment of men.

> Today, the presence of women on the *bimah* is common—though not a commonplace. Brides accompany their grooms on the Shabbat before their wedding, to recite together the *berakhot* and the *sheheheyanu*.[48] Mothers are called to the Torah for their *bar mitzvah* sons or *bat mitzvah* daughters to read for them. Young mothers . . . come to bless their newborn sons, or name their newborn daughters. And women of all ages rise to chant the benedictions, when the forthcoming week marks the *yahrzeit*[49] of a dear one.
> And the men? Oh, they get an *aliyah*—once in a while.[50]

During the 1950s, the congregation gradually began to implement women's equality more fully. Not only did women receive aliyot with increasing frequency, but they also began to chant Torah and haftarah (passages from the prophets).[51] In 1952, the SAJ established a Junior Congregation, in which boys and girls participated equally, and that same fall the SAJ equalized the traditional Simchat Torah celebration honoring a *hatan Torah* and a *hatan bereshit* through the institution of a *kalat bereshit*.[52] In 1953, the SAJ appointed the first woman board member (or rather, first whose role was other than Women's Division president),[53] and in 1957 elected the first woman officer to the board.[54]

The Reconstructionist Synagogue of the North Shore (RSNS) began to organize at this period, as part of a concerted effort by the Jewish Reconstructionist Foundation to grow Reconstructionism as a distinct religious denomination.[55] Young Jewish couples founded the congregation in Great Neck, Long Island, in the late 1950s as a Reconstructionist study group,[56] and by May 1960 members had rented a meeting place and established a school, and were running their own services.[57]

Purim *shpiels* from the early 1960s provide rich insight into how the members of RSNS understood themselves as a new congregation. Well-written shpiels, composed by members and usually performed to large crowds at a carnival-like celebration, tended to comically dramatize key dynamics, events, or self-understandings within congregational life. In the early 1960s, RSNS was self-consciously Reconstructionist and extremely well-informed about Reconstructionist principles; thus the following ditty illustrated members' sense of commitment to the movement:

> (to the tune of the "Battle Hymn of the Republic")
> We are fighting for our movement,
> We are Reconstructionists
> A fourth denomination
> With some very modern twists.
> In theory and in practice

We're religious naturalists.
Our faith is marching on!

Another shpiel featured religious equality for women as one of the "modern twists" that defined the new congregation, and also pointed to expanded roles for women's religious participation.

(To the tune "of Utzu Etzah")
Prospective Member:
Women here with men are on a par.
That means my wife can be a Jewish star!
A lady sometimes blows the shofar
That is something I can go for
When I'm a Reconstructionist![58]

Women played key roles in the establishment of the congregation, and both they and their husbands recognized their centrality to the synagogue. In a jointly written remembrance, three founding female members reported feeling that their personal and professional lives were significantly influenced by their experiences establishing the congregation.[59] But even though women had been central players in the establishment of the synagogue, and though all members insisted upon the full equality of women in all aspects of Jewish ritual, the postwar norms of the feminine mystique continued to shape women's experiences within the institution. Women served on the synagogue's board from its founding, but no woman held the office of president until the 1970s. Even as women helped to generate such outreach and education programs as Reconstructionist Facts and Fables, throughout the 1960s women alone served as hostesses when refreshments were served afterward.[60] Such limitations fell away only when American social norms shifted.

At the same time that the Jewish Reconstructionist Foundation (JRF) seeded new congregations, it pursued other strategies to expand the Reconstructionist movement, including the establishment of a Women's Committee. In spite of the movement's progressive stance toward women's religious equality, the mission and activities of the Women's Committee did not differ from those of the Reform movement's National Federation of Temple Sisterhoods or the Women's League for Conservative Judaism.[61] Essentially an outgrowth of the Women's Division of the SAJ,[62] the JRF Women's Committee sought to attract women to Reconstructionism, to educate them about its philosophy and general Jewish topics, and to provide support for particular projects within the Reconstructionist movement. The Women's Committee organized Reconstructionist study groups in people's homes and mounted a midday forum series in public halls, featuring outstanding speakers.[63] The Women's Committee supported Tehiyah, a youth fellowship geared at exposing college-aged students to Reconstructionism. In a conventional approach combining education and fundraising, the women raised money to place Reconstructionist bookshelves in college libraries and to support retreats and other programs, but the program was primarily directed by staff members of the foundation.[64] That is, in this effort to support the growth of Reconstructionism, the Women's Committee limited women's roles to those conventionally accepted by postwar American society.

Scholars assess Reconstructionist thought as profoundly influential within postwar Jewish thought and practice. They point especially to the understanding of Judaism as a civilization, a concept that functioned as an organizing principle for many leaders across denominational and organizational lines, and which thus became an unnamed framework within which most liberal Jews experienced the Jewish community. An expansive embrace of peoplehood, of unity with all Jews and of the legitimacy of diverse expressions of Jewishness, also defined the postwar Jewish experience.[65] However, gender equality in the religious realm stood in marked contrast to these other widely accepted ideas, especially in comparison to the fast-growing Conservative movement that shared so many origins and aspirations with Reconstructionism. The status of women stands out as one way that American Judaism adopted, though more slowly, Reconstructionist thought, and thus can serve as a way of distinguishing between expressly Reconstructionist synagogues established in the postwar period and Conservative synagogues of the era, with their fainter impression of Kaplan's influence.

The Reconstructionist movement shared with Reform Judaism in America a willingness to cast off elements of traditional Judaism, but the two movements had different emphases, with different implications. Where the Reform movement embraced individual autonomy and pursued a vision of Judaism that prioritized its universal religious aspects, Reconstructionism stressed democracy and diversity in Jewish life while seeking to maintain a deep sense of continuity with the Jewish past, including a sense of connectedness with all other Jews. This focus transformed Reconstructionism's relationship to traditional Jewish decision making but did not sever it. Reconstructionists embraced grassroots activism and voting by positively identified Jews, in place of traditional halakhic decision making, as authoritative means of change.[66] In terms of the status of women, such a process led to an expansion of the sphere of religious involvement, thereby shattering the classical Jewish dualism that reserved the public sphere for men. In matters of nonreligious roles, American social mores remained in place until the early 1970s; the critique, deeply influenced by American political philosophy, affected only one area.[67] Nonetheless, the Reconstructionist ideological and practical stance toward the religious status of women limned the far-reaching nature of discussions of the status of women, and the Reconstructionist activism that precipitated change anticipated and likely seeded Ezrat Nashim and other efforts that emerged as part of second-wave American feminism. Thus the fact of Reconstructionist activism calls into question the periodization of twentieth-century Jewish feminism that usually locates its origins in the late 1960s.[68] In fact, activism around women's roles and women's participation in traditionally oriented Jewish religious activities began as early as the 1940s.

The negotiations around greater religious equality for women reflected an awareness of the possibility of women's ordination, especially in light of decisions by liberal Christian denominations, but Reconstructionist proponents for equality paid close attention to structural inequities that limited women's participation and prospects in myriad other ways as well, and they sought remedies that were just and comprehensive rather than oriented toward any single issue.[69] In their efforts to balance the Jewish past with the modern American future, Reconstructionists tried to live fully in two civilizations, to the mutual enrichment of both.

NOTES

1. Mel Scult, *Judaism Faces the Twentieth Century: A Biography of Mordecai Kaplan* (Detroit: Wayne State University Press, 1993), 41, 52.

2. Mordecai M. Kaplan, *Judaism as a Civilization: Toward a Reconstruction of American Jewish Life* (New York: Macmillan, 1934), 80–87.

3. As Noam Pianko has demonstrated, Kaplan deliberately employed the term *civilization* rather than *culture*, both to ensure that Judaism was equated with the highest values in American society and also to function as a counterweight and corrective to totalizing claims emerging out of American nationalist and Zionist circles. "Reconstructing Judaism, Reconstructing America: The Sources and Functions of Mordecai Kaplan's Civilization," *Jewish Social Studies*, n.s. 12, no. 2 (Winter 2006): 39–55.

4. Deborah Dash Moore, "Judaism as a Gendered Civilization: The Legacy of Mordecai M. Kaplan's Magnum Opus," *Jewish Social Studies*, n.s. 12, no. 2 (Winter 2006): 178.

5. Beth S. Wenger, "Making American Civilization Jewish: Mordecai Kaplan's Civil Religion," *Jewish Social Studies*, n.s. 12, no. 2 (Winter 2006): 56–63. See especially Mordecai Kaplan, J. Paul Williams, and Eugene Kohn, *The Faith of America* (New York: Henry Schuman, 1951).

6. Charles Liebman, "Reconstructionism in American Jewish Life," *American Jewish Year Book* 17 (1970), 192, 220–221.

7. Deborah Ann Musher, "Reconstructionist Judaism in the Mind of Mordecai Kaplan: The Transformation from a Philosophy into a Religious Denomination," *American Jewish History* 86, no. 4 (December 1998): 397–417.

8. Charles Liebman, "Reconstructionism in American Jewish Life," 276; Deborah Dash Moore and Andrew Bush, "Mitzvah, Gender, and Reconstructionist Judaism," in *Women Remaking American Judaism*, ed. Riv-Ellen Prell (Detroit: Wayne State University Press, 2007), 147–148.

9. "The Status of the Jewish Woman" was published in the February 2, 1936 (vol. 2, no. 1) edition of *The Reconstructionist*, republished in 1936 *Jewish Reconstructionist Papers* and, in a slightly different form, in Kaplan's influential 1948 *Future of the American Jew* (New York: Macmillan, 1948; rpt., New York: Macmillan, 1981). Page numbers are from the 1948 version.

10. Kaplan, *Future of the American Jew*, 402.

11. Ibid., 409.

12. Ibid., 411. Emphasis in original.

13. Ibid., 412.

14. The Conservative Committee on Law addressed this narrow topic repeatedly in the 1930s, 1940s, and 1950s. Each time, the prospect of overturning the halakhic prescription for women's inferior status prevented the committee members from coming to a definitive conclusion. In 1954, a joint committee of the Rabbinical Assembly and the Jewish Theological Seminary finally issued a *takkanah*, or rabbinical decree, calling for the insertion of a clause into the *ketubah* (marriage contract) that would provide for a rabbinic court to force the man to offer a divorce if he continuously refused to grant one in spite of legitimate grounds for divorce. See Shuly Rubin Schwartz, "The Tensions that Merit Our Attention: Women in the Conservative Movement," in *Women Remaking American Judaism*, 156–158. The Reconstructionist response dismissed the *takkanah* because it did nothing to address the inferior status of women in Jewish law and simply added a layer of patronizing protection in the narrow matter of divorce law. See Jack J. Cohen, "A Wrong Solution to the Divorce Problem," *The Reconstructionist* 20, no. 16 (December 10, 1954/Kislev 15, 5715): 12.

15. Kaplan, *Judaism as a Civilization*, 108–125.

16. Michael A. Meyer, *Response to Modernity: A History of the Reform Movement in Judaism* (Detroit: Wayne State University Press, 1988), 257.

17. See the editorial, "Resuming Our Task," after the first summer's publication hiatus in 1936 (vol. 1, no. 11 [October 4, 1936/Tishri 7, 5696]): 3.

18. From the unattributed Realities and Values section of *The Reconstructionist* 12, no. 9 (June 14, 1946/Sivan 15, 5706): 9.

19. From the unattributed Realities and Values section of *The Reconstructionist* 13, no. 12 (June 27, 1947/Tammuz 10, 5707): 7.

20. See Eugene Kohn, "Here and There," *The Reconstructionist* 21, no. 9 (June 10, 1955/Sivan 20, 5715): 7, and editorial, "Eve and the Rights of Women," *The Reconstructionist* 22, no. 8 (June 1, 1956/Sivan 22, 5716): 5. On Reform discussions on women's ordination in the 1920s and 1950s, see Karla Goldman, "Women in Reform Judaism: Between Rhetoric and Reality," in *Women Remaking American Judaism*, 117, 119–120.

21. As noted above, this was a barb at the Conservative movement and, to a lesser extent, at Orthodox control of personal status issues in the new State of Israel. Eugene Kohn, "Here and There," *The Reconstructionist* 25, no. 5 (April 17, 1959 [magazine no longer using Hebrew dates by this time]): 14.

22. "Know How to Answer," *The Reconstructionist* 16, no. 13 (November 3, 1950/Heshvan 23, 5711): 31.

23. *The Reconstructionist* 16, no. 20 (February 9, 1951/I Adar 3, 5711): 15. The title is a reframing of a Talmudic teaching urging that women's advice be taken seriously.

24. Here Kaplan launched a veiled barb at Reform practice; see *Judaism as a Civilization*, 115.

25. "Know How to Answer," *The Reconstructionist* 17, no. 10 (June 29, 1951/Sivan 25, 5711): 29.

26. The conformity to American domestic norms was consistent with Jewish acculturation to modern, Western society. See Riv-Ellen Prell, "Introduction," in *Women Remaking American Judaism*, 6–7.

27. I have not been able to document the date of this shift in practice, only the decision to alter it further—see subsequent paragraph. In his 1953 summary of the move toward religious equality at the SAJ, Ira Eisenstein records the occasion of the shift in practice only as "some years later," Eisenstein, "Sex Equality in the Synagogue," *The Reconstructionist* 19, no. 2 (March 6, 1953/Adar 19 5713): 19. See Regina Stein, "The Road to Bat Mitzvah in America," in *Women and American Judaism*, ed. Pamela S. Nadell and Jonathan D. Sarna (Hanover, NH: Brandeis University Press, 2001), 226.

28. Kaplan was rabbi emeritus.

29. Simchat Torah marks the conclusion of the annual cycle of reading the Torah in the synagogue. *Hakafot* refers to carrying the Torah scrolls around the sanctuary as part of the celebration.

30. Ira Eisenstein, "Sex Equality in the Synagogue."

31. March 20, 1945, SAJ minutes. Note the expanded parameters of the discussion to include confirmation as sufficient educational preparation for an aliyah. Anecdotal evidence from conversations with adults who grew up at the SAJ suggests there was a preference for group confirmation over individual bat mitzvah ceremonies (personal conversations with the author, New York, NY, December 8, 2002). Hence, this expansion would have included more girls than would discussion limited solely to bat mitzvah.

32. Even though Reconstructionists were deeply concerned with adult education and with declining levels of knowledge among all Jews, it is unlikely that any such conversation would have occurred around calling a male to the Torah: according to Jewish law and tradition, if he were of majority and could stumble his way through the appropriate blessings, a man would be eligible for an aliyah, regardless of the occasion or his level of education. This framing also misses the point of the solo ceremony of bar mitzvah (though not of the group-oriented confirmation, which had its origins in Christian practice). According to traditional teaching, a boy becomes bar mitzvah (he does not "have" a bar mitzvah) when he achieves majority—defined by Maimonides as puberty—and therefore becomes obligated to observe the mitzvot, or commandments. The Torah honor marks and celebrates this occasion; it does not create it.

33. E.g., *kol ishah*, the practice of preventing women from singing in public to avoid male arousal.

34. Beyond a "retreat into domesticity" in the larger American environment, one reason for the deferral may have been events immediately following this meeting. In May 1945, the Jewish Reconstructionist Foundation published the *Sabbath Prayer Book*, which applied Reconstructionist ideology to the traditional liturgy. The prayer book was received ambivalently, even with some hostility, by Kaplan's fellow faculty members at the Conservative Jewish Theological Seminary, with whom he had a turbulent relationship. See Eric Caplan, *From Ideology to Liturgy: Reconstructionist Worship and American Liberal Judaism* (Cincinnati: Hebrew Union College Press, 2002), 123; and Jack Wertheimer's "Kaplan vs. 'The Great Do-Nothings': The Inconclusive Battle over *The New Haggadah*," *Conservative Judaism* (Summer 1993): 20–37. These faculty members' displeasure was muted, however, by the violent reaction of the ultra-Orthodox Agudat Harabanim (Union of Orthodox Rabbis). In June 1945, members of the Agudah met in a New York hotel to place Kaplan in *herem* (excommunication) and to burn a copy of the *Sabbath Prayer Book* (Charles Liebman, "Reconstructionism in American Jewish Life," 220). Those SAJ members who opposed the notion of calling girls to the Torah had their fears realized: the actions of the rabbis signaled a perception that the Reconstructionist leaders had broken with *klal yisrael* (greater Israel) and were open to more than ridicule, even to violence. Ultimately, the press coverage that this incident generated, in both the *New York Times* and the Jewish press, and the resulting widespread condemnation created "an unprecedented demand for the *Sabbath Prayer Book* and introduced a larger number of Jews to Reconstructionism than anything previously had been able to do," according to Marc Lee Raphael, *Profiles of American Judaism: The Reform, Conservative, Orthodox, and Reconstructionist Traditions in Historical Perspective* (San Francisco: HarperCollins, 1984), 184. The two issues—women near the Torah and the Reconstructionist prayer book—are possibly linked, as embodied symbols that generated intense reaction far more than could any theoretical argument.

35. The *gabbai* (convener of the Torah service) called up *vekol hanashim*, "all the women," making explicit the radical act. This practice was also adopted at Rockaway Hebrew Congregation. See Robert Gordis, "Simhat Torah—A Triumph of the Democratic Spirit," *The Reconstructionist* 13, no. 11 (October 3, 1947/Tishri 19, 5708): 47.

36. Ira Eisenstein, "Sex Equality in the Synagogue."

37. June 17, 2002, interview by the author.

38. *SAJ Bulletin,* November 10, 1950. Kaplan was present at this meeting, and his reaction to the minority opposition was vividly recalled by Benjamin William Mehlman, who reported that Kaplan thundered at the gathered group: "The name of this organization is the Society for the ADVANCEMENT of Judaism. You are responsible for the REGRESSION of Judaism." Interview of Benjamin William Mehlman by the author, New York, May 20, 2002.

39. *SAJ Bulletin,* November 10, 1950.

40. Ira Eisenstein, "Sex Equality in the Synagogue," 18. The process of a vote for radical, non-halakhic change at lay initiation and on the basis of social justice is a distinct yet parallel Reconstructionist process of replacing mitzvot with "folkways," according to Deborah Dash Moore and Andrew Bush, "Mitzvah, Gender, and Reconstructionist Judaism," 135–153.

41. These are Yiddish references to the system of *kashrut,* Jewish dietary laws. *Fleishig* is meat; *milchig* is dairy. The colors refer to a system of coding to indicate which dishes should be used for which category.

42. Raised platform from which services are conducted and the Torah is read, traditionally reserved for men during religious services, except in Reform synagogues.

43. Yiddish, "to grow weak."

44. Candle lighting to mark the onset of the Sabbath and holidays, traditionally a woman's mitzvah.

45. Prayer shawl.

46. Yiddish, "synagogues."

47. Ira Eisenstein, "Sex Equality in the Synagogue," *The Reconstructionist* 19, no. 2 (March 6, 1953/Adar 19 5713): 19

48. Prayer said upon attaining a special moment.

49. Anniversary (annual) of a death.

50. Ira Eisenstein, "Sex Equality in the Synagogue": 20. In 1955, the Rabbinical Assembly's Committee on Law and Standards adopted a responsum allowing women to be called to the Torah on special occasions; see *1955 Proceedings of the Rabbinical Assembly of America* (New York: The Rabbinical Assembly, 1955), 33–41.

51. Benjamin William Mehlman interview, New York, May 20, 2002.

52. *SAJ Bulletin,* October 31, 1952. The first two are honors for men specific to this holiday; each is a metaphor of a *hatan* or groom. The new honor created a *kalah* (bride) role for women.

53. SAJ minutes, May 25, 1953.

54. SAJ minutes, May 13, 1957.

55. Charles Liebman, "Reconstructionism in American Jewish Life," 224–225. At roughly this time, the foundation also established a Women's Committee toward this end, as here discussed.

56. 1959 President's Letter, February 9, 1959, letter from Herman Levin, Folder 18, Box 1, Jewish Reconstructionist Foundation (I–71), American Jewish Historical Society.

57. 1960 President's Letter, May 1960 letter from Ira Eisenstein,. Folder 19, Box 1, Jewish Reconstructionist Foundation (I–71), American Jewish Historical Society. See also the Reconstructionist Synagogue of the North Shore's Twenty-fifth Anniversary Journal, June 11, 1985 (unattributed, unpaginated). RSNS is located, at the time of this writing, in Plandome, NY.

58. Adelle Blumenthal, a founder of RSNS with her husband Samuel, composed both sets of lyrics in roughly 1963, and blew the shofar for the congregation. Both shpiels are from the files of RSNS.

59. Carole Kessner, Adelle Blumenthal, and Harriet Feiner, "After Twenty-Five Years," RSNS, Twenty-fifth Anniversary Journal.

60. See, for example, announcement of November 20, 1964, seminar with Rabbi Paul Ritterband, "Reconstructionist Facts and Fables." From the RSNS files.

61. Karla Goldman, "Women in Reform Judaism," 118; Shuly Rubin Schwartz, "The Tensions that Merit Our Attention," 155.

62. See names included on invitation to first meeting on April 16, 1958, Folder 1: "Women's Organization of the JRF,," Box 42, Jewish Reconstructionist Foundation (I–71), American Jewish Historical Society, and comparison to SAJ membership lists (SAJ files).

63. Report 1959–60, Folder 1: "The Women's Organization, "Box 42, Jewish Reconstructionist Foundation (I–71), American Jewish Historical Society .

64. Ludwig Nadelmann, "In the Reconstructionist Movement," *The Reconstructionist* 23, no. 17 (December 27, 1957 / Tevet 4, 5718): 31.

65. Charles Liebman, "Reconstructionism in American Jewish Life," 276–280.

66. For a related discussion on the Reconstructionist relationship to halakhah, see Deborah Dash Moore, "Judaism as a Gendered Civilization."

67. For an example of how Judaism served as a source of critique of American culture, see Riv-Ellen Prell, "America, Mordecai Kaplan, and the Postwar Jewish Youth Revolt," *Jewish Social Studies* 12, no. 2 (Winter 2006): 158–171.

68. See Sylvia Barack Fishman, *A Breath of Life: Feminism in the American Jewish Community* (New York: Free Press / Macmillan, 1993), 6–8. Reflecting in a scholarly forum on her experience as one of the organizers of Ezrat Nashim, Paula Hyman acknowledged that there were predecessors to the women's activism around religious equality for women, but that she and her colleagues were unaware of these at the time. Riv-Ellen Prell's treatment of how and why activists in the 1960s and 1970s distanced themselves from Kaplan suggests one dynamic behind this lack of awareness (Prell, "America, Mordecai Kaplan, and the Postwar Jewish Youth Revolt," 158–171).

69. In her history of women's ordination, Pamela Nadell addressed some of the halakhic issues around the status of women that were faced by the Conservative movement: the narrow focus on women's ordination is illuminating on some matters, she noted, especially across denominational lines, but this focus both distorts and occludes key points in the overarching issue of the religious status of Jewish women. See her chapter "The Debate in the Conservative Movement," in *Women Who Would Be Rabbis: A History of Women's Ordination, 1889–1985* (Boston: Beacon Press, 1998), 170–214.

6

Beyond the Myths of Mobility and Altruism

JEWISH IMMIGRANT PROFESSIONALS
AND JEWISH SOCIAL WELFARE
AGENCIES IN NEW YORK CITY,
1948–1954

REBECCA KOBRIN

On a cold December morning in 1950, Dr. K., an Austrian-trained dentist, single mother, and Holocaust survivor exploded in frustration to her case aide, a Ms. Hibble at the New York Association for New Americans (NYANA), proclaiming:

> The four years in concentration camps and the four years after the war in the starving Germany did not bring me tuberculosis. But five months mainte-nance in NYANA gave me tuberculosis! I am in despair. I have a young child. I know only one thing: Something has to be done so that I should get well because I must study for my exam to become qualified in this country. But you cannot get well from attending appointments at your agency! I would have been better off if I had remained in Germany![1]

In response, her case aide, a woman close to her own age, argued with Dr. K. that she must place "motherhood before career," refusing to help her find an orphan-age to care for her son so that she could devote herself fully to reestablishing herself. At this, Dr. K. broke down in tears. Indeed, Dr. K.'s experiences were far from exceptional: tuberculosis, childcare, and numerous supervision meet-ings at NYANA exasperated many Jews who arrived in the United States among the 393,542 European refugees admitted under the Displaced Persons Act of 1948.[2] The larger narrative of Jewish displaced persons', or DPs', encounter with America has long celebrated these Jewish migrants' rapid economic and social integration—and has long submerged the stories of Dr. K. and other profession-ally trained Jewish DPs who entered the nation under the special provisions accorded to refugees with medical training.[3] In contrast to the triumphant myths of Jewish immigrant upward mobility dominant in historical scholarship and popular writings, Dr. K.'s experience was not one she would depict as triumph "against all odds," as sociologist William Helmreich describes the general experience of Jewish DPs in America;[4] nor would she say, as Nathan Glazer did in 1960, that her success, like the "successes" of other Jewish DPs in America, could be credited to the organizational apparatus set up by the American Jewish community.[5] Dr. K.'s experiences in Europe as a respected medical professional made her view "the promised land" not as a place of opportunity but rather as one of an unwelcoming medical establishment, frustrating social service agencies, and downward mobility.[6] Indeed, as a European professional woman in 1950s America, she faced unparalleled challenges in her quest to support her family through her career. Whereas, in Europe, university education had "emancipated middle class women," as one historian notes, from the "cult of domesticity," enabling women to move beyond the conventional roles of wives and mothers, in the United States, as Dr. K.'s case aide often reminded her, 1950s Jewish women were expected to see motherhood as their top priority.[7]

Our understanding of Jewish women's experiences in 1950s America can be expanded through an analysis of the experiences of female medical professionals who arrived in the United States through the Displaced Persons Act, and their encounters with social workers who were part of the growing system of American Jewish social welfare organizations. The overriding questions regarding professionals who were migrants of the DP era, such as Dr. K., are indeed the central questions shaping the entire field of immigrant historiography: On what terms have immigrants come to live in the United States? What waste of human abilities has occurred as a result of migration? How did social service agencies help or hinder immigrants' integration into U.S. society? The questions become particularly clear in this context since, although organizations had existed in the American Jewish community to aid immigrant adaptation since the turn of the twentieth century, the involvement of Jewish social welfare agencies in overseeing DP adjustment was more extensive than any before.

In studying these questions, I have drawn upon a randomly selected group of case files from the New York Association for New Americans (NYANA). Comparison of the sagas of male and female doctors and dentists captured in these case files provides a new vision of this era, an era in which Jewish social welfare organizations and their female employees played such an unprecedented role in guiding the process of immigrant adaptation. To be sure, one must approach such case files with circumspection: each file covers periods spanning weeks to years and demonstrates that the agency's goals were often quite different when applied to individual cases. Moreover, each file is far from univocal: the numerous reports from neighbors, licensing agencies, and case aides all come together to illustrate both the particular challenges and the universal struggles facing postwar Jewish immigrants and the female workers with whom they interacted at Jewish social work agencies. But NYANA's case files, like the files of many Jewish social welfare agencies, contain exceptionally rich sources through which scholars can access the stories of those whose tales are submerged in the historical narrative.

NYANA's case files vividly capture not only the variables that shaped lives of Jewish immigrants in the 1950s, but also the larger dynamics set in motion by the expansion, feminization, and transformation of the field of Jewish social work in the aftermath of the Second World War. Inundated with refugees to serve, organizations such as NYANA hired many Jewish women who simultaneously sought to address their "clients'" concerns and lay claim to identities as professionals in this increasingly feminized world of Jewish social work. To be sure, women had been active in social work agencies since the turn of the twentieth century, but they had explained their benevolence in terms of "feminine virtues of piety and sympathy."[8] By the 1950s, with the expansion of Jewish social service into government-sponsored refugee resettlement as a result of the 1945 Truman Directive and the Displaced Persons Act, practitioners pushed to position social work as professional service, where "case aides" (instead of volunteers) would be paid for their expertise based on training in scientific method. However, in the late 1940s, these case aides were still mostly untrained women, and they not only shaped their immigrant clients' first encounters with America but also altered how professionals in the larger matrix of Jewish communal life viewed the promise and pitfalls of Jewish social work.

These circumstances provided the backdrop for Dr. K.'s interaction with her case aide, an American Jewish woman struggling to define her own work identity, and who exemplified, in historian Daniel Walkowitz's terms, "many of the tensions and contradictions that riddled the lives of people navigating the murky waters of class identity during the second half of the twentieth century."[9] In advising Dr. K. against recertification if that would require sending her son away to a home, the case aide harbored clear ideological beliefs about childrearing, proper gender roles, work, and the path to integration in postwar America. "Containment," as historian Daniel Horowitz has astutely observed, "referred not only to American policy toward the USSR but also to what happened to aspirations at home."[10] A wave of conformity swept across much of the nation, wreaking havoc on the increasingly feminized world of Jewish social work by claiming a connection among women's "role," anticommunism, and domestic conformity. This ideology posited that mentally and sexually healthy women first needed to nurture their children and "satisfy" their husbands, thereby reining in their ambitions in order to protect American democracy and the free world. Thus, case aides at NYANA advised their clients to reshape their ambitions and goals to fit with such societal needs even while the aides simultaneously unionized to limit their workload—so that the aides too could juggle work and family in pursuit of a new form of the American dream.

The encounter between European Jewish survivors of the World War II and American Jewish women working in such organizations as NYANA only occurred as a result of Truman's 1945 directive on DPs. The directive had forever altered the course of European Jewish refugee resettlement in the United States.

In response to "the immensity of the problem of displaced persons and refugees," Truman commanded that more refugees be allowed to settle in the United States through specified welfare agencies, which would issue "corporate affidavits" acknowledging responsibility to support these refugees while they adjusted to American life.[11] Immediately in 1946, Jewish communal leaders founded the United Service for New Americans (USNA) to develop programs to resettle as many Jews as could gain admittance to the nation. Despite initial hopes that masses of Jewish refugees would be allowed to enter, the 1948 DP Bill was, as Will Maslow of the American Jewish Committee caustically described it, "a bill to exclude DPs, particularly Jews, and to admit Hitler's collaborators."[12] Indeed, as a result of the cold war and the growing sympathy for its victims, the DP act and its implementation worked against, rather than facilitated, the entry of Jewish Holocaust survivors, who, many feared, had leftist leanings. In the end, only Jews with special skills, such as dentists and doctors, found it easy to gain entrance to the United States.

Between 1948 and 1954, 140,000 Jewish refugees reached the United States under the Displaced Persons Act. The vast majority received help from the USNA, which saw its staff expand from a few dozen in 1946 to over 600 by 1947, an expansion achieved precisely by hiring hundreds of young case aides, and its budget ballooned to over $9,153,500, making it the second largest welfare agency in the United States, second only to the Red Cross.[13] Working with local Jewish federations and social welfare agencies throughout the country, USNA coordinated a massive resettlement effort. But many refugees did not desire to resettle in the remote corners of the country, preferring to remain in New York City, where there was a rich Yiddish culture and where many had friends, former compatriots, and relatives; thus USNA formed a special organization focused specifically on refugee adaptation to New York City. Indeed, the major objective of NYANA, from its founding in 1949, was, aside from protecting the legal status of Jewish aliens, to assist Jewish displaced persons in economic, social, and cultural adjustment to life in New York City.[14]

Offering medical care, housing, living stipends, and vocational counseling, NYANA had an unofficial program focused on one main task: finding jobs for clients so they would not become wards of the state. Thus, the organization allocated much of its resources to its Vocational Services Department (VSD), a group of hundreds of case aides whose work was supervised by several social workers whose task it was to make sure that "each client become a self-sufficient and independent member of American society."[15]

This seemingly simple task was far from easy in postwar New York City. As Hayim Hartman vividly described in the New York Yiddish daily *Farheit*:

> The first months are indescribable. Everything is new and strange. Everything is confused and hazy but one thing is clear. He [the displaced person] must

get started to live again—that is the only way to a complete victory over Hitler. . . . But it is difficult. He has no relatives. There is little available work. He must live in a crowded shelter. . . . He does not wish to be dependent on charity; he wishes to find work, furnish a home and begin to live as a person.[16]

Beyond providing the expected challenges to immigrants in a new land, postwar New York was far from welcoming to Jewish refugees. Most displaced persons were considerably older than previous waves of Jewish immigrants to arrive on American shores, and many had young children. Few American employers were willing to accommodate to the needs of such a group, provoking agency workers to push their clients to take any job offered, even one outside their field of training. NYANA, as historian Beth Cohen observed, expected clients to "take any job" they could get.[17] To be sure, this strategy addressed immediate economic concerns, but it deeply wounded many of these emotionally frail survivors, who, as Cohen has argued, were trying to regain their former status as they endeavored to rebuild their lives.[18]

Vividly narrating the costs of NYANA's "employment above all else" agenda are the case files of the Physicians' Unit, a special sub-unit dedicated to helping the 2,800 Jewish doctors, dentists, and scientists who arrived in New York City under the DP Act's special provision for medical professionals.[19] Loaning foreign-trained doctors and dentists money to support their families while studying for relicensing exams, or supplying them funds to buy equipment, the Physicians' Unit was established in recognition of the distinct concerns and needs of these immigrants, who differed radically from the Jewish immigrants who had arrived in New York earlier in the century, many of whom had had no postsecondary education (and in some cases no secondary education).[20]

Helping these displaced professionals develop new careers in a hostile medical profession proved the greatest challenge facing the Physicians' Unit.[21] Far from holding doctors with European degrees in high esteem, American physicians, as a result of their declining professional incomes during the Great Depression, saw the influx of foreign physicians as a threat, provoking the American Medical Association to demand numerous relicensing requirements, from exams to internships, that made reestablishing oneself as a doctor a long and arduous process.[22] But even those who did succeed in passing all the requisite exams and obtaining a medical license found few positions open. Most jobs available were in rural communities, or in public community hospitals developed by the government in the 1940s and where few American physicians would work, given the lower pay scale in such institutions.[23] Consequently, incoming foreign physicians were channeled into the lower-tier institutions, where they worked on the periphery of the American medical establishment and were offered few opportunities for upward mobility.[24] Only one doctor, among the eighty-five physicians included in this case study, found a placement in a well-paying private research hospital.[25] Further, although the Physicians' Unit proved successful in finding rural areas in dire need of trained physicians, through placements hailed in the popular press and seen by NYANA as "securing highly favorable reactions from the larger field of American medicine," few women could be placed in such positions.[26] By 1954, when the unit disbanded, it had found employment for 1,600 physicians among its 2,800 clients, placing these either in distant locales or in mental institutions, elder-care facilities, or public hospitals, where the maximum a doctor could earn could not support a family of four in a lifestyle to which most European doctors were accustomed.[27]

Jewish refugee doctors and dentists also found their efforts stymied by their age, which many case aides considered "too old" to be hired. As a reporter noted in the New York Yiddish newspaper *Forverts* (Jewish Daily Forward), "the greatest difficulty . . . is found among older [DP] immigrants who desperately desire to work and become useful people [but] are rarely able to secure jobs."[28] DP doctors were in general older than the general DP population, as a 1949 report of the NYANA Physicians' Unit report noted, as a result of their long training, which most had acquired prior to the war.[29] Thus, although the average age of a non-professional Displaced Person was between twenty and forty,[30] DPs with professional degrees were, on average, a decade older, with a significant number of arriving doctors in their sixties.[31]

Table 1   Age Distribution of DP Population upon Arrival in United States

Age Distribution of General DP Population		Age Distribution of Sample Population of DP Doctors and Dentists (N = 55)	
AGE (YEARS)	% OF TOTAL	AGE (YEARS)	% OF TOTAL
Under 9	19.0		
10–19	10.5		
20–29	22.5	20–30	25.9
30–39	20.1	30–40	35.2
40–49	15.5	40–50	20.4
50–59	8.7	50–60	14.8
60–69	2.8	60–70	3.7
70+	0.9	70+	0.0
Total	100.0	Total	100.0

Sources: DP Commission, *The DP Story*, 368; sample of NYANA case files compiled using SPSS software.

Table 2   Age Distribution of DP Population Resettled in NYC prior to
           March 1950

Age (years)	% of total
Under 16	22.4
16–20	4.3
20–30	24.0
30–40	20.7
40–50	13.8
50–60	7.9
60+	6.8
Total	100.0

Sources: E. Ross, "Age Distribution of Jewish Immigration Post-WWII," Folder 114, Statistical and Administrative Files, NYANA Archives; W. Karp, "Physicians' Unit Report," November 15, 1949, Table II, Folder 63, Statistical and Administrative Files, NYANA Archives.

The file of Dr. M., who had been the chief surgeon at a leading hospital in Munich, and was one of the five members of the International Red Cross Medical Screening Board in a DP camp, poignantly conveys the toll that age discrimination took on NYANA's Jewish medical professional clientele. After being rejected as a resident at Beth Israel Hospital due to his age, fifty-year-old Dr. M. questioned the entire myth of "America as promised land" and whether he would ever be able to rebuild his life.[32] As he told his case aide: "I am no longer young, I am quite tired and it is very difficult to start again. . . . Often I feel that it is too hard for I am too old, and it would have been better to stay in Germany where I had already been successful and recognized in my field. . . . I am often very discouraged and depressed about my whole situation."[33] Dr. Moritz Infeld echoed Dr. M.'s anguish and depression. Arriving in New York at the age of eighty-one "ready to start his life anew," Infeld felt eager to begin again, but most American medical institutions only saw him as an elderly foreigner who would not have time left to pass all the necessary requirements.[34] Indeed, as one scans the copious records of the Physicians' Unit, one recognizes that these cases were far from exceptional. DP doctors, particularly those with a high degree of professional achievement in Europe, often developed clinical depression as they began to realize that the system created by the American Medical Association made it practically impossible to reclaim their former lives.[35]

Although many doctors and dentists, regardless of gender, found themselves rebuffed by their American counterparts, all expressed shock by the discouragement and lack of class sensitivity exhibited by the case aides hired to aid their adjustment to America. One caseworker, for instance, reported after her encounter with fifty-six-year-old Dr. N, "He is no longer a young man and he cannot plan to work much longer so I am greatly worried. How will he manage to put away some money for his future when he really would no longer be able to support himself?"[36] Such disheartening sentiments were not only penned into reports, but appear to have been conveyed during the "supervision" meetings that each client was forced to attend to receive financial support from NYANA. Indeed, case aides did not appreciate, as William Helmreich has pointed out, that for doctors, dentists, and their families arriving as DPs, "respect as a professional and the chance to meaningful work was equally as important" as being economically self-sufficient.[37] Thus one case aide, who felt that a client was not trying hard enough to find a job outside the field of medicine, cut off all agency financial support which he and his family depended upon, leaving them homeless.[38] Deeply shaped by their education and upper-class status prior to the war, professionally trained immigrants disdained relying on support by a charity organization and the interventions of their so-called case aides. As one DP doctor summed up, "We all dread the adjustment experience here," since the requirements for professional relicensing required they be "subjected" to the "meddling case aide" for a significantly longer period than were their nonprofessional colleagues.[39]

This "meddling" became more intrusive when doctors or their wives harbored unrealistic expectations. Indeed, the wives of professionals found adjustment to their new class status especially difficult. Because of the prominence of the needle trades in the New York City economy, women were three times more likely to be successfully placed in a job throughout this period, but the wives of doctors and dentists, such as Mrs. S., refused to take unskilled work in a factory since such a woman saw herself as "a doctor's wife [for whom] such work is highly inappropriate."[40] Such tenacious and unrealistic clinging to their former class identities irritated clients' case workers, as it prevented these workers from fulfilling NYANA's main objective: finding employment for all incoming Jewish DPs. Mrs. S. was admonished by her case aide, who cut her stipend in half. Another woman, whose husband had been a dentist in Lithuania, refused to take a job taking care of an elderly woman, feeling it necessary for a woman of her status to find some form of "white collar work which has status and lack[ed] physical endeavor."[41] Caseworkers, however, did not understand their clients' class background or the psychological toll of adaptation. When the wife of a Yugoslavian doctor tried explaining to her case aide her reason for refusing work—"If my husband maintained the household and cared for our daughter, he would become more nervous and depressed because it would be evident that he had failed at assuming his responsibilities [as principal wage earner]"—her case aide chastised her for turning down a job.[42] Dr. C., who was not only a doctor herself but was married to one, informed the agency, "It was absolutely necessary for a man of [her husband's] stature to be able to buy a new suit more than just once a year."[43] In their constant arguments with the case aides, the wives of medical professionals echoed their husbands, noting how sorely they missed "their lives in Europe, where they could rely upon themselves for all their own needs," having in Europe been donors rather than recipients of philanthropy.[44]

Although the wives of medical professional expressed frustration with the failure of case aides to appreciate their predicament, contempt for the case aide appeared most evident among the files of female medical professionals who saw these women as uneducated nuisances. The difficult "question of balancing marriage, medicine, and motherhood," noted the historian Regina Morantz-Sanchez, plagued the entire American medical profession in the 1940s and 1950s.[45] Balancing among these demands proved even more difficult for female DP professionals, who had attended university "to emancipate themselves from conventional roles as wives and mothers" and saw their case aides, whom they assumed would help them reestablish their careers, harboring gender ideologies that sought to discourage them from seeking to recapture their former status, income, and prestige.[46] The conflicts between these social workers and their female clients who chose career advancement over home life highlights what historian Daniel Horowitz has identified as the inner paradox of social-worker class identity in the 1950s: while female social workers were employed outside their homes, they devoted themselves to policing gender norms that kept women in the domestic sphere, a paradox made abundantly clear as they interfaced with postwar professional immigrant women.[47]

It was in fact female doctors and dentists who suffered the greatest losses, both professionally and personally, by immigrating to the United States. Perhaps because many individuals had met their spouses while pursuing professional training, a quarter of the families in the files surveyed included both husband and wife with advanced medical training.[48] To be sure, these female medical professionals displayed a range of understandings of the "proper" balance among family, medicine, scientific objectivity, and career advancement, but each woman came from a world that viewed "marriage as an option, not a necessity," and career as essential.[49] These professionals were appalled to learn of the agency's implicit gender ideology, which favored the retraining of male professionals and forbade supporting the retraining of two professionals in one family unit.[50] Consequently, over half of the professionally trained women in this sample were forced to abandon their professions and to support their families through menial labor.[51] For example, three women who had been doctors in Europe were required to work as housekeepers to support their families. Another woman, formerly dentist, obtained an unskilled job as an instructor in a factory.[52]

Formatively shaped by their training in Central European universities, these female professionals firmly believed they deserved equal treatment and opportunities with males. They often shared with their case aides their disappointment at not being offered the same support as their husbands. These case aides, who reported their own reactions as part of the casework process, remained perplexed as to why these women were not happy to be employed and in America. They could not understand the women's hostility, a fact vividly captured in the case file of Dr. A.:

> This was a lengthy interview during which Dr. A expressed freely a good deal of her bitterness and unhappiness about the difficulty her family was having in getting established here. . . . She has considerable ambivalence about her husband's training program for she recognizes that it makes it very difficult for her, who has to carry a larger share of the responsibility for maintaining the family. . . . The focus of her bitterness [stems] from the fact that she was a dentist in Europe but when the family arrived here, the agency, in agreement with her husband, decided that they were going to make the investment in re-establishing [only her husband's] professional status. . . . She feels like she has made a great sacrifice since she put a great deal into her training in Europe and it is hard for her to accept that a professional adjustment on that level is not possible for her in the United States. She had attempted to work for a period of time as a dental assistant but found that the jobs were poorly paid and also that it was really more painful to be working as an apprentice in her own profession than [to be] moving into a different field.[53]

Coldly advising her client to "stop dwelling on the past," Dr. A.'s case worker exemplified the insensitivity with which NYANA caseworkers addressed their female clients' aspirations. Perhaps as a result of the ambiguity, fragility, and marginality of their own class position, case aides exhibited an almost complete disregard of the great frustration, excessive pressure, and discriminatory gender regulations facing their female clients, as exemplified by the tragic tale of Dr. T., a forty-two-year-old woman, whose brother wrote the following to her caseworker in 1951:

> My sister had never been ill before and her present [nervous] breakdown was clearly due to overwork. She, remarkably, had been self-supporting since her arrival in the U.S. and had been working extremely hard to establish herself as a physician here. She had obtained for herself a residency at Mt. Sinai Hospital and had taken another short residency at Pilgrim State Hospital. Her last job was at Fordham Hospital. . . . [This] job taxed her strength too much because she was assigned to the Emergency Admitting Department for no other doctor wanted to work there, where the pressures were excessive and she also had to prepare for her State Board Examination. . . . Her landlady called to tell me how disturbed she was and helped make arrangements for her to enter Bellevue [the public city mental institution], a task which you should have helped arrange.[54]

While clearly the medical professional world in New York, which placed great burdens on women and foreigners,[55] contributed to this doctor's nervous breakdown, the neglect of her case aide, who offered her little guidance or support (as her brother's letter implied), bore some blame for the tragic result.[56] Indeed, as NYANA's files narrate, case aides rarely helped female professional immigrants negotiate what historian Mary Walsh called "the long tradition of hostility to women physicians by the male medical profession that reinforced the stereotype of medicine as a man's world." As for this tradition, a 1949 poll of one hundred hospital chiefs of staff included, among many other negative comments about women physicians, "Women doctors are emotionally unstable . . . they talk too much. . . . Women were created to be wives."[57] As Dr. S., a young female doctor, told her case aide, "I am the only woman on staff among seventy-five men and [consequently there are] many jokes about that."[58] Her case aide responded by advocating she enter another field of work.

Another arena in which case aides regularly offered advice to their female clients was in the realm of childrearing, a pressing issue for many immigrant professionals. Like the larger DP population, the families serviced by the Physician's Unit had a highly disproportionate number of children under the age of fifteen.[59] As one U.S. Army officer, Phillip Bernstein, reported in 1948, the DP community had the highest birthrate of any Jewish community in the world, with at least one new baby born every day in the camp in Germany where he was stationed.[60] Particularly in regard to childcare, case aides' conceptions of appropriate behavior diverged strikingly from their female clients.' For example, after one female dentist gained admission into a prestigious relicensing program, her caseworker, rather than commend her achievement, remarked:

> In a sense, it is very unfortunate that you have been admitted to dental school. You could probably make a faster, less costly and more satisfactory adjustment in some other field. Let us just say that you do somehow manage to struggle through to a degree in dentistry. Then what?! . . . [The major problem] is how your ambition and strong desire for a career has prevented you from caring properly for your young child.[61]

Ignoring her caseworker, this dentist placed her child in an orphanage so as to devote herself fully to her studies. Her caseworker never forgave this dentist for this allegedly "uncooperative" and "unmaternal" decision. When the caseworker sought to find out about the child's well-being, she asked the dentist: "how she felt about being separated from the child. . . . she [the dentist] said this was the first time in her life she had been separated from her son. . . . She had tears in her eyes as she spoke of this but I really wondered as I watched her if it was her true feeling [and I challenged her] if she really found it difficult to be separated from her child."[62]

The prevalent gender ideology of the postwar era, which upheld the role of homemaker for women and that of breadwinner for men, prodded most case aides to urge their highly educated clients to work from their homes so that they could continue assuming all childcare responsibilities. Thus, for example, case aides placed several women who had been doctors or dentists in interwar Poland in jobs as seamstresses working from their homes. Other professional women took in boarders, and one gave private French lessons to children in her neighborhood.[63] One caseworker threatened to cut off the support of Dr. M., a female physician, claiming she was not caring properly for her child, and only after an American physician called on Dr. M.'s behalf did the agency continue support.[64]

Not only women suffered as caseworkers implemented gender ideology in practice: one caseworker, for instance, stopped sending financial aid to a doctor and his family when she felt that "he was falling into an inappropriate pattern of dependency." Stopping short of describing him as acting "like a woman," the case aide explained she had decided it was her responsibility to teach the man about "his responsibilities as head of a family."[65]

As such depictions indicate, the case files of NYANA's Physicians' Unit not only reveal up close the trials faced by DP professionals but also shed light on NYANA's case aides, a group of dedicated young women who were struggling for recognition as respected Jewish professionals and whose full stories, though beyond the scope of this study, demand further analysis.

It should for now be noted that the founding of the National Jewish Welfare Board [JWB] in 1917 and the establishment of the Graduate School of Jewish Social Work in New York City in 1925 marked a shift toward scientific methods and professionalism in the field of Jewish welfare. Subsequently, the fifteen years between 1933 and 1948 constituted a critical historical moment in the development of the Jewish social work profession in the United States, with the rise of Nazism bringing thousands of refugees to American shores, a development demanding the recruitment of many new caseworkers—and their hiring set in motion a silent revolution as it remade the gender complexion of this field. As Jewish social work expanded and feminized its ranks, social workers in Jewish agencies developed new definitions of their work, a process, Daniel Walkowitz has noted, that was complicated by "the elusive nature of professionalism, particularly in feminized occupations such as social work."[66] Tsedekah, or charity, had long been central to Jewish communal life and praxis, but during this era a large group of social workers developed a professional association and articulated a distinct vision of their professional identities; by 1950, the JWB had over 502,000 members, representing 331 agencies.[67]

The questions remain of who the women were whom NYANA employed as case aides, and how they fit into the growing matrix of Jewish communal welfare agencies. Although no personnel files exist on specific case aides, NYANA's central administrative personnel files are filled with humor-filled poems, composed for celebratory dinners, that poke fun at a case aide's thankless job. One poem, written in December 1949 and called "How a Case Aide Was Made," vividly depicts a common path of recruitment for these social workers:

> This is about a union maid
> whose fare was to be a case aide.
> For the record I'll call her Ruth
> Simply because that's not the truth.
> . . . The year was '46
> USNA was in its usual fix
> Caseworkers just were not on hand
> Personnel could just not understand.
> So Ruth who was a receptionist at first
> which she found was not the worst
> . . . got the notion
> that she would apply for a promotion.
> So then Ruth became a case aide
> she was but slightly better paid.
> Housed was she in a cubby hole
> getting more space became her goal.[68]

As the poems and anecdotal evidence suggest, ambitious women with little or no graduate training in social work were promoted from the secretarial ranks to address the growing flood of arriving Jewish immigrants. Clerical work, as economist Claudia Goldin has observed, had emerged as a female sphere already in the 1930s and quickly become a low-status job.[69] Thus, it is not surprising that these American Jewish women quickly embraced the opportunity to work in what was perceived as professional employment. And they strictly adhered to the standards of their new jobs, following the directive to find employment for their clients, rarely taking into account the psychological impact their efforts might have upon these sister Jews. As noted farther on in the poem here quoted, Ruth "was given supervision / Sometimes made a rash decision," yet celebrated the day she was approved as a case aide. Like many early-twentieth-century social workers, she contended with her supervisor's attempts to further rationalize her work and constantly struggled both to address her and her family's desire for a higher standard of living and to see herself as "a social welfare professional." However, as historian Daniel Walkowitz has pointed out, here as in the larger field of social work "professionalism as an ideology obscured shifting work conditions" that made it practically impossible for these workers to maintain either their autonomy or their middle-class standard of living."[70]

In 1948, case aides at NYANA, even while advancing a self-identification with professionalism and the middle class, also began to unionize. In the 1930s, powerful professional-worker unions, such as the Social Service Employees Union (SSEU), had already been established by figures such as Jacob Fisher, an employee of the Bureau of Jewish Social Research.[71] Although the women case aides at NYANA succeeded in joining a union, their ultimate goal of limiting their caseload failed, however, as a result of the shifting landscape of social work in America. The rise of McCarthyism saw leaders such as Fisher, who critiqued postwar economic policies, ruined and expelled from the field of social work. Unions in social work saw their ranks and power decimated by the McCarthyist purges. The United Public Workers of America (UPWA), for example, saw its membership drop from 80,000 in 1947 to 2,500 in 1952.[72]

But these women wanted more than a lighter caseload and more pay; they demanded respect as professionals, as the 1949 poem eloquently concludes:

> Ruth can now be irate
> No longer a martyr to her fate.
> In organized activity
> she strives for greater clarity.
> To agency request is made
> "Tell us please, what is a case aide?"
> When the case aide's job is defined
> Ruth's confidence is undermined
> She's told counseling she shouldn't do
> nor should she try to relate to
> The client's emotional state
> or to the problems he has with his mate.
> But by far the hardest pill
> was that case aides don't need skill!
> Thus this case aide
> became a union maid.

Refusing to relinquish a vision of themselves as professional social welfare workers, the case aides did not see unionization as an act of joining the proletariat, but rather as a way of solidifying their professional claims. They moved beyond the label of *altruists*, which the many wealthy women working in nineteenth-century Jewish welfare organization had claimed. These case aides were, rather, professional workers, who entered the labor force to maintain their families' middle-class lifestyles, but who did not see their work as compromising their commitment to middle-class gender values, particularly in relation to marriage and motherhood. Unlike earlier generations of Jewish female welfare workers, they did not see their job as playing a nurturing supportive role. Rather they were "efficient" professionals who formed a critical part of the growing Jewish community social welfare network.

The experience of Jewish displaced persons in America has generally been narrated as a victory. But the postwar reality was much more complex, particularly

Figure 6.1 *New Neighbors*, published by the United Service for New Americans between 1949 and 1954, constantly featured stories on the adjustment of DP doctors.

for those who arrived with professional degrees and saw their education as entitling them to upper-class status. That America and their middle-class case aides did not interact with them in such a manner complicated their adaptation. Although the 1949 cover of *New Neighbors*, a publication issued by the USNA to discuss the DP experience in America, celebrated the triumphs of DP doctors in America, proclaiming "America has embraced the DP doctor," in reality most doctors and dentists saw America as the land of bothersome social work agencies and downward mobility.

The trials and tribulations of professionally trained Jewish immigrants, particularly those arriving under the DP Act, shed light on the larger challenges facing immigrant professionals in America, whose numbers would continue to grow over the course of the twentieth century.[73] The copious files of NYANA's

Physicians' Unit provide a significant window through which to view the highly problematic encounter between social work and the immigrant. Despite the resurgent interest in the historical role played by Jewish communal agencies in facilitating immigrant resettlement in the United States,[74] few scholars have devoted attention to analyzing the adjustment and resettlement of the Jewish DPs, the largest refugee immigrant group to enter and be acculturated by public welfare agencies in American history. These immigrants' story, as Beth Cohen noted, deserves more attention. Far from the fairytale portrait William Helmreich painted of the Jewish DP experience in America, in which the mobilization of the American Jewish community, along with the DP's "hard work," "determination," "skill," intelligence, luck, and willingness to take risks"[75] enabled DPs to not "allow their past tragedies to defeat them," Jewish DPs experienced irrevocable loss and saw America as far from welcoming.[76]

The adjustment was particularly difficult for women with foreign certifications. The above analysis of NYANA's Physician's Unit suggests a need to rethink one of the major tenets of American immigration history: the alleged correlation between education and upward mobility. As is evidenced through the experiences of the numerous highly educated female doctors in this sample, because of the insecurities of the American medical community, education only facilitated mobility if obtained within the United States. Whereas scholarship on other groups of professional immigrants in America notes how these immigrants only rarely accepted menial jobs in the United States, in the Physician's Unit, as a result of its gender-biased program, many women found themselves having to work in menial jobs.[77] Gender, as the Physicians' Units papers narrate, played a crucial role in shaping the DP experience.[78]

The field of Jewish social work demands further sustained and systematic analysis. A comprehensive understanding of the experiences of DPs in America cannot be formed unless more attention is paid to these refugees' case aides, women who did not see themselves as altruists seeking to help immigrants overcome painful pasts, but rather as dispassionate professionals. The expansion and feminization of the field of Jewish social work in the 1950s not only internally transformed this field, but also fundamentally shaped the experiences of DPs.

By 1954, when immigration under the DP Act ceased, NYANA, which had employed over six hundred employees in 1949, pared down its staff to forty-six—firing, mostly, female case aides.[79] But, although the New York Association for New Americans may have closed its doors, the legacy of its commitment to work-above-all-else lingers in our own time. It turns out that the questions shaping the Jewish social welfare network of the immediate postwar era involved a complex matrix of issues concerning gender, immigration, and work that have become the lasting concerns of American social policy.

ACKNOWLEDGMENTS

The author would like to thank Jose Moya, Rachel Kranson, and Shira Kohn for their helpful feedback. To protect the privacy of those discussed, I have used pseudonyms or initials when referring to individuals who appear in the unpublished case files of the New York Association for New Americans (NYANA). Although I have used full names of individuals discussed in *New Neighbors*, a publication of the United Service for New Americans, an agency affiliated with NYANA, any name of public officials or agency personnel that appears in the unpublished files has been changed. I thank NYANA for granting me access.

When this study was originally conducted, some files could not be found in the vast repository of NYANA's archives. The original research model for this study employed the requirements of clustering random sample theory to select case files. Unforeseen obstacles resulting from the archive's loss of numerous case files, along with faulty numbering of other files, resulted in the construction of a sample that does not totally accord with random sampling theory. I am well aware that the findings of this study, therefore, are not considered statistically representative, yet, nevertheless, I hope that other historians will see the richness of these records for gaining a glimpse into the inner world of the Displaced Person.

NOTES

1. E. K. to S. Hibble, July 11, 1950, Case File N9945, NYANA Archives, Center for Jewish History, New York.

2. On the larger debate concerning DP resettlement, see Leonard Dinnerstein, *America and the Survivors of the Holocaust* (New York: Columbia University Press, 1982); Mark Wyman, *DPs: Europe's Displaced Persons, 1945–1951* (Ithaca, NY: Cornell University Press, 1998); Michael Marrus, *The Unwanted: European Refugees in the Twentieth Century* (Oxford: Oxford University Press, 1985); Ariel Kochavi, *Post-Holocaust Politics: Britain, the U.S., and Jewish Refugees, 1945–1948* (Chapel Hill: University of North Carolina Press, 2001); Haim Genizi, *America's Fair Share: The Admission and Resettlement of Displaced Persons, 1945–1952* (Detroit: Wayne State University Press, 1993), 114–127.

3. With the exception of Beth Cohen's *Case Closed: Holocaust Survivors in Postwar America* (New Brunswick, NJ: Rutgers University Press, 2007), most scholarly or popular accounts of Jewish displaced persons in America celebrate these immigrants' triumphant and rapid adjustment to life in America; see William Helmreich, *Against All Odds: Holocaust Survivors and the Successful Lives They Made in America* (New Brunswick, NJ: Transaction Publishers, 1996); Dorothy Rabinowitz, *New Lives: Survivors of the Holocaust Living in America* (New York: Knopf, 1977).

4. Helmreich, *Against All Odds*, 266.

5. Nathan Glazer, "Social Characteristics of American Jews" in *The Jews: Their History, Culture, and Religion*, vol. 2, ed. Louis Finkelstein (New York: Harper and Row, 1960).

6. See Cohen, *Case Closed*.

7. Harriet Freidenreich, *Female, Jewish, and Educated: The Lives of Central European University Women* (Bloomington: Indiana University Press, 2002), 1. The "cult of domesticity" that shaped the opportunities offered Jewish women in the nineteenth century is described in full by Marion Kaplan in *The Making of the Jewish Middle Class: Women, Family, and Identity in Imperial Germany* (New York: Oxford University Press, 1991).

8. Regina Kunzel, "The Professionalization of Benevolence: Evangelicals and the Social Workers in the Florence Crittenton Homes, 1915–1945," *Journal of Social History* 22 (Fall 1988): 21–43.

9. Daniel Walkowitz, *Working with Class: Social Workers and the Politics of Middle-Class Identity* (Chapel Hill: University of North Carolina Press, 1999), 10.

10. Daniel Horowitz, *Betty Friedan and the Making of The Feminine Mystique: The American Left, the Cold War, and Modern Feminism* (Amherst: University of Massachusetts Press, 1998), 124.

11. Lyman Cromwell White, *300,000 New Americans* (New York: Harper, 1957); Gil Loescher and John Scanlan, *Calculated Kindness: Refugees and America's Half-Open Door, 1945–Present* (London: Collier Macmillan, 1986), 5–12.

12. Will Maslow and George Hexter, "Immigration—or Frustration?" *The Jewish Community* 3 (September 1948): 17.

13. Cohen, *Case Closed*, 21.

14. General Description of the Agency, NYANA, February 27, 1948, Folder 1, 1, Administration Folders, NYANA Archives. Joshua Friedland, *The Lamp beside the Door: The Story of the New York Association for New Americans* (New York: NYANA Press, 1999[?]), 40.

15. Folder 6, Vocational Services Group, 1, Administration Folders, NYANA Archives.

16. H. Hartman, "The First Days in New York of a New Jewish Immigrant," *Farheit*, October 3, 1950, 2.

17. Cohen, *Case Closed*, 61.

18. Friedland, *The Lamp beside the Door*, 24.

19. Ibid., 33.

20. For most of the nineteenth and early twentieth centuries, Jewish immigrants arrived in the United States with little secondary or postsecondary education that might push them to embrace America's educational system for their children, an embracing that scholars argue facilitated Jewish economic and social mobility. See Thomas Kessner's *The Golden Door: Italian and Jewish Immigrant Mobility in New York City, 1880–1915* (New York: Oxford University Press, 1977); Stephen Brumberg's *Going to America, Going to School: The Jewish Immigrant, Public School Encounter in Turn-of-the-Century New York* (New York: Praeger, 1986). Many historians of immigration posit a strong correlation between education and social mobility. Examples can be seen in George Pozzetta, ed., *Education and the Immigrant* (New York: Garland Publishing, 1991); Nathan Caplan, John Whitmore, and Marcella Choy, *The Boat People and Achievement in America: A Study in Economic and Educational Success* (Ann Arbor: University of Michigan Press, 1989); Selma Berrol, "Education and Economic Mobility in New York City, 1880–1920," *American Jewish Historical Quarterly* 65 (March 1976); Michael Olneck and Marvin Lazerson, "The School Achievement of Immigrant Children, 1900–1930," *History of Education Quarterly* 15 (winter 1974): 453–482; Charles Hirschman and Morrison Wong, "The Extraordinary Educational Attainment of Asian Americans: A Search for Historical Evidence and Explanations," *Social Forces* 65 (September, 1986): 1–27.

21. For more on the numerous legislations concerning the licensing of doctors, see Kathleen Pearle, *Preventive Medicine: The Refugee Physician and the New York Medical Community (Bremen: University of Bremen, 1981)*, and Eric Kohler, "Relicensing Central European Refugee Physicians in the United States, 1933–1945," *Simon Wiesenthal Center Annual* 6 (1989): 3–36.

22. Rosemary Stevens and Joan Vermeulen, *Foreign Trained Physicians and American Medicine* (New Haven: Yale University Press, 1972), 3.

23. Paul Starr, *The Social Transformation of American Medicine* (New York: Basic Books, 1982[?]), 347–351, 359–363.

24. See Eui Shin and Kyung-Sup Chang "Peripheralization of Immigrant Professionals: Korean Physicians in the United States," *International Migration Review* 22, no. 4 (1988): 609–625, where the authors discuss, through a case study of Korean doctors, how the American medical profession peripheralizes immigrant doctors and prevents their structural assimilation and economic success.

25. A. Cohen, "Summary of Contact," Case File #N12834, p. 1, NYANA Archives.

26. "Highlights of Activities," a report of NYANA's Vocational Services Department, September 21, 1951 quoted in Friedland, *The Lamp beside the Door*, 33.

27. J. Coler, Summary of Contact, Case File #N9448, p. 6, NYANA Archives; in this case, the client is earning only $175/month, a salary not sufficient to support his wife and two children.

28. Anonymous, "31, 000 D. P.'s Have Adjusted Themselves in New York," *Forverts*, April 13, 1950, 1.

29. W. Karp, "Physicians' Unit Report," November 15, 1949. See Appendix A: Table A1 and Table A4, Folder 63, 3, Administrative and Statistical Files, NYANA Archives.

30. See Appendix A: Table A1 and A3.

31. See Appendix A: Tables A1, Table A2, and Table A3.

32. B. Lazaroff to L. Rubin, October 12, 1950, Memo; M. Lantz, Summary of Contact. Both in Case File N9449, 2, NYANA Archives.

33. M. Lantz, Summary of Contact, Case File N9449, 2 and 4, NYANA Archives.

34. USNA notion.

35. See the Summary of Contact reports for the following cases: N9933, 18; N10713, 3; K2089, 7, 13; N9449, 1–4, 12; A32245, 6; K13562, 3. All in NYANA Archives.

36. M. Blum, Summary of Contact, Case File A32245, 6, NYANA Archives.

37. Helmreich, *Against All Odds*, 110–111.

38. I. Kaplan, Summary of Contact, Case File N14638, 6–7, NYANA Archives.

39. M. Lantz, Summary of Contact, Case File N9449, 2 and 4, NYANA Archives.

40. Anonymous, January 1950 Statistical Report, Folder 115, 20, Statistical and Administrative Files; R. Levy, Summary of Contact, Case File N3752, 10, NYANA Archives.

41. A. Pascoe, Summary of Contact, Case File 10713, 5, NYANA Archives.

42. See the following case files: N9624, 4; B21289, 19; N9532, 7; K13562, 13, NYANA Archives. In particular, M. Mittel, Summary of Contact, Case File N9933, 10, NYANA Archives.

43. F. Konig, Summary of Contact, Case File K9017, 10, NYANA Archives.

44. Y. Butman, Summary of Contact, Case File A32245, 15, NYANA Archives.

45. Regina Morantz-Sanchez, *Sympathy and Science*, 338–339.

46. Freidenreich, *Female, Jewish, and Educated*, 1; NYANA Archives.

47. Daniel Horowitz, *Working with Class: Social Workers and the Politics of Middle-Class Identity* (Chapel Hill: North Carolina Press, 1999).

48. See the following case files: K2089; A32245; C9856; K13562, all in NYANA Archives.

49. Freidenreich, *Female, Jewish, and Educated*, 2.

50. For an elaboration of this policy, see S. Kaltman, Summary of Contact, Case File K2089, 9–10, NYANA Archives.

51. It is interesting to note how this directly contradicts the prevalent supposition of many postwar immigrant historians asserting that professional immigrants never take menial jobs. For more on this assertion, see Alejandro Portes and Rueben Rumbaut, *Immigrant America: A Portrait* (Berkeley and Los Angeles: University of California Press, 2006), 18–20.

52. See the following case files: N2987F; A32245; N2468; K13562, all in NYANA Archives.

53. K. Aizen, Summary of Contact, Case File N2468F, 35, NYANA Archives.

54. A. Cohen, Summary of Contact, Case File 12834, 2, NYANA Archives.

55. For more about women and discrimination in various professional fields, see Mary Walsh, *Doctors Needed: No Women Need Apply: Sexual Barriers in the Medical Profession, 1835–1975*

(New Haven, CT: Yale University Press, 1977); Donna Gabaccia, *From the Other Side: Women, Gender, and Immigrant Life in the United States, 1820–1990* (Bloomington: Indiana University Press, 1994), 95–109. For information about foreign doctors and discrimination in New York, see Pearle, *Preventive Medicine*.

56. G. Charnow, Summary of Contact, Case File N9079-R, 6, NYANA Archives.

57. Walsh, *Doctors Wanted*, 244–246.

58. S. Kaltman, Summary of Contact, Case File 2089, 7, NYANA Archives.

59. Almost 38 percent of the individuals in this study's sample are under the age of fifteen.

60. P. Bernstein, "Fifteen Months as a U.S. Army Jewish Advisor," *American Jewish Times* (January 1948): 9. Bernstein's article is quoted in Helmreich, *Against All Odds*, 129.

61. B. Lazaroff to M. Stevens, Physicians' Committee Memo, August 29, 1950, Case File N9945, NYANA Archives.

62. S. Hibble, Summary of Contact, Case File N9945, 6, NYANA Archives.

63. See Summary of Contact from the following case files: N2775F, 3–4; N14638, 9; N2621F, 8; A32245, 34, all in NYANA Archives.

64. A. Serzane, Summary of Contact, Case File N26334, 2, NYANA Archives.

65. H. Berg, Summary of Contact, Case File N9933, 6 and 13, NYANA Archives.

66. Daniel Walkowitz, "The Making of a Feminine Professional Identity: Social Workers in the 1920s," *American Historical Review* (1990): 1052.

67. Herbert Stein, *Jewish Social Work in the United States, 1654–1954*, Ph.D. diss., Columbia University, 1958, 72–73.

68. Anonymous, "How a Case Aide Was Made" (December 1949), Folder 104, Personnel Files, 1949–1978, NYANA Archives.

69. Claudia Goldin, *Understanding the Gender Gap: An Economic History of American Women* (New York: Oxford University Press, 1990), 145–148.

70. Walkowitz, "The Making of a Feminine Professional Identity," 1053.

71. Michael Reisch and Janice Andrews, *The Road Not Taken: A History of Radical Social Work in the United States* (Ann Arbor: University of Michigan Press, 2001), 70.

72. Ibid, 96–97.

73. While there is a general absence of scholarship on this issue, the following articles have addressed these questions and have played a formative role in shaping several aspects of this study: William Glaser and Christopher Habers, "The Migration and Return of Professionals," *International Migration Review* 8 (Summer 1974): 227–244; Pyung Min, "From White-Collar Occupations to Small Businesses: Korean Immigrants' Occupational Adjustment," *Sociological Quarterly* 25 (1984): 333–352; Raul Moncraz, "A Model of Professional Adaptation of Refugees: The Cuban Case in the U.S., 1959–1970," *International Migration Review* 4 (Spring 1973) : 171–183; Raul Moncraz, "Professional Adaptation of Cuban Physicians in the U.S., 1959–1969," *International Migration Review* 4 (Spring 1970): 80–86.

74. Portes and Rumbaut, *Immigrant America*, 175–176; Alejandro Portes and Jozsef Böröcz, "Contemporary Immigration: Theoretical Perspectives on Its Determinants and Modes of Incorporation," *International Migration Review* 23 (Fall 1989): 606–630; E. Kunz, "Exile and Resettlement: Refugee Theory," *International Migration Review* 15 (Spring/Summer 1981): 42–51; and J. Berry, "The Acculturation Process and Refugee Behavior," in *Refugee Mental Health in Resettlement Countries*, ed. Carolyn Williams and Joseph Westermeyer (Washington, DC: Hemisphere Publishers, 1986), 25–37.

75. Helmreich, *Against All Odds*, 265.

76. Ibid., 266; Cohen, *Case Closed*, 174.

77. Portes and Rumbaut, *Immigrant America*, 18–20. The authors supply a summary of the widely accepted arguments concerning professionals' immigration.

78. For a discussion of how gender played a formative role in shaping the relationship of female professional immigrants to menial labor in the 1930s, see Gabaccia, *From the Other Side*, 95–98.

79. Estimates of Needs for 1954, NYANA Central Administration, Folder 17, NYANA Archives.

7 Negotiating New Terrain

EGYPTIAN WOMEN AT
HOME IN AMERICA

AUDREY NASAR

"When I came here [Brooklyn], it was so hard," recalled Denise Z. of her immigration from Egypt to the United States in 1962. "I used to have two maids in the house [in Egypt]. When I came, first do the dishes, or go take care of the kids, or clean the house, or go wash, it was really hard. . . . You don't know what to do first."[1] Like many other female Jewish immigrants from Egypt during the postwar years, Denise Z. found domestic chores a cause of particular anxiety as she adjusted to American life. Like these other migrants, she had moved to America for political rather than economic reasons, and she underwent the painful process of downward financial mobility at the same time that she experienced the many cultural changes of settling in a new country. No longer able to afford the household servants that had made their homes in Egypt so comfortable, newcomers like Denise struggled with such basic homemaking tasks as shopping, childrearing, and cooking. Although the role of family caretaker was not new for these women, life in the United States imbued the position with unanticipated challenges. When Egyptian Jewish women remember their immigration, their attempts to master household duties and purchase consumer goods emerge among the most salient difficulties in their adjustment.

In the midtwentieth century, Egypt was transformed from a country of Jewish immigration to one of Jewish emigration. Throughout the 1950s and 1960s, the overwhelming majority of Egyptian Jewry abandoned their homes, livelihood, and, for many, their sole familiar way of life to rebuild their lives in new environments. These refugees escaped a regime that was becoming increasingly intolerant of non-Muslim minorities—especially of Jews, as a result of Egypt's involvement in the Arab-Israeli conflict.[2] Approximately ten thousand Egyptian Jewish refugees entered the United States, and most settled in Brooklyn, New York, in close proximity to the existing Syrian Jewish communities of Bensonhurst and Flatbush.[3] In the course of this transition, Egyptian Jews confronted the challenges of negotiating a way into a foreign society that had unfamiliar cultural norms and expectations, and where they could no longer depend on a stable or secure household income.

This migration challenges the dominant narrative of Jewish immigration to the United States, which has tended to focus on the experiences of migrants pulled to America by its economic opportunities. But such a focus privileges the experiences of Eastern European Jews, who went so far as to dub the United States the *goldeneh medina*;[4] not every group of American Jews was drawn to the United States for economic opportunity. Egyptian Jews, like many other refugee populations that settled in America during the postwar decades, had been pushed out of their land of origin and underwent, in migrating, a decline in socioeconomic status.[5]

Not only does the story of the Egyptian Jewish migration challenge this dominant paradigm of Jewish immigration; it also focuses on a population long ignored by practitioners of American Jewish history. General historiography on the adaptation of Jews to American norms and values has often ignored the effects of relocation on Middle Eastern Jews, and on Middle Eastern Jewish women in particular. At most, the Egyptian Jewish migration receives only minimal attention among the plethora of works chronicling immigrant Jewish experiences.[6]

The scarcity of archival documents concerning Egyptian American Jews, and specifically concerning the women in this population, adds to the challenge of recording this history. It is in such cases that historians must especially rely on oral testimonies, which serve the necessary function of "bringing recognition to substantial groups of people who had been ignored in the historical narrative."[7] Oral history is particularly essential to the study of women's history, for the experiences of women have so often been left out of the archival record.[8] Further, this method is uniquely suited for the study of adjustments made by Egyptian Jewish women upon arrival in America, as these women have suffered a double marginalization, both as women and as members of a community whose history has been ignored by scholars of American Jewish history and by most archival repositories of the American Jewish experience. For instance, the archives of the American Sephardi Federation, an organization dedicated to representing the heritage of Sephardic Jews, do not currently hold any information concerning the acclimation of Egyptian Jewish immigrants to their adopted country.

Oral history has also transformed the study of family history, unlocking hitherto secret areas by providing evidence about marital relations, childrearing, domestic work, conflicts, and other aspects of family life.[9] As the historian Paul Thompson asserts, the use of oral history to study familial dynamics has broadened the scope of women's history, "given the dominance of the family through housework, domestic service, and motherhood in the lives of most women."[10] With regard to Egyptian Jewish women immigrants to America, who have tended to view their adjustments through the lens of domesticity and class, oral history thus emerges as the most appropriate and possibly the only vehicle to transmit their story and how they understood their experiences.[11]

Here, I rely on sections taken from interviews I conducted with eight Jewish women who immigrated to America from Egypt in the 1950s and 1960s, to construct a women's community oral history. Seven of the women married and bore children while living in Egypt. The other, who immigrated to America unmarried at the age of nineteen, wed after settling in New York.[12] I became acquainted with these women through familial relationships and my own membership in the Egyptian Jewish community.

My status as a familiar community member undoubtedly shaped the content of the interviews. Considering the insular nature of the Egyptian Jewish community, it is certain that community membership provided me with unprecedented access to the women who had migrated in the immediate postwar decades.[13] Speaking to "one of their own" may have made them more comfortable and open: they were unafraid of judgment in my presence. At the same time, it is also possible that the interviewees may have concealed some details that they considered disturbing, such as severe economic difficulties, changes in religious observance, and the hardships they faced as a result of the rise of anti-Semitism in Egypt. While acknowledging the possibility of these or other distortions, I would argue that oral history must serve as the medium for exploring the impact of relocation on Egyptian Jewish women—because, without it, their voices would not be heard.[14]

The Jewish community of Egypt, which existed for two thousand years, experienced a tremendous increase during the end of the nineteenth and the beginning of the twentieth centuries. This increase was primarily a result of Jewish emigration from the Ottoman Empire, Greece, the Balkans, Corfu, Italy, North Africa, Yemen, Aden, Russia, Romania, and Poland. Immigrants were, in many cases, escaping economic and political upheavals in their native lands, or were driven out as a result of religious persecution, and came to Egypt seeking financial opportunities and hoping to benefit from the country's policies of economic liberalism. These policies derived from the British occupation of Egypt, beginning in 1882, which provided protection for foreigners and minorities.[15]

Consequently, Egyptian Jewry could not be defined as a homogenous community. Sephardim / Orientals, Ashkenazim, and Karaites each made up a portion of the larger Jewish population. By 1947, the Jewish community contained seventy-five thousand to eighty thousand members, with a significant majority identifying themselves as Sephardim, the group whom the Egyptian authorities recognized as the official representatives of Jewish interests in Egypt.[16] The heterogeneity of the Egyptian Jewish community was most apparent in what the historian Gudrun Kramer describes as the "babel of tongues" among the many Jews who continued to speak their native languages long after settlement in the nation.

Following World War I, this linguistic diversity declined, and European languages, particularly French, dominated among upper- and middle-class Jews. French was not the exclusive property of the upwardly mobile Jews, but had indeed become the lingua franca of other minorities, as well as of the elite within Egyptian society.[17] Joel Beinin, in his work on Egyptian Jews, explains that a French education "was not a marker of otherness or a political liability. It was a prestigious symbol of modernity and progress common to the sons of the landed elite, the business community, and many leading intellectuals of the early twentieth century, Muslims and Christians as well as Jews."[18] As Egyptian Jews associated more with Western culture, they tended to view Arabic as the language of the poor indigenous Jews still residing in the Harat al-Yahud, the Jewish quarter of Cairo.

The value placed on Westernization demonstrated itself most profoundly in the sphere of education. French was the primary language of instruction in the schools attended by Jewish children, from the French-based Alliance Israelite Universelle to the schools maintained by the Jewish communities.[19] Many Jewish children, specifically those belonging to the middle and upper classes, also attended French, German, British, or American missionary schools or secular schools, most notably the Lycées de la Mission Laïque Française. This "modern" education, along with Western influences, led to a decline in the commitment to maintaining strict religious observance, and the decline became exacerbated as a number of Jews reached privileged social and economic rank under British rule.[20] Gudrun Kramer, in discussing Egyptian Jewry's rapidly increasing middle class, described the class structure of the Egyptian Jewish community as resembling an onion, with a small upper class (5–10 percent), a large upper-middle class, and a broad lower-middle class, this last merging into the lower class. The Egyptian Jews who migrated to the United States in the 1950s and 1960s tended to derive from the middle and upper classes.[21]

As Egyptian Jews sought Western values and education, some found ways to attain Western citizenship. Western nationality provided them with benefits via the capitulation system, which offered guarantees of life and property for those with foreign protection and exempted Egyptian Jews with foreign citizenship from local taxes and from trials in Egyptian courts. Desirous of these benefits of foreign citizenship, many Jews obtained it from countries such as Italy, Greece, France, England, and the Austro-Hungarian Empire, at a time when these nations also expressed an interest in increasing their influence in Egypt. During the period that Egypt was a British protectorate, statistics from the years 1914–1922 record approximately 25 percent of Egyptian Jewry as foreign nationals, 25–30 percent as Egyptian citizens, and over 40 percent as stateless, lacking any form of citizenship.[22] Toward the end of the 1930s, as relations between Jews and their Muslim neighbors deteriorated, the Jews' lack of Egyptian nationality caused them to be viewed as aliens. This problem failed to be easily rectified, for the Egyptian government often prevented the naturalization of non-Muslims. The lack of citizenship became, for a large number of Jews, especially hazardous after the abolishment of the system of capitulations in 1937.

The rise of pan-Islamic nationalism in the late 1930s, coupled with the escalation of violence between Arabs and the Jews of the Yishuv in Palestine, placed the Jews of Egypt in a perilous situation. Additionally, as nationalists fought British military occupation, Jews and other minorities found themselves accused of benefiting from the British presence and of contributing to foreign influences in Egypt.[23] As these nationalistic tendencies grew, the Egyptian authorities passed the Company Law in 1947, requiring that 75 percent of a joint stock company's salaries be paid to Egyptian nationals and mandating that all firms furnish lists of their employees, including their nationality and salary. This legislation particularly affected the majority of Egyptian Jews, who were not Egyptian nationals, and the government was very slow in responding to Jewish applications for naturalization.[24]

The 1948 Arab-Israeli War further aggravated the status of Jews in Egypt. During that conflict, sporadic acts of violence targeting the Egyptian Jewish community arose, and authorities arrested between 600 and 1,000 Egyptian Jews.[25] Thus began the modern exodus of Jews from Egypt, and although most Egyptian Jews expressed an indifferent attitude toward Zionism, many, mostly from the lower and lower-middle classes, decided to settle in Israel. Then, following the rise of Gamal Abdel Nasser in 1954 and the advent of the 1956 Suez War, the situation for Jews deteriorated dramatically; Jewish properties were seized, approximately 900 Jews were detained or imprisoned; other Jews received police summonses followed by orders to leave Egypt. Initial panic was followed by mass departures of Jews in the late 1950s and early 1960s, with these post-1956 refugees, who had more accumulated wealth and ties to the West, tending to choose to settle in Europe or America. By 1967, the Jewish population in Egypt was diminished from approximately 75,000 before the 1948 Arab-Israeli conflict to at most 3,000.[26] In 1967, Egypt's loss in the Six-Day War led to the arrest of at least 425 Egyptian Jews and further emigration, and, by the summer of 1970, only 550 Jews still resided in Egypt.[27]

The women interviewed for this study arrived in America in the period between the 1956 and 1967 Arab-Israeli wars. All of their families had migrated to Egypt from Syria in the late nineteenth and early twentieth centuries; they had come to Egypt seeking economic opportunities and quickly rose to the middle class. Their children and grandchildren then followed the pattern of the majority of the Jewish middle class of Egypt, acquiring the accoutrements of Westernization.[28] Thus it is the descendents of these Syrian merchants who were the core of the migration to Flatbush and Bensonhurst, Brooklyn.[29]

This brief history does not express the hardships and emotional strain that the Jewish community of Egypt faced as its members sought new places of refuge and escaped once comfortable homes and settled lives. The women interviewed remembered those comfortable and secure lives in Egypt. All spoke several languages growing up, and were educated primarily in Arabic and French. In Egypt, Jewish wives and mothers were not required to leave their homes to visit the market or to make purchases; financial security and social class enabled most of these women's households to employ at least one servant who would be sent to purchase groceries and other items for them. Many of the women recalled their husbands going to the market, sometimes on a daily basis, to buy fresh produce, a practice necessitated by lack of refrigeration. Rita M. explained: "They used to pass by our house, we shopped [for] the vegetables, and if we need something extra we send the maids, she buy from the market. The butcher send the meat, chicken. I never went shopping for the food."[30] Fortune M. insisted that butchers' delivery service was often necessary because, although she sent a housekeeper on daily shopping errands, she was apprehensive about asking a non-Jewish servant to purchase kosher meat. She explained: "We give her [the maid] the money and go get us the peas and tomatoes, everything fresh, no freezer. Only the meat they send us because kosher, or we go, or we tell her [the maid] go, we don't give her money, she go to him, he give her. If she has money maybe we afraid she go to a goy. [We have to] make sure kosher, kosher!"[31]

In Egypt, many of the women had not found it necessary, either, to leave their homes to shop for clothing. They wore custom-made clothing, and shopping consisted of picking out fabrics for the seamstress. Sometimes seamstresses brought their fabrics directly to the homes; at other times, the women went to department stores and chose fabrics for complete outfits, with matching hats, handbags, and shoes. Often, these women, or their mothers, would sew clothing for themselves and their children. Ready-made clothing was available, but the women described it as a more expensive option. Elizabeth N. explained that ready-made clothes were "very expensive, you have to be rich to buy them."[32]

Further, the women did not have to venture from home to launder their families' clothing. These interviewees discussed a laundress, hired in addition to their household servants, who came once a week to wash clothing. Esther C. explained: "Besides the housekeeper, there used to come one lady to wash by hand. . . . They used to come, sit down with water, that's how I remember. . . . She used to come and wash and hang. You know, we had no dryer. They used to hang up the clothes on the line."[33] Women also received assistance in cleaning the home. For these women, then, a woman's role consisted of light housework and overseeing the performance of servants. Some had two maids, "one to do the house, one to take care of the kids."[34]

Yet, although servants often helped with the children, the women claimed that in Egypt they saw themselves primarily as caretakers for their children, and most of these women declared, "Our life [was] the kids."[35] Many recalled taking their children to the park, summering with them on the beaches of Alexandria, and spending time with them after the school day. In addition, a large part of their social lives included their children, such as taking walks with other mothers and children or sitting in the parks with other women as the children played. The fact that they had housekeepers made life easier, providing the women with

Figure 7.1 Nazli M., at age eighteen, mother of Esther C. and mother-in-law of Rita M. This photograph was taken in Cairo, Egypt, in 1918. Nazli, with her children and grandchildren, left Egypt in 1960 and traveled to France before settling in New York. Notice the very fashionable ensemble of matching hat, shoes, and dress, representative of the custom-made clothing that Egyptian Jewish women often wore. Courtesy of Audrey Nasar.

more free time and an extra hand to assist with the children. Thus, women could spend all day with their children and then go out at night: there was always a babysitter at hand. Denise Z. recalled: "Every other night we used to go out, Sunday we used to go to the movies, Saturday night we must go out. . . . And we go with friends, I always had someone home for the kids."[36]

The women's role as caretaker, with its familiar responsibilities, was challenged after settlement in America. And the difficulties and uncertainties accompanied the entire emigration from Egypt. Even though their husbands made the final decision of when and where to go, this was a family migration, and the women had viewed themselves as partners in the decision to leave. Many declined to move to Israel, feeling that it held limited opportunities, particularly since Israel had only recently become a state. Rita M. explained, "My father [who had moved there in 1950] said Israel was very hard to live. . . . I had six kids . . . and [my husband] don't speak Hebrew. He speak better English. We said to come to America."[37] America, viewed as the land of opportunity, became these families' destination of choice. In addition, very probably the fact that this particular subset of Egyptian Jews were descendents of migrants from Syria led them to settle in Brooklyn, home to an established Syrian Jewish community. This assumption is supported by the fact that many of the women mentioned assistance that their families received from distant cousins among Brooklyn's Syrian Jews.

None of the women interviewed vocalized much about what prompted the mass exodus from Egypt; most referred to the reason vaguely as "terrorism," referencing the Arab-Israeli wars. However, three women offered more explanation; they recalled events such as the shouting of "Zionists" on the streets and the throwing of dirt at Jewish houses on Friday afternoons while the women were preparing for the Sabbath.[38] The Mansoura family owned a popular bakery in Egypt, and Mrs. Mansoura described her family decision to leave, declaring "They threw a bomb, Molotov, on the store. . . . We didn't close, but we stay, but business wasn't the same and we had to leave. It wasn't for the Jews to be there."[39]

The conversations became more informative when the women discussed packing for the move. They explained their packing decisions by emphasizing how uncertain they were about their destination. In the documentary film *I Miss the Sun*, filmmaker Mary Halawani interviewed her grandmother about her move from Egypt to Brooklyn. Halawani's grandmother explained her decision to pack her sewing machine: "I need it. I think when I'm coming out of my country maybe I don't have a money, so I can sew something and I have a money."[40] This anxiety and insecurity about the future arose in all of my interviews. Women bemoaned the fact that they were only allowed to travel with small amounts of jewelry and money, and shared their fears of having their luggage searched by the Egyptian authorities. Traveling with food and clothing was permitted, so Jewish emigrants took as much as possible of these two items, since they were uncertain what they would find or be able to afford at their future destinations. Esther C. recalled: "We couldn't take any money, any jewelry, anything at all. So we packed whichever money we had." Fearful about what necessities, such as household cleaners, dried goods, or clothing, could be found in America, Esther C. spent a substantial sum prior to emigrating on "nonsense stuff," items such as shoe polish, beans, Ajax, and clothes for her infant son in varied sizes, which she hoped would last him until his teenage years.[41] Purchasing large amounts of clothing for family members prior to departure appears to have been a common practice, but Esther C., like other women interviewed, bought these items and transported them to their new homes only to discover that the Egyptian apparel could not withstand American winters. Fortune M. described having to discard many items she had packed: "When we came here after that [leaving Egypt via Paris], we had a lot of clothes with us, we throw them. Our shoes don't match [the American climate]. We buying the shoes in Egypt. [There] we don't have rain, we don't have snow, we don't have nothing. We don't need [strong footwear]."[42]

The majority of the women did not go straight to America but rather took a boat to France, where they often had to stay for approximately six months awaiting U.S. entrance visas, and then continued on by plane to the United States. The description of the boat trip varied. Two women could not describe it beyond their feelings of seasickness; for example Esther C. said, "To tell you the truth I don't remember anything. I remember on the boat I was dizzy. I had a baby; I don't know who took care of him."[43] Others discussed going into the kitchen to prepare food for the babies; as Rita M. recollected, "I had Joey, ten months old when I left Egypt, ten months! I had to go cook the cranberry on the boat. They had a big burner—not burner, just hot—you heat the food and you cook it and I feed him."[44] One woman described subsisting on jelly and olives for seven days because of a lack of kosher food, but dismissed the difficulties, saying, "Thank G-d we were young, we were together, everyone—laughing, fun."[45] Although this trip must have been a tremendous ordeal for a young mother contemplating an unknown future, this interviewee avoided dwelling on the hardships. It is possible that the stable life she eventually established in America overshadowed those early hardships, or that her denial might be protecting herself from recalling the stressful transition.

Upon arrival in Paris, the Egyptian Jewish families lived in hotels while they awaited their U.S. visas.[46] They were not permitted to work during this time, and depended on support from Jewish organizations, such as the Hebrew Immigrant Aid Society (HIAS), which provided them with meals and with tickets to tourist attractions. The greatest discomforts that the women expressed about their time in France were the cold weather and the difficulties of bathing children in a hotel without a proper shower facility. Their knowledge of French, and the awareness that this was a temporary situation, may well have aided them.

Language was not a major source of difficulty in France but it turned into a major cause of anxiety in America. However, in the United States, their knowledge of at least one Western language eased the transition, assisting them as they slowly became familiar with using English. Nor was English a completely foreign language in Egypt, since the British schools and British military presence had imported the language into the country. In America, the women learned English with their children or by listening to the radio and watching television; a minority took English classes upon arrival in New York. Learning English was a concern for the women, yet some implied that acquiring proficiency in the language was more of an immediate necessity for their husbands, who were required to find employment immediately.

The women's lack of facility in English became problematic, however, in the context of shopping for food and clothing. Early shopping experiences often brought on uncomfortable situations, quite traumatic for a woman trying hard to conform. Yvonne H. recalled going to the butcher to buy veal, but forgetting the word; when she told the man at the counter, "I need a piece of meat, but not the regular cow meat and not lamb,"[47] the only response was laughter, and she walked out of the store crying. She refused to utter another word of English for the first six months of her stay in America, because she was too embarrassed to make further mistakes. She remarked: "I couldn't adjust to the life here at all comparing to the Egyptian life, I couldn't at all. The language was a problem for me; I didn't know English so well. I was very shy. I didn't want to make mistakes at all so I went for six months . . . I was like a person who doesn't talk, you know, doesn't talk. . . . By contrast my husband used to just throw in sentence [in] past, present, just to get by. . . . But I wouldn't, so I suffered inside, over here, a lot."[48] In Egypt, she had received a respectable education, including gaining fluency in French and Arabic, and she could not tolerate the fact that in America her inability to communicate made her the object of ridicule.

In addition to remembering such insecurities, some women expressed particular concern that their children would be affected because the children did not speak English well yet and because they spoke with an accent. Language is considered a primary stepping stone in the process of assimilation: through their speech, these children were automatically identified as foreigners. Some mothers feared that their children would be teased for being strangers. One mother remembered how hurt her children were, and thus how hurt she was, when her children were taunted and called "French boys."[49]

But language was not the only source of stress that the women had encountered while shopping for food. Purchasing groceries became a new experience for these women. Rather than sending servants, now they themselves became the primary food purchasers for their families. Immediately after arriving in New York, Rita M.'s family stayed in a hotel in Manhattan for three months, trying to find an apartment with a landlord willing to rent to a family with six children. In Manhattan, she avoided doing the food shopping, instead sending her husband. She explained this with the simple statement "I didn't know [how and where to shop]."[50]

Once apartments were secured in Brooklyn, however, and their husbands found employment, the women became responsible for all food purchases. Although impressed by the proximity of food stores and the tremendous variety available in Brooklyn supermarkets, some women remarked that the very number of options made decisions difficult: they did not know which specific product would be best for a particular recipe. Yvonne H. described the difference between food choices in Egypt and in America: "The variety is much more here than in Egypt. You go buy, let's say, a tomato here; there is six kinds of tomato. You go buy lettuce; there is three kinds. You don't have this in Egypt—just a lettuce is a lettuce, a tomato is a tomato."[51] Often, a relative who had arrived in Brooklyn earlier would assist them and take them to the appropriate stores. Most of the women also received food deliveries from a fellow Egyptian Jew who would carry rice, cheeses and spices to their homes and would allow them to buy on credit. Denise Z. fondly recalled these deliveries: "I remember he used to carry the rice, *hazeet*, on his back and bring it, and he don't ask me even for money . . . and then come [later] to collect . . . he was nice man."[52] *Hazeet* was a common slang term employed by the Syrian-Egyptian Jewish community of Brooklyn, implying a sense of pity. This same man later opened a store, Setton's, specializing in Middle Eastern products. The store, along with Khasky's, another store opened by an Egyptian Jewish immigrant, became a shopping haven for these new immigrants, a place where they could buy familiar products and use their mother tongues of French or Arabic.

Ensuring that they were purchasing kosher products also became an issue, because in Egypt they had used raw ingredients, while American products often consisted of processed foods, which required greater kosher supervision. The women, familiar with reading Western languages, learned to read ingredients and searched for key words, such as *lard*, to determine if the product should not be purchased. One woman explained that the guidance of a family rabbi who had migrated with them alleviated the problems associated with maintaining a kosher home.[53]

Purchasing food and learning about American food-ways were only one aspect of cultural adaptation, but an important one, since the women were each responsible for preparing daily meals for their families, just as they had been in Egypt. Traditional food preparations there tended to be extremely labor intensive, requiring major amounts of cleaning, stuffing, rolling, and, perhaps most important, a substantial amount of time. All the women maintained that they cooked the same foods in their American and Egyptian kitchens; as one said, "We are not too American about food."[54] Yet for many Egyptian Jewish families, foods traditionally associated with holidays or special meals became more common fare at their American dinner table. Additionally, the majority asserted that the quantities—of food, work, time spent—changed. One woman described this phenomenon by saying, "Here, there is more work, more food. We didn't eat like that in Egypt. . . . Here every day is a holiday—in Egypt we didn't make *kaak* [a Middle Eastern cookie] every day, we never had *kibbe*—only special occasions."[55] Mary Halawani's grandmother announced during a Passover Seder that she, like the ancient Israelites, had left Egypt, but her journey took her to an American kitchen.[56] And in the women's American kitchens, no housekeepers could be hired to help with the chopping and cleaning.

The emphasis on food perhaps arose because Egyptian cooking became a symbol of Egyptian identity that was easy to maintain yet did not prohibit assimilation into American society. Thus, the women, by cooking large amounts and an extensive variety of foods reminiscent of a previous life, were providing a sense of continuity with a past identity. At the same time they were also adjusting to the idea of the United States as the "land of plenty."

Shopping for food was not the only aspect of consumer culture that changed for the women; they also encountered new experiences in shopping for clothing. In Brooklyn, custom-made clothing was usually the more expensive option; the women learned to buy ready-made attire at local shops and in major department stores. As with their food shopping experiences, some of the women sought the assistance of a relative, someone who had arrived in New York earlier and was thus considered an expert through longer exposure to Brooklyn shopping modes. Others described shopping with family members, sisters and sisters-in-laws, who had migrated with them. The style of clothing was different, and some women articulated the sense that daily wear in America seemed less proper than that expected in Egypt. One woman recalled her Egyptian-Israeli aunt's first visit to New York. The aunt looked at her niece's clothing and inquired, "So this is how you dress in America?" apparently shocked by the casualness of American clothing.[57] Not only did the women feel that the manner of dress in America was less formal, but they also expressed shock at how freely people wore the color black. In Egypt, black clothing was considered a symbol of mourning and thus would be worn only during the mourning period.[58]

The women interviewed also felt that the role played by Egyptian Jewish women in maintaining the home changed with their immigration. Without domestic helpers, and thus with household responsibilities now solely on their shoulders, one woman remembered thinking, "You don't know what to do first."[59] They felt overwhelmed by having "to take care of the house from head to toe."[60] Doing laundry became particularly trying, because the majority did not own a washing machine immediately upon arrival; the women remember with dread walking, accompanied by their children, to laundromats while carrying loads of laundry. For these women, the change of having to drag their own laundry and then wait their turn for a washing machine left a less than favorable impression of American lifestyles. One expressed this succinctly: washing and laundry "were my nightmare."[61] Purchasing cleaning supplies posed a problem, too, for some women, who found that American cleaning products, like the foods in supermarkets, offered too many options. Following a failed attempt to shop for laundry soap, one woman recalled anxiously calling her sister because she did not know what product or what brand to buy. In Egypt, she explained, they had simply used plain soap, a rag, and a washing board.[62]

Within the context of maintaining the home, all the women felt responsible for childrearing. However, the requirements of the role of caretaker, and their perception of parenting, were changed with immigration. One woman described the differences between raising children in America and in Egypt: "It's a different life [there]—we didn't have so much pressure. The women was in the house, raise the kids."[63] In America, on the other hand, the majority of the women worked in the home and took care of their children, but felt that they could not offer the children as much attention as in Egypt. In the early stages of their arrival, many women said, they had felt alone, without any help—implying that in Egypt they had received some assistance in childrearing from servants or from family members. Most viewed the American lifestyle as fast-paced and constantly busy, and they felt that this affected their level of involvement in their children's lives, even though they were, for the most part, stay-at-home mothers. However, though the mothers were so busy, they often kept the children with them while they preformed the many errands necessary to maintain an American household. In the beginning, many women, nervous about their new adopted country, insisted that the children accompany them on all errands, whether to the laundromat, the supermarket, or family visits. Children were brought along because they were too young to stay home (and there was no housekeeper to look after them) or because their mothers had insecurities and uncertainties about the new environment. In addition, children, who in many cases had learned the English language faster than their mothers, were able to help with making purchases and speaking to salespeople.

Some women also believed that raising children in America was more difficult because of the freedoms that children received in the new country. One woman explained that, in Egypt, "a child is born disciplined."[64] Another woman elaborated: "In Egypt what a parent says, goes."[65] Both women asserted that in America children answered back and refused to accept no as an answer. Thus, for these women, not only did the way they spent time with their children change, but the entire parent/child dynamic also transformed. However, both women asserted that their own children still showed respect and followed the patterns established in Egypt. They thus ascribed the changes they had mentioned to the third generation, or claimed these were a negative aspect of American culture that they themselves had been able to overcome.[66]

For a minority of the women, working outside the home became another determinant of the time they could spend with their children or use to take care of their homes. Only two women recalled working outside the home in Egypt, one as a French teacher in the Jewish community school, the other in a bank. Both had left their jobs before they married. It was not common, the interviewees explained, for women to work in Egypt. In the United States, the majority of these women continued to stay at home. However, two mothers did work immediately upon arrival in New York. One worked for a short while as a seamstress at a local dressmaker. Although she did not describe that experience, or the hours it took, as affecting her childrearing and home maintenance, she did state, in discussing some major differences between life in Egypt and life in America, "over there, it was our life, the kids; we didn't know anything else besides. . . . Not like here."[67] Thus, it is likely that working, coupled with the loss of household help, did affect her role as caretaker. The other woman worked from 9 A.M. to 9 P.M. in the bakery that she and her husband opened two weeks after their arrival. Her husband had owned a bakery in Egypt, but there she had not been involved in the business; in Brooklyn, however, their financial situation did not enable them to hire any employees, and so she had to assist. The experience of becoming a working mother overshadowed her entire description of her adjustment to life in America. The first statement she made in her interview concerned this transition: "In Egypt, we don't work. . . . In Egypt, we had a nice store and everything was nice. We had so many employee and the women she doesn't work. . . . There we had to take care of the house with the maid . . . we used to have maids. In Egypt, the life was very easy, not like here. When we came, we had to get adjusted and then—and here we are [the interview was conducted in her family bakery]."[68] She described the Brooklyn bakery as a family business, with all family members, including the children, pitching in. Her children came right after school to help their parents and spend time with them. They were required to help with chores at home, as well. She explained, "My kids, everyone had to do something . . . you go do the laundry, you gonna make the house, you gonna go shopping . . . and the kids after school they used to come here—it was close, you know—and they used to come and we used to stay till nine o'clock at night and they managed and they give us also, the children, a very good hand."[69] Even though the children may have helped out in Egypt, their responsibilities became much more extensive in their new country. When asked about the changes that she encountered in adjusting to American life, this woman responded: "There are very good opportunities here. . . . It was very easy in Egypt. Here it was very hard . . . we had to work from nine to nine."[70] Although appreciating the opportunities in America, she saw the transition to a working mother as difficult.

The adjustment from one country to another required a redefinition of the women's roles in their families. Although they primarily maintained their positions as wives, mothers, and caretakers, and, in most cases, continued to stay in the home, their responsibilities and expectations within the household took on new forms. This, in turn, led to a reshaping of their identity. None of the women expressed anger at the imposition of newfound responsibilities; they seemed to see their daily tasks as clearly falling under the rubric of their definition of wives, mothers, and caretakers. That is, although the roles clearly entailed more physical labor in America, these women did not articulate a sense that they were involved in anything beyond the boundaries of what was expected of a woman in their community. This view may be attributable to the fact that they witnessed other women in their migration taking on the same new responsibilities. It is also possible that these women recognized that, in Egypt, their privileges were a result of social class, and they now had, with their families, to struggle to achieve stability and success in the United States.

NOTES

1. Interview with Denise Z., November 2006.

2. The Jews escaping Egypt were referred to as refugees by American Jews involved in the campaign to grant entrance visas to Egyptian Jews seeking refuge in the United States. See Sidney Liskofsky, "Immigration," *American Jewish Yearbook* 59 (1958): 99–101.

3. Aviva Ben-Ur, *Sephardic Jews in America: A Diasporic History* (New York: New York University Press, 2009), 46.

4. Central European Jews and Eastern European Jews alike shared the experience of migrating to the United States for economic opportunity. See Hasia Diner, *A Time for Gathering: The Second Migration* (Baltimore: Johns Hopkins University Press, 1992).

5. Silvia Pedraza-Bailey, "Cuba's Exiles: Portrait of a Refugee Migration," *International Migration Review* 19, no. 1 (1985): 8. An interesting parallel can be drawn when observing the early wave of Cuban immigration to the United States immediately following Fidel Castro's takeover in 1959: the Cuban exiles arriving in the United States between 1959 and 1962 were disproportionately drawn from the upper and middle classes of Cuban society. For more on this, see Miguel Gonzalez-Pando, *The Cuban Americans* (Westport, CT: Greenwood Press, 1998), 32–33. Like their counterparts in Egyptian Jewish society, Cuban immigrants deriving from the middle and upper classes experienced downward class mobility upon arrival in the United States. These refugees, many of whom were required to leave without financial assets, had to accept that their migration would require a transition to both a new environment and a new class standing. Gonzales-Pando discusses this phenomenon in stating: "Former Cuban entrepreneurs and professionals parked cars, washed dishes, drove taxis, waited on tables, delivered newspapers, and performed a variety of menial tasks for which they were undoubtedly overqualified. . . . Housewives who had never held a job in Cuba found employment as waitresses, maids, seamstresses, factory workers, and vegetable pickers in the fields" (36). However, among the myriad differences between the Egyptian and Cuban migrations, two must be highlighted: the distance between land of origin and the United States; the fact that early Cuban migrants anticipated that their stay in America would be temporary. Egyptian-American Jews were not awaiting a return to Egypt, and they chose America as their new homeland over closer locations, such as Israel, because they felt that there were more opportunities for success in the United States.

6. Hasia Diner, *The Jews of The United States, 1654 to 2000* (Berkeley and Los Angeles: University of California Press, 2004), 284, mentions the arrival of one thousand Egyptian Jews in the early 1960s. Historian Aviva Ben-Ur has made the first tentative steps toward such a reframing of the narrative of American Jewish history, in her work *Sephardic Jews in America: A Diasporic History* (New York: New York University Press, 2009). She correctly asserts: "Studies of American Jewry focusing on the nineteenth and twentieth centuries reserve at best a one-sentence nod at Eastern Sephardim (Iberian-origin Jews transplanted to the Balkans and the Anatolian Peninsula) and Mizrahim (Jews indigenous to North Africa and the Middle East), who came to these shores from the disintegrating Ottoman Empire. The non-Ashkenazic Jew then plunges precipitously off the page into the abyss of historical oblivion" (2). Yet, in her attempt to fill in the gaps in the study of American Jewish history by focusing on the "minority within a minority" (6), Ben-Ur continues the prevalent policy of excluding, for the most part, the experiences of Jews from Middle Eastern lands. Ben-Ur divides non-Ashkenazi Jews in the United States into three categories, characterized by three language groupings: Sephardic Jews, who speak Spanish, Portuguese, or Ladino; Romaniote

Jews, who speak Greek; and Mizrahi Jews, who speak Arabic. Although Mizrahi Jews form the majority of non-Askenazi Jews in America today, the emphasis of Ben-Ur's work is on Sephardic Jews in the first half of the twentieth century, who at that time outnumbered Mizrahi Jews. When Mizrahi Jews are mentioned, it is generally within a few paragraphs comparing Syrian Jews' experiences to the experiences of Sephardic Jews, who receive the bulk of the author's attention. The only mention of the immigration of Egyptian Jewry is within a brief account of the "subethnic makeup" of the Syrian community, where Ben-Ur claims that, "in time, these new [Egyptian Jewish] arrivals became an inseparable part of the Syrian Jewish community" (46). Thus the struggles, accommodations and negotiations of Egyptian Jewish immigrants are submerged under the category of the larger Syrian community, denied their historical significance, and excluded from the historical narrative.

7. Paul Thompson, "The Voice of the Past: Oral History," in *The Oral History Reader*, ed. Robert Perks and Alistair Thomson (London: Routledge, 1998), 26; Robert Perks and Alistair Thomson, "Introduction," in *The Oral History Reader*, ix.

8. Robert Perks and Alistair Thomson, "Critical Developments: Introduction," in *The Oral History Reader*, 4; Joan Sangster, "Telling Our Stories: Feminist Debates and the Use of Oral History," in *The Oral History Reader*, 87.

9. Thompson, "The Voice of the Past," 25–26.

10. Ibid., 26.

11. Thompson explains the value of this method: "Oral history is a history built around people. It thrusts life into history itself and it widens its scope. It allows heroes not just from the leaders, but from the unknown majority of the people." Ibid., 28.

12. Three of the women in this group, Esther C., Fortune M., and Rita M., are related through marriage. These three sisters-in-law are also related to me through my stepfather, who is the son of Rita M.

13. Evelyn Nakano Glenn, *Issei, Nissei, War Bride: Three Generations of Japanese American Women in Domestic Service* (Philadelphia: Temple University Press, 1986), x. Nakano Glen sees her status as an in-group member as an advantage in recording her oral histories of Japanese American women. She argues that her position provided her with access to the community, as well as firsthand knowledge that allowed her to "direct her inquiry toward the most relevant issues."

14. Joan Sangster argued: "We might be less concerned about imposing our interpretations on women's voices if we were dealing with a written source; we are particularly sensitive about judging women because of the personal relationship—however brief—established between ourselves and our interviewees. But this is not necessarily positive, for it may lead us to shy away from critical conclusions about their lives." See Joan Sangster, "Telling Our Stories: Feminist Debates and the Use of Oral History," in *The Oral History Reader*, 93. For more on some of the problematic elements of oral history, such as distortion, see Alessandro Portelli, "What Makes Oral History Different?" in *The Oral History Reader*, 70–71.

15. For more on Jewish immigration to Egypt, see Michael M. Laskier, *The Jews of Egypt: 1920–1970* (New York: New York University Press, 1992), 5. A concise discussion of British policies in Egypt and of Jewish responses to them can be found in Gudrun Kramer, *The Jews in Modern Egypt* (Seattle: University of Washington Press, 1989), 36–37.

16. Laskier writes, "Statistically, of the seventy-five to eighty thousand Jews in Egypt during the 1940s, there were approximately six thousand Ashkenazim, at least thirty-five hundred Karaites, and ten thousand indigenous Jews, the rest being Orientals and Sephardim who were recent emigrants, or their descendents." In Laskier, *Jews of Egypt*, 7.

17. Kramer, *Jews in Modern Egypt*, 27.

18. Joel Beinin, *The Dispersion of Egyptian Jewry: Culture, Politics, and the Formation of a Modern Diaspora* (Cairo: American University in Cairo Press, 2005), 46.

19. Kramer, *Jews in Modern Egypt*, 27–28. Also see Rachel Marlerne Barda, "The Migration Experience of Jews from Egypt to Australia, 1948–1967" (PhD diss., University of Sydney, 2006), 82–84.

20. Barda, "Migration Experience," 86–87. Britain declared Egypt a protectorate in 1914. However, Egypt was granted limited independence in 1922, with British maintaining control over foreigners and local minorities until 1936. For more on the decline of Egyptian Jews' religious observance, see Norman A. Stillman, *The Jews of Arab Lands in Modern Times* (Philadelphia: Jewish Publication Society, 1991), 36.

21. Kramer, *Jews in Modern Egypt*, 55, 57; Beinin, *Dispersion of Egyptian Jewry*, 71.

22. Laskier, *Jews of Egypt*, 8; Kramer, *Jews in Modern Egypt*, 29–32.

23. Kramer, *Jews in Modern Egypt*, 220.

24. Ibid., 206–207.

25. Ibid., 203; Stillman, *Jews of Arab Lands*, 151–153.

26. Kramer, *Jews in Modern Egypt*, 217–218; Stillman, *Jews of Arab Lands*, 169.

27. Laskier, *Jews of Egypt*, 209 and 293. For more on middle- and upper-class ties to the West, see Barda, "Migration Experience," 106; Kramer, *Jews in Modern Egypt*, 55.

28. Kramer, *Jews in Modern Egypt*, 15–16, explains that Jewish immigrants to Egypt who originated from other Arab countries tended to merge socially and culturally into the poorer class of indigenous Jews, many of whom resided in the Jewish quarter of Cairo. However, Kramer sites as one exception Syrian merchants, many of whom were able to attain the middle and upper classes.

29. Victor D. Sanua, "A Study of the Adjustment of Sephardi Jews in the New York Metropolitan Area," *Jewish Journal of Sociology* 9, no. 1 (1967): 28.

30. Interview with Rita M., November 2006.

31. Interview with Fortune M., November 2006.

32. Interview with Elizabeth N., January 2007.

33. Interview with Esther C., November 2006.

34. Interview with Regine S., November 2006.

35. Ibid.

36. Interview with Denise Z., November 2006.

37. Interview with Rita M., November 2006.

38. Interview with Fortune M., November 2006; interview with Elizabeth N., January 2007.

39. Interview with Mrs. Mansoura, December 2006.

40. *I Miss the Sun*, dir. Mary Halawani, perf. Rosette Hakim, VHS, Sphinx Productions, 1983.

41. Interview with Esther C., November 2006.

42. Interview with Fortune M., November 2006.

43. Interview with Esther C., November 2006.

44. Interview with Rita M., November 2006.

45. Interview with Fortune M., November 2006.

46. Sanua, "A Study of the Adjustment," 26–27, explains that the U.S. quota for Egyptians was one hundred. Sanua discusses efforts made by Jews in America to gain entry for Egyptian Jewish refugees.

47. Interview with Yvonne H., December 2006.

48. Ibid.

49. Ibid.

50. Interview with Rita M., November 2006.

51. Interview with Yvonne H., December 2006.

52. Interview with Denise Z., November 2006.

53. Interview with Esther C., November 2006.

54. Interview with Yvonne H., December 2006.

55. Interview with Denise Z., November 2006.

56. *I Miss the Sun.*

57. Interview with Denise Z., November 2006.

58. Interview with Yvonne H., December 2006.

59. Interview with Denise Z., November 2006.

60. Interview with Esther C., November 2006.

61. Interview with Regine S., November 2006.

62. Interview with Yvonne H., December 2006.

63. Interview with Regine S., November 2006.

64. Interview with Esther C., November 2006.

65. Interview with Regine S., November 2006.

66. Other scholars have noticed similar patterns of transitioning parent-child relationships in immigrant cultures across diverse ethnic backgrounds and historical periods of immigration. For example, see Virginia Yans, *Family and Community: Italian Immigrants in Buffalo, 1880–1930* (Urbana: University of Illinois Press, 1977); Jennifer Lansford, et al., eds., *Immigrant Families in Contemporary Society* (New York: Guilford Press, 2007); and Xiaojian Zhao, *Remaking Chinese America: Immigration, Family, and Community, 1940–1965* (New Brunswick, NJ: Rutgers University Press, 2002).

67. Interview with Regine S., November 2006.

68. Interview with Mrs. Mansoura, December 2006.

69. Ibid.

70. Ibid.

8

The Bad Girls of Jewish Comedy

GENDER, CLASS, ASSIMILATION, AND
WHITENESS IN POSTWAR AMERICA

GIOVANNA P. DEL NEGRO

In the late 1950s and early 1960s, the bawdy humor of Belle Barth, Pearl Williams, and Patsy Abbott, a trio of working-class Jewish stand-up comics, enjoyed enormous popularity in the United States. Today largely forgotten or dismissed, they released bestselling LPs known at the time as "party records," which, though intended for respectable, middle-class consumers, were often sold under the counter and banned from radio airplay. With their earthy, old-world sensibility and strategic use of Yiddish, these middle-aged performers railed against societal mores that told them to be quiet, well behaved, and sexually passive. During the period in which these comics flourished, many working-class Jews experienced upward mobility and suburbanization, acceptance as racial whites, and substantial pressures to assimilate into mainstream American culture. This chapter explores the ways these comics placed Jewish identity and highly sexual subject matter at the center of their humor and, in so doing, negotiated issues of gender, Jewish ethnicity, class, and whiteness in the 1950s.

In their heyday, the albums that these comics recorded proved enormously popular with American audiences across the country. Belle Barth, who released eleven LPs with sexually suggestive titles such as *If I Embarrass You, Tell Your Friends*; *I Don't Mean to Be Vulgar, But It's Profitable*; and *This Next Story Is a Little Risqué*, reportedly sold two million records in her career, while Pearl Williams, who released seven albums including *A Trip around the World Is Not a Cruise*; *Bagels and Lox*; and *Pearl Williams Goes All the Way*, sold over a million copies—or even more, given the recording companies' habit of undercounting sales in order to avoid paying taxes and sharing profits with artists.[1] The least prolific of the cohort, Patsy Abbott, only recorded two albums, *Suck Up, Your Behind* and *Have I Had You Before*.[2] By the conservative estimates of critic Michael Bronski, "the three performers may have released . . . more than five million records."[3] At the peak of their careers, these comediennes played to sold-out crowds in the nation's top venues. Barth headlined at Carnegie Hall, Caesar's Palace, and El Morocco and owned her own club, named Belle Barth's Pub. Williams, who commanded a $7,500 weekly salary, regularly performed at luxury hotels and swanky clubs like the Foutainebleau, Maxine's, the Hotel Windsor, Chez Paris, and Place Pigalle.[4] After a successful run as a comedic singer on the stage and in the club circuit around the country, in 1958 Abbott opened her own establishment, Patsy's Place.

The trio performed regularly across the United States and Canada during the first decades of their careers, but audiences in the 1960s associated them most closely with Miami, and their success in this city was directly tied to the social transformations of Jewish American life that occurred after World War II. During this period, over one hundred thousand Jews migrated to Miami, which they jokingly dubbed the "Southern Borsht Belt"; many more went there for their holidays.[5] In Florida's tourism capital, the trio found lucrative work catering to vacationing Jewish suburbanites, retired Jewish snowbirds, and transplanted second- and third-generation Jews who nostalgically longed to remember the homes that they had left behind.

It was not only their nightclub performances that linked the trio to these social transformations; the emerging genre of the party album did so as well. After the war, an increasing number of returning Jewish servicemen with specialized skills in technical fields or management moved to the suburbs. Transmitting the sounds, images, and narratives of the older, working-class Jewish culture directly into the new suburban living rooms, the party albums that many of these recently married ex-soldiers and their families enjoyed offered fresh representations of Jewishness and American life. The listeners were far away from the ethnic enclaves of their childhood, and many found in these albums a way of feeling connected to their old community. Played in the home, but during social situations that weren't fully private, these albums encouraged their audiences to think about the cultural transitions between the ethnic and the mainstream, the urban and the suburban, the public and the private. Thus, on the nightclub stage or the living room stereo, the humor of Barth, Williams, and Abbott addressed conflicting attitudes about gender, sex, intergroup relations, and the politics of whiteness and ethnic integration in post–World War II American society.

Belle Barth

Although not as widely recognized as other female comics of her era, Barth had an enormous influence on the stand-up comics who followed her. According to Linda Martin and Kerry Seagrave, she was the "first to use the format of short jokes, as opposed to the monologues of [Beatrice] Herford and [Ruth] Draper."[6] Born Annabelle Salzman in New York City in 1911, Barth, who took her first husband's name, started her career doing imitations of "Al Jolson, George Jessel, and 'devastatingly funny take-offs' of strippers Lili St. Cyr and Gypsy Rose Lee."[7] She grew progressively raunchier from the 1930s onward, doing more and more risqué songs and X-rated material. Called the female Lenny Bruce, even though she preceded him, Barth periodically battled the obscenity laws in court. Banned from radio and television, she spent most of her career performing in nightclubs and hotels until her death in 1971.

In many ways the bawdy and irreverent Barth emulated the style and attitude of the female vaudeville performers she had seen at the B. F. Keith Theater while growing up in East Harlem during the 1920s. Dubbed the "Hildegard of the Underworld" and the "Doyenne of the Dirty Ditty," Belle Barth played the piano and sang in a gravelly voice. Mixing the red-hot mama style of performers like Sophie Tucker with that of more demure entertainers like Carol Channing, she often punctuated her sexually explicit jokes with a childlike manner of speech reminiscent of Betty Boop.[8] Barth's live LPs featured scatological and sexual jokes and covered topics like hemorrhoids, rectal exams, baby's feces, douching, masturbation, and intercourse. Excerpts from her party album *I Don't Mean to Be Vulgar, But It's Profitable* give an idea of the style and content of her comedy. Describing the mayhem that ensues when a kosher chicken is snuck into the movies, Barth said:

> There was a woman, she was so kosher that she didn't trust the cook in the kitchen. She sent her husband to a poultry market to bring her a live chicken. She wanted to kill it herself. On the way to the kitchen, he puts it under his arm, then he wanted to go to the movies, so he stuck it in his pants. You know, the chicken had to breathe. Two women sat next to him. One nudged the other, she said, "Sadie, what's doing?" Sadie, referring to the bulge in his pants says, "What are you so nervous. You've seen one, you've seen them all." The other says, "But this one is eating my potato chips."

In another joke from the same LP, an unfortunate hunting accident turns even more absurd by the medical advice given to the victim.

> Here is a story about two men who went hunting. One was [a] little cross-eyed hunter. Shotgun went off, hit the guy in the *citriolle*—it's Italian for cucumber. He had nine holes in it. He ran to the doctor. The doctor got scared and says, "I think I'll send you to Schwartz." The guy says, "Who's Schwartz, a specialist?" Doctor says, "No, he's a piccolo player, who'll show you how to finger it."

In material such as this, Barth transgressed the boundaries of female decorum, performing the kind of absurd, sexual gags usually reserved for male comics, and Jewish identity is introduced with a light and skilled touch. In the chicken joke, Jewish dietary laws provided the impetus that set the comic situation in motion. Likewise, Barth allowed the hunter joke to subtly reference the tensions surrounding ethnic upwardly mobility by making Schwartz, who bore an iconically Jewish name, appear to have the high status profession of a medical specialist, when in fact he was a lowly musician.

Although Barth filled her comedic repertoire with absurdly sexual or scato-logical jokes, such as the line about the precocious child who complains about having to "share a breast with a cigar smoker," she interspersed her bawdy rou-tines with material that directly confronted issues of discrimination and assimila-tion. In *I Don't Mean to Be Vulgar, But It's Profitable*, she said,

> [This is a story] about the Jewish man who wanted to check into the Kennelberry [Kennelworth] Hotel in Miami Beach, and the clerk says, 'It's restricted.' The guy says, [with Yiddish accent] "Who's a Jew?" "If you're not a Jew, you wouldn't mind answering three questions," the guy says. "Fire away." [The clerk] said, "Who was our Lord?" He says, "Jesus Christ." "Where was He born?" "In a stable." "Why was he born in a stable?" He says, "Because a rat bastard like you wouldn't rent him a room."

Barth then continued, "Think if I get a nose job, I can work in the Kennelworth?" On the album, the nightclub's live audience applauded aggressively at the remark and one fan replied, "Touché." Barth added, "You know what kills me, the rich Jews never know what I'm talking about [with that joke]. Yeah, you want to hear that, go to Miami Beach. 'Very wealthy,' she [a rich Jew, with a Yiddish accent] says. 'I'm very sorry, I don't know what you're talking [about].' I says, 'Where did you get the accent?' She [the rich Jew] says, 'I travel.'"

Here, Barth relayed an unambiguous commentary on the cultural amnesia to which some upwardly mobile Jews had succumbed: even as she attacked the anti-Semitism of the day, she skewered those wealthy Jews who eagerly aban-doned their immigrant past. In this bit, she develops a wealthy Jewish character who has tried to obscure her working-class roots. Her accent, this character claims, does not come from something as lowly as immigration, long a mark of marginalization for diasporized Jews, but from the archetypical form of leisure-class activity, tourism.

Pearl Williams

The daughter of a Russian immigrant tailor, Pearl Williams (née Pearl Wolfe) was born in 1914 in the Lower East Side of Manhattan. A former legal stenogra-pher, she developed into an aggressive, zaftig, husky-voiced, piano-playing comic with a penchant for double entendres and naughty stories.[9] According to *Miami Herald* reporter Andres S. Viglucci, the twenty-three-year-old Williams, who at the time had aspirations of becoming a lawyer, unexpectedly got a very differ-ent big break in 1938 during her lunch hour, when she played piano for her friend's singing audition. The agent was apparently so taken with her musical tal-ent that he hired her on the spot, and "that same night she went on stage at the Famous Door, on 53rd Street, opposite Louis Prima's Band."[10] Although she had no intention of going into show business, the $50 weekly salary paid her to per-form was almost three times higher than what she earned as a legal secretary.

Williams, who came from a poor family, found the lucrative pay too attractive to turn down.[11]

Williams eventually graduated from performing at Maxine's in the Bronx to headlining at the Aladdin and the Castaway Hotel in Las Vegas, as well as in numerous clubs in Detroit, Chicago, Toronto, and Montreal. After regularly doing winter gigs in Miami, Williams eventually bought a home in North Beach Miami; there, she spent the last eighteen years of her career as the main attraction performing to houses packed with busloads of Jewish retirees from nearby condos.[12] After forty-six years of nonstop entertainment, Williams finally retired at age seventy, and she died in 1991 following a battle with heart disease.

Williams's repertoire of jokes ran the gamut from tame to risqué to sexually explicit, and in many of her albums, mild one-liners existed directly alongside X-rated material. Like Barth, Williams broached topics not permitted on television: breasts, pubic hair, ejaculation, douches, *knish* (vagina), *shlong* (penis), and cunnilingus. Deftly appropriating and inverting the canonical wife joke genre so common among male Catskill comics of the period, Williams often made the man the butt of her humor. In *A Trip around the World Is Not a Cruise*, she nonchalantly said, "There's a woman ironing her brassiere, and her husband says. 'What the hell are you ironing that for. You don't have anything to put in it.' The wife replies, 'I iron your shorts, don't I?'" At her raunchiest, Williams could compete with any male comedian: in *Second Trip around the World*, she says, "Did you hear about the broad who walked into a hardware store to buy a hinge and the clerk says, 'Madame, would you like a screw for this hinge,' and she says, 'No, but I'd blow you for the toaster up there.'"[13] In her album *A Trip around the World Is Not a Cruise*, she joked, "Tonight I think I'll go home and douche with Crest. It will reduce my cavity by 40 percent." Touting the sexual prowess of French-Canadian men in *Bagels and Lox*, she said, "Are[n't] those French-Canadian men gorgeous? They're the only guys who know what your belly button is for. That's where they leave their gum on the way down. Oh that's nothing, then they put ice in your knish; they eat you on the rocks."

In performance, Williams typically underscored her punch lines with brief piano interludes and hummed recognizable tunes, such as "Hava Nagila." Her racier anecdotes, however, were ironically demarcated by demure sighs and a nasal, almost innocent laugh. Indeed, her ironic sentimentality and melodramatic interpretations of standard Jewish popular songs, obscene puns, and energetic musical interludes capitalized richly on her "hyphenated," Jewish American identity and the broad humor of the 1930s Yiddish theater and Borscht Belt *tummlers* (social directors). Her comedic tool kit contained a number of "definition" jokes ("Definition of indecent? If it's long enough, hard enough, far enough, then it's in decent") and sexually suggestive rhymes ("[sings] By the sea, by the sea [C]UNT").[14]

Williams filled her comic narratives with frustrated Jewish characters who would speak with thick accents and joyfully mete out their own brand of social justice. One bit in *Second Trip around the World* begins with a Jewish character who makes a long-distance phone call:

> All of sudden, in the middle of his conversation—he's talkin' about a half a minute—he's cut off. [Yiddish accent] "Hello operator, give me back the party." She says, "I'm sorry sir, you'll have to make the call over again." He's [he says] "Operator, I'm entitled to three minutes. I was only talkin' half a minute. Give me back the party." She says, "I'm sorry, sir, you'll have to make the call all over again." He says, "Operator, vhat do you want for my life? . . . I got no money, I'm broke, give me back the party." She says, "I'm sorry, sir, you'll have to make the call over again." He's, "Operator, you know vhat, take the telephone and shove it you know vhere," and he hangs up.

Later, two large men from the phone company arrive and tell him that they will take away his phone if he doesn't call and apologize to the operator. He makes the call, saying:

> "Give me Operator 28. Hello operator, remember me? Two days ago I insulted you. I told you, take the telephone." And she says, "Yeah." He says, "Well get ready. They're bringin' it to you."

For middle-aged Jews in the 1950s, this comic narrative of working-class resistance would resonate with the well-known "Cohen" albums, a hugely popular series of comedy records released by Joe Hayman in the 1910s and 1920s. In Williams's routine, the Jew's frustration is transformed into retribution, and the shame of accented English becomes an auditory icon of toughness and guile.

Gentile oppressors often took the form of belligerent Texans in Williams's stories, and these aptly illustrate the aggressive style of comedy with which the cohort became associated. In one story from *Second Trip around the World*, an exhausted Jewish traveling salesman is lucky enough to get the last room in a hotel. Shortly thereafter, a large Texan man bullies him into giving up the room. As the Jew leaves the hotel lobby, he swears that he will get his vengeance. The next day, the Texan wakes up

> with a big heavy load on his chest. He takes a look. There's manhole [cover] on his chest. He starts laughing and says, "Ah the little Jew wanted to get even with me." Gets up out of bed, picks up the manhole cover, walks up over to the window of the twenty-second floor, flings it out of the window. He's walking back to the bed, laughing. He gets back to the bed. There's a big note waiting for him on the bed. It says, "And now, you big bastard, you have fifteen seconds to untie the cord that's attached to your *beardzall* [testicles]."

As she did with the "Operator 28" narrative, Williams drew on well-known comic stereotypes to symbolically invert the power relations of American society. Here, the hulking Texan stands for the arrogance of mainstream white

America, and the marginalized figure of the scrawny Jew uses cunning to outwit and emasculate him.

Patsy Abbott

Raised in the Bronx, Patsy Abbott, née Goldie Schwartz, was born in 1921 and started her career as a vocalist with the Teddy King Orchestra. Journalist Gail Meadows reports that Abbott credited her training to the time she spent at the Catskills resorts, where entertainers presented fresh shows every night. Early in her career, she "sang popular songs to tourists, gamblers, and mobsters" at the Paddock Club in New York, and she performed for the military with the USO during the war.[15] Although her co-starring role in the hit musical *The Borscht Capades* made her the hit of Broadway in 1951, a series of illnesses abruptly cut short her rise to stardom. While she recuperated in Miami, she started doing one-woman shows at resort hotels, and eventually she decided to purchase her own nightclub, which she named Patsy's Place and which she ran from 1958 to 1965. After suffering two strokes, Abbott finally retired from show business, but she continued to work locally as a theatrical coach. In 1988, "she wowed the crowds again with [the show] 'The Golden Girls of Music and Comedy' ... which became the longest, continuously running musical revue in South Florida's history."[16] She died at the Miami Jewish Home and Hospital in 2001, days before she was to stage a show with fellow residents.

Both *Have I Had You Before* and *Suck Up, Your Behind* captured the comedienne's ear for dialects, impromptu flair for a salty line, and gusto for singing lighthearted, lusty musical numbers. In her stage act, Abbott warmly dispensed philosophical wisdoms in a faux high-class voice and showed off her sparkling evening gowns. She would frequently ask young married couples embarrassing questions. In her first party album, recorded live at Patsy's Place, she asked a bride, "How long have you been married?" The woman replied, "A week." "May I ask you a personal question?" Abbott then asked, "Is it nice?" and, when the woman answered, "Yes," Abbott asked, "What do you have to compare it to?"

Her jokes dealt with married couples lacking in sexual excitement, with the limitations imposed by Jewish holidays, with infidelity, with birth control.[17] Discussing marital boredom, Abbott joked in *Have I Had You Before*, "There's a couple married for fifteen years. . . . Wedded boredom—but you know, bored or not you got to make hay. Comes time to make hay, and they're in bed, one hour. Nothing happens. Finally she looks at him and says, 'What happened, you can't think of anybody either?'"

Commenting on Jewish strictures on marriage in *Have I Had You Before*, Abbott said,

> In [the] Jewish religion, you can't get married when you want to, right? See, you just go through the holidays. They got you by the holidays. Now they just

go through *Tishabov*. That holiday you can't get married. And you can't go swimming. It's ridiculous that you can't get married, and you can't get wet. It is. Then you have a holiday like *Pesach* and *Shavues* where you can't get married, and you can't have any music played. And you can't get married without an organ. And if you're not Jewish, darling, it's Lent, right, and you can't get married. You gotta borrow somebody else's. That's why they got you by the holiday.

Insinuating the topic of sex into a discussion of religious holiday practices was indeed quite taboo, and Abbott's elegant demeanor and highbrow accent made the candid treatment of earthy bodily pleasures particularly amusing.

Abbott's routines conjured up a plethora of recognizable Jewish characters, ones who uttered malapropisms or told cautionary tales about counting their blessings, even in times of economic hardship. The following story from the LP *Suck Up, Your Behind*, calls to mind the Jewish stock character of the *kvetch*, or complainer:

People are complaining with two loaves of bread under one arm. I hear a man goes to temple every single day, and he's praying to God, and he says [in a Yiddish accent], "God, I'm here every day. Every day, I'm here. I know you by your first name. God. Got no second name. Every day, I'm here. I want you to know I don't have a job, and my children starving, and my vife is sick. But I don't mind, mind you. I don't mind, mind you. But why you see Feldman down the street who doesn't go to temple, don't go to church. He's gotta a mansion, with a Cadillac, with a Jaguar, [stuttering] hees vife with minks, with chinchillas. Why he got? Why I ain't got? Why? Why? Why should he have when I ain't got? Why? Tell me why!" All of sudden there is bolt of lighting and the voice out of the blue says, "'Cause you're *nudging* me. That means you bug me, man."[18]

Like many of the trio's stories, this joke follows the long tradition of what folklorists refer to as "dialect jokes." Just as such humor may reflect immigrant anxiety about language use and social exclusion, it may also allow third- and fourth-generation ethnics to emphasize their own social mobility and distance themselves from those of the older generation who were less assimilated.[19] The joke quoted is a particularly striking example of the genre; inverting the traditional stigma associated with the Yiddish-accented kvetch, the joke sets the heavily accented speaker as a traditional loser, only to reveal that the English of God himself is peppered with hip Yiddishisms.

In the smoke-filled nightclubs of the late, late, show, Barth, Williams, and Abbott spoke candidly about sex, cursed in Yiddish, and openly criticized what they saw as the hypocritical values of bourgeois culture. These tough women with working-class roots not only condemned the oppressive gender ideologies of the 1950s, they also highlighted the growing tensions that existed both within the Jewish community and between Jews and non-Jews. The trio's bawdy party records offered the consumers of suburban America an opportunity to enjoy the exciting, uncensored atmosphere of the nightclub while safely ensconced in the privacy of their own living rooms. The recordings represented an alternative to mainstream forms of entertainment, which seldom acknowledged the existence of conflicting attitudes toward gender, sex, intergroup relations, and the politics of ethnic integration. In some ways, these comics can be seen as enacting their ethnic difference for a mass market and helping to make Jewishness more palatable for non-Jews. But at this transitional moment when Jews found themselves accepted in the American mainstream, these performances of esoteric knowledge also served to reaffirm ethnic boundaries. They cautioned Jews to resist the tide of cultural assimilation and not to fall victim to a false sense of security.

During the period after World War II, Jews saw both upward class mobility and a redefinition of the nature of their identity as white ethnics. As Mathew Frye Jacobson has shown, Jews and southern Europeans were, over time, increasingly seen by mainstream Americans as racial whites marked by a distinctive, non-mainstream ethnicity or religion, rather than as a racial group "less white" than Americans of English descent yet "more white" than African Americans, Native Americans, or Asian Americans.[20] This shift was directly tied to changes in large-scale American institutions. Before the outbreak of World War II, Franklin Roosevelt's notion of inclusive nationalism allowed Jews to begin to gain admittance into the public sector and government, and the growing anti-Semitism of the period led Jews to question race-based definitions of Jewish character.[21] With the reduction of restrictive admission policies in universities, and increased entrance into merit- and exam-based professions such as teaching, medicine, and law, Jews entered the middle class in ever greater numbers. As Karen Brodkin Sacks observes, the "whitening" of Jews continued after World War II; for example, federal assistance programs, offered returning Jewish veterans cheap home mortgages, and the GI Bill allowed them to pursue higher education and thus to develop expertise in specialized occupations from which they had been barred and which were in great demand after the war.[22] Although these government programs may seem to speak to issues of class, rather than of race and ethnicity, the pervasive discrimination of the day guaranteed the linkage of these forms of identity. African Americans continued to experience exclusion in housing, education, and employment, while such barriers began to fall for Jews. As a result, Jews saw new opportunities for upward mobility that were unavailable to other nonwhite groups, and with this upward mobility came a new sociopolitical climate, reinforcing the definition of Jews as an ethnic, rather than racial, group.

Although the comics did not often explicitly discuss race in their routines, we would be projecting contemporary notions of race onto 1950s America if we understood the intergroup politics of the trio's humor strictly in terms of class and ethnicity. In a period in which notions of race were being contested, the trio and their audience, I suggest, were negotiating whiteness whenever ethnicity and class were on the table.

This is not to say, of course, that class wasn't the focus of much of their humor. Quick to refresh the memories of successful Jews keen on forgetting the harshness of their working-class immigrant past, Patsy Abbott commonly used "You don't remember?" as a coda to her jokes. Here is an example from her second album, *Suck Up, Your Behind*:

> You pick up the paper, you want to throw up. It's better [in] the old days. We took the paper, and we put it on the kitchen floor. Remember? Remember when we had wall-to-wall papers? You don't remember the good old days? You had nothing to eat. Go ahead, remember. The only good thing about the good old days is a bad memory. We used to have a toilet. We used to have a toilet in the hall. Remember the toilet in the hall . . . ? You don't remember? You was always rich? . . . There's a man that had a toilet in the hall for years, and he vowed himself that someday he'd make enough money to have a bathroom in the house. Today he's a millionaire in Miami Beach. Got three toilets in the house. *Ken nisht geyt.* [To one particular audience member] That means he can't have a B.M. He can't go to the bathroom. I'm explaining, honey. If you listen to me, darling, I'll explain everything. But if he's [to another audience member] busy explaining to you, then you won't hear me explaining either. Understand? Thank you.

Here, Abbott acerbically reminds Jews that, as Eric L. Goldstein has phrased this, "despite the social and [economic] benefits whiteness has conferred upon them, [they will never] feel the kind of freedom whiteness is *supposed* to offer—the freedom to be utterly unselfconscious about one's cultural or ethnic background."[23] We know from the recordings that other European ethnics attended performances by the trio, and in many ways the women's anti-assimilationist message could be viewed as a kind of protomulticulturalism for those who had recently crossed the color line, such as Italian Americans.

Although some second- and third-generation Jewish Americans may have nostalgically identified with the world that these comediennes evoked, many of the non-Jews in the audiences saw Jews as exotic. Jewish women represented a female, cultural *other* whose more assertive displays of identity could flourish only in the marginalized atmosphere of after-hours nightclub and underground record labels—even as their male Jewish counterparts tamed their routines and capitalized on their gender privilege to gain greater access to radio, television, and film. In the face of an increasingly sanitized media to which Jewish entertainers were allowed entrance only at the expense of attenuating expressions of their ethnic identity, the adult-oriented party records helped to fill a cultural gap by providing an arena for the expression of an ethnically assertive counterdiscourse. By tapping into an underserved consumer need, the trio helped labels such as Chess, Laff, Surprise, Riot, Roulette, and After Hours carve out a profitable market niche. In so doing, they inadvertently became what Joel Foreman would call "agents of cultural subversion," and paved the way for the production and dissemination of cheap media products that deviated from the norm.[24]

Although many Jewish women of childbearing age in the postwar period sought to fulfill themselves through domesticity, and grappled with what the Jewish feminist author Betty Friedan would call the "nameless problem," lingering anti-Semitism and the growing vilification of Jewish women as materialistic, guilt-inducing, status seekers colored their experience.[25] In such an era of ethnic social exclusion and female scapegoating, these brassy women comics offered Jews a respite from the puritanical values of their middle-class suburban neighbors, whose attitudes told them to suppress their Jewishness and their desire to be anything other than a standard housewife. Instead, these loud-mouthed, nonconformist comics did not shy from being "too Jewish." Even though they challenged the religious tenets of Jewish female refinement and cleanliness—*edelkiet* and kashrut[26]—their unorthodox career choices reflected other Jewish traditions of female outspokenness, such as the more egalitarian gender values of East European society that "reinforced the acceptance of female participation in the world of work and politics."[27] These aging "ghetto girls" turned "vulgar, garish, uncultivated . . . plebeian ways" into emblems of honor.[28] And their racial ambiguity gave them the license to tackle forbidden subjects. As Ruth Frankenberg's work on whiteness reveals, although Jewish women are either relegated to the borders of whiteness or marked as racial *others*, they are never viewed as "constitutive of the cultural norm."[29] Interestingly, their African American counterpart Moms Mabley, a wise-cracking grandmother who lusted after young men, also enjoyed a huge following. Unlike the trio, Mabley made, at the height of the civil rights movement, a successful transition to television, appearing on afternoon and evening slots on the *Merv Griffin Show*, the *Smothers Brothers Show*, and the *Flip Wilson Show*, as well as in a series of specials hosted by well-known celebrities such as Harry Belafonte. With humor that was more assertive in its politics and franker in its subject matter, the trio had little chance to attain the mainstream success that Mabley enjoyed. The rather unconventional, though affable, role of the grandmother that Mabley embraced on stage was far less threatening to American television viewers than the trio's aggressively bawdy humor.

But finally, in an era when mainstream stereotypes represented Jewish women as greedy consumers who dominated their husbands and sons, why did this trio of outspoken women hold such appeal? If the Jewish men of the period feared the emasculating power of Jewish wives and mothers, nevertheless many frequented these shows by women who embodied many of the qualities that they resented.[30] In a time when many Jews enjoyed unprecedented financial success but limited social acceptance, jokes at the expense of non-Jews, a core theme in these comics' repertoire, provided an outlet for the frustrations that male as well as female Jews faced. And, more generally, although the routines about impotence or philandering might deflate the male ego, these comics were motivated less by any desire to castrate men than by the pleasure of "shock[ing] the audience with their naughty Jewish girl" act.[31] Further, these comediennes mocked both Jewish men and Jewish women; male discomfort brought on by the penis jokes was quickly mitigated by the jokes about women's sexual dalliances, cavernous knishes threatening to swallow up men, and nouveau riche Jewish wives trying to hide their ethnicity behind expensive minks. In these scenarios, both men and women were ridiculed, and everyone took their lumps.

The women's negotiation of gender, ethnicity, and class intertwined with their role as transgressive, trickster-like figures. Delivering their humor in the nightclub, a site associated with adult indiscretion, with shows as late as midnight or even 4 A.M., targeted to audiences enjoying their annual Miami vacation, the women's performances took place in liminal spaces that encouraged both transgression and the kind of candid, cultural reflexivity that would not have been appropriate in mainstream venues. Further, by reflexively commenting on their own performances with phrases such as "I know I'm weird," the comics marked themselves, too, as liminal. The scatological references further served to frame their performances as boundary breaking. This helped to prepare the crowd for the outrageous transgressions of gender and sexuality and the occasionally painful reflections on ethnicity and class referenced by their jokes.

Unruly "red hot mamas," the trio flagrantly embodied the carnivalesque, and in the erotically charged atmosphere of the nightclub they championed the principles of chaos, disorder, and excess, both orally and visually. Confronting the conservative gender ideology of the post–World War II era, they pronounced their refusal to hide at home. They used features of their identities that had been repressed—features such as flagrant ethnic Jewishness and women's sexuality— as weapons to mock social norms. These lusty, fleshy, obviously menopausal women with sequined dresses and painted-on eyebrows flaunted their girth to mitigate the threat of their jokes. While mainstream 1950s magazines depicted a world of normative sexual relations and bourgeois family live, the emergence of *Playboy* (first published in 1953) and the release of the *Kinsey Reports* (in 1948 and 1953) complicated the public discourse about gender and sexuality.[32] Thus, far from sleek-looking classical beauties, these outrageously blue, sexually frank performers obviously touched a nerve with middle-class audiences who longed to escape the unquestioned blandness of their white-collar existence and the climate of cultural conformity.

Relegated to the liminal space of the late, late show, Belle Barth, the self-described "maven on *drek*" and her cohort offered many slumming middle-class patrons an opportunity to enjoy the rowdiness of "lower-class leisure" without discernible damages to their reputation.[33] Like the abject bodily functions from which polite society averts its gaze, Jews in the white suburbs of America of the 1950s had to hide their working-class roots and sanitize their ethnicity and difference. Given this context, the trio's scatological humor, no less than their working-class dialects or omnipresent Yiddishisms, served as a metaphor for the return of the ethnic and working-class culture that assimilating Jews had repressed. Like the joke tellers that Simon Bronner discusses in his work on anal humor in Pennsylvania Dutch culture, these comics engage in "act[s] of verbal aggression, [symbolically] hurling 'shit,' at the establishment that 'looks down' upon them like dirt."[34]

By denuding sex of its seriousness and placing a uniquely female perspective on the subject matter, these brash comics ultimately challenged the male-centered visions of female sexuality that dominated vaudeville, burlesque, and the Borscht Belt. The trio replaced the "badgering mother-in-laws, homely naggers, ball and chain wives, or dumb bombshells" that dominated male comedians' routines with strong-minded, willful women, always ready to offset their opponent with a cheeky remark.[35] Rather than playing the hapless victims of a male comic's jokes, the trio cast themselves as the instigators of humor and mayhem. In their topsy-turvy world, annoying men are taunted by menacingly large mammary glands or those all-consuming knishes. Here, indeed, exaggerated female body parts (oversized breasts, buttocks, and vaginas) conspired to ridicule men and render them powerless. By playing on male fears about women's sexuality and by drawing on comedic devices historically used by male comics to demean women, these comediennes strategically employed the tools of their male-dominated trade to highlight the asymmetries that existed between the sexes. In the work of these talented performers, allusions to orifices and overabundant attributes associated with the feminine form become a source of strength, rather than embarrassment, and terms which had been used to objectify and silence women's sexual enjoyment served to destabilize the power and privilege exerted by men on the public stage and in the wider patriarchal culture.

The performances of Barth, Williams, and Abbott offer powerful insights, not only into Jewish identity, but into class, assimilation, and whiteness. Even as these women highlighted the very real and suppressed cultural differences of Jews in the postwar years, their over-the-top acts also uncovered the constructedness of ethnic and racial identities. In other words, the women's humor focused on the tensions between being a Jew, with all the distance from mainstream American culture that this implied, and playing the Jew, being white and playing white, being middle class and playing middle class.[36] Certainly, the trio did not perform any type of realistic Jewish identity that they would have embraced off-stage: they would not have agreed that Jews were or should be hypersexual, loud, and crude. To the contrary, these women's parodies of working-class ethnic identity mirrored the everyday, sometimes strained performances of whiteness that they saw enacted by certain upwardly mobile Jews in the affluent, assimilated suburbs. The trio saw with great insight the constructedness of proper, middle-class white identity for Jews and non-Jews alike. Projecting their voices into the living room, the trio reminded the new Jewish suburbanites where they had been, and brought to light the parts of their audience's lives that audience members found difficult to express to their neighbors. These comics carried the tensions of Jewish private life into the marginalized public space of the late, late night comedy stage, then returned that public discourse to the domestic realm of the living room stereo, where it could be safely acknowledged. To be sure, their routines were sympathetic to the pressures that Jews faced in the ethnic and class environment of the era. Even as their humor unmasked the constructedness of whiteness and Jewishness, they warmly recognized the social dilemmas that their audiences faced. Seen in this light, their live and recorded performance of ethnic working-class identity highlighted the everyday performance of whiteness that Jews, though no more than white Anglo-Saxon Protestants themselves, engaged.

ACKNOWLEDGMENTS

The data for this project come almost exclusively from newspaper articles and writings that I found at the New York Public Library for the Performing Arts, the Museum of Television and Radio in New York City, and the Historical Museum of Southern Florida. I would like to thank Harris M. Berger, Simon Bronner, and Barbara Kirshenblatt-Gimblett for their insightful remarks on earlier drafts of this text.

All albums cited in this article were recorded between the late 1950s and the late 1960s. Belle Barth, *If I Embarrass You, Tell Your Friends*, After Hours Records LAH 69; *I Don't Mean to Be Vulgar, But It's Profitable*, Surprise 169; and *This Next Story Is a Little Risqué*, After Hours Records LAH 69. Pearl Williams, *A Trip around the World Is Not a Cruise*, After Hours Records LAH 70. 192; *Bagels and Lox*, LAFF 127; and *Pearl Williams Goes All the Way*, Riot Records R309. For more on record company practices, see Ronald L. Smith, *Comedy on Record: The Complete Critical Discography* (New York: Garland Publishing, 1998).

NOTES

1. Ronald L. Smith, *Comedy on Record: The Complete Critical Discography* (New York: Garland Publishing, 1998).

2. Patsy Abbott, *Suck Up, Your Behind*, Abbott LP 1000; and *Have I Had You Before*, Chess LP 1450.

3. Michael Bronski, "Funny Girls Talk Dirty," *Boston Phoenix*, August 15–21, 2003.

4. Andres S. Viglucci, "Pearl Leaves Her Setting," *Miami Herald*, March 29, 1984.

5. Deborah Dash Moore, "Jewish Migration in Postwar America: The Case of Miami and Los Angeles," in *A New Jewry? America since the Second World War*, ed. Peter Y. Medding (New York: Oxford University Press, 1992), 105–109.

6. Linda Martin and Kerry Seagrave, *Women in Comedy: The Funny Ladies from the Turn of the Century to the Present* (Syracuse, NY: Citadel Press, 1986), 141.

7. Ibid.

8. Although Barth, Williams, and Abbott owe a great deal to the sexually assertive, self-mocking "red-hot mama" persona that Jewish entertainer Sophie Tucker made famous in the early 1900s, Tucker's song lyrics and banter, though suggestive, were neither overtly blue nor as sexually aggressive as the trio's. Although the 'red-hot mamas,' too, played independent-minded, feisty older women with voluptuous bodies and healthy sexual appetites, and although all used Yiddishisms for comedic effect, the trio were considerably more graphic. The trio also helped contribute to and build upon the Borscht Belt tradition most often linked with Jewish male comics of the Catskills, comedy that was characterized by insults, fast-paced one-liners, and amusing anecdotes about deeply flawed whiners and losers who would persevere, despite various forms of victimization, self-inflicted or externally imposed. Even though these comics are not associated with the hip, new, rebellious, anti-establishment stand-up comedy that emerged in the intimate clubs of New York, Chicago, and San Francisco in the early 1960s, they did in many ways pave the way for it.

9. Marjorie Valbrun, "Pearl Williams, Well-Known Singer, Comedienne," *Miami Herald*, September 20, 1991.

10. Viglucci, "Pearl Leaves Her Setting."

11. Ibid.

12. Ibid.; Valbrun, "Pearl Williams."

13. Pearl Williams, *Second Trip around the World*, Surprise Records 75.

14. Both examples are from *A Trip around the World Is Not a Cruise.*

15. Gail Meadows, "Patsy Abbott, Miami Beach Entertainer, Impresario," *Miami Herald*, August 3, 2001; Irene Lacher, "At Patsy's Place, There Was Always a Party Going On," *Miami Herald*, October 6, 1985; *Borscht Capades* Playbill, September 24, 1951, 26, Zan T282, *Borscht Capades* Clip File, The New York Public Library for the Performing Arts.

16. Meadows, "Patsy Abbott."

17. Particularly relevant here is a passage from Pearl Williams's album *Pearl Williams at Las Vegas: "She's Doin' What Comes Naturally"* (Riot R303), in which the comic engages in a dialogue with Barth, who is in the audience, and a member of the crowd. Describing the damage that the comic and "her mother" Barth could unleash upon the conservative broadcast television of their day, Williams sarcastically howls, "We're doing the *Tonight Show.* We really are, honey. Don't get hysterical. We're going on television. We're gonna blow the entire network. She'll take one end, I'll take the other end. We'll bring back radio." When an audience member brings up Patsy Abbott, Williams dismisses Abbott as merely a "nice girl." The mere fact that she needed to do so, though, shows how these three were linked in the public imagination.

18. Although such dialect jokes were often seen as insulting to immigrant Jews, as Dan Ben-Amos points out in his 1973 article on "The 'Myth' of Jewish Humor" (*Western Folklore* 81: 129–130), "the fact that Jews tell jokes about each other demonstrates not so much [Jews' alleged] self-hatred as perhaps the internal segmentation of their society." He writes, "The recurrent themes of these anecdotes are indicative of areas of tensions within the Jewish society itself, rather than the relations with outside groups."

19. Simon J. Bronner, "Dialect Story," in *Encyclopedia of American Folklife*, ed. Bronner (Armonk, NY: M. E. Sharpe, 2006), 307–310; Ben Amos, "The 'Myth' of Jewish Humor"; see also James P. Leary, "Dialect Story," in *American Folklore: An Encyclopedia*, ed. Jan Harold Brunvand (New York: Garland Publishing, 1998), 200–201; and Stanley Brandes, "Jewish-American Dialect Jokes and Jewish-American Identity," *Jewish Social Studies* 45 (1983): 233–240.

20. Mathew Frye Jacobson, *Whiteness of a Different Color: European Immigrants and the Alchemy of Race* (Cambridge, MA: Harvard University Press, 1998). For related perspectives on this issue, see Eric L. Goldstein, *The Price of Whiteness: Jews, Race, and American Identity*

(Princeton, NJ: Princeton University Press, 2006); Karen Brodkin Sacks, "How Did Jews Become White Folk?" in *Race*, ed. Steven Gregory and Roger Sanjek (New Brunswick, NJ: Rutgers University Press, 1994), 78–102; and Eli Lederhendler, *New York Jews and the Decline of Urban Ethnicity, 1950–1970* (Syracuse, NY: Syracuse University Press, 2001).

21. Goldstein, *The Price of Whiteness*, 189.

22. Brodkin Sachs, "How Did Jews Become White Folk?" 97.

23. Goldstein, *The Price of Whiteness*, 236.

24. Joel Foreman, *The Other Fifties: Interrogating Midcentury American Icons* (Urbana: University of Illinois Press, 1997), 10.

25. See Riv-Ellen Prell, "Rage and Representations: Jewish Gender Stereotypes in American Culture," in *Uncertain Terms: Negotiating Gender in American Culture*, ed. Faye Ginsburg and Anna Lownhaupt Tsing (Boston: Beacon Press, 1990), 248–266; and Prell, *Fighting to Become Americans: Assimilation and the Trouble between Jewish Women and Jewish Men* (Boston: Beacon Press, 1999).

26. Sarah Blacker Cohen, "Unkosher Comediennes: From Sophie Tucker to Joan Rivers," in *Jewish Wry: Essays on Jewish Humor*, ed. Cohen (Detroit: Wayne State University Press, 1987), 105–124.

27. Paula E. Hyman, *Gender and Assimilation in Modern Jewish History: The Roles and Representation of Women* (Seattle: University of Washington Press, 1995), 111–113.

28. Prell, *Fighting to Become Americans*, 23.

29. Ruth Frankenberg, *White Women, Race Matters: The Social Construction of Whiteness* (Minneapolis: University of Minnesota Press, 1993), 224.

30. A variety of scholars have examined depictions of Jewish women in post–World War II America as greedy, guilt inducing, domineering, and sexually aggressive. See, for example, Roberta Mock, "Female Jewish Comedian," *New Theater Quarterly* 58 (1999): 99–109; Joyce Antler, *You Never Call! You Never Write!: A History of the Jewish Mother* (New York: Oxford University Press, 2007); Prell, "Rage and Representations"; Alan Dundes, "The J.A.P. and the J.A.M in American Folklore," *Journal of American Folklore* 98 (1985): 456–475.

31. Cohen, "Unkosher Comediennes," 112.

32. On the complex reality of sexism and women's resistance to it in 1950s America, see Joanne Meyorwitz, *Not June Cleaver: Women and Gender in Postwar America, 1945–1960* (Philadelphia: Temple University Press, 1994).

33. Kathleen Spies, "'Girls and Gags': Sexual Display and Humor in Reginald Marsh's Burlesque Images," *American Art* (Summer 2004): 33–57.

34. Simon J. Bronner, "Analyzing the Ethnic Self: The Hinkel Dreck Theme in the Pennsylvania-German Folk Narrative," *Columbia Journal of American Studies* 8 (2007): 34.

35. Spies, "Girls and Gags," 45.

36. In *Acting Jewish: Negotiating Ethnicity on the American Stage and Screen* (Ann Arbor: University of Michigan Press, 2006), Henry Bial explores how Jewish performers manage their ethnic identity by referencing a set of aural and visual cues, cues that are "double coded" (intended to be read differently by audiences of differing ethnic backgrounds). In such a situation, Jewishness is not a question of ethnic or religious affiliations, but a set of behaviors, gestures, and manners that are acted out for viewers who can or cannot, respectively, attend to messages expressing esoteric or exoteric knowledge.

9

Judy Holliday's Urban Working-Girl Characters in 1950s Hollywood Film

JUDITH SMITH

A Jewish-created urban and cosmopolitan working-girl feminism persisted in the 1950s as a cultural alternative to the suburban, domestic consumerism soon eloquently critiqued by Betty Friedan in *The Feminine Mystique*. The film persona of Jewish, Academy Award–winning actress Judy Holliday embodied this working-girl feminism. Audiences viewed her portrayals of popular-front working-girl heroines in three films, all written by the Jewish writer and director Garson Kanin (sometimes in association with his wife, the actress Ruth Gordon) and directed by the Jewish director George Cukor in the early 1950s: *Born Yesterday* (1950), *The Marrying Kind* (1952), and *It Should Happen to You* (1954). Holliday's working-girl feminism conveyed women's wage earning as ordinary and unexceptional, women workers as competent, spunky, active in their own behalf, and unwilling to back down in the face of authority. Significantly, this working-girl feminism assumed the necessity of male allies, and envisioned the possibility of male support and admiration for working women, enabling the requisite, heterosexual, romantic denouement.[1]

In the 1930s and 1940s, Jewish cultural producers, among others, enthusiastically participated in the creation of popular theatrical, musical, and film works that offered up images of sassy, sexy, and tough working women and their male counterparts, and of multiethnic and sexually sophisticated urban cosmopolitans.[2] Images of working-girl feminism, shaped in the 1930s and 1940s, then made their way into 1950s popular culture underneath or interspersed with the more dominant celebration of consumerism, domesticity, and compulsory heterosexuality. At the same time, the prevalent anticommunism of the era led many who helped to create the images of working-girl feminism to camouflage these counterthemes, hoping to avoid right-wing scrutiny and protest. Anticommunist blacklisting closed off the public space for popular-front left-wing feminism, publicly silenced Holliday herself, and made it harder for subsequent audiences to recognize the traces of the independent, politically engaged woman at the center of her star power and distinctive persona.

Jewish cultural producers were primarily responsible for making Holliday a star. From the point of view of current conceptions of Jewish identity, their willing merger of Jewish ethnicity into a kind of urban ethnic style, and the reframing of Jewish ethnicity as a more generic urbanity, might seem a form of *passing* that hid Jewish particularity. However, within the context of the 1930s and 1940s, when American Jews moved from immigrant provincial and parochial associations into new forms of community and collaboration (within the labor movement and on the progressive left), particularly at a time when challenging fascism's externally imposed racial categorizations appeared urgent, the presence of Jewishness as part of urban cosmopolitanism seems less like a form of hiding and more like an explicit political choice.[3]

Women film critics of the 1970s such as Molly Haskell and Marjorie Rosen, influenced by the enthusiasms of women's liberation, largely failed to recognize the traces of working-girl feminism in 1950s culture. From these critics' perspective, films of the late 1940s and the 1950s that featured working-girl heroines did not look all that feminist, because most did not encourage female autonomy and because these films' celebration of the heterosexual couple seemed to reinforce domestic retreat. Although these feminist critics could find compelling women characters in the anarchic screwball comedies and heroic women's films of the 1930s and the war years, they found themselves disappointed by harsher forms of containment for women's aspirations after the war and by romantic resolutions that compromised women's independence. Brandon French was one of the few feminist critics to find some affinities between the rebellious female characters lionized by the women's liberation movement and the women heroines in films of the 1950s. She identified Judy Holliday's characterization of Florence Keefer in *The Marrying Kind* as an example of a transitional woman "on the verge of revolt," as she titled her study.[4] However, French's text-based reading of the film paid no attention to the Popular Front backgrounds of the writers and director responsible for creating the rebellious film character whom Holliday would enact. Many of those who gravitated to the left in the 1930s and 1940s were in fact interested in some version of the "woman question" as a central dimension of the sexual modernity to which they aspired.

The emergence of gay liberation in the 1970s, and the resulting polarization of the categories of homosexual and heterosexual, may have also had the effect of obscuring working-girl feminism's subtler challenges to male dominance. But, in the face of the 1950s' overwhelming public celebration of heterosexual domesticity, some qualities associated with working-girl characters, such as sexual cosmopolitanism, assertive female sexuality, and publicly acknowledged female desire and pleasure in sexuality, presented challenges to normative heterosexuality.[5] The working-girl films that playfully highlighted the performance of heterosexual courtship and those that, somewhat less playfully, disclosed the potential disappointments of courtship and marriage, provided popular cultural alternatives to more circumscribed notions of women's aspirations.

The world of the wartime and postwar Popular Front left shaped Judy Holliday as a performer; this is the same world that historian Daniel Horowitz has shown to have been formative for Betty Friedan, whose work in the 1963 *The Feminine Mystique* popularized a critique of suburban domesticity. Judy Holliday was born in 1921 to a family with ties to the Jewish immigrant left. Her grandmother Rachel Gollumb was a devoted socialist, and her mother Helen grew up in the overlapping New York worlds of the socialist labor movement and Yiddish literary and theatrical circles. Her uncle Joseph Gollumb joined the Communist Party for a period of time and wrote for the *Daily Worker*. Her father Abe Tuvim, at one time a labor union activist, traveled in the same Jewish leftist community. Holliday's parents met each other at the Rand School of Social Science, a gathering place for Greenwich Village socialists, and socialized at the Café Royale, where the Yiddish intelligentsia and the stars of Yiddish theater congregated.[6]

Holliday's career as an entertainer began during the Popular Front period of the late 1930s, developing through World War II and into the late 1940s. As Michael Denning has argued, the interactions in these years, between the new social movements associated with labor and the CIO, civil rights, and antifascism, and the emergence of the new culture industries of radio and film, provided unprecedented opportunities for left-wingers to be involved in American cultural productions attracting a popular audience, and indeed Popular Front spaces nurtured Holliday's own performing career. Holliday secured her first job in the theater, as a switchboard operator for Orson Welles's Mercury Theater Company in 1938, after graduating first in her class from Julia Richmond High School. At the same time, she began to write original material to perform with friends and aspiring entertainers Adolph Green and Betty Comden; they formed part of a troupe, eventually to call themselves the Revuers. Their original humor and songs, parodying Hollywood and Broadway, radio and advertising, also played off news headlines. They critiqued European fascism and opponents of the New Deal and of the left, such as newspaper publisher W. R. Hearst and Congressman Martin Dies. They drew on the format of the European cabaret and on the topical musical revue style popular in Yiddish Catskill resorts, in labor movement summer camps, and in the ILGWU-sponsored hit *Pins and Needles*, which played on Broadway from November 1937 to 1940. When Holliday first proposed that her troupe perform at Max Gordon's Village Vanguard, then a meeting place for bohemian poets, Gordon recognized her promise of "skits and songs of satire and social significance" as part of what he had just enjoyed seeing in *Pins and Needles*.[7]

Word of mouth and enthusiastic press built up a loyal audience for the Revuers' song parodies and skits, both in New York and beyond. In addition to appearing at the Village Vanguard in 1939 and in 1941, the troupe performed at many venues in Manhattan, including the upscale Rainbow Room at Rockefeller Center in the fall of 1939, at the 1939 and 1940 World's Fair, on their own show on NBC radio from March to November 1940, on an experimental television broadcast in 1940 and 1941, at Radio City Music Hall in 1941, and at Barney Josephson's left-wing Café Society Uptown and Downtown in 1942 and 1943. In the summer of 1943, they toured nightclubs outside New York as far away as in the Midwest and Canada, and they played at Popular Front benefits. In these years, Holliday's social world included people associated with the Popular Front left, such as Leonard Bernstein, John Houseman, and Nicholas Ray. She had an important relationship with a left-wing Jewish woman, Yetta Cohen, with whom she lived in the Village in the early 1940s and remained close for the rest of her life. The Revuers moved to Hollywood in September 1943 on the promise of a film with Twentieth Century–Fox and a long-term contract for Judy Tuvim, now officially renamed Holliday by the studio, but their performance scene ended on the cutting-room floor. When the Revuers split up, Comden and Green collaborated with their friend Leonard Bernstein; together, they wrote the hit 1944 musical *On the Town*, in which Comden and Green also performed. Holliday had small parts in two unimportant films, and when the studio let her option lapse in December 1944, she returned to New York.[8]

After a small but prize-winning supporting part in her Broadway debut in 1945, Holliday's big breakthrough came in 1946 in *Born Yesterday*, a first play written and directed by Garson Kanin, who also came from a left-wing Jewish family, and also was part of the Popular Front left. *Born Yesterday*'s political satire proved a surprise hit for Kanin, who had began his career on the New York stage as an actor and director and had worked steadily in Hollywood in the late 1930s with the left-wing writers and directors Dalton Trumbo, Paul Jarrico, and Herbert Biberman. After serving in an army film unit during the war, Kanin lent his support to the Civil Rights Congress and the Henry Wallace campaign; then he wrote the part of Billie Dawn, the streetwise and brazen "dumb blonde" mistress of a crooked junk dealer, for Jean Arthur—a part based, he commented retrospectively, "on a stripper [I] once knew who read Karl Marx between shows."[9]

Holliday took over the part at the last minute and developed the "dumb blonde" characterization of Billie Dawn's chorus girl into a smart and spirited working-girl citizen. She invented a distinctive talk and walk for Billie Dawn that audiences adored, and that was identified with Holliday for the rest of her life. According to Kanin's retrospective account, the play's producer resisted casting Holliday, that "fat Jewish girl from the Revuers," citing Richard Rodgers's pronouncement at an audition that "this show is *by* Jews and *for* Jews but it can't be *with* Jews." Reportedly, Kanin defended Holliday by calling her "not so fat" and "not so Jewish. But she's funny and a hell of a good actress." *Born Yesterday*'s exposé of Washington, D.C.'s postwar return to "politics as usual" centered around Holliday's character, representing the hopeful promise of the postwar social contract. The play, set in 1945, inscribed Billie Dawn's political awakening with Popular Front references: she allies herself with the woman hotel cleaner who measures the price of a hotel room against her weekly earnings, and she learns to invoke Tom Paine and the Bill of Rights from the young *New Republic* writer who has become her teacher. The play refers to New Deal standard-bearer Henry Wallace and jabs at the rhetoric of "free enterprise" used by conservatives to oppose the social safety net protections of the New Deal.[10]

When *Born Yesterday* opened in February 1946, audiences loved the play's humor and warmly responded to its political sensibilities. They especially delighted in Holliday's stunning performance, which *New York Times* theater critic Brooks Atkinson would later describe as "the spectacle of her character in development out of cold brassiness into human enthusiasm and revolt." A critic at the Philadelphia opening depicted the audience euphoria: "After the final curtain came hand-clapping (mere clapping couldn't raise that din), whistles, and even cheers . . . the crowd didn't want to leave. Utter strangers nodded beamingly to each other. They had to put out the lights to get them into the streets." As the crowds kept coming, reviewers widely credited Holliday as key to the play's success. Atkinson wrote that the central point of the comedy, Billie Dawn's transformation "into a human being aroused by a new interest in the life of other people," was "conveyed by Holliday's acting as vividly as by the script Mr. Kanin has written." Holliday performed the part of Billie Dawn for the next three-and-a-half years, dazzling the sold-out crowds who flocked to see her perform, nightly, from February 1946 through May 1949. When she left the play in 1949, audiences dwindled. In January 1948, she married a musician, David Oppenheim, whom she had met through Leonard Bernstein. In the years of her *Born Yesterday* celebrity, Holliday campaigned for Henry Wallace, protested the blacklist in radio and film, supported the Hollywood Ten, and lent her name as a sponsor of the World Peace Conference held in New York City in the spring of 1949. Later that fall, she would publicly protest the attack, in August 1949, on Paul Robeson's Peekskill performance.[11]

Born Yesterday's remarkable box office success led to a lucrative film deal for Kanin. Harry Cohn and Columbia Pictures paid a million dollars for the screen rights, top money in 1947 for a stage play. Kanin wanted Holliday to reprise her star turn as Billie Dawn in the movie version, but she did not fit the usual Hollywood categories for women actresses: wholesome girl next door, femme fatale, long-legged dancer, or glamour queen. Her speech associated her with New York Jewish ethnicity, but within studio system representational practices, only comics and supporting players could be marked as Jewish. Like the play's producer, Harry Cohn resisted casting Holliday as Billie Dawn, publicly referring to her as "that fat Jewish broad" and circulating names of Columbia contract players, such as Rita Hayworth or Lucille Ball, instead.

It took two years for Columbia to cast Judy Holliday as the "Brooklyn Galatea" character that she had created on Broadway. Hollywood insider accounts credit Holliday's eventual casting to Garson Kanin and his wife—the actress Ruth Gordon, also part of the theatrical left—who schemed with their friend and fellow progressive Katherine Hepburn to showcase Holliday in their 1949 film *Adam's Rib*. Holliday filmed the New York scenes while continuing to play Billie Dawn on stage, then left *Born Yesterday* to finish filming *Adam's Rib* in Hollywood at the end of May 1949. In the latter film, Holliday's character, Doris Attinger, picked up a gun and shot at her cheating husband and his mistress, motivating the defense of women's equal rights by her lawyer, Katherine Hepburn's Amanda Bonner. Holliday's small but memorable part as the wronged housewife on trial for murder provided her with a kind of public screen test for Columbia: Gordon, Kanin, and Hepburn orchestrated a publicity campaign that circulated the claims that Holliday "stole" the picture, and, after Holliday was announced a runner-up for the New York Film Critics Award for her performance in *Adam's Rib*, Columbia cast her to play Billie Dawn on screen.

However, this "Hollywood insider" account elides attention to Holliday's star-power bargaining, with which she resisted ceding control over her career to the studio via the usual unfavorable long-term contract asked by Columbia. The contract that Holliday signed in January 1950 for *Born Yesterday* required her only to do one film a year for seven years, enabling her to continue living in New York and working in theater, along with the additional unusual contractual concession of complete autonomy to appear on radio and television. Publicity pieces, including those by nationally syndicated Hollywood columnists Louella Parsons and Hedda Hopper, revealed Holliday's aspirations to be a star on her own terms without "going Hollywood," emphasizing her preference for living and working in New York and her resistance of film pressures to constantly diet, to dress as a star, and to aspire to a Hollywood social life.[12]

George Cukor, director of *Adam's Rib*, also directed the film version of *Born Yesterday*. Cukor had been working in Hollywood since 1930, and his circle included many people active in the Hollywood left, although he saw himself as less politically engaged than many of his friends. Working with Kanin and Gordon reoriented Cukor's filmmaking away from Hollywood theatricality and artifice toward postwar styles of social realism, including filming on location in ordinary public spaces and experimenting with camera subjectivity.[13]

Although the film version of *Born Yesterday* removed most of the political references that had identified the play, Holliday's performance of a "dumb blonde who gets smart" circulated her distinctive version of a working-girl heroine even more widely, to highly enthusiastic audiences who made the film, like the play, a tremendous hit. A former chorus girl who had achieved a speaking part, the daughter of a worker for the gas company with modest aspirations for honest work and a hot lunch, Holliday's Billie Dawn is savvy and sexually forthright even before she puts on her glasses, studies the dictionary, rejects her mobster former boyfriend as a "fascist," and exposes his corruption scheme as a cartel. As the filming began and Holliday was interviewed by the local Hollywood press, she praised Billie Dawn as "complex . . . in almost every performance I find new

and fascinating facets of the dumb gal who actually is one of the smartest women
I've ever known." Many of the reviewers recognized and applauded the message
of the film's political satire, "the thought that the 'little people' will eventually
fight back and topple tyrants, and that education is the levering power," and
almost all credited Holliday's performance as key to the film's success. "'Born
Yesterday' is all Judy Holliday," wrote the trade newspaper *Hollywood Reporter*;
Life Magazine gushed that "the whole picture is Judy's"; the *Los Angeles Examiner*
exclaimed that "Judy Holliday is Born a Star in this Satirical and Highly Amusing
Comedy."[14]

By the time of the film's release, in December 1950, anticommunist activists
had begun to aggressively challenge the wartime's progressive left, although it
was not yet clear how much clout they could muster and whether they could dis-
lodge the Popular Front's widespread and far-flung cultural presence. The serious consequences of red-baiting were becoming, however, increasingly apparent
throughout 1950, beginning with the perjury conviction for New Dealer Alger
Hiss, the wide publicity for Senator Joe McCarthy's February 1950 charges about
communists in the State Department, the government's successful prosecution
of the Rosenbergs as atomic spies, the failure of the appeals efforts for the
Hollywood Ten's jail sentences for challenging the 1947 House Un-American
Activities Committee (HUAC) investigation, and especially the outbreak of the
Korean War. Judy Holliday, Garson Kanin, and Ruth Gordon were among the 151
writers, directors, and actors listed in *Red Channels: The Report of Communist
Influence in Radio and Television*, a volume released by three former FBI agents
that then served as a reference tool for blacklisting within radio and television
broadcasting. The anticommunist blacklisters fumed at the star power of Popular
Front celebrities, their popular appeal, and their potentially unlimited impact to
ever-larger audiences via appearances on radio and television. With their primary
employment in the theater, Kanin and Gordon felt less vulnerable to blacklisting,
but Holliday had more to fear over its potential impact.

Although *Born Yesterday* found itself the subject of an attack by conservative
Catholic William H. Moorling, its Popular Front political satire expressed a still
recognizable popular democratic sensibility, and the film community rallied
around it. Moorling, a film reviewer syndicated in the Catholic diocesan press,
singled out Kanin's support of Wallace in 1948 and his active defense of the
Hollywood Ten to discredit him, and turned against the Popular Front framework of the play. Moorling called it "the most diabolically clever political satire I
have encountered in almost 30 years of steady film reviewing," and identified the
William Holden's writer character as "making arguments for all the world as if
he'd freshly graduated 'summa cum laude' from the University of Karl Marx."[15]
But, at this moment, the film community closed ranks in support of Kanin's highly
praised comedy. Louella Parsons asserted in her column for the anticommunist
Hearst-owned *Los Angeles Examiner* that, "if there are any pink ideas infiltrated

into *Born Yesterday*, they are way over my head." The Motion Picture Association of America (MPAA), the industry lobby, sent out a wire to all the Catholic papers where Moorling's article appeared, challenging Moorling's review, arguing that "the picture gives warmth and positive support to the democratic ideals, principles, and institutions of America." The editorial in *Motion Picture Herald*, edited by Martin Quigly, the author of the film industry's production code and arguably the industry's most important Catholic, defended the picture's "important meaning with respect to . . . honesty, democratic principles, integrity, and good citizenship," although the editorial noted that the "low moral tone" and some of the "baldest and bawdiest dialogue sequences" could have benefited from its preferred mode of "moral remonstrances."[16]

Escalating publicity for Holliday led to increased attacks. Holliday's acclaim for her performance as a comedienne and romantic lead in this film initially resulted in radio appearances and awards nominations, including an Academy Award nomination. In late March 1951, however, HUAC began a new round of hearings on the entertainment industry, and groups of picketers from the Catholic War Veterans set out to discourage people from attending the film, at two movie theaters in New York and New Jersey, with signs that attacked Holliday and Kanin as "Reds." Still, as *Variety* noted, "some patrons thought the [picket] line was a publicity stunt and the box office returns were higher than on previous Saturdays." Just a few days later, Holliday won 1950's Oscar for Best Actress. Shortly after that, she headlined a list of stars accused by HUAC of having links to "Red Groups." Columbia stood by its new star, hiring Kenneth Bierly, a former FBI agent and *Counterattack* researcher, to analyze the evidence against Holliday, in an effort to help her clear her name. Holliday attempted to save her ability to work as an actress without compromising her political convictions, producing a statement in June 1951 in which she invoked antifascism while also making the requisite nod to anticommunism.[17]

Holliday hoped to use her new movie celebrity status to challenge Hollywood norms for female stars, and to expand her dramatic range beyond what she had conveyed as Billie Dawn. In interviews before she won the Oscar, she defended the "feminine figure" and the sex appeal of actresses with curves, and rejected the dieting and bleaching regime required by the studios and television cameras. Although she praised Billie Dawn as "honest and brave and nobody's fool," she hoped for a part where "I can use my own hair, my own voice, and maybe even be literate."[18] Kanin and Gordon wrote her next Columbia-contracted film, *The Marrying Kind*, with such aspirations in mind. A drama of class-inflected and sex-conflicted modern marriage, *The Marrying Kind* paid unusual attention to female as well as male subjectivity and challenged the conventions of Hollywood romantic comedy. Kanin wrote to Cukor differentiating the film from his previous style of polished comedy, saying the new film's "aim is realism, its tone is documentary rather than arty, its medium is photography rather

Figure 9.1 Judy Holliday and Aldo Ray in *The Marrying Kind*.
Courtesy of the Academy of Motion Picture Arts and Sciences.

than caricature . . . the closest we have ever come to 'holding up the mirror to nature.'"[19] Holliday played the film's working-girl heroine, Florence Keefer, who exhibited no social marks of ethnicity but spoke lines written in syntax suited to her distinctive cadence. Kanin and Holliday used pre-film publicity interviews to try to reorient Billie Dawn's fans. Kanin described the new film as a comedy in "another key"; Holliday more directly argued that "this picture isn't a comedy. Not at all," but a "quiet love story" about a settled married couple.[20]

The Marrying Kind opens in Manhattan's divorce court, and signals its political intentions to explore the social institution of marriage, rather than individual problems, with the wife's answer to the judge's query about the cause of their incompatibility: "Because we're married." The narrative is constructed by the difference between women and men's experience of their courtship and shared married lives, with voice-over narration by both wife and husband that diverges from what we see on screen. The film is consistently sympathetic to both the wife's unfulfilled longing for intimacy and connection and the husband's relentless feelings of strain to achieve beyond his limited income as a machine fixer in the post office. When an accident puts him temporarily out of work, she returns to the job she held before marriage, suggesting that the wife's competence can flourish only when her husband is down, but also that reliance on two wage earners might reduce the pain of his situation by redistributing the pressure to provide. The narrative incidents eloquently critique the marriage ideal characterized by upward mobility, acquisition, a male breadwinner, and a female homemaker. The wife's concerns are as poignantly illuminated as the husband's; her dissatisfactions are as fully a challenge to the success of the marriage as are his. A freak accident leading to a child's death leaves a burden not of blame but of painful loss, which falls heavily on both parents. The film shows the wife claiming the same right to slam out the door during an argument that the husband has previously assumed. Ther final willingness of the two to try again rejects superficial promises of personal transformation, instead proposing the hope of comfort based on potential mutuality and an acceptance of the fragility of marriage.

After Holliday completed filming *The Marrying Kind*, public anticommunist accusations against her continued to appear and work opportunities began to disappear. Winning the Oscar resulted not in offers for lucrative radio and television appearances but rather in a subpoena to appear before Pat McCarren's Senate Internal Security Subcommittee, even though a 1950 FBI investigation had turned up no evidence that Holliday had ever been a member of the Communist Party. NBC cancelled scheduled and contractual radio appearances and dropped a proposal for a network television show. Anticommunists organized against *The Marrying Kind* when it arrived in theaters, and the film community was divided and on the defensive in the face of continued congressional investigation. Catholic War Veterans picketed the New York opening of the film with posters proclaiming "While Our Boys Are Dying in Korea, Judy Holliday Is Defaming Congress," and "Judy Holliday Is the Darling of the *Daily Worker*." A group calling themselves the Wage Earners Committee picketed the opening in Los Angeles, their signs proclaiming "Red Dogs Bark but the Pickets March On."[21]

At her Senate Subcommittee hearings, postponed by studio request until after the film opened, Holliday, who was accompanied by her Columbia-financed counsel, former judge Simon Rifkind, fell back on Billie Dawn's "dumb blonde'" style of confused answers, which distanced her from the Communist Party without incriminating left-wing friends or associates. She did not give the committee the names the members wanted, and she tried as best she could to hold her political ground. "The few things I actually participated in were things I couldn't possibly have thought were subversive," Holliday insisted, while still managing to refer to the Peekskill attacks as "a civic outrage," to attack censorship, and to cite General Douglas MacArthur's signing onto a *New York Times* ad congratulating the Red Army. Still, she felt demeaned and humiliated by having to cover her chosen progressive affiliations as being a "sucker" for the underdogs, and to describe her sophisticated intellectual self as "irresponsible and slightly—more than slightly—stupid." As she reported afterward to her friend, the journalist Heywood Hale Broun, who had helped prepare her on the previous night, "Maybe you're ashamed of me because I played Billie Dawn. Well, I'll tell you something. You think you're going to be brave and noble. Then you walk in there and there are the microphones and all of those senators looking at you—Woodie, it scares the shit out of you. But I'm not ashamed of myself, because I didn't name names. That much I preserved."[22]

Apparently, the picketers did not affect the initial ticket sales for *The Marrying Kind*, but the film enjoyed only modest success and Holliday hardly mentioned it in later accounts of her career. Columbia's promotional materials suggest how a chilling atmosphere encouraged the studio to try to mask the film's social concerns, instead potentially misleading audiences by promising a repeat of *Born Yesterday*'s comedy or a sweet, wedding bells romance. Representations of intelligent independent working women, and the film's implicit working-girl feminism, constituted a red flag for anticommunists. Studio publicity described the film as "hilarious" and recommended publicity stunts and tie-ins featured weddings, cakes, and rings. But when the ads encouraged audiences to look forward to a reprise of Holliday as a dizzy, wise-cracking blonde or a celebration of marital bliss, ticket buyers were likely to be disappointed and upset by the depths of her character. Although reviewers continued to admire Holliday's talents, a number of them, and presumably audiences as well, found the film's efforts to "dissect married life, with its joys and sorrows," too naturalistic, its drama too contentious.[23] After the congressional release of her supposedly private testimony in September 1952, another round of unsettling articles appeared, some portraying her as "duped by Reds" while angry anticommunist columnists accused her "dumb blonde" performance of duping the investigators.[24]

Holliday's efforts to clear herself meant that she could continue to make movies with Columbia according to her contract. She made a few appearances on television, though enhanced enforcement of the blacklist on *Philco-Goodyear Playhouse* meant that its producer, Fred Coe, had to negotiate a special deal to cast Holliday in a dizzy-blonde part written especially for her in the NBC television drama "The Huntress," broadcast in February 1954. Still, the anticommunist picketing, hate mail, furious phone calls, and blacklisting scarred her personally and professionally and silenced her public political voice. She had told the Senate subcommittee that she would be careful not to "side on anything": in her words, "I don't say 'Yes' to anything now except cancer, polio, and cerebral palsy, and things like that." In nationally published interviews after 1952, she spoke as an aspiring working actress, and later as a divorced woman, but she retold the story of her career to emphasize her lucky timing, her comic roles, and her weight problems without revealing the left politics or the Popular Front feminism that created the supportive context for her spirited working-girl persona.[25]

The space created by Popular Front writers for Holliday's specialty of spunky and sexy working girls narrowed, although it did not disappear altogether. Holliday worked with the *Born Yesterday* team one more time, in the 1954 *It Should Happen to You*, written by Kanin and directed by Cukor. In this film,

Holliday plays another savvy and sexy working girl, Gladys Glover, who has left her job in a shoe factory upstate and come to New York City to find work and try to make a name for herself. When she gets fired from her job modeling girdles, she rents a billboard in Columbus Circle, in one last try at making herself known. Traces of Popular Front humor and working-girl feminism are visible here: the film spoofs Madison Avenue promotions, and Holliday's character holds her own against high-powered soap company corporate executives who want that billboard for their own marketing campaign. She maintains her ambitions in the face of disapproval from Jack Lemmon's documentary filmmaker, shows remarkable self-possession in a seduction attempt by the wealthy soap company heir played by Peter Lawford, and ultimately stands up to the radio promoter who merchandises her billboard appeal. The film ends with her abandoning her self-generated stardom for marriage to the filmmaker, but the sight of a blank billboard can still catch her attention.[26] Reviewers praised writer Kanin's satirical take on "advertising endorsement, celebrity-worship, television . . . panel shows," and welcomed the return of Holliday's character with its familiar combination of "confusion and self-delusion . . . gumption and native honesty."[27]

Two of the remaining three films Holliday made for Columbia made no use of her working-girl persona, and, perhaps not coincidentally, achieved less success with critics and ticket buyers. Reviewers continued to admire her acting ability as Nina Tracy, a stylish and successful television soap opera writer, in the 1954 film divorce/remarriage comedy *Phffft*, directed by Mark Robson, and as Emily Rocco, housewife and expectant mother in the 1956 Italian family film *Full of Life*, directed by Richard Quine. Although her *Phffft* costumes recalled her Billie Dawn outfits, Holliday's character had none of the popular appeal of "the poor man's Pygmalion" in writer George Axelrod's comic premise, repeated from his first hit in *The Seven Year Itch*, of "the confusion and embarrassment of two people who think they want to be devils but don't." John Fante's script, based on his novel exploring ethnic cross-generational acceptance, broke Hollywood taboos with its explicit and earthy depiction of pregnancy and of Catholic practice. But Holliday's part as the perpetually hungry and anxious mother-to be, which called for her to develop a newfound passion for cleanliness, to fall through the kitchen floor, and to go through with a Catholic wedding to please her Italian father-in-law, used her provocative talents to support mainstream conforming values, in what one trade reviewer identified as "an ardent tribute to both Motherhood and (as its communicants term it) the Mother Church."[28]

Broadway's relative freedom to resist the political pressures of the blacklist shaped the two parts through which Holliday's working-girl feminist persona persisted into the second half of the 1950s. She portrayed the anticorruption crusader Laura Partridge in *The Solid Gold Cadillac*, a 1953 satire on big business, written by George S. Kaufman and Howard Teichman and rewritten as a 1956 film for Holliday by 1940s left-winger and comic writer Abe Burrows. Holliday also played the telephone-answering-service operator Ella Peterson in *Bells Are Ringing*, a 1956 hit musical written for Holliday by her old friends and fellow Revuers Betty Comden and Adolph Green. Holliday appeared on Broadway in *Bells* for nearly a thousand performances, from 1956 to 1959, and the film version premiered in 1960.

The 1956 film version of *Solid Gold Cadillac*, directed by Richard Quine, reunited Holliday with her Broadway *Born Yesterday* co-star Paul Douglas in a plot which teamed them as opponents of corporate scandals and as romantic partners. Reviewers delighted in the reincarnation of *Born Yesterday*'s key ingredients: the "little people," represented by Holliday's character, standing up against the "vested interests," and the topical satire, noting for instance that "references to Washington, Senatorial investigations, and big-business chicanery have been missing from the movies for so long that even the modest raillery that goes on here seems brash and daring." They cheered Holliday's performance, recognizing Laura Partridge to be a "sister under the skin to Judy's Billie Dawn."[29]

In *Bells Are Ringing*, Holliday played a romantic telephone operator who gets involved in solving the problems of the people whose phones she answers, taking, as one reviewer noted, "her switchboard and humanity seriously." The *New York Times* theater critic Brooks Atkinson noted happily that "nothing had happened to the shrill little moll whom the town loved when Miss Holliday played in 'Born Yesterday,'" and he hailed her *Bells* song and dance routines making fun of advertising and show business pretensions, and celebrating ordinary New Yorkers, as carrying on in the tradition of the Revuers. The film reviewers gave Vincent Minelli's screen adaptation mixed praise, but they unanimously applauded the delights of Holliday's performance, crediting her with carrying the show via what one critic called her signature "mix of innocence and savvy mixed in dry martini proportions."[30]

For those who knew how to read them, Holliday's working-girl characters represented what Holliday herself, silenced by the anticommunist blacklist, could no longer directly articulate. The title role in *Laurette*, a biographical play about the legendary actress Laurette Taylor, represented her final effort to perform a mature, independent, and powerful woman. However she left the show, which closed shortly after, for the hospital in the fall of 1960, when a doctor diagnosed the breast cancer from which she would die a few years later. If New Yorkers read Holliday's obituary in the *Herald Tribune* in 1965, they were reminded of the Popular Front left affiliation that proved so generative for Holliday and her creative circle. The obituary included a pre-blacklist quote that urged artists toward political engagement: "We actors, like most highly specialized professionals, tend to live in a world of our own. . . . Do you become less of an artist because you refuse to accept inflation, war, and lynching? I don't think so. We can't turn to the theater page first."[31] But even if the blacklist diminished Holliday's public political voice during the 1950s, her working-girl depictions on stage and screen maintained a public cultural presence of urban, worldly, sexy, and rebellious female characters to counter that period's more publicized images of middle-class, suburban domesticity.

NOTES

1. On Popular Front feminism, see Michael Denning, *The Cultural Front: The Laboring of American Culture in the Twentieth Century* (London: Verso, 1996), 136–151; David Horowitz, *Betty Friedan and the Making of the Feminine Mystique: The American Left, the Cold War, and Modern Feminism* (Amherst: University of Massachusetts Press, 1998); Kate Weigand, *Red Feminism: American Communism and the Making of Women's Liberation* (Baltimore: Johns Hopkins University Press, 2001); Dorothy Sue Cobble I, *The Other Women's Movement: Workplace Justice and Social Rights in Modern America* (Princeton, NJ: Princeton University Press, 2004).

2. Denning, *The Cultural Front*, 152–159; Paul Buhle and Dave Wagner, *Radical Hollywood* (New York: New Press, 2002); Paul Buhle, *From the Lower East Side to Hollywood: Jews in American Popular Culture* (London: Verso, 2004); Paul Buhle, ed., *Jews and American Popular Culture* (Westport, CT: Praeger, 2007); Frank Krutnik, Steve Neale, Brian Neve, and Peter Stanfield, ed., *"Un-American" Hollywood: Politics and Film in the Blacklist Era* (New Brunswick, NJ: Rutgers University Press, 2007).

3. Judith E. Smith, *Visions of Belonging: Family Stories, Popular Culture, and Postwar Democracy, 1940–1960* (New York: Columbia University Press, 2004), 140–165.

4. Molly Haskell, *From Reverence to Rape: The Treatment of Women in the Movies* (New York: Holt, Rinehart and Winston, 1974); Marjorie Rosen, *Popcorn Venus* (New York: Coward, McCann, and Geoghegan, 1973); Brandon French, *On the Verge of Revolt: Women in American Film of the Fifties* (New York: Frederick Ungar, 1978).

5. Smith, *Visions of Belonging*, 242–280. William Mann, *Kate: The Woman Who Was Hepburn* (New York: Henry Holt, 2006); William Mann, *Behind the Screen: How Gays and Lesbians Shaped Hollywood, 1910–1969* (New York: Viking, 2001), 162–170.

6. On Holliday's family background, see Will Holtzman, *Judy Holliday* (New York: G. P. Putnam, 1982), 25–29; Max Gordon, *Live at the Village Vanguard* (New York: St. Martin's Press, 1980), 34.

7. Gordon, *Live at the Village Vanguard*, 33–34; Whitney Balliett, "Profiles: Night Clubs [Max Gordon and Barney Josephson]," *New Yorker*, October 9, 1971, 60; Lee Israel, "Judy Holliday and the Red-Baiters: An Untold Story," *Ms.*, December 1976. See also Holtzman, *Judy Holliday*; and Gary Carey, *Judy Holliday: An Intimate Life Story* (New York: Seaview Books, 1982).

8. Holliday's testimony to the U.S. Senate Internal Security Subcommittee (SISS) on March 26, 1952, in Subcommittee on Internal Security of the Committee on the Judiciary, *Subversive Infiltration of Radio, Television, and the Entertainment Industry, Part 2: Published Hearings* (Washington, DC: Government Printing Office, 1952); activities of other Revuers on pp. 145, 155, 184. On Yetta Cohen and her importance to Holliday, see Israel, "Judy Holliday and the Red Baiters," and the biographies by Holzman and Carey.

9. "Garson Kanin," in *Current Biography* (1941), 453–454 and (1952 ed.) 294–296; Jerry Tallmer, "Garson and Kate and Spencer," *New York Post*, November 13, 1971; Richard Stayton "There's Nothing Retiring about Kanin," *Los Angeles Herald-Examiner*, June 25, 1988.

10. Garson Kanin, *Hollywood* (1967: rpt. New York: Limelight, 1984), 373; Kanin, *Born Yesterday: A Comedy* (New York: Viking, 1946).

11. Brooks Atkinson, "Acting the Jokes: Essence of Theatre Is in 'Born Yesterday,'" *New York Times*, May 18, 1947, X1. The Philadelphia opening night critic was quoted in a profile of

Holliday, "It's a Living," *Colliers*, June 15, 1946, 84. In the *New York Times*, see Lewis Nichols, "Play in Review," February 5, 1946, 30, and Lewis Nichols, "Broadway Comedy," February 10, 1946, 45. See "list of supposedly subversive organizations, March 30, 1951," in the Judy Holliday clippings file, Margaret Herrick Library of the Academy of Motion Picture Arts and Sciences (MHL, AMPAS); the file on Holliday as part of the *Counterattack* papers at the Tamiment Library, New York University; Holliday's testimony in front of the SISS, March 26, 1952; Ronald D. Cohen, *Rainbow Quest: The Folk Music Revival and American Society, 1940–1970* (Amherst: University of Massachusetts Press, 2002), 50, 68.

12. Edwin Schallert, "Smart Girl Role Sought by Judy Holliday," *Los Angeles Times*, July 3, 1949; Hedda Hopper, "Judy Holliday Had to Be 'Born' 1200 Times to Land Film Role," *Los Angeles Times*, July 3, 1950. See also Kanin, *Hollywood*, 375–376; Irving Drutman, "Came the 'Dawn' for Judy Holliday," *New York Times*, January 22, 1950; and Louella Parsons, "Louella Parsons in Hollywood," *Los Angeles Examiner*, March 5, 1950. Radio and (early) television were important venues for the Revuers in the early 1940s, and Holliday performed in radio dramas in 1945 and 1948, and in a live television drama in 1949: "Judy Holliday's Chronology, 1921–1951, prepared by Glenn McMahon, at www.wtv-zone.com/lumina/judy/chrono1.html, accessed June 11, 2008.

13. Patrick McGilligan, *George Cukor: A Double Life* (New York: St. Martin's, 1990), 194; Ezera Goodman's column, *Los Angeles Daily News*, July 16, 1951.

14. Lowell E. Redelings, "Hollywood Scene: One Minute Interview," *Hollywood Citizen News*, June 6, 1950. The quoted review was from *Cue*, December 30, 1950; other reviews that mention *Born Yesterday*'s "attempt to inject social significance" include *Time*, December 25, 1950 ("Ordinary citizens cannot be pushed around"); *Los Angeles Daily News*, December 26, 1950 ("When the people are educated to the meaning of Democracy they will turn on corruption in government and destroy it"). Reviews of *Born Yesterday* that single out Holliday's performance include: *Hollywood Reporter*, November 17, 1950; *Independent Film Journal* November 18, 1950; *Life Magazine*, December 25, 1950; *Los Angeles Examiner*, December 26, 1950; *Los Angeles Times*, December 26, 1950; *Look*, January 16, 1951.

15. William L. Moorling, "Clever Film Satire Strictly from Marx," *The Tidings*, December 1, 1950.

16. Louella Parsons's comment was quoted in "Catholic Lay Opinions Pile Up in Opposition to Moorling," *Variety* (weekly), December 6, 1950; in Thomas Brady, "Hollywood Checks: 'Born Yesterday' Controversy Sheds Light on Another Delicate Censorship Issue," *New York Times*, December 10, 1950; and in "Mis-Directed Zeal," editorial, *Motion Picture Herald*, December 9, 1950.

17. The other nominees for Best Actress included Bette Davis, Anne Baxter (*All About Eve*), and Gloria Swanson (*Sunset Boulevard*). See "Veterans to Picket 'Born Yesterday,'" *Hollywood Reporter*, March 26, 1951; "Catholic War Vets Picket 'Born' on B'Way; Patrons Deem it Ballyhoo; Biz Up," *Variety* (daily), March 26, 1951; "Two Catholic Vet Groups Picket 'Yesterday' in Rap at Holliday-Kanin," *Variety* (weekly), March 28, 1951. For HUAC headlines, see Thomas J. Foley, "Oscar Winners Judy Holliday and Jose Ferrar Linked to Red Groups: House Probers Name Stars, 47 Others," *New York Times*, April 5, 1951, 1, 4. In October 1951, the American Legion directed its local organizations to publicize entertainment "Reds"; an article naming Holliday as a "Communist sympathizer" appeared in *American Legion Magazine*, December 1951.

18. And see "Judy Holliday: She Wasn't Born Yesterday," *Quick*, February 19, 1951; Judy Holliday, "Women Men Like," *Hollywood Album*, 1951; Helen Markel Herrmann, "Hey-Hey-Day of a 'Dumb' Blonde," *New York Times Magazine*, March 4, 1951, 16, 44; Winthrop Sargeant, "Judy Holliday: 'Born Yesterday's' Not So Dumb Blonde Prefers Slacks to Mink, Likes Proust, Hates Hollywood, Hopes Someday to Play Ophelia," *Life*, April 2, 1951, 107–108, 111–118.

19. Garson Kanin to George Cukor, July 12, 1951, and September 9, 1951; see also Cukor to Kanin and Gordon, July 27, 1951, in *The Marrying Kind* folder, Correspondence with Kanin, George Cukor Collection, MHL, AMPAS.

20. "Marrying Blonde," *New York Times*, April 22, 1951; Howard Thompson, "The Local Scene," *New York Times*, September 25, 1951. New York–based reviewers identified the Keelers as "second generation of various stocks," and Holliday as a "Brooklyn-Bronx-Manhattan type" and as a "Bronx yenta." See Gilbert Seldes, "SR Goes to the Movies," *Saturday Review of Literature*, March 22, 1952, 31; Bosley Crowther, "More on Miss Holliday and 'The Marrying Kind,'" *New York Times*, March 23, 1952; Manny Farber in *The Nation*, April 26, 1952, 410.

21. Holliday's FBI file, "Judy Holliday's Chronology, 1921–1951, at www.wtv-zone.com/lumina/judy/chrono1.html, accessed June 11, 2008. The FBI opened its investigation in June 1950, after Holliday had signed her Columbia contract and shortly before *Red Channels* was published, and concluded by September 1950. "Catholic War Vets Picket 'Kind' in NY," *Variety* (daily), March 17, 1952; "Wage Earners Committee Pickets 'Marrying Kind,'" *Variety* (daily), April 14, 1952. Both articles note that neither Holliday nor Kanin was called before HUAC or named as communists by anyone who testified before HUAC.

22. Holliday testimony to SISS, March 26, 1952, 181, 151, 165, 175; Holzman, *Judy Holliday*, 9–24, 158–168. Holzman referred to the conversation with Broun on p. 24. It was initially quoted by Lee Israel, "Judy Holliday and the Red-Baiters."

23. Pressbook for *The Marrying Kind*, University of California Cinema Television Library; Kay Proctor, "'Marrying' at Three Theaters," *Los Angeles Examiner*, April 12, 1952; John L. Scott, "New Film Blends Comedy and Drama," *Los Angeles Times*, April 12, 1952; "New Films," *Newsweek*, March 24, 1952, 109–110.

24. For an example of the first, see "Judy Holliday Not Red, Just 'More than Slightly Stupid,'" *Los Angeles Daily News*, September 23, 1952; for the latter, see Victor Riesel's column in *Los Angeles Daily News*, October 1, 1953.

25. Judy Holliday, "The Role I Liked Best . . . ," *Saturday Evening Post*, July 26, 1952; Bob Thomas, "Oscar Winner's Life No Cinch, Says Judy," *Mirror*, June 13, 1953; Judy Holliday, "Unless I Watch Out, I'm a Fat Girl," *Los Angeles Examiner: American Weekly*, February 27, 1955; Betty Randolph, "An Intimate talk with Judy Holliday," *TV and Movie Screen*, 1955; Virginia Bird, "Hollywood's Blonde Surprise," *Saturday Evening Post*, December 31, 1955; William Peters, "Judy Holliday," *Redbook*, 1957; all in the Judy Holliday clipping file at MHL, AMPAS. On the difficulties in casting Holliday on Philco-Goodyear, see Delbert Mann interview in Gorham Kindner, *The Live Television Generation of Hollywood Film Directors: Interviews with Screen Directors* (Jefferson, NC: McFarland, 1994), 150–153.

26. Kanin's preferred original ending imagined more collaboration, and less disciplining of Gladys: "Pete and Gladys play a little scene about stopping at a motel overnight and him bringing her breakfast in bed, and so on, with the climax of him pointing off at the sign which read, Mr. and Mrs. Pete Shepperd; sign blown off, under it, the end," in Garson Kanin to George Cukor, June 30, 1953, in Folder 1: Ruth Gordon and Garson Kanin, George Cukor Collection, MHL, AMPAS.

27. Otis Guernsey Jr., "Screen: 'It Should Happen to You,'" *New York Herald Tribune*, January 16, 1954; Bosley Crowther, "The Screen in Review," *New York Times*, January 16, 1954; "The New Pictures," *Time*, January 25, 1954. Other reviews that saw the part as a repeat of Billie Dawn included Lynn Bowers, "New Comedy Delightful," *Los Angeles Examiner*, April 1, 1954, "Movies," *Fortnight*, March 3, 1954, and "SR Goes to the Movies: The Not So Weaker Sex," *Saturday Review*, February 6, 1954, 28, which used the term "sisters under the skin."

28. "Phffft," *Time*, November 15, 1954; Bosley Crowther, "The Screen in Review," *New York Times*, November 11, 1954; "Phffft," *Variety* (daily), October 19, 1954; "New Films," *Newsweek*, November 8, 1954. The review quoted is James Powers, "Kohlmar, Quine Pic

Warm and Amusing," *Hollywood Reporter*, December 19, 1956; see also "Full of Life," *Variety* (daily), December 19, 1956; "Holliday Hit in Repartee," *Los Angeles Times*, December 26, 1956; "Full of Life," *Cue*, February 16, 1957; Bosley Crowther, "Screen: Father-in-Law," *New York Times*, February 13, 1957, 38. See also memos and censorship reports in "Full of Life" folder, Motion Picture Association of America/Production Code Administration (MPAA/PCA) collection, MHL, AMPAS.

29. "Solid Gold Cadillac," in *Variety* (daily), August 15, 1956, and in *Hollywood Reporter*, August 15, 1956; "Solid Gold Judy," *Saturday Review of Literature*, September 29, 1956.

30. Brooks Atkinson, "'Bells Are Ringing' for Judy Holliday," *New York Times*, November 30, 1956, 18; Archer Winston, "Bells Are Ringing," *New York Post*, June 24, 1960. See also reviews in *Variety*, *Hollywood Reporter*, and *Motion Picture Daily*, June 8, 1960; *New York World Telegram and Sun*, *New York Mirror*, and *New York Herald Tribune*, June 24, 1960; and *Los Angeles Mirror-News*, June 30, 1960.

31. M. C. Blackman, "Judy Holliday Dead of Cancer at 41: That Wonderful Dumb Blonde with the 172 IQ," *New York Herald Tribune*, June 8, 1965.

10

The "Gentle Jewish Mother" Who Owned a Luxury Resort

THE PUBLIC IMAGE OF JENNIE
GROSSINGER, 1954–1972

RACHEL KRANSON

After Jennie Grossinger's death in 1972, the *New York Times* characterized her as "the gentle Jewish mother who transformed a modest Catskills family hotel into a luxurious resort." This description echoed the maternal and ethnic imagery that had propelled the hotelier to national fame during the decades after World War II.[1] Throughout her career as the co-owner and spokesperson of Grossinger's Hotel and Country Club, Jennie Grossinger presented herself both as a nurturing mother figure and as the grateful beneficiary of the Jewish immigrant dream. The American public enthusiastically embraced this persona, and Grossinger became a national celebrity whose fame hinged upon her status as both a mother and a Jew. Examining the evolution of Grossinger's public image reveals the constraints that she faced as a Jewish woman in postwar America, as well as the opportunities that this hybrid identity opened up for her.

Grossinger reached the apex of her career in the postwar era, a time of important changes for American women and American Jews. As Betty Friedan pointed out in *The Feminine Mystique* in 1963, American women in the postwar years faced a dominant culture that valorized their roles as homemakers, wives, and mothers and discouraged them from engaging in nondomestic occupations.[2] Yet, even as Friedan condemned these conservative gender ideals, increasing numbers of American women were challenging societal expectations by taking on responsibilities outside the home. In fact, in spite of the broad emphasis on female domesticity, the actual number of employed American women doubled between 1940 and 1960, while the number of working mothers swelled by 400 percent. Increasingly, American women experienced the postwar years not as an era of domestic limitation but as a time of flux, with growing opportunities to engage in wage employment, entrepreneurial endeavors, and other activities outside the home. As a highly visible businesswoman, Jennie Grossinger joined the growing ranks of postwar American women who found ways to defy the conventions of the feminine mystique.[3]

American Jews also experienced the postwar era as a time of crucial change. The postwar years brought rapid, even meteoric, financial mobility to American Jews, and numerous surveys documented their growing affluence. A survey of American college graduates in 1947 revealed that more Jews than non-Jews established careers as professionals, proprietors, managers, and public officials, even though fewer parents of the Jewish students had enjoyed these high-income occupations. And as Jews moved into such middle-class professions, their salaries rose as well. A 1951 study of New York area families, for instance, found that 12 percent of Jewish households in the city reported incomes of more than $10,000, as opposed to 5 percent of the non-Jewish population, with 29 percent of Jewish households earning less than $4,000, in comparison to 49 percent of the non-Jewish population.[4]

The story of American Jews' financial success functioned as a central trope in American culture of the postwar years. The new, middle-class status of American Jews provided the backdrop for such bestselling works of fiction as Herman Wouk's 1955 novel *Marjorie Morningstar* and Philip Roth's 1959 novella *Goodbye, Columbus*. Scholars such as Oscar Handlin celebrated Jewish upward mobility in *Adventure in Freedom*, published in honor of the 1954 tercentennial anniversary of Jewish settlement in America, and in 1963 Nathan Glazer and Daniel Patrick Moynihan extolled Jewish economic success in *Beyond the Melting Pot*.[5] For American Jews, this conspicuous upward mobility served as a point of pride, as well as a source of anxiety for those who feared that newfound Jewish wealth might aggravate anti-Semitic stereotypes of Jewish materialism and vulgarity. During a time when over one third of the American public believed that Jews held "more economic power. . . . than was good for the country," many American Jews were convinced that their striking economic rise could potentially expose them to criticism or attack.[6]

In many ways, Jennie Grossinger's personal history reads as an archetypical example of the Jewish success story that suffused American culture in the postwar era. Born in 1892 in Balingrod, a small village in Galicia, Grossinger immigrated to the United States in 1900. By age thirteen, she illegally left school to work in a Lower East Side sweatshop and contribute financially to her poverty-stricken family. When Grossinger's father fell ill in 1914, the family left the city in search of a healthier environment and purchased a ramshackle farm in the Catskill region of upstate New York. After trying unsuccessfully to earn a living through agriculture, they decided to rent rooms to summertime boarders from the city to boost their income.

The Grossingers flourished in the hospitality business. By 1919, they sold their dilapidated farmhouse and purchased a new building, equipped with electric lights and running water. The hotel grew steadily during the economic boom of the 1920s and continued to prosper even during the lean years of the Depression. By this time, the family had hired publicist Milton Blackstone, who thought to add to the luster of the resort by inviting prizefighters to train on the property. The presence of famous figures succeeded in generating newspaper coverage and guests, and the Grossingers and their publicist carefully cultivated the reputation of the Grossinger Hotel as a favored celebrity haunt. By the end of World War II, the Grossinger Hotel and Country Club had grown into a 1,200-acre resort that boasted its own airfield and federal post office and could accommodate up to 150,000 guests a year. The resort sat at the apex of the hundreds of Jewish-run hotels and bungalow colonies that made up the Catskills vacation region, where thousands of American Jews vacationed during the postwar era. Although ordinary, middle-class Jews made up the majority of the guests, a variety of famous figures, both Jewish and gentile, frequented Grossinger's in these years. The celebrities included former first lady Eleanor Roosevelt, baseball player Jackie Robinson, Israeli statesman Chaim Weitzman, author Herman Wouk, and Dr. Jonas Salk, inventor of the polio vaccine.[7] Eventually, the journalists who had followed the celebrities and athletes to Grossinger's Hotel began to show interest in Jennie Grossinger herself. By the 1950s, she had become one of the celebrities whose presence enhanced the prestige of her hotel.

The newspaper articles, books, and television programs that recounted Jennie Grossinger's rise to fame offered a gendered variant of the typical American Jewish narratives of success that were circulating during the postwar years. Generally, popular accounts of Jews' economic mobility attributed their accomplishments to such factors as hard work, a particularly keen business sense, and a respect for education defined as inherent in Jewish culture. By and large, these Jewish success stories assumed that male protagonists built the prosperous businesses and professional practices that led to their rapid economic rise.[8]

In contrast, the personality profiles of Jennie Grossinger bowed to the ideals of the feminine mystique, crediting her kindness, motherliness, and goodhearted nature as the keys to her achievements. Throughout her career, advertisements, television promotions, and newspaper profiles painted her as a nurturing Jewish mother, emphasizing her domestic qualities over any business savvy. This, in turn, made it possible for Jennie Grossinger and her business exploits to be not merely tolerated, but also celebrated, by the American public. Grossinger's winning combination of domestic virtue and Jewish success protected her from criticisms that could have targeted her both as a working woman during an era of conservative domestic ideals, and, during a time of conspicuous Jewish upward mobility, as a particularly successful American Jew.

In her dress, speech, and manner, Jennie Grossinger embodied a carefully conceived image of a modern and elegant Jewish mother. Not content to look old-fashioned or dowdy, Grossinger eschewed the "kerchief, long coat, dark hose, and high-buttoned shoes" associated with old-world Jewish women. Instead, she dressed in understated, well-tailored clothing that signaled her financial success in a discreet manner. She refused to wear the mink coats, dubbed

We have put into this folder some of the things we think you'd like to know about The "G." One thing we *couldn't* put into it ... that we can't capture in picture or print ... is our desire to leave nothing undone which would help in making our guests happy that they visited with us. This is the concept of hospitality that my husband Harry and I have followed for four decades ... that our children Paul and Elaine have known all their lives. This is what our friends call "*The Grossinger spirit*" ... and *that* makes us proud!

Jennie Grossinger

FOR THE GROSSINGER FAMILY
AND STAFF ...

Grossinger's

ON GROSSINGER LAKE

GROSSINGER, NEW YORK

Figure 10.1 Brochure for the Grossinger's Hotel.
Courtesy of Bunny Grossinger.

"Jewish security blankets" in a mocking 1965 portrayal of her hotel, that had become the much-derided garb of the newly affluent Jewish women in the Catskills. As one journalist remarked, "any suggestion of personal ostentation makes her uncomfortable." Trim and blonde, often dressed in simple, dark-colored dresses with a strand or two of pearls draped around her neck, Jennie Grossinger presented a visual figure of grace and elegance.[9]

Grossinger's unpolished speech, with its liberal sprinkling of Yiddish words, malapropisms, and convoluted grammar, belied her refined mien and reminded listeners of her background as a Jewish immigrant to America. Captivated by the dissonance between her elegant demeanor and her unpretentious conversation, Grossinger's admirers highlighted her distinctive way of talking. When *Time* magazine reported on the marital troubles between singer Eddie Fisher, a former staff member at Grossinger's, and actress Debbie Reynolds, they quoted Jennie's response in dialect: "Two nicer people they don't come. I hope it'll blow over like little grey clouds."[10] As had much of the commentary during her lifetime, Grossinger's obituary tied her Yiddish-inflected speech to her domesticity, mentioning that "although she spoke fluent English, occasionally tangled . . . she sprinkled Yiddishisms in her speech and professed a simplicity that encompassed all the homely virtues. 'I don't know from those hochmas [I do not understand such lofty subjects]' she might say, referring to sophisticated expositions that abounded in casuistry."[11] Jennie Grossinger's skillful combination of refined elegance and unassuming charm created a new image of the Jewish mother.[12]

The American public, even those who had never visited Grossinger's hotel, caught their first glimpse of this modern and elegant Jewish mother in November 1954, when the General Baking Company began to mass-produce Grossinger's Rye and Pumpernickel breads. The company enlisted Jennie Grossinger as the spokesperson for the breads, printing her face on every package of Grossinger's Rye, along with her warm wish of a "hearty appetite." Television and radio commercials, posters, postcards, supermarket displays, and promotional photographs featured images of Jennie affectionately inviting customers to sample Grossinger's Rye. "Try a loaf. I'm sure you'll love it," exhorted one postcard, designed to look like a personal letter from the hotel owner.[13]

This national advertising campaign increased the visibility of both Grossinger's hotel and Grossinger's Rye Bread, and also promoted Jennie Grossinger's reputation as a nurturing figure. In fact, the portrait of Jennie Grossinger pictured on packages of Grossinger's Rye greatly resembled the 1950s incarnation of Betty Crocker, the fictitious icon of domesticity whose visage had graced packages of baking products since the 1920s. Both products featured images of women with neat curls, wide, white collars, and encouraging smiles. Much as Betty Crocker was seen as the motherly persona of cake and cookie mixes, Jennie Grossinger became known in the postwar era as the maternal face of Jewish food.[14]

The new medium of television helped create this widespread recognition. In 1954, an estimated forty million viewers watched the December episode of *This Is Your Life* that looked back on Jennie Grossinger's career. In addition to praising her philanthropic endeavors, the program emphasized her ability to make people of all ethnic, racial, and religious backgrounds feel cared for and comfortable. Baseball player Jackie Robinson, perhaps the most prominent African American figure of the postwar years, endorsed Grossinger's motherly hospitality on the program. "Jennie's always made me and my family feel welcome," Robinson told the host of the show as he put his arm around Grossinger's shoulder. "As a matter of fact, when we go to Grossinger's, it's just like going home. And we are proud to consider her one of our real friends." At a time when many American hotels restricted both Jews and African Americans from their guest lists, Robinson's accolades created a particularly compelling television moment. Robinson's public acknowledgment of his close relationship with Jennie Grossinger reinforced her reputation as a nurturing hostess and also reflected the liberal values of civil rights and racial equality that both Jewish and African American organizations espoused in the decades after World War II. This episode of *This Is Your Life*, which featured other celebrated, non-Jewish admirers of the hotelier, including Catholic priest Father Fred Gehring and James G. McDonald, a former U.S. ambassador to Israel, proved so popular that the station replayed the show in September 1955, again promoting Jennie Grossinger as the consummate icon of gracious American Jewish motherhood.[15]

The Art of Jewish Cooking, a cookbook featuring the recipes of the Grossinger's Hotel, also boosted Jennie Grossinger's fame as a domestic figure, although it ironically misrepresented her actual role in the hotel enterprise. This cookbook enjoyed great success throughout the postwar period. First published by Random House in 1958, it had been released through seven hardcover and eleven paperback printings by 1965.[16] The introduction of the book, attributed to Jennie's son Paul, projected a motherly image of Jennie Grossinger by promoting her mastery of Jewish cuisine. "More than most women, mom had to be a good cook," insisted the introduction, "For if a good cook is the heart of the American home, how much more so is a good cook the heart of the American-plan hotel?"

Although the cookbook emphasized that Jennie Grossinger's cuisine accounted for the success of her hotel, she did not, in fact, cook the meals for the 1,600 people that could be accommodated at any one time at the mammoth resort. As of 1970, 150 kitchen workers toiled in the Grossinger's kitchen preparing food for the guests.[17] Jennie Grossinger's many responsibilities as the public spokesperson for the hotel and its related businesses never included cooking or even supervising the resort's kitchen. In spite of this, *The Art of Jewish Cooking* valorized this hotel owner's domestic tasks, even ones that she did not perform, and deemphasized her accomplishments as an entrepreneur and public figure. It presented Grossinger's Hotel as a larger, idealized version of an American Jewish home, and Jennie Grossinger as the mother of that home.[18]

Scores of publicity photographs followed *The Art of Jewish Cooking* in promoting Jennie Grossinger's culinary skills, despite her lack of experience in the hotel kitchen. One 1958 photograph placed her in that kitchen, proudly presiding over a team of chefs. Another image, printed in her 1970 biography, captured her sitting in front of a table laden with bagels, pancakes, matzah, cheeses, and other American Jewish breakfast foods served at the Grossinger's resort.[19] Journalists followed resort publicity in associating her with cooking skills, mentioning, as did one reporter for the *Boston Herald*, that she "ladled out affection as lavishly as the food at Grossinger's."[20] Jennie Grossinger's image depended on her reputation for feeding and nurturing her guests, though few of them would ever sample an item that she had personally prepared.

As television appearances and best-selling cookbooks catapulted Jennie Grossinger to the status of a celebrity, the brochures and advertisements for

Grossinger's hotel began to capitalize on her fame in order to draw guests. The many charms of the Grossinger's Hotel, insisted one brochure, included "the justly-cherished *Grossinger* spirit of warmth and friendliness, as much a local landmark as the famous smile of the beloved *Jennie*" (emphasis in original).[21] Similarly, a 1967 advertisement attributed Grossinger's genial atmosphere to the owner's influence: "Fifty-three years ago, Jennie Grossinger realized that pleasant people attracted other pleasant people. The hotel has followed that rule ever since. As a result, we have entertained thousands of pleasant families and pleasant single guests for more than half a century."[22] These advertising campaigns emphasized Jennie Grossinger's doting presence as much or more than the abundant food, nightclub acts, and other amenities that the hotel offered. With a figure like Jennie Grossinger presiding over the hotel, Grossinger's could promise not only opulent surroundings but also a friendly, and even familial, social environment.

Grossinger delivered on these guarantees of motherly solicitude through elaborate rituals aimed at making her paying guests feel like valued family members. As resort-goers enjoyed their sumptuous meals in the hotel dining room, she visited each table, chatted with the guests, and took note of any special requests. Her presence in the dining room, insisted *Holiday Magazine*, resembled an "obstacle race of handshaking, smiling, waving, and pauses for conversation."[23] And, even after Grossinger's failing health no longer permitted her to move from table to table, she sat on a high stool at the entrance of the dining room to greet her entering guests.[24] She delivered speeches of welcome when her guests gathered together for High Holiday services or weekend entertainment, prompting one *Commentary* journalist to comment that, "although she addressed several hundred of us on Yom Kippur . . . she was able to project the impression that she saw each of us as a special guest of the Grossinger family, and that it was her pleasure to have us visit her private establishment."[25] Through the doting concern that she lavished upon her guests, Jennie Grossinger played out her image as a motherly hostess.

Grossinger's emphasis on maternal attentiveness followed her clients even after they left the resort premises, a business strategy well suited to an establishment that counted on guests returning year after year. In her name, the hotel sent care packages of pickled lox, cakes, and other resort delicacies to clients in honor of their birthdays, weddings, and other special occasions. Guests serving in the army could expect to receive a nonperishable fruitcake from Grossinger's, as could any engaged couple that met at the hotel. These gifts from "Jennie" helped Grossinger establish her reputation as a hostess who truly cared for her guests, and reminded them of her remarkable hospitality long after they left her hotel.[26]

If Jennie Grossinger's reputation as a kind, motherly hostess drew guests to her resort, her particular background as a Jewish immigrant ensured her status as an iconic figure of the postwar era and a symbol of American Jewish success. Newspaper articles and resort-sponsored books elaborated on her rise from humble sweatshop worker to resort owner. Reporters like Quentin Reynolds, who was working on a biography of Grossinger before his death in 1965, delighted in comparing the "shabby and ramshackle" farmhouse that housed Grossinger's first boarders in 1914 to the resort's opulent luxury during the postwar era.[27] The conditions endured by the resort's first guests could only be described as "primitive," added Morris Freedman of *Commentary*, with "light being provided by kerosene lamps, ablutions taking place in a nearby lake, the guests providing their own entertainment and occasionally making their own bed."[28] *Holiday* quoted Jennie Grossinger's recollection that the $81 her family earned in the first week that the boarding house opened represented "more money than we'd ever dreamed of."[29] Throughout the postwar years, journalists recounted Grossinger's modest beginnings and eventual triumph, citing her personal history as one particularly spectacular example of a fulfilled American dream.

Resort publicity also celebrated Jennie Grossinger's success, maintaining that she had learned important and valuable lessons from her lowly, immigrant beginnings. A 1970 biography, penned by a member of the resort's publicity staff, claimed that the years Grossinger endured as a Lower East Side factory worker compelled her to treat her employees in a maternal and protective manner. According to the biographer, a factory foreman had once berated Jennie in front of her coworkers for missing a day of work. After being so humiliated, she swore that if she ever became an employer, she would never publicly reprimand an employee. "It was a promise she was not to forget," insisted her biographer, "a forerunner of the strongly maternalistic attitudes she would develop towards her employees in years to come. The ruthlessness that often underscored the fanatical hard work of many rising immigrant businessmen was always unknown to her." According to her biographer, Grossinger's "softness," instead of being a sign of weakness, proved an "important asset" in the hospitality business.[30] In this way, Grossinger's biography offered an important twist on the typical story of immigrant success. Unlike the immigrant tales of Jewish men, which attributed their success to determination, hard work, or "ruthlessness," Jennie Grossinger's biography credited her motherly kindness and decency for her triumph in America.[31]

Resort materials also highlighted Grossinger's immigrant past to protect her, and her hotel, from criticism. Henry Taub's *Waldorf-in-the-Catskills*, a resort-sponsored history of the hotel, used the owner's background as a garment worker to justify her hotel's labor practices. Grossinger's Hotel, like most resorts of the Catskills, did not employ union labor and repeatedly resisted attempts to unionize resort staff. This position could potentially have alienated resort guests. Many American Jews, particularly New Yorkers, supported unions; indeed, earlier in the century, the city's labor movement had been dominated by Jews, and that legacy persisted even as Jews moved out of the working class. Grossinger herself, recounted Taub, had been a union member when she worked as a button-maker

in a Lower East Side sweatshop. Her current horror at the thought of unionization at her own hotel, explained *Waldorf in the Catskills*, derived specifically from
her own experiences as an exploited worker: she could not accept that her own
caring, maternal relationship with her staff could be likened in any way to what
she had suffered in the sweatshops. "What she remembered about the unions,"
wrote Taub, "was that they were spokesmen for frightened people who resented
and feared their bosses. That any of her people could feel that way about her was
a thought to give her palpitations." Jennie Grossinger, according to *Waldorf-in-the-
Catskills*, cared too much about the members of her staff to enter into an imper-
sonal union contract with them. "If they had to deal with grievance committees
instead of individual friends," explained Taub, "if they had to treat everybody
alike, like machines, and were unable to give a raise to the man with the new
baby, or a promotion to an unusual talent, then Grossinger's would be just a big
business. Under those conditions, it couldn't be everyone's home, like it is
now."[32] The workers at Grossinger's Hotel would never enjoy union benefits,
but Jennie Grossinger's immigrant experience helped shield her and her business
from censure.

As Catskills hotels developed a reputation for gaudiness and conspicuous
consumption, observers used Jennie Grossinger's history as a motherly, Jewish
immigrant to rationalize the resort culture itself. "By espousing luxury and glut,
the Catskills have invited criticism as vulgar and ostentatious," wrote journalist
and New York University professor David Boroff in a 1965 piece for the *New York
Times*.[33] Boroff argued that Jennie Grossinger's reputation for domestic virtue
and "traditional" Jewish values humanized, perhaps even justified, the opulence
of her hotel. As he compared Grossinger's Hotel to The Concord, another
renowned Jewish-owned resort of the Catskills, Boroff elaborated on the air of
authenticity that Grossinger lent to her own establishment:

> The Concord, in terms of its size and opulence, has indeed pulled away from
> the field. . . . On the other hand, Grossinger's has Jennie Grossinger, daugh-
> ter of the founders of the place (in 1914) and herself a priceless resource. . . . It
> is Jennie Grossinger who has enabled the hotel to maintain a traditional
> Jewish piety and familial flavor despite the inroads of Broadway sophistica-
> tion. Veterans of the resort circuit are likely to describe the Concord as beau-
> tiful but cold, while Grossinger's is *heimish* [homelike].[34]

Boroff invoked Grossinger's image as a pious, Yiddish speaking, Jewish mother
and noted that she mitigated the opulent atmosphere of her hotel by being a living reminder of the humble, immigrant Jewish roots that she and her guests
shared.

Grossinger's well-publicized philanthropic ventures added to her reputation
for kindheartedness and lent her a measure of legitimacy as a public figure. Her list-
ing in the 1966 version of *Who's Who of American Women* noted her involvement

in an array of Jewish, nonsectarian, and even Christian charities, including the National Federation of Jewish Philanthropies, Father Duffy Canteen, City of Hope National Medical Center, the National Foundation for Muscular Dystrophy, and the National Foundation to Combat Blindness.[35] Her image as a charitable figure worked in tandem with her reputation as motherly hostess by testifying, as one reporter put it, to her "warm and generous heart."[36]

Charitable work has long been an acceptable avenue for maternalist women to influence public opinion, and Grossinger enjoyed such opportunities in her role as a philanthropist. As a well-known Jewish celebrity who contributed to Catholic and Protestant charities as well as to Jewish ones, Grossinger participated in a broad, postwar-era movement that emphasized the positive impact of interfaith relationships. During Grossinger's 1954 episode of *This Is Your Life*, for instance, World War II navy chaplain Father Frederic Gehring testified to her generosity, claiming that "Jennie Grossinger, of the Jewish faith, is one of the finest Christians I know." Even her philanthropy in Israel took on an ecumenical tone on that program, when the U.S. diplomat to Israel, James MacDonald, praised her for sponsoring a convalescent home overlooking the Sea of Galilee "where Jesus once walked."[37] Grossinger's 1970 biography also emphasized her relationships with non-Jewish religious leaders. It opened with an anecdote describing Francis Cardinal Spellman's special trip to visit Grossinger, after a surprise visit from New York's governor Nelson Rockefeller prevented her from attending Spellman's speech at a local church.[38] As a Jew who also embodied the idealized virtues of the feminine mystique, Jennie Grossinger showed how American Jewish success might benefit Americans of all faiths. She presented a kind, generous, and motherly vision of Jewish affluence that the American public found safe and unthreatening.

Within the Jewish milieu, leaders who might otherwise have considered Jennie Grossinger and her hotel to be embarrassing symbols of alleged American Jewish frivolity felt compelled to take Jennie Grossinger seriously as a public figure, in part because of her many contributions to Jewish causes. In 1960, for instance, Israeli statesman Abba Eben delivered a speech thanking Grossinger for donating a library to the Weizman Institute of Science in Israel. Eben offered a somewhat reluctant tribute to her hotel, stating that "Certainly nobody who visits that place, whatever doubts he may have about the future of American Jewry, can have any hesitation in reaching a verdict concerning its pulsating vitality." Eben considered the most positive aspect of Grossinger's Hotel to be the Zionist sympathies widely held by its guests. "Anybody who finds themselves there, invariably is surrounded by great waves of sympathy and emotion and pride revolving about the saga of Israel's resurgence," he said. He attributed this pro-Israel sentiment to the work of Jennie Grossinger, and praised her as "an authentic benefactor."[39]

Other Jewish leaders, more optimistic about the prospects for Jewish culture in America, also commended her. Rabbi Judah Naditch of New York's Park Avenue Synagogue thanked her for turning the Grossinger Hotel into an "extraordinary institution in American Jewish life." Similarly, at a 1954 testimonial dinner in her honor, during the year that marked the three hundredth anniversary of the Jewish presence in America, Meyer Pesin from the Jewish National Fund painted Grossinger as one of the great Jewish figures contributing to American culture. "It is altogether fitting that this celebration is being held during the year of the Tercentenary of American Jewry," declared Pesin; "The name of Jennie Grossinger, for her contributions to the welfare of America, may well take its proper niche in the bright galaxy of Americans of her faith who have in these three hundred years done so much to aid the building of the great institutions and traditions that are America."[40]

But if Jennie Grossinger's reputation as a generous Jewish mother protected her and her hotel from critique, it also led to the popular assumption that she lacked talent as a businesswoman. Newspaper articles and promotional materials implied that Jennie Grossinger catered to her guests out of instinctual, familial duty. Many either obscured or downplayed her skills as a businesswoman by attributing her success to natural friendliness rather than to her years of experience in the hospitality industry. A 1960 profile of Grossinger in *Newark Evening News* declared that her most "vital success quality" derived from her "gift for gladness."[41] Similarly, *Holiday* reported that Jennie Grossinger "fidgets" during meetings of the planning board "if business seems to be cutting into time she has allowed herself for a trip to the nursery camp." *Holiday*'s description of Grossinger, meant as high praise, portrayed a motherly figure whose interest in business could barely compete with her greater passion for children.[42] Even *National Business Woman*, a magazine aimed at celebrating women's entrepreneurial accomplishments, belittled her skills, writing that "Mrs. G's main contribution to the success of the hotel is not her fantastic store of business knowledge, but her own personality. A long time ago she was aware that she would have to rely on others to handle business details."[43]

Other characterizations of Jennie Grossinger minimized her contribution, crediting her husband Harry's keen business sense for its success. In fact, Jennie Grossinger partnered with Harry in running the resort. She took the lead role in public relations, which ensured that Grossinger's would continue to attract clients, while Harry spearheaded the maintenance, ordering, and other behind-the-scenes responsibilities. Although the contributions of both Grossingers proved indispensable to the hotel's profitability, Harry Grossinger's 1964 obituary in the *New York Times* relegated Jennie Grossinger's role to that of a figurehead: "In the public eye, Mr. Grossinger was obscured by his wife, Jennie. . . . But intimates said it was Mr. Grossinger who actually ran the hotel."[44] And Jennie Grossinger's biographer went so far as to assert that while she functioned as the "symbol" of the resort and its "grand lady," her husband Harry eclipsed her as "the center of power."[45] Reflecting the era's gender conventions, these writers downplayed Jennie Grossinger's crucial skills as the spokesperson of a major resort enterprise.

Other descriptions of Jennie Grossinger acknowledged her business savvy, but portrayed them as secondary or even trivial in comparison to her motherliness, kindness, and friendliness. *Commentary* writer Morris Freedman described her "embracing, glowing femininity that covered over and made unimportant her obviously sharp business sense."[46] Similarly, when the college sorority Phi Sigma Sigma honored Grossinger as their National Patroness in 1960, they praised her as a person "whose greatness of heart has made her revered, whose personal charm and beauty have made her adored, whose astuteness and business acumen have made her admired and respected." The sorority reporter acknowledged Grossinger's expertise in business, but mentioned her heart, charm, and beauty as her primary attributes.[47] Such portrayals of Grossinger, which either denied or mitigated her professional abilities, neutralized the contradictions that some might have perceived between her image as a kindly mother figure and her actual formidable success in business.

Resort materials also publicized Grossinger's supposed naïveté, adding to her image as a kindly mother figure whose success stemmed from her innocent goodheartedness instead of her business acumen. *Waldorf-in-the-Catskills*, for instance, described her listening to golfer Ross Sobel tell an obviously fabricated story about teaching an Indian maharajah how to play golf while they both rode on elephants; according to the publication, "the tale was made more delightful for everyone by Jennie's inability to distinguish between fact and a clubhouse story. Heedless of the laughter around her, she went on questioning Sobel about his fictitious job, while he kept inventing more details." She then offered the storyteller a position as the resort's golf instructor, because she felt that "a man who has all the patience you showed with that Maharajah would be just the right one" to teach her guests how to play—and subsequently, the anecdote concluded, Sobel's great success as Grossinger's golf instructor attracted guests and enhanced the resort's prestige. This story attributed Grossinger's skillful decision to hire a golf instructor to her kindhearted gullibility rather than to her sharp sense of what would appeal to her guests.[48]

Some people who knew and worked with Jennie Grossinger have offered a view of the hotelier very different from the maternal image that appeared in newspapers, television, and resort materials. For Tania Grossinger, a cousin of Jennie whose mother worked at the hotel, Jennie Grossinger's kindly and motherly attitude came across as affected and contrived. In a 1975 memoir, Tania mocked the hotelier's fawning manner with her guests, particularly her tendency to thank them "from the bottom of her heart"; "'Thank you from the bottom of my heart' has become a cliché that to this day will bring a full-fledged laugh, if not a guffaw, from any ex-staffer and most ex-guests of the fifties," insisted Tania, who had heard the phrase so many times that it ceased to be meaningful. Although Tania grew up at the hotel, she said, Jennie Grossinger did not pay her much attention, as she was a distant cousin and not a close member of the owning family. Consequently, she believed that the care that Jennie lavished on the guests amounted to insincere posturing.[49]

Similarly, Ann Landau, whose husband Rabbi Abraham Landau worked as a ritual slaughterer and religious functionary at Grossinger's Hotel, called Jennie a "tough, strong, lady . . . not the sweet little hostess everyone thought she was." The Landaus, who spent every Sabbath and Jewish holiday at Grossinger's from 1947 until the resort closed in 1986, respected Jennie Grossinger's skills as a hostess but certainly did not regard her as a mother figure. Although the Landaus ate in the same dining room as the paying guests, Jennie Grossinger's ubiquitous presence there made them feel uncomfortable rather than welcomed. Whereas the guests looked forward to an affectionate greeting from the hotelier as they entered the room, the Landau family filed past her as quickly as they could, without stopping to wish her a pleasant Sabbath or a happy holiday. "She would never have said anything bad to us if we had stopped to talk to her," recalled Ann and Abraham's daughter, "but she made it clear that she wouldn't have liked it." From the Landaus' perspective, Jennie Grossinger proved an intimidating employer, and a far cry from the gentle Jewish mother encountered by journalists and guests.[50]

Even grandson Richard Grossinger, who shared a warm relationship with his grandmother Jennie, did not take her image as the consummate Jewish mother at face value. In his own memoir of growing up within the Grossinger milieu, he contended that his grandmother cultivated her public persona and performed it perfectly: "She invented Jennie Grossinger and became her. Perhaps she was no more than a clever business woman, but she *seemed* to be Eleanor Roosevelt and Molly Picon."[51]

These alternative views of Jennie Grossinger as a pretentious socialite, an intimidating employer, and a brilliant performer provide an important counterpoint to the maternal image that circulated throughout the postwar years. Not everyone who encountered Jennie Grossinger viewed her as a "gentle Jewish mother" whose success derived from her innate kindness rather than from her experience and skill. These candid characterizations, though not intended to be complimentary, paint a more complicated and less saccharine portrait. They hint at a woman who had more control and self-consciousness over her role as a hostess and public figure than the postwar publicity materials projected.

During the postwar years, Jennie Grossinger's image emphasized her motherly qualities while also camouflaging her resounding success as the public face of a large business concern. This strategy paved a path for her to become a renowned entrepreneurial figure in an era that celebrated domestic virtue, and contributed to the growth of her hotel and its related businesses. Grossinger used the trappings of the feminine mystique to achieve successes that challenged, however obliquely, the power of that ideology.

Grossinger's motherly persona also had important implications for her as a prominent Jewish figure. Although the rapid economic success of American Jews became the stuff of legend in postwar popular culture, it also created an under-current of anxiety among American Jews. Many feared that their conspicuous, newfound affluence would aggravate anti-Semitic stereotypes of Jewish materi-alism and would jeopardize the growing acceptance enjoyed by American Jews in the postwar years.[52] As a successful Jew who also happened to be a woman, Grossinger could temper her possibly threatening image by promoting herself as a nurturing mother. By adopting the maternal qualities revered by Americans at large, Grossinger domesticated the public conception of Jewish achievement. In her capacity as a celebrated icon of the postwar period, she projected a safe, unthreatening, even beloved image of Jewish success in America.

ACKNOWLEDGMENTS
I would like to thank Hasia Diner, as well as the members of the History of Women and Gender workshop at New York University, for insightful comments on this piece. I would also like the thank the Jewish Women's Archive for awarding me a research fellowship that led to the development of this chapter, Phil Brown for sharing his unparalleled knowledge of the Catskills, Jesse Aaron Cohen at YIVO for patiently guiding me through Jennie Grossinger's papers, and Tracy Figueroa for allowing me access to the cache of Grossinger ephemera held at the Bronfman Center for Jewish Life at New York University.

NOTES
1. Richard F. Shepard, "Jennie Grossinger Dies at Resort Home," *New York Times*, November 21, 1972, NJ89.

2. Betty Friedan, *The Feminine Mystique* (New York: Norton, 1963). Other historical works that focus on the impact of this domestic ideology include Elaine Tyler May, *Homeward Bound: American Families in the Cold War Era* (New York: Basic Books, 1988); Wini Breines, *Young, White and Miserable: Growing Up Female in the Fifties* (Boston: Beacon Press, 1992); Benita Eisler, *Private Lives: Men and Women of the 1950s* (New York: Franklin Watts, 1986); Carol A. B. Warren, *Madwives: Schizophrenic Women in the 1950s* (New Brunswick, NJ: Rutgers University Press, 1987); Myra Dinnerstein, *Women between Two Worlds: Midlife Reflections on Work and Family* (Philadelphia: Temple University Press, 1992); Brett Harvey, *The Fifties: A Women's Oral History* (New York: HarperCollins, 1993).

3. William Chafe, *The American Woman: Her Changing Social, Economic, and Political Roles, 1920–1970* (New York: Oxford University Press, 1972), 218. Chafe also notes theat the propor-tion of the employed middle-class women grew from 7 percent in 1950 to 25 percent in 1960, showing that opportunity, rather than economic necessity, sent many of these women into the work force. It is worth noting that Jewish women tended to work outside the home at a lower rate than did other American women in the postwar years. Although 33.9 percent of American women participated in the labor force in 1950, regional studies of Jewish commu-nities demonstrated employment rates ranging from 26 percent to 14 percent for Jewish women. See "Socio-Economic Data: Jewish Population in the United States, 1956," *American Jewish Yearbook* 58 (1957): 70–71.

4. Nathan Glazer, "The Attainment of Middle-Class Rank," in *The Jews: Social Patterns of an American Group*, ed. Marshall Sklare (Glencoe, IL: The Free Press, 1958), 141.

5. Herman Wouk, *Marjorie Morningstar* (Garden City, NY: Doubleday, 1955); Philip Roth, *Goodbye Columbus* (Boston: Houghton Mifflin, 1959); Oscar Handlin, *Adventure in Freedom: Three Hundred Years of Jewish Life in America* (New York: McGraw-Hill, 1954); Nathan Glazer and Daniel Patrick Moynihan, *Beyond the Melting Pot: The Negroes, Puerto Ricans, Jews, Italians, and Irish of New York City* (Cambridge, MA: MIT Press, 1963).

6. As per a 1947 opinion poll from *Fortune*, discussed in William Kephart, "What Is the Position of Jewish Economy in the United States?" *Social Forces* 28 (December 1949): 156, and cited in Lila Corwin Berman, "American Jews and the Ambivalence of Middle-Classness," *American Jewish History* 93, no. 4 (December 2007); I elaborate further on Jewish concerns over upward mobility in my dissertation, "Grappling with the Good Life: Jewish Anxieties over Affluence in Postwar America."

7. Harold Taub, *Waldorf-in-the-Catskills: The Grossinger Legend* (New York: Sterling Publishing, 1952); Joel Pomerantz, *Jennie and the Story of Grossinger's* (New York: Grosset and Dunlap, 1970).

8. See the chapter on Jews in Glazer and Moynihan's *Beyond the Melting Pot* as an example of a study that tried to explain Jewish economic success through some of these factors.

9. Upon seeing a photograph of Grossinger, an audience member at one of my talks commented "The New York Times should have called her a 'gentile' Jewish mother instead of a 'gentle' Jewish mother." Numerous photographs of Jennie Grossinger, as well as of her mother Malka Grossinger, are held in the Grossinger Collection at the YIVO archives, RG1195. The description of old-world Jewish mothers comes from Morris Freedman, "Grossinger's Greener Pastures, Part I," *Commentary* 18, no. 1 (July 1954): 58. The "Jewish security blankets" comment comes from Mordecai Richler, "The Catskills: Land of Milk and Money," *Holiday* 38 (July 1965): 58; I also discuss the way that critics targeted female Catskills guests for showiness, in my dissertation, "Grappling with the Good Life." On Grossinger eschewing personal ostentation, see "She Can't Be Duplicated," *National Business Woman* 45, no. 1 (January 1966): 11; Joyce Antler, *You Never Call, You Never Write: A History of the Jewish Mother* (Oxford, New York: Oxford University Press, 2007), 116–117.

10. "Just Friends," *Time Magazine*, September 22, 1958, 44.

11. Shepard, "Jennie Grossinger Dies at Resort Home." *Hohma*, a Yiddish word meaning wisdom, is used in this sense sarcastically.

12. For a history of how Jewish mothers have been perceived, see Antler, *You Never Call, You Never Write*. For analyses of Jewish mother jokes, see Riv-Ellen Prell, *Fighting to Become Americans* (Boston: Beacon Press, 1999), 142–176; Esther Romeyn and Jack Kugelmass, *Let There Be Laughter: Jewish Humor in America* (Chicago: Spertus Press, 1997), 52–54; Gladys Rothbell, "The Jewish Mother: Social Construction of a Popular Image," in *The Jewish Family: Myths and Reality*, ed. Steven Cohen and Paula Hyman (London: Holmes and Meier Productions, 1986).

13. Letter from Harry E. Adamson, Manager of General Baking Company, Folder 4, Box 1, RG1195, the Grossinger Collection at the YIVO archives (hereafter, RG1195); Letter from J. A. Adamsen of the General Baking Company, Folder 5, Box 1, RG1195; Photograph of a Supermarket Display of Grossinger's Rye, photograph no. 1077, Folder 64, Box 12, RG1195; Advertising Posters for Grossinger's Rye, Folder 14, Box 2, RG1195. Postcard of Grossinger's Rye, from Irwin Richman, *Sullivan County Borscht Belt* (Charleston: Arcadia Press, 2001), 110.

14. Photograph of a Supermarket Display of Grossinger's Rye, RG1195; Advertising Posters for Grossinger's Rye, RG1195; Susan Marks, *Finding Betty Crocker: The Secret Life of America's First Lady of Food* (New York: Simon and Schuster, 2005), photograph of 1955 image of Betty Crocker on p. 227. I first elaborated on the similarities between the images of Grossinger and of Betty Crocker in "Staging the Ideal Jewish Community: Women Hotel Owners in the Catskills," a paper I delivered during the Catskills Institute Conference on August 26, 2005. Citing from that paper, Joyce Antler compared the images of Grossinger and Crocker in *You Never Call, You Never Write*, 119.

15. Producer Ralph Edwards, *This Is Your Life*, December 1954, NBC, Tape no. 30, , RG1195; Letter from Ralph Edwards to Jennie Grossinger, September 7, 1955, Folder 3, Box 1, RG1195. On Grossinger's relationship with Jackie Robinson, see Stefan Kanfer, *A Summer World* (New York: Farrar, Straus, Giroux, 1989), 262–263. On the liberal stances taken by Jewish

organizations in the postwar years, see Marc Dollinger, *Quest for Inclusion: Jews and Liberalism in Modern America* (Princeton, NJ: Princeton University Press, 2000), and Stuart Svonkin, *Jews against Prejudice* (New York: Columbia University Press, 1997).

16. Jennie Grossinger, *The Art of Jewish Cooking* (New York: Random House, 1958). Bantam books began printing paperback editions in 1960.

17. Pomerantz, *Jennie and the Story of Grossinger's*, 286.

18. Grossinger, *The Art of Jewish Cooking*, vii. In Catskills parlance, an "American-plan hotel" referred to an establishment whose rate included three meals a day.

19. Photo of J. Grossinger in the Kitchen, photograph no. 222, RG1195, Folder 28, Box 4, RG1195; Photo of J. Grossinger in Front of a Breakfast Buffet, printed in Pomerantz, *Jennie and the Story of Grossinger's*, photographic insert.

20. Marjorie Mills, "Jennie Grossinger has Love for Fellow Man," *Boston Herald*, May 4, 1961, 26. Clipping found in, Folder 12, Box 2, RG1195.

21. Brochure, "This is Grossinger's," circa late 1950s–early 1960s, Schweitzer Collection, National Museum of American Jewish History.

22. Advertisement for Grossinger's, *Commentary* 44, no. 6 (December 1967): 18.

23. Al Hine, "Grossinger's," *Holiday* 6, no. 2 (August 1949): 105.

24. "She Can't Be Duplicated," *National Business Woman* 45, no. 1 (January 1966): 9.

25. Morris Freedman, "The Green Pastures of Grossingers, Part II," *Commentary* 18, no. 2 (August 1954): 153.

26. Gifts to couples who met at Grossinger's: Letter from Jennie Grossinger to Newlyweds Mr. and Mrs. Wise, November 20, 1954, Folder 2, Box 1, RG1195; Freedman, "The Green Pastures of Grossinger's, Part II," 151. On care packages to soldiers, see Taub, *Waldorf-in-the-Catskills*, 202–203.

27. Quentin Reynolds, "Jennie," *Look*, July 13, 1965, 86–97.

28. Freedman, "Grossinger's Greener Pastures, Part I," *Commentary* 18, no. 1 (July 1954): 58.

29. Hine, "Grossinger's," 100.

30. Pomerantz, *Jennie and the Story of Grossinger's*, 54–55.

31. Abraham Cahan's *The Rise of David Levinsky* (New York: Harper and Brothers, 1917) is arguably the best-known immigrant tale of this genre.

32. Taub, *Waldorf-in-the-Catskills*, 174–180.

33. I discuss criticism of the Catskills in far greater detail in my dissertation, "Grappling with the Good Life."

34. David Boroff, "Don't Call It the Borscht Belt," *New York Times*, May 9, 1965, SM53.

35. "Jennie" Grossinger, *Who's Who of American Women*, 4th ed., 1966–1967 (Chicago: A. N. Marquis, 1965), 462.

36. "Jennie Grossinger Becomes First National Patroness in Moving Ceremony," *The Sphinx of Phi Sigma Sigma* 38, no. 4 (fall 1960), Folder 11, Box 2, RG1195.

37. Producer Ralph Edwards, *This Is Your Life*, RG1195.

38. Pomerantz, *Jennie and the Story of Grossinger's*, 3–11.

39. "Jennie Grossinger—An Authentic Benefactor," Address by Abba Eben, Delivered on July 28, 1960, Folder 61, Box 11, RG1195.

40. Letter from Rabbi Judah Naditch, May 16, 1960, Folder 11, Box 2, RG1195; *The Grossinger News*, no. 23, November 9, 1954, 4, Folder 14, Box 2, RG1195.

41. "Grossinger's Success Saga," *Newark Evening News*, August 24, 1960, clipping found in Folder 2, Box 10, RG1195.

42. Hine, "Grossinger's," 104.

43. "She Can't Be Duplicated," 9.

44. "Harry Grossinger Is Dead at 76," *New York Times*, July 23, 1964, 27.

45. Pomerantz, *Jennie and the Story of Grossinger's*, 248.

46. Freedman, "The Greener Pastures of Grossinger, Part II," 154.

47. "Jennie Grossinger Becomes First National Patroness in Moving Ceremony," 2.

48. Taub, *Waldorf-in-the-Catskills*.

49. Tania Grossinger, *Growing Up at Grossinger's* (New York: Skyhorse Publishing, 2008), 122–123. Originally published by David McKay and Company, 1975.

50. Interview with Ann Landau and her daughter, July 29, 2008.

51. Richard Grossinger, *Out of Babylon: Ghosts of Grossinger's* (Berkeley: Frog, Ltd., 1997), 48–49.

52. I elaborate on this further in "Grappling with the Good Life: Jewish Anxieties over Affluence in Postwar America"; also see Berman, "American Jews and the Ambivalence of Middle-Classness": 409–436.

11 Reading *Marjorie Morningstar* in the Age of the Feminine Mystique and After

BARBARA SICHERMAN

Herman Wouk's *Marjorie Morningstar* appeared, to great fanfare, in September 1955: Book-of-the-Month Club selection, *Reader's Digest* Condensed Book, a *Time* cover story, and an initial print run of 100,000. At over 190,000 copies, it was the best-selling novel of the year and went on to sell more than 1.7 million copies in the next decade; a popular 1958 movie version starred Natalie Wood and Gene Kelly.[1] Wouk's previous novel, *The Caine Mutiny* (1951), had won a Pulitzer Prize and racked up the largest U.S. sales since *Gone With the Wind*, but the popularity of a story with a young Jewish heroine was something of a surprise.[2]

The novel is the coming-of-age story of Marjorie Morgenstern, whose upwardly mobile immigrant parents move from the Bronx to Central Park West as the story begins. It is 1933 and Marjorie is a seventeen-year-old Hunter College student enjoying a grand social whirl, overseen rather ineffectively by her anxious and status-conscious mother. She also aspires to a career in the theater: Morningstar is her stage name. The plot centers on Marjorie's on-again, off-again romance with Noel Airman, a bohemian and renegade Jew (formerly Saul Ehrmann) whom she meets at a Jewish summer resort in the Catskills. He is a songwriter who personifies the sophisticated artistic world she hopes to inhabit. When he finally proposes, five years later, she turns him down and settles for a conventional attorney, orthodoxy, and suburban domesticity.

Marjorie Morningstar was widely reviewed in the general and Jewish press, in the "little magazines" favored by intellectuals, and even in Catholic journals and the recently launched *National Review*.[3] Reviews were mixed, ranging from "singularly undistinguished" (*Binghamton Press*) to "damned nearly the Great American Novel (Urban Division)"—this last from the (London) *Spectator*.[4] More commonly, reviewers praised it as a good yarn; many also noted that it might profitably have been cut.

Marjorie Morningstar's initial success and its continuing cachet with Jewish women provide me with an ideal opportunity to explore responses to a book published in my lifetime, a project that builds on a longstanding interest in women's reading in the late nineteenth century. My work has been influenced both by literary critics who challenged the view that texts have a single and controlling meaning, and by historians who tried to make sense of reading practices in their infinite variety, fluent or halting, oral or silent, solo or communal—and how these practices changed over time.[5] Collectively, this work has demonstrated the significance of social location and historical context not only in *what* books are read, but in *how* they are read and what they mean to the reader—a meaning often quite different from what authors intend or critics allow. The larger point is that texts don't just happen to readers but that readers actively create their own texts.

This essay examines the cultural work of *Marjorie Morningstar*, first, by placing it in its historical context as a cross-over novel (as a Jewish subject appealing also to non-Jews), and second, by examining the responses of its early readers. The contrasting reactions of two groups of readers—the first, married women who wrote the author at the time of publication, the second, women now mainly in their early sixties who read the novel in their early to mid-teens—highlight the importance of an often overlooked category in discussions of reading: the stage of life at which a work is read. The responses also suggest that, notwithstanding the author's male view of a Jewish woman's coming of age, the novel addressed issues—sexuality, ambition, and life choices generally—that resonated with female readers of a particular time and place.[6]

As with Levy's rye bread, one did not have to be Jewish to enjoy *Marjorie Morningstar*. The success of this cross-over book, in which virtually all the characters are Jews and anti-Semitism does not raise its ugly head (except perhaps among Jews), occasioned considerable comment. Meyer Levin spoke for many when he declared that the "novel succeeds in making the Jewish milieu an unquestionable area in American life."[7] Reviewers attributed its appeal to the new interfaith tolerance in an era of detente between Jews and Gentiles, an assessment with which historians agree and which they variously attribute to horror or guilt over the Holocaust, the democratic promise of the new state of Israel, or the rapid ascent of Jews into the middle class.[8] The virulent and open anti-Semitism so prevalent in the 1930s had receded, although it persisted in less obvious ways, such as quotas at Ivy League colleges. With Bess Myerson crowned Miss America in 1945, and Rabbi Joshua Loth Liebman's *Peace of Mind* a best seller the following year, Jews were well on their way to a new kind of acceptance.[9] The spirit of the times is exemplified by the success of the novel and movie *Gentleman's Agreement* (1947), the story of a crusading journalist who poses as a Jew to expose anti-Semitism.[10]

The postwar years were also years of prosperity for many Americans, and of unprecedented social and economic mobility for Jews, as the second and third generations attended college out of proportion to their numbers, entered prestigious professions, and moved headlong into the middle class. Jews were in the forefront of a new national ritual, the move to suburbia, migrating at an estimated four times the rate of Americans as a whole.[11] From their new economic and geographic vantage points, Jews not only built synagogues and mounted lavish bar mitzvahs, but also participated in such sanctioned rituals of bourgeois America as joining country clubs. In his influential book *Protestant–Catholic–Jew*, published the same year as *Marjorie Morningstar*, Will Herberg concluded that the three religions constituted a triple melting pot that subsumed formerly diverse ethnic traditions. In the new dispensation, celebrating bar mitzvahs and Chanukah became a way of being American.

The reviews of *Marjorie Morningstar* made clear that not all Jews welcomed this trend. Rather unexpectedly, this novel about a young Jewish woman's romantic coming of age became a lightning rod that revealed fractures among Jews, in particular between traditionalists and secular literary intellectuals. That so many prominent Jews weighed in on the subject marked *Marjorie Morningstar* as an "important" as well as a best-selling book. It even became the subject of Rosh Hashanah sermons.[12]

Observant Jews lamented the threat posed by Americanization to traditional religious practices and to group survival; they viewed Marjorie's defiance of dietary laws, albeit temporary, and her fall from sexual grace as signs of the breakdown of Jewish life and of the inability of parents like the Morgensterns to keep their children in the fold. A virulent editorial in *The Sentinel* (Chicago), "Sin and Sex Served 'Kosher Style,'" reproved Wouk for "catering to the most decadent cultural tastes of our times" and for equating Judaism with observance of ritual rather than with living Torah "24 hours a day." Trends like this, the author believed, were creating a generation of "lamebrains."[13] In addition to the anxieties of orthodox and Zionist Jews about group survival, reviewers were troubled by Wouk's satiric treatment of upwardly striving Jews, the lavish bar mitzvah and raucous seder scenes, the grasping and often uncouth characters unleavened by any genuinely spiritual or inspiring types. The book was, according to Maurice Samuel, a prominent author on Jewish and Zionist subjects, writing in *Midstream*, "the shameless exaltation of certain unsavory elements in the Jewish social body." In this rendering, *Marjorie Morningstar* was bad for the Jews. Some even charged the author with self-hatred, and could not fathom how Wouk, an observant Jew who had helped establish synagogues on Long Island and Fire Island, could have written it.[14]

From the opposite direction, avant-garde literary intellectuals, many of them secular Jews with leftist politics and a modernist aesthetic, joined their attacks on Wouk with the critiques of conformity prevalent in the 1950s.[15] Wouk's endorsement of bourgeois values, his sexual conservatism, and his religious orthodoxy, not to mention the middle-brow literary aesthetic much praised by *Time*, all drew heated attacks. Leslie Fiedler, in "What Makes Herman Run?" in *The New Leader*, considered the novel "a kind of Cook's tour of comfortable bourgeois Judaism" as well as a rejection of the main thrust of serious fiction at least since Flaubert. The young Norman Podhoretz, who considered the novel "obscurely doctrinal," observed in *Commentary* that some customs, like kashruth and virginity, "die of their own irrelevance." In "For God and the Suburbs," fiction writer and critic Isaac Rosenfeld blasted Wouk, in *Partisan Review*, for suggesting that "the accumulated folk wisdom of the Bronx and Central Park West is superior to sex, bohemianism . . . and the eating of crustaceans and pork." Mordecai Richler summed it up in the *Jewish Observer and Middle East Review* when he deemed Wouk the most gifted and widely read of the new "booster writers" on the right who had replaced the anticapitalist writers of the nineteen-thirties.[16] These critics were outraged as well by Wouk's anti-intellectualism, manifested by his negative portrayal of Noel, a posture some may have taken personally at a time when intellectuals were under political attack.[17]

Despite such divergent outlooks, critics in both camps rejected accommodation to American mainstream values, secular in one case, bourgeois in the other. Both sets of partisans also observed that, despite its Jewish milieu, the novel paid scant attention to religion. Some also partook of the prevailing misogyny of the time. "Sin and Sex Served 'Kosher Style,' " decried temple sisterhoods for what its author called "their degrading card parties, stupid programs, and other myriad evidences of intellectual and spiritual decay," while Rosenfeld, who considered Mrs. Morgenstern the epitome of Jewish bourgeois vulgarity, excoriated Wouk for his "Mom is always right" approach.[18] The negative view of Jewish matrons by both sides is striking at a time when, as several essays in this volume make clear, women were becoming central to Jewish institutional life, a striking reversal of traditional practice.[19]

Like the novel itself, Marjorie was marketed by the publisher and accepted by reviewers as all-American, "a classic American heroine," in Meyer Levin's words. John P. Marquand, in *Book-of-the-Month Club News*, proclaimed her "as much in the American tradition as Abraham Lincoln and Daniel Boone." *Time* declared her "an American Everygirl who happens to be Jewish," and went on to quote the author that she was "Betsy Jones, Hazel Klein, or Sue Wilson. She is every girl who ever dreamed of seeing her name on a Broadway marquee, who fell in love and set out to land a man."[20]

If Marjorie was an American icon, what kind of icon was she? She is a beautiful girl-woman who is never at a loss for dates and relishes her popularity with the opposite sex, but who also dreams of seeing her name in lights, of being someone in her own right. In love with Noel, she rebels, though hesitantly, against traditional expectations for nice Jewish girls: marriage to a good provider and adherence to the faith. Wouk may have fallen in love with his heroine, but reviewers tended to dismiss her as "silly," "flannel-headed," altogether an

"unworthy subject." They considered her desire to be an actress banal or mis-
guided, and assumed that she overestimated her talent or did not work hard
enough.[21] The reviewer for the liberal Catholic magazine *Commonweal* noted the
"wastes of Marjorie's girlish imagination," while William Du Bois in the daily
New York Times disdained the novel's point of view as "the treacherous prism of a
girl's mind."[22] They did not mention Marjorie's spunk in seeking a career on the
stage, or her ability to spar with Noel as they ate, smoke, and drank their way
through fashionable New York. The almost universal dismissal of the heroine
and her aspirations conveys the repressive aspects of an era in which women
were not taken seriously. Girls, evidently, were not appropriate subjects for
serious literature.

Marjorie's authenticity and individuality are challenged in the novel by Noel,
a model of the male flight from commitment in the 1950s most often associated
with the Beats.[23] In a long diatribe, Noel declares that however modern Marjorie
appears on the surface, she is really "Shirley." Shirley is "the respectable girl, the
mother of the next generation, all tricked out to be gay and girlish and carefree."
In time, however, she will become her mother, smug and self-righteous, the epitome of dullness. "She's going to paint, that's what—or be a social worker, or a
psychiatrist, or an interior decorator, or an actress, always an actress if she's got
any real looks—but the idea is she's going to *be* somebody. Not just a wife." All
she really wants, as Noel sees it, "is what a woman should want . . . big diamond
engagement ring, house in a good neighborhood, furniture, children, well-made
clothes, furs—but she'll never say so." She may talk like Hemingway's free-
spirited Lady Brett Ashley, but she doles out her sexual favors with care.[24] In fact,
it takes Noel a full 417 pages to get Marjorie into bed, a space the author does not
allow her to enjoy.

Noel is no hero to Wouk, but the author saddles Marjorie with the predicted
fate. In an epilogue set in 1954, some fifteen years after her marriage, Marjorie,
now Mrs. Milton Schwartz, lives in Mamaroneck with her husband and four children. She keeps a kosher home, attends synagogue, and is active in local Jewish
organizations. Not yet forty, she has gray hair, and a former admirer, now a successful writer, at first takes her for someone's grandmother. He finds her seemingly happy, but "dull, dull as she can be, by any technical standard. You couldn't
write a play about her that would run a week, or a novel that would sell a thousand copies. There's no angle."[25]

Wouk, of course, did write a novel about Marjorie, a very long one, and one
that engaged many readers. Unlike the reviewers who disliked wading through
the "wastes of Marjorie's girlish imagination," many girls and women identified
with Marjorie and found her story compelling; for some the novel had a long
afterlife. Marjorie may have been "average," a recurrent description in letters to
the author, in reviews, and by Wouk himself, but, perhaps for that very reason,
readers responded to her story, which in its immediacy if not in every detail

might have been their own—or, in the case of younger readers, might be theirs in the future. I base these conclusions on the responses of two groups of early women readers; the first wrote the author at the time of publication, the second answered a questionnaire I distributed in 2007.

Wouk received fan mail from a diverse group of men and women, many of whom identified themselves by religious or other background.[26] Female correspondents were especially enthusiastic, some even ecstatic, about a novel many found difficult to put down. Christians commented favorably on the sympathetic portrait of Jews; some said the characters reminded them of their Jewish friends. Jews remarked on the novel's realism, some recounting their own moves from the Bronx to Manhattan's West Side. A few, like the Methodist minister who recommended *Marjorie Morningstar* to older teenage girls in his congregation, or the Shreveport businessman who bought fifty copies to give to his non-Jewish friends, became publicists in their own right.[27] Women of varied backgrounds reported losing themselves in the book to the point of neglecting their studies or family obligations.[28]

The most interesting letters came from women, many of whom identified themselves as housewives, often suburban. They ranged in age from the early twenties to the late thirties. Almost all had Jewish names. Some chided Wouk for emphasizing the seamy side of Jewish life; a few were disappointed that Marjorie did not marry Noel. But most identified with Marjorie and found the story realistic; for many, it was deeply moving. It is "the story we have waited for," one reader declared; a second, who had experienced "an eerie sense of identity" while reading the novel, felt she was speaking for "practically every other Shirley, now gracefully approaching 40." Another woman gave her husband a copy so he would better understand his own Marjorie Morningstar.[29]

It was the novel's conclusion that elicited the most pointed comments, many of them questioning Wouk's dismissal of Marjorie's aspirations, and her confinement to suburban domesticity. These observations provide clues about the writers' views on the Shirley-esque lives they were leading. Wouk himself refused to say whether the novel's conclusion was a happy one, on the grounds that he was "not sure what happiness is"; the most he would say was that he considered the ending "truthful."[30]

Only one correspondent, a twenty-eight-year-old Pittsburgh mother of two, "one of your 'Shirleys,'" offered an unqualified, if perhaps defensive, approval of Marjorie's choices, which mirrored her own:

> The past couple years or so, I've been coming to the realization that for me and so many like me, there is nothing more poetic in life than wiping grubby little noses, tying stiffly starched ribbons in a first grader's hair, and cooking a decent meal for my man after he's put in a hard day's work at his "dull" job. Your book has strongly reinforced and nourished my embryo belief that

perhaps the concrete accomplishments of a conscientiously performed task in our local community chest campaign is worth more to the total picture (whatever that picture might be) than all the brilliant, vague, every-directional fantasies of what I might have accomplished.[31]

A note of resignation came from a woman with "two 'Marjories'" of her own who identified with Mrs. Morgenstern. Perhaps responding to the contemporary insistence on the importance of early "maturity," she took this identification as proof that she "had finally grown up. It's a sad and sweet thought."[32]

Less acquiescent readers were distressed by Wouk's endorsement of what they viewed as a deep-seated cultural prejudice against housewives. A mother of three in her early thirties, president of her sisterhood, declared herself haunted by the specter of mediocrity she saw in Wouk's depiction of the middle-aged Marjorie. A member of a book discussion group composed of suburban mothers "who sincerely desire to eradicate the threat of dullness" inquired: "Aren't there those among us who must reach out on their own to discover their capabilities and to know whether or not their aims are worthwhile?" And a third woman, who found the novel absorbing, but "the ending abrupt, almost tacked on," demanded: "Don't you think it's time we housewives stopped getting a beating for being dull, dull, DULL? . . . Why must contentment, sweetness, and children add up to dullness?"[33]

Other correspondents more explicitly rejected what they saw as the narrow life the author had foisted on Marjorie. A woman who proudly identified herself as a Shirley who had once desired a career on the concert stage considered middle-aged Marjorie a "shell of a person" and thought she had worked too hard at becoming an actress and gone too far in her love life to be happy in such a conventional marriage: "She seemed to have done more than the average American girl toward breaking out of the pattern of Shirley."[34] A woman in her early twenties, who said she had lost her battle to escape women's "preordained" destiny two years earlier, felt "an intense state of depression because I recognized what many American Jewish girls must feel on reading it: it is the story of my life."[35] A Syracuse University sophomore who read the first five hundred pages with "entire fascination" stated flatly that the last few chapters were such "a radical departure" that "I cannot even accept them as a part of the story."[36]

The most strenuous protest came from a woman in West Hartford, Connecticut, who defended Wouk against the charge that he had defamed Jews, believing that his "greatest sin was against Marjorie herself." Rejecting his depiction of the heroine as a dull matron, she exclaimed, "I fail to understand why in hell the desertion of Marjorie," and went on to rewrite the ending:

> Inasmuch as I grew to know Marjorie quite well having worried about her, listened to her, applauded her, been offended by her, and laughed with her, I thought I'd drive out to Mamaroneck to see for myself. When I arrived

Marjorie Schwartz was still sitting on the terrace, reading the *Theatre Arts Magazine* in Bermuda shorts, drying her black hair in the sun.

This correspondent cared deeply about the character and, despite the demurral, like many others read the novel with a lump in her throat.[37]

The challenges of some readers to Wouk's portrait of suburban domesticity may seem muted to our post-second-wave-feminist ears, but they are no less significant for that. In 1955 there was not yet a public language in which to discuss such issues. In retrospect, it is striking how little reviewers said and how much they took for granted about Wouk's endorsement of what anthropologist Sherry Ortner has called "the girl track."[38] An occasional woman reviewer, like Elizabeth Hoyt in the *Cedar Rapid Gazette*, who thought Marjorie had "the normal ambition of thousands of American girls," intimated that women might have legitimate interests outside the home.[39] But, for the most part, female ambition was treated patronizingly if at all, a silence that underscores the pervasiveness of the domestic ideology that only a few years later Betty Friedan would label the feminine mystique. Of course, that ideology had a long history, but in the postwar era, with its early marriages and high birth rates, it was exceptionally intense and unmediated by the countervailing pressures of depression and war.[40] Gender practices were in fact more fluid than acknowledged; a growing number of women, including middle-class mothers with young children, worked outside the home—a challenge that may help account for the repressiveness of the ideology. Unlike the cult of domesticity in the nineteenth century, this one was accompanied by overt misogyny and mother-bashing, exemplified by Philip Wylie's *Generation of Vipers* (1942, reissued and annotated in 1955), which added the term "momism" to the language.

In contrast to the rather hesitant responses of Wouk's early correspondents, many of them married women with children, were the assertive replies of those who answered my questionnaire, most of whom had encountered *Marjorie Morningstar* while in their early to mid-teens—roughly between 1957 and 1964. Whereas women in their twenties and thirties tended to consider the novel a more or less realistic description of their lives thus far, those who read it at younger ages were caught up in Marjorie's coming-of-age story for what it might tell them about their own futures.[41] Far from finding Marjorie silly or pathetic, these readers, Christians as well as Jews, were impressed by her assertiveness.

A generation for whom virginity was a "big issue" also found the book "sexy."[42] A woman whose mother was Jewish remembers "a strong feeling of empathy with Marjorie and wanting desperately to be her, envying her ability to rebel and 'be true to her real self.'" A classicist who read the novel while attending a Catholic boarding school recalls: "I was overwhelmed with Marjorie's vigor, life and passionate drive. I think the book opened me to a sense of sexual possibilities that I had previously not recognized." On a long train trip to Vancouver when she was fifteen, a Mennonite from a small farming village in Iowa found "the story of a young Jewish woman in NYC who loses her virginity . . . pretty thrilling." The most pointed comment on the novel's sexual daring came from a woman who defined herself as coming from "in many ways a stereotypical New England WASP family." To her, "MM was a book that I would have been too embarrassed to read in front of the family, nor did I admit to having read it to anyone . . . because I was reading—and clandestinely enjoying—it for . . . its adult (sexual) content." She had not even dared to read Peyton Place, a scandalous 1956 novel that treated subjects like incest, rape, and abortion.[43] Of course we know that retrospective memories are filtered through subsequent experiences. But these responses had a uniformity that astounded me, particularly since today Marjorie Morningstar seems so tame and even prudish.

These testimonies bear out Janice Radway's analysis of her own reading experience as a fourteen-year-old in 1963. Quoting Marjorie's dreams of " 'Amounting to something. Being well known, being myself, being distinguished, being important, using all my abilities, instead of becoming one more of the millions of human cows,' " Radway recalls reading Marjorie Morningstar as a novel of desire that "taught [her] how to want." But the longings awakened by the tantalizing depictions of art and theater, "the excitement of the wider world, the thrill of a freer sexuality," are thwarted by Marjorie's domestic fate, from which Radway suspects she learned that "none of these are easily obtained, especially if you are a woman."[44]

Radway still remembered her disappointment at the ending, years later, but several informants told me that they had completely forgotten it. It is possible that, even as teenagers, some readers simply ignored the tacked-on epilogue about the forty-year-old Marjorie, written in a different voice, much as generations of readers have ignored Jo March's marriage to the ungainly Professor Bhaer in Little Women.[45] In a similar manner, readers intrigued by Marjorie's sexual evolution may have overlooked the fact that both she and her fiancé regarded her transgression as a "deformity." Unlike nineteenth-century transgressors, Marjorie not only lives but marries and goes on to a life of unimpeachable respectability, a denouement that had to have been encouraging to adolescent girls negotiating relations with the opposite sex in an era of mixed messages.

The early adolescent readers I have discussed so far came from middle-class backgrounds. A differently situated reader, Olga Litvak, who emigrated from Russia to Brooklyn at the age of ten, also read Marjorie Morningstar as a novel of possibility, but of a somewhat different kind. The novel was her first window into American life, and years later she acknowledged in print that "Beautiful, blue-eyed, shapely Marjorie . . . was the most glamorous Jewish girl I had ever met. She didn't simply live: she played center stage in the America of my dreams. Her glimmering girlhood, her adventurous, desiring soul seemed sweetly familiar and bitterly beyond the reach of Flatbush." To the awkward youngster who "sought nothing less than a vocabulary of personal expression and an intimate grammar of experience" as she groped toward American adolescence, the heroine's quest for individuality beckoned, as did her comfortable middle-class status and the assurance that a Jewish girl could be beautiful by American standards. No wonder Litvak was shocked when, years later, the college students to whom she assigned the novel dismissed Marjorie as "a vapid, self-absorbed prude."[46]

What seemed passé and prudish years after the sexual revolution, was a matter of vital importance to adolescent girls in the late 1950s and early 1960s, as Wouk explicitly recognized.[47] In his account of the central romance, he had in fact captured with some precision the narrow line of permissible sexual conduct for a girl who wanted to be popular with boys while keeping her reputation intact: she had to dole out sex, as Marjorie does.[48] So when Mrs. Frieda Clark Hyman declared, at the second annual Jewish Book Festival in Hartford, that Marjorie "had really no problems worth writing about," it is likely that she was a long way from her own adolescence. The heroine of Sylvia Plath's *The Bell Jar* believed there were two kinds of people, those who had slept with someone and those who had not, and that "a spectacular change would come over [her] the day [she] crossed the boundary line."[49] Girls of course negotiated the sexual tightrope in their own ways. From the Kinsey report on female sexuality, published in 1953, we know that despite cultural proscriptions against "going all the way," 50 percent of the women surveyed had crossed the line prior to marriage, as Marjorie had.

The intense if divergent responses to *Marjorie Morningstar* suggest that the novel touched sensitive nerves in the postwar era: for religious Jews, loss of adherence to traditional religious practice and concern about group survival; for avant-garde Jewish writers, conservatism in its many varieties and the numbing conformity that accompanied the cold war. For American women, the novel raised a host of issues related to their place in the sun: sexuality, domesticity, and most of all whether they could have legitimate aspirations beyond those of marriage and motherhood.[50]

As the first best-selling American novel with a Jewish heroine, *Marjorie Morningstar* had special resonance for Jewish women, many of whom considered it "'our' book."[51] Contemporary readers rejoiced at having a realistic Jewish heroine with whom they could identify, one who was also an all-American girl. Given the concerns of many Jewish girls about whether they measured up to American beauty standards, it is likely too that Wouk's frequent emphasis on Marjorie's good looks was a factor in the character's appeal to insecure teenagers, much as it was to Olga Litvak. Although Marjorie is represented as flawed for falling away from traditional sexual and religious norms, she succeeds in fulfilling her womanly destiny in the only way a woman legitimately could in the 1950s: through marriage and motherhood. In presiding over a Jewish home and participating in organized religious life, she embraces her destiny as a Jewish woman as well.

But there was nothing exclusively Jewish about the gender issues raised by the novel. Wouk's early correspondents, whether observant or not, made no mention of a Jewish dimension to their lives as wives and mothers. In that sense, they exhibited no identifiably "Jewish feminine mystique." But, like other women who had arrived at the material comfort and social status afforded by suburbia, some Jewish housewives were finding the life of "Shirley" not all it was cracked up to be.[52] This was the kind of incipient questioning that Friedan would tap into a few years later.[53]

Marjorie Morningstar's early readers encountered the book at a historical moment that devalued female autonomy. Most cultural arbiters of the time would have answered the question raised by Friedan—whether a woman could honorably be anything other than a wife and mother—in the negative. It was a moment, too, just before the sexual revolution of the 1960s, when standards were in flux but female virginity was still highly prized. If today, the novel reads like a period piece, the responses of these early readers bear out the truth of Janice Radway's suggestion that the novel was so popular with women in the 1950s and early 1960s "because it captured with almost perfect precision the tensions and uncertainties of profound social change as it was about to erupt and explode."[54]

Beyond the long and abortive romance at the novel's center, beyond its satire of bourgeois Jewish life, *Marjorie Morningstar*, by its very ability to elicit such considerable interest—even passion—in its readers, suggests that it raised questions, in however problematic a manner, of central concern to middle-class women's present and future place in American life. At a time when few novels addressed middle-class women's identity at all, perhaps this was the ultimate reason for the novel's popularity.[55]

ACKNOWLEDGMENTS

I want to thank Joan Jacobs Brumberg, Joan Hedrick, and Dolores Kreisman for reading an earlier version of this essay, Alexandra Bernet for assistance with the Herman Wouk Papers, Patricia Bunker for computer research tips, Mary Curry for her interlibrary loan expertise, and Margaret Mair for research assistance at the Hartford Jewish Historical Society. Thanks as well to Richard Rosenzweig and his family for inviting me to deliver a talk on Marjorie Morningstar as the Linda W. Rosenzweig Memorial Lecture in Wellfleet, Massachusetts, on August 9, 2007. Finally, I wish to thank Herman Wouk and Jennifer B. Lee for permission to cite material from the Herman Wouk Papers, Rare Book and Manuscript Library, Columbia University.

NOTES

    1. Herman Wouk, *Marjorie Morningstar* (Garden City, NY: Doubleday, 1955), hereafter *MM*. Publication information comes from Box 22, Folder 749, and Box 23, Folders 751 and 753, of the Herman Wouk Papers, Rare Book and Manuscript Library, Columbia University. This collection is hereafter cited as HWP. Sales figures are from Alice Payne Hackett, *70 Years of Best Sellers, 1895–1965* (New York: R. R. Bowker, 1967), 20, 199.

2. The movie not only changed the setting from the 1930s to the 1950s, thereby omitting a brief but important section on the plight of Jews in Nazi Germany, but sidestepped Marjorie's suburban domestication by projecting a romance with a successful playwright.

3. Many reviews have been collected, in no discernible order, in Folders 751–753, Box 23, HWP. Where not otherwise identified, reviews cited in the notes come from these folders. For brief published discussions of reviews of MM, see Arnold Beichman, "Bewitched, Bothered, and Bewildered: *Marjorie Morningstar*," in *Herman Wouk: The Novelist as Social Historian* (New Brunswick, NJ: Transaction Books, 1984), 51–58; Laurence W. Mazzeno, *Herman Wouk* (New York: Twayne Publishers, 1994), 52–66; and Gordon Hutner, "The Meanings of *Marjorie Morningstar*," *Key Texts in American Jewish Culture*, ed. Jack Kugelmass (New Brunswick, NJ: Rutgers University Press, 2003), 46–56.

4. J. A .D., "Marjorie Morningstar," *Binghamton Press*, September 4, 1955; John Metcalf, *Spectator* (London), October 7, 1955, both in Folder 751.

5. The book based on this research, *Well-Read Lives: How Books Inspired a Generation of American Women* (Chapel Hill: University of North Carolina Press, 2010), has been greatly influenced by the work of Janice Radway and Roger Chartier. For the former, see *Reading the Romance: Women, Patriarchy, and Popular Literature* (Chapel Hill: University of North Carolina Press, 1991 [orig. 1984]); for the latter, see *The Order of Books: Readers, Authors, and Libraries in Europe between the Fourteenth and Eighteenth Centuries* (Stanford, CA: Stanford University Press, 1994), among others.

6. Several women reviewers questioned Wouk's ability to write from a female viewpoint. See, for example, Deborah Walker, "A Quasi-Feminine Ghost," Folder 751, and Nora Magid, "The Girl Who Went Back Home," *The New Republic*, September 5, 1955, 20.

7. Meyer Levin, "With Novel 'Marjorie Morningstar' Wouk Hits Full Stature as Author," *National Jewish Post*, [September 16, 1955], Folder 751.

8. For contemporary views, see Leslie A. Fiedler, "What Makes Herman Run?" *The New Leader*, October 3, 1955, 23; Harold U. Ribalow, "Jewish Fiction since the War: A Promising Decade," *National Jewish Monthly* (October 1955), 38–30, Folder 753; and Levin, "With Novel 'Marjorie Morningstar.' " For historians' views, see Jonathan D. Sarna, *American Judaism: A History* (New Haven, CT: Yale University Press, 2004), especially pp. 272–282, and Edward S. Shapiro, *A Time for Healing: American Jewry since World War II* (Baltimore: Johns Hopkins University Press, 1992).

9. Sarna, *American Judaism*, 275–278.

10. *Gentleman's Agreement* was one of several cultural products of the time that portrayed ostracized class, ethnic, and racial minorities in universal terms and in ways that questioned the hard and fast boundaries between "us" and "them." See Judith E. Smith, *Visions of Belonging: Family Stories, Popular Culture, and Postwar Democracy, 1940–1960* (New York: Columbia University Press, 2004).

11. Sarna, *American Judaism*, 282. The suburban population doubled between 1950 and 1970, by which time more people lived in suburbs than in cities and on farms. Kenneth T. Jackson, *Crabgrass Frontier: The Suburbanization of the United States* (New York: Oxford University Press, 1985), 283–284, and passim.

12. Sherry B. Ortner, *New Jersey Dreaming: Capital, Culture, and the Class of '58* (Durham, NC: Duke University Press, 2003), 138; Ruth Missal to Wouk, September 19, 1955, Box 5, HWP. Wouk later defended himself against attacks by Jews who considered the bar mitzvah scene disrespectful. *This Is My God* (Garden City, NY: Doubleday, 1959), 142–143.

13. J. I. Fishbein, "Sin and Sex Served 'Kosher Style'!" *The Sentinel* (Chicago), Folder 753, Box 23, HWP.

14. Maurice Samuel, "Not Simply Rubbish," *Midstream* 1 (1955–1956): 92–98 (quotation, 98). See also Allan G. Field, "The Strange Case of Mr. Wouk," *Jewish Spectator* 21 (January 1956): 28–30;

AE., "Forever Marjorie," *Young Israel Viewpoint* (November–December 1955), 19–22, Folder 753; and [Charles Angoff], review of *Marjorie Morningstar* in *Hadassah Newsletter* (December 1955), a Xerox copy of which was provided by Tom Blunt of *Hadassah Magazine*. The novel received harsh treatment at the second Annual Jewish Book Festival in Hartford, Connecticut. See Melvin Kalpus, "Three Lash Wouk's Book as Inferior," *Hartford Courant*, December 5, 1955, and Father Victor Donovan to Wouk, December 5. 1955, Folder 192, Box 22, HWP; Donovan describes the meeting as "really a 'neck-tie' party" in which Wouk was "left 'hanging' in effigy.'" Not all reviews in Jewish publications were so critical; see, for example, the appreciative review by Ludwig Lewisohn, himself a distinguished writer, "Mr. Wouk's New Novel," *The Jewish Horizon* (December 1955), 14–15, Folder 753, Box 23, HWP, and Robert E. Segel, "As We Were Saying," *The American Israelite* (a Reform publication), October 6, 1955, Folder 751. Louis Harap, in *Jewish Life: A Progressive Monthly* (November 1955), and Milton Hindus, "An American Girl," *Jewish Frontier* (December 1955), Folder 751, were more mixed.

15. These range from influential critiques by social scientists, such as David Riesman, with Reuel Denney and Nathan Glazer, *The Lonely Crowd: A Study of the Changing American Character* (New Haven, CT: Yale University Press, 1950), and William H. Whyte, *The Organization Man* (New York: Simon and Schuster, 1956), to "Little Boxes," a well-known satirical song by Malvina Reynolds that caricatured bourgeois conformity.

16. Fiedler, "What Makes Herman Run," 22; Fiedler, "The Breakthrough: The American Jewish Novelist and the Fictional Image of the Jew," *Midstream* 4 (Winter 1958): 30–31; Norman Podhoretz, "The Jew as Bourgeois," *Commentary* 12 (February 1956): 187; Isaac Rosenfeld, "For God and the Suburbs," *Partisan Review* 22 (Fall 1955): 565; Mordecai Richler, "Mr. Wouk Attacks the Intellectuals," *Jewish Observer and Middle East Review*, October 14, 1955, 565, Folder 753. See also William Du Bois, "Books of The Times," *New York Times*, September 1, 1955, 21, where Du Bois claims that Marjorie is unable to make "an all-out surrender at the altar of art" because she "can never really rise above her soundly orthodox upbringing." For analytic purposes, I have highlighted some of the most critical reviews. More sympathetic assessments include: Meyer Levin, "Central Park West Revisited," *Saturday Review* 38 (September 3, 1955): 9–10; Maxwell Geismar, "The Roots and the Flowering Tree," *New York Times Book Review*, September 4, 1955, 1; Florence Haxton Bullock, *New York Herald Tribune Book Review*, September 4, 1955, 1; and many in the HWP.

17. Arthur M. Schlesinger Jr. discussed *Time*'s cover story on Wouk in the context of the magazine's attack on intellectuals: "*Time* and the Intellectuals," *The New Republic*, July 16, 1956, 15–17.

18. Fishbein, "Sin and Sex Served 'Kosher Style'!"; Rosenfeld, "For God and the Suburbs," 566. On popular, largely negative, views of Jewish mothers in the 1950s, see Joyce Antler, *You Never Call! You Never Write!: A History of the Jewish Mother* (New York: Oxford University Press, 2007), 102–121; the chapter begins with Noel's "Shirley" diatribe in *MM*.

19. On Jewish women's activities in suburbia, see also Marshall Sklare and Joseph Greenblum, *Jewish Identity on the Suburban Frontier: A Study of Group Survival in the Open Society*, 2nd ed. (Chicago: University of Chicago Press, 1979), especially pp. 255–259. In surviving fragments of a response to *MM*'s critics that he never published, Wouk observed that what he called "The Morningstar-Negative Factor" "is most widespread in avant-garde literary circles, and among suburban ladies who dislike their husbands." He also noted, "A few critics have earned considerable money in recent months merely by touring women's clubs to denounce *Marjorie* and her creator, Herman Wouk." "The Morningstar Syndrome," Folder 747, Box 22, HWP; see also "The Morningstar Panic," Folder 747. The Wouk papers indicate that the novel aroused controversy on the women's lecture circuit, but I found no evidence that any of Wouk's correspondents disliked their husbands.

20. Levin, "Central Park West Revisited," 9; John P. Marquand, *Book-of-the-Month Club News*, Folder 753, Box 23, HWP; Wouk quoted in "The Wouk Mutiny," *Time*, September 5, 1955, 48.

21. R. T. Horchler, "Life and the Dream," *Commonweal* 43 (November 4, 1955): 123.

22. Horchler, "Life and the Dream"; Du Bois, "Books of the Times."

23. Barbara Ehrenreich, *The Hearts of Men: American Dreams and the Flight from Commitment* (New York: Anchor Books, Doubleday, 1983), includes MM and Noel in her discussion of the Beats' rejection of responsibility and maturity (17, 27–28).

24. MM, 168–179; quotations, 172, 173. For the impact of "Shirley" on a Jewish journalist who read MM shortly after it came out while attending Choate, see Paul Cowan, *An Orphan in History: One Man's Triumphant Search for His Roots* (New York: Anchor Books, Doubleday, 1982; 1989 edition). Cowan, who identified with Noel, recalls finding Marjorie "a shallow self-deluded girl . . . a composite of well-to-do Jewish girls." He looked back on the novel "as a symbolic turning point in my romantic life," before which he dated only Jewish girls, and afterwards, usually, non-Jewish ones (111–112). In this vein, Riv-Ellen Prell suggests that Marjorie (along with Brenda Patimkin in Philip Roth's *Goodbye, Columbus*) is a prime example of "the poisoned postwar prize"; *Fighting to Become Americans: Jews, Gender, and the Anxiety of Assimilation* (Boston: Beacon Press, 1999), 223–227, and see also 144, 145.

25. "Wally Wronken's Diary," MM, 557–565; quotation, 562.

26. The letters to Wouk analyzed in the text come from Boxes 2–6, HWP, where general correspondence is filed alphabetically by author. With the help of an archival list, I checked all correspondence for 1955 and 1956. There are many letters from men, including members of the military who had enjoyed *The Caine Mutiny*, and some from adolescent girls, though not so many of the latter as I expected. Except for a few naysayers who objected to what they viewed as Wouk's negative portrait of Jews, most correspondents were enthusiastic.

27. Chester E. Hodgson to Wouk, October 11, 1955; Sam Sklar to Wouk, September 27, 1955.

28. It was not only suburban women who lost themselves in MM. John Griggs to Wouk, August 28, 1955, said of his "marathon 'read' " of MM, that it was a book "you can 'live in.' " And an African American social scientist, who read MM while attending grade school in Memphis, recalled it as a book she "could get lost in": Alvia Branch e-mail communication to author.

29. Emma Schlesinger (Mrs. Isadore), October 14, 1955; Celeste Muschel (Mrs. Seymour), November 3, 1955; and Etta Solnick (Mrs. Clarence), January 12, 1956, all to Wouk. See also letters from Mrs. Louis Leopold, September 25, 1955, and Barbara Szold Sloan, October 23, 1955, among many others. A number of women identified themselves as Marjorie's contemporaries. Men, too, considered the novel realistic, and some claimed they had traversed a path like Marjorie's from the Bronx to Manhattan's West Side. An English professor who knew Wouk considered the novel "a feast of recognition" for Jewish families in New York: Everett Carter to Wouk, October 2, 1955.

30. Herman Wouk, "My Search for Marjorie," *The American Weekly*, May 11, 1958: 10–12. The search was for an actress to play Marjorie in the movie.

31. Pearl Brostoff (Mrs. Gerald) to Wouk, October 24, 1955.

32. Edna Koretsky (Mrs. Leo) to Wouk, August 24, 1955.

33. Sylvia Altman to Wouk, September 27, [1955]; Mildred Eichen (Mrs. Marvin) to Wouk, December 1, 1955; Pat Feder (Mrs. Ben) to Wouk, November 1, 1955.

34. Jean Levy Collat (Mrs. Robert) to Wouk, October 13, 1955.

35. (Mrs.) June Wallach to Wouk, Jan. 1, 1956.

36. Vivian Greczka to Wouk, October 25, 1955. The author had neglected her homework for two days to finish the book.

37. Paula Shirley Farber to Wouk, December 7, 1955. Farber had not liked the ending of *The Caine Mutiny*, either—she considered it "mularkey"—but thought that, in the case of the earlier novel, Wouk might have "sublimated to the possible pressure of public opinion."

38. Ortner, *New Jersey Dreaming*, 238. Ortner's insightful ethnographic and historical study of her largely Jewish 1958 Newark high school class examines classmates' life trajectories over the course of thirty-five years, as well as their changing sensibilities on gender, race, class, and ethnicity.

39. Elizabeth N. Hoyt, review, *Cedar Rapids Gazette*, September 4, 1955, Folder 751, Box 23, HWP. Bella K. Milmed wished that Wouk had considered whether Marjorie had real talent, a matter of concern for her; *The Jewish News*, October 14, 1955, Folder 751.

40. Although birth rates among Jews remained lower than the national norm, as had long been the case, they too rose from the low point of the Depression years. See Robert Gutman, "Demographic Trends and the Decline of Antisemitism," in Charles Herbert Stember et al., *Jews in the Mind of America* (New York: Basic Books, 1966), especially pp. 360–362. See also Erich Rosenthal, "Jewish Fertility in the United States," *American Jewish Year Book* (1961), 3–27.

41. I distributed the questionnaire by e-mail in 2007 to randomly selected friends and colleagues who I thought might have read the novel. Despite the informal nature of the sample, the responses were amazingly consistent. They were also enthusiastic: some women could still conjure up Marjorie's horseback ride in Central Park or the Jewish resort at which she met Noel.

42. Joan Jacobs Brumberg, e-mail communication to author.

43. Quotations from Rhoda Adam, Judith Perkins, Amy Robinson, and Catherine Bermon, all e-mail communications to author. A former student at Randolph-Macon Academy, an all-male Methodist military academy, recalls an episode from the mid-1950s in which his English teacher removed a copy of *MM* from the school library with great fanfare: John H. Chatfield, e-mail communication to author.

44. Janice A. Radway, *A Feeling for Books: The Book-of-the-Month Club, Literary Taste, and Middle-Class Desire*, 325–331 (quotations, 328, 330; the lines from "Amounting to someone . . . cows" are from *MM*, 195). See endnote 51 below for the comments of other women also entranced by the grown-up pleasures of New York City.

45. Barbara Sicherman, "Reading *Little Women*: The Many Lives of a Text," in *U.S. History as Women's History: New Feminist Essays*, ed. Linda K. Kerber, Alice Kessler-Harris, and Kathryn Kish Sklar (Chapel Hill: University of North Carolina Press, 1995), 245–266.

46. Olga Litvak, "Me and Marjorie," *Princeton University Library Chronicle* 63 (Autumn 2001–Winter 2002): 159–60. In a similar vein, many years earlier a Jewish immigrant claimed *Little Women* as her entry into American life; Sicherman, "Reading *Little Women*," 262–263.

47. Wouk also adhered to traditional values with regard to female chastity, and would have been distressed to learn that readers found new sexual possibilities in the novel. Wouk to Father Victor Donovan, September 10, 1955, Folder 192, Box 2, HWP, and "The Morningstar Syndrome," Folder 747, Box 22.

48. For a discerning analysis of the sexual tightrope, see Wini Breines, *Young, White, and Miserable: Growing Up Female in the Fifties* (Boston: Beacon Press, 1992), 84–126. Breines is writing about the 1950s, but many features of the sexual dating code she describes were in place by the 1930s, the period of Wouk's youth in which *MM* is set. See John Modell, "Dating Becomes the Way of American Youth," in *Essays on the Family and Historical Change*, ed. Leslie Page Moch and Gary D. Stark (College Station: Texas A&M Press, 1983), 91–126.

49. Kalfus, *Hartford Courant*, December 5, 1955, 23; Sylvia Plath, *The Bell Jar* (New York: Bantam Books, 1971; [orig. 1963]), 66.

50. In a thoughtful analysis, Gordon Hutner highlights the novel's regressive gender politics: "The Meanings of *Marjorie Morningstar*," 46–56.

51. Lois Wyse, "The Way We Are," *Good Housekeeping*, January 1993, quoted in Dan Vogel, "Remembering *Marjorie Morningstar*," *Studies in American Jewish Literature* 13 (1994): 21–26 (quotation, 22). Hasia Diner, email communication to author, recalls that Jewish girls in her

Milwaukee junior high school "recognized in [*MM*] something special, 'ours' as it were." A woman growing up in Albuquerque, who was mystified by her family's Jewish identity, "was fascinated by the Jewish content of the book," which "conjur[ed] up the east coast Jewish world" (Helen Lang, e-mail communications to author).

52. A decade after *MM*'s publication, Zionist writer Marie Syrkin observed that there was nothing specifically Jewish about Marjorie's dilemmas: "Jewish Awareness in American Literature," in *The American Jew: A Reappraisal*, ed. Oscar I. Janowsky (Philadelphia: Jewish Publication Society of America, 5276–1965), 221–222. Several non-Jewish respondents to my questionnaire, some of whom grew up far from New York, suggested that they had been particularly struck by the novel's glamour and sophistication, rather than by its Jewish content: e-mail communications from Jane De Hart, Amy Robinson, Mary Ellen White, and telephone conversation with Mary Kelley. Rock singer Linda Ronstadt, on the other hand, was impressed by the novel's Jewish milieu: "In retrospect, it was terrible for a young girl—it screwed me up about love and romance and everything. But I loved it then, and it made me wish I was Jewish." *Washington Post*, May 4, 1978, quoted in Beichman, "Bewitched, Bothered, and Bewildered," 58.

53. Historians have recently argued that the "feminine mystique" was never as blanketing an ideology in popular culture as has sometimes been assumed. See, for example, Joanne Meyerowitz, "Beyond the Feminine Mystique: A Reassessment of Postwar Mass Culture, 1946–1958," in *Not June Cleaver: Women and Gender in Postwar America, 1945–1960*, ed. Joanne Meyerowitz (Philadelphia: Temple University Press, 1994), 230–262. Ortner, *New Jersey Dreaming*, also notes the inconsistencies of the era.

54. Radway, *A Feeling for Books*, 325. See also Brandon French, *On the Verge of Revolt: Women in American Films in the Fifties* (New York: Frederick Ungar, 1978).

55. On the scarcity of novels focusing on middle-class female identity, see Hutner, "The Meanings of *Marjorie Morningstar*," especially pp. 53–55. The situation changed dramatically with the advent of the feminist movement.

12

"We Were Ready to Turn the World Upside Down"

RADICAL FEMINISM
AND JEWISH WOMEN

JOYCE ANTLER

One of the most significant outcomes of the postwar feminine mystique was the
rebellion against it. Second-wave feminism, the seeds of which were planted in
the "mystique" decade of the 1950s, blossomed in the 1960s and early 1970s, forever changing the landscape of family life, social relationships, and individual
consciousness. Many young women who grew up in the postwar years, struggling with the period's ambivalent, gendered messages, would have agreed with
women's liberation pioneer Amy Kesselman that "feminism saved my life."[1] The
women's movement that grew out of and in response to postwar domesticity is
widely acknowledged to have been among the most transformative social movements of modern times.

With *The Feminine Mystique*, Betty Friedan put her name on second-wave
feminism. Recent scholarship has asserted that Friedan's Jewishness, even her
avoidance of her own Jewish identity, must be considered a potent factor in her
critique of domesticity and in her urging of social change.[2] Yet a similar scrutiny
has not been given to the Jewish backgrounds and identity of the younger Jewish
women who stood front and center of women's liberation, which was the more
radical wing of the movement. Despite commonalities, the differences between
these wings, including their adherents' ethnic and religious background, age and
political philosophy, must be addressed.[3]

Women's liberation, though the term is often broadly applied to second-wave
feminism, in fact referred to the radical wing of the feminist movement, as distinguished from Friedan's liberal or "equal rights" feminism.[4] Whereas liberal
feminists called for a broadening of women's roles within the family, and for the
movement of women into meaningful careers, women's liberation (or *liberation
feminism*) demanded a full restructuring of society and culture, including the
abolition of normative gender roles and, for some proponents, of the nuclear
family itself.[5] Organization profiles, strategies, and tactics also differed. Based in

organizations like NOW and state commissions for equal rights, liberal feminism pursued traditional forms of protest like lobbying, picketing, marches, and lawsuits; nevertheless, it highlighted individual change. Radical feminists joined in more fluid, amoeba-like consciousness groups, and preferred theory and analysis rooted in collective action and the vision of a developing social movement. Although strategies and ideas of the two branches drew closer together by the mid-1970s, early differences remain instructive.[6]

Feminisms were indeed "plural," writes Benita Roth in her study of feminism's second wave, characterized by "racial/ethnic organizational distinctiveness."[7] Yet her book on racial and ethnic feminism, as well as other important works, including Winifred Breines's study of black and white women in second-wave feminism, does not accord a place to Jewish feminists.[8] Breines refers to many radical feminists who are Jewish—for example, Meredith Tax, Robin Morgan, Marge Piercy, Linda Gordon, Vivian Gornick, and Vivian Rothstein—but the identification is not made and the category not explored. The major general histories of second-wave feminism by Sara Evans, Alice Echols, Ruth Rosen, and Susan Brownmiller also do not identify the contributions of Jewish women, as such, to the women's liberation movement.[9] Such identifications may be problematic for a movement that posited, in its early years, the unity of sisterhood and the universality of women's oppression, even though it self-consciously recognized itself as diverse. As historian Paula Hyman notes, the feminist belief that "gender trumped all other aspects of identity" compounded the avoidance of Judaism then widespread within American ideological and political culture.[10] An aversion to a narrow "tribalism," as some Jews referred to ethnic particularism, also contributed to the invisibility of Jews within radical feminism.

Yet, just as Jewish ideals and experiences helped to shape Betty Friedan's critique of the feminine mystique, Jewish influences, including the *Jewish* feminine mystique, informed radical feminism's vision and actions. Although not the case for all Jewish-born participants, for many in the radical women's movement, Jewish background, values, and group consciousness provided examples of activism and a vision of a better future with more equal roles for men and women.[11] Such ideals reflected a rebellion against postwar American domestic ideals and an appreciation for alternative models.

Interrogating the connections between radical feminism and Jewish identity may help to revise the "homogenized narrative" of the second wave, in Sara Evans's words, and create what Stephanie Gilmore describes as a "more capacious definition of feminism."[12] Focusing on Jewish women's involvement in the early years of women's liberation uncovers previously obscured connections and motivations. To this end, I have reexamined writings by second-wave Jewish feminists and participated in discussions with several key figures in the movement. I am grateful to the Chicago "Gang of Four," Heather Booth, Amy

Kesselman, Vivian Rothstein, and Naomi Weisstein, key founders of the influen-tial Chicago Women's Liberation Union, who explored their involvement in women's liberation in an article published in Rachel DuPlessis and Ann Snitow's anthology, *The Feminist Memoir Project*, in 1998. A decade later the four women graciously followed up with me in a series of conversations, examining the ques-tion of Jewish identity in both a personal and political context.[13] These conversa-tions helped me to understand complex constructions of political identity and the ways in which ethnicity, gender, education, religion, and other factors shape pat-terns of activism. In revealing these multiple influences and the ways that previ-ously unacknowledged Jewish backgrounds played a role in stimulating feminist responses, the conversations may serve as a model for analyzing the intersection of Jewish and feminist identities.

Setting the Scene: Women's Liberation, Chicago, 1967

Jewish assimilation in postwar American culture seemed so inexorable that, in 1964, *Look* magazine published a widely read article, "The Vanishing American Jew," noting this trend.[14] But postwar assimilation also contributed to the resur-gence of feminism, according to Judith Rosenbaum of the Jewish Women's Archive. "The otherness that many Jewish women felt as Jews in postwar America dovetailed with their experiences as women," Rosenbaum has written. "Though often painful, the parallelism of these experiences bolstered their determination to fight for inclusion and equality." In addition, Jewish women's high levels of education and the fact that they grew up in upwardly mobile, middle-class house-holds integrated within mainstream America allowed them to identify with per-sons beyond the boundaries of their own communities; this, too, became a powerful impetus for feminism.[15]

Second-wave feminism connected to other movements for political and social change in the turbulent 1960s. For many participants, the lever that pro-voked activism was the civil rights movement. Hundreds of women, including many Jews, traveled south on Freedom Rides, joined the Student Non-Violent Coordinating Committee (SNCC), or rallied against segregation and discrimi-nation in the North.[16] Many thousands became deeply involved in New Left politics, protesting the war in Vietnam and arguing issues of class and racial oppression. Although the issue of sexism had already been raised repeatedly, by 1967, the continuing dismissal of gender as a "secondary contradiction" sparked, in some women, ideas about forming an autonomous, independent women's group.[17]

One event that helped trigger a break from the New Left occurred Labor Day weekend, 1967, at the National Conference for New Politics in Chicago.[18] At the conference, the outspoken civil rights activist Jo Freeman and the twenty-two-year-old Shulamith Firestone, an Orthodox Jew from St. Louis, Missouri, came together to create a resolution giving women delegates 50 percent of the convention votes, to reflect the percentage of women in the general popula-tion.[19] Freeman tells the story:

> We waited all day for the women's resolution to be put on the floor, passing
> our minority report around, recruiting support, and preparing for a floor
> fight. When the time came, four of us were standing at the microphones, our
> hands raised to move a substitute. After reading the resolution, meeting chair
> William Pepper recognized none of us [but addressed a different motion].
> "All in favor, all opposed, motion passed," he said. "Next resolution." As we
> stood there in shock, a young man pushed his way in front of us. He was
> instantly recognized by the chair. Turning to face the crowded room, he said,
> "Ladies and gentlemen, I want to speak for the forgotten American, the
> American Indian." Infuriated, we rushed the podium, where the men only
> laughed at our outrage. When Shulie reached Pepper, he literally patted her
> on the head. "Cool down, little girl," he said. "We have more important
> things to do here than talk about women's problems." Shulie didn't cool down
> and neither did I. . . . The other women responded to our rage. We contin-
> ued to meet almost weekly, for seven months . . . we talked. And we wrote.[20]

Firestone was an "unidentified comet," in Susan Brownmiller's words, a "studious,
nearsighted yeshiva girl" who transformed herself into a "fearless dynamo . . .
consumed by a feminist vision."[21] Following the incident at the National Conference
of New Politics, Firestone and Freeman organized West Side, Chicago's first
women's liberation group. The *Voice of the Women's Liberation Movement*, the
newsletter of the West Side women, gave the burgeoning movement its name.[22]

The West Side group included core movement organizers like Heather
Booth and Naomi Weisstein, whose course on women at the Free University at
the University of Chicago served as a significant catalyst for Jo Freeman. Among
the other women who met with Firestone and Freeman after the Labor Day snub
were Amy Kesselman, Fran Rominski, and Shulamith's younger sister, Laya;
Vivian Rothstein, Sue Munaker, and Evie Goldfield joined the group later.
According to Brownmiller, the West Side group probably constituted the first
women's liberation organization in the country. Naomi Weisstein describes the
moment:

> We talked incessantly. We talked about our pain, we discovered our right-
> eous anger. We talked about our orgasms, and then we felt guilty for talking
> about our orgasms. Shouldn't we be doing actions? After all, the New Left
> was about action. We talked about the contempt and hostility that we felt
> from the males on the New Left, and we talked about our inability to speak
> in public. Why had this happened? All of us had once been such feisty little
> suckers. But mostly we were exhilarated. We were ecstatic. We were ready
> to turn the world upside down.[23]

Jo Freeman gave Heather Booth the credit for spinning off new women's liberation groups in Chicago through the New Left network. "She had the connections," Freeman recalled, "and she had the commitment."[24] Shulamith Firestone, who soon left Chicago for New York, helped organize the first women's liberation meeting in that city just two months following the Labor Day conference in Chicago. By the following spring, Firestone had prodded the New York group, which took the name of New York Radical Women, into producing its first collection of writings, *Notes from the First Year*.[25] When Kathie [Amatniek] Sarachild, another New York feminist activist, visited Boston, she persuaded her school friend Nancy Hawley to join the growing women's liberation movement. In 1968, Hawley, Marya Levenson, and a few other Boston women went to a Thanksgiving weekend women's liberation retreat in Lake Villa outside Chicago; when they returned, they shared the excitement of the retreat by holding meetings with other activists, and, in September 1969, they and other organizers formed the Boston feminist collective, Bread and Roses.[26] At about the same time, Hawley and a small group of women began to teach and write on Women and Their Bodies; soon they had formed the Boston Women's Health Book Collective (of which nine of the twelve founding members were Jewish).[27] The movement was spreading like wildfire.

Out of the first small groups in Chicago grew the citywide Chicago Women's Liberation Union (CWLU), described by Naomi Weisstein and Vivian Rothstein as an "explicitly radical, anti-capitalist, feminist . . . organization committed to building an autonomous, multi-issue women's liberation movement."[28] Rothstein, who had gone South in the summer of 1965 as a civil rights worker, found new opportunities in feminism and Chicago women's liberation; she became the first staff worker for the CWLU. In addition to founding and running the Liberation School for Women, Rothstein organized working-class white women on Chicago's North Side.[29]

Amy Kesselman, a past full-time anti–Vietnam War organizer, moved to Chicago because it seemed to her "like the belly of the beast: the perfect place to build a revolutionary movement."[30] Initiated into feminism and the Chicago women's liberation movement, Kesselman taught a course on women's roles at a Chicago high school and worked with local youth. She recalled women's liberation "exploding" in the city in 1967–1970 as she and the West Side group members listened to one another and began to find their political voices.

> Together we developed a shared vision of the independent women's movement . . . that was both rebellious and pluralistic, one that both confronted the prevailing notions about femininity and was sympathetic to women's varied approaches to survival. . . . It would be a movement that organized women to confront the myriad forms of sexism in their lives . . . and challenged the power relations of gender in both private life and social institutions. We envisioned a

radical transformation of society, but we believed that we had to build a movement around the specific injustices women experienced.[31]

Heather Booth recounted the common feeling that "We could change the world, and we can change ourselves in the process." Booth, who founded the first campus women's movement organization in 1965, had also started Jane, an underground abortion counseling service that assisted more than ten thousand women prior to the legalization of abortion with *Roe v. Wade*.[32]After the establishment of the CWLU, Booth organized the Action Committee for Decent Childcare (ACDC), a multiracial organization of parents and providers.

Naomi Weisstein recalled, "We couldn't wait to go to meetings, where we talked ecstatically about everything."[33] The CWLU's most dynamic and popular speaker, Weisstein organized the Chicago Women's Liberation Rock Band, the first feminist rock band. Listening to Mick Jagger and Janis Joplin on the radio one day, Weisstein experienced a eureka moment: "Rock is the insurgent culture of the era," she thought. "How criminal to make the subjugation and suffering of women so sexy! We've got to do something about this. . . . Why not see what would happen if we created visionary, feminist rock? . . . The task would be to change the politics while retaining the impact." [34] Although short-lived, the band was remarkably successful—"an image of feminist solidarity, resistance, and power," in Weisstein's words, "absolute democracy, the players and the audience together in a beloved community."[35]

In the first years of the Chicago women's liberation movement, Rothstein, Kesselman, Booth, and Weisstein formed a remarkable friendship, chronicled in "Our Gang of Four: Friendship and Women's Liberation," an essay by Kesselman, with contributions from the others, for DuPlessis and Snitow's *Feminist Memoir Project*. Relationships like these women's formed an important part of the history of second-wave feminism, Kesselman believed, "central to the energy and insights that emerged among women's liberation activists in the 1960s." The article focused on family and movement backgrounds, the women's disappointment with the left, and their emergence as feminists. What they did not consider at the time was the bond of their common Jewish background, the values it instilled and models it created. Fuller reflections would wait until 2008, when the four friends, at my urging, interrogated the question of a missing Jewish link to women's liberation.

Introduction to the "Gang of Four"

Born in 1939 (Weisstein) and the others in 1944–1946, the four women grew up, three of them in New York City, in the golden age of the "feminine mystique": Heather Booth in Bensonhurst, Brooklyn; Amy Kesselman in Jackson Heights, Queens; Naomi Weisstein on the West Side of Manhattan, and Vivian Rothstein in Los Angeles.[36] Although the messages that they received from their parents were often positive and purposeful, the values of the surrounding society left them, in Amy Kesselman's words, "feeling alienated from just about everything." Kesselman absorbed "political consciousness" from her left-activist parents but "in the fearful atmosphere of the McCarthy era" such messages seemed "muted and confused." Nonetheless, she became an activist, organizing a high school discussion group even though she was told that "politics, sex, or religion" were forbidden topics. In her senior year, Kesselman was suspended for several days for protesting the civil defense drills that perpetuated the belief that "standing against the wall could save us if a nuclear bomb dropped on New York City."[37]

Naomi Weisstein's high school experience was little better. After two years in an all-girls school, she transferred to the prestigious Bronx High School of Science, and her world "collapsed":

> All my music, my art, my writing, my acting in plays, my power, standing, and popularity, that I enjoyed in the first fourteen years of my life vanished in a day, as it became clear that the only thing that girls were judged on was their ability to negotiate the world of heterosexuality. . . . I can still feel my resentment, rage, and despondency at this state of affairs, especially because it seemed as if my future were closing down on me. It seemed like all my girl-friends were grooming themselves, first, for boyfriends, and ultimately for husbands and families.[38]

Like Kesselman, Weisstein had grown up "in the church of socialism." Intuitively, she recognized that politics would be a part of what she did with her life, while even in this prefeminist era, she assumed that the domestic mystique would not. "I knew that my life could not be devoted to husband and children," Weisstein wrote, "that I must have a career, and it wouldn't be such a bad thing if I didn't marry at all." But, in what she described as the "harsh, repressive, and wildly woman-hating decade" of the 1950s, she could not openly proclaim her beliefs. Thus she remained "in the closet most of the time on two accounts—my socialism and my feminism."[39]

High school also presented a challenge to Heather Booth, whose family moved from Brooklyn to Long Island when she was a teenager. Booth became head of several high school clubs, but could not find a way to engage the values of social responsibility passed on by her parents. Like Weisstein and Kesselman, she began protesting even before college, dropping out of the school sorority and one of the cheerleading teams "when it was clear that they discriminated against blacks and girls who did not fit some standard definition of 'pretty.'" Like the others, she was ready for other meaningful activity.[40]

As a child of German-Jewish immigrants who had fled from the Nazis in the late 1930s, Vivian Rothstein's coming-of-age years differed from those of her friends. Rothstein recounts her sense of being part of a refugee community and her "keen sense that they could come after us at any time." This feeling, combined with the absence of her father (who had separated from her mother) made Rothstein feel "like an outsider looking into mainstream America." She, too, was a "ripe candidate" for 1960s activism.[41]

The moment came soon enough. Amy Kesselman entered City College in 1962, interested in "read[ing] Marx instead of doing homework." Soon, she was president of the campus committee against the war in Vietnam. Yet, with her male colleagues, Kesselman felt "stupid and inadequate," her activism filled with "petty humiliations and frustrations."[42] After college, she moved to Chicago to work with an organizing project with high school students, but again found herself stymied by male leaders' hostility to women peers.

Vivian Rothstein became a scholarship student at the University of California at Berkeley, a member of the first generation in her family to go to college. Although she participated in many civil rights actions, there seemed, no matter how active she was, to be room for her "only as a body going limp in mass demonstrations." Rothstein dropped out of school and moved to Chicago to work for an SDS organizing project. But neither the civil rights nor New Left movement welcomed her as a "leader or as an intellect."[43]

Naomi Weisstein flourished in Wellesley's all-female atmosphere, but she had a difficult time as a Ph.D. student in Harvard's psychology department, where she faced sexism and the "heterosexual juggernaut." Moving to New Haven for her dissertation work, she joined CORE but was shocked to find that she was terrified to speak publicly. "I didn't understand it at all," she recalled in the *Feminist Memoir Project* article. "I didn't understand it until Chicago, until Heather and I started talking about women's position in these movements for social change."[44]

In 1960, still in high school, Heather Booth joined the effort to aid CORE's sit-ins supporting African American students' boycott of Woolworth's, the five-and-dime chain whose stores in the South remained segregated. At the University of Chicago, which she entered in 1963, she joined SNCC and went on the Mississippi Freedom Summer Project the next year. In 1965, after learning that a friend from the Summer Project had become distraught over an unwanted pregnancy, Booth began Jane, the abortion counseling service. But she chafed at the sexism in the student movement around her. At one large meeting, when a male student told her to "shut up," she did. But "That was the beginning of our own organization, the Women's Radical Project (WRAP), which became one of the most dynamic groups on campus."[45]

As Vivian Rothstein declared, "We had hit the glass ceiling on the left and there was nowhere for us to go. We were hungry for political discussion with others who took us seriously, and slowly we began to find each other."[46] In Chicago, the four women became friends. Weisstein and Booth met at a University of Chicago sit-in in 1966; they "shared their consternation about how few women were speaking, and talked about their own struggles and frustrations."[47] For two summers, they co-taught a course at the University of Chicago's Free University. Kesselman met Booth at a draft counseling office in Chicago at about this time. After their first two-hour conversation, Kesselman felt as if she "had been awakened from a deep sleep. . . . Together we figured things out." Later, she met Weisstein, who was "astounded" by Kesselman's comments about the importance of agency in people's lives. "I wanted to talk to Amy forever," she recalled.[48]

"Throughout 1966 and '67," Kesselman wrote, "Heather, Naomi, and I talked about what it meant to be female in our society at every possible opportunity. Each time we talked, we generated new insights. The world seemed to be coming dramatically and miraculously into focus."[49] Rothstein joined the West Side feminist group later in 1967, and became the fourth member of the "gang," the others drawn to her "sense of moral purpose, her intelligence, and her unshakable commitment to organizing." Kesselman recalled, "Our appreciation of each other was like fertilizer, liberating energy long stifled by the sexism of the male leadership of the New Left."[50] And Booth remembers, "We were so different, we were so similar. We were so courageous. We were so insecure. We called forth the best in each other. We called forth what we did not even know was there. We were more than the sum of our parts."[51]

The Gang of Four Moves Along (2008): On the Steps of the Synagogue

Growing up Jewish during the years of the postwar feminine mystique significantly influenced each woman's maturation into left activists and feminists.[52] "Even though our families were dissenting Jews," as Weisstein framed it in our group conversation in 2008, "Jewish values permeated our lives." Yet this influence went unacknowledged. As Weisstein put the matter, "we *never* talked about it."[53]

Several reasons explain this silence. Weisstein suggests, for one thing, that there was a tacit agreement to ignore the substantial presence of Jews in the New Left and women's liberation. Any undue attention might have compromised the notion of universality. "Our holding back about our Jewish backgrounds related in part to a general approach to Jewishness that was widespread in the New Left," Weisstein noted.

> I had grown up in the hothouse of New York City Red Diaper Baby politics—
> for me this included participation in the Young Communist League and the
> Bronx High School of Science Forum—and when the New Left and then feminism began to emerge, we wanted to build a broader movement than those
> we had grown up in, and wanted to convey that our new movements were
> not just a repeat of the Old Left, which we identified, I think correctly, as
> disproportionately Jewish.[54]

Like Weisstein, Amy Kesselman rejected "the creation of separate communities, the fierce defense of 'our kind' of people, blind loyalty to a group." She recalled

> a vivid memory of sitting in my parents' kitchen in my senior year in high school while my mother listened to the radio. Someone was reading the list of all the winners of merit scholarships in New York City. My mother was counting the number of Jews and cheering for each Jewish name. I found it deeply disturbing and in contradiction to what I thought we all believed in— the desire for all people to excel.[55]

This "antipathy to tribalism," Kesselman suggested, represented a strong element in the politics shared by the Gang of Four and others who worked toward building a "larger and more diverse movement."[56] Vivian Rothstein added: "Our identification with the outside world, in opposition to our parents' narrow (and self-protective, fearful) views was rebellious and progressive . . . a response against the broader society's divisions by ethnicity and religion. Why would we identify ourselves as Jews when we wanted to promote a vision of internationalism and interfaith and interracial solidarity?"[57] The women were further distanced from contemporary Jewish life by what they saw as Jews' consumer affluence, a far cry from the working-class milieu of earlier generations. The conservatism and affiliated blandness of synagogue life further alienated them from mainstream Jewish culture.

Despite such reasons for the lack of explicit identification as Jews, the influence of Jewish values and experience on the women was significant. "I definitely feel my Jewishness played a role in my ability to be a critic of American culture and in becoming a feminist," Rothstein told us. "My parents fled Nazi Germany and already felt at risk and outsiders in the [United States]. So I naturally shared some of their sense of alienation and separateness. Plus I was aware that their European social values clashed with the Puritanical American standards of the general society."[58]

Kesselman noted that growing up as the child of secular left-wing Yiddishists was a formative influence on her developing political views.

> My parents were . . . communists until the fifties. They had both rejected the religion of their immigrant parents, but in the wake of the Holocaust they embraced their Jewish identity as a political act and were determined to communicate a secular Jewish identity to their children. We never went to synagogue except when visiting my grandparents, who spent the high holidays at a Jewish Old Age home. But we did celebrate Chanukah and Passover. The menorah always stood at the window to show people in the neighborhood that we were Jews, and we sang the spiritual "Go Down, Moses" at our seder. After the war, my parents joined with other secular, progressive Jews to

organize a shul in our community that would teach their children Jewish history, Jewish folksongs, and the rudiments of Yiddish, all of which was infused with progressive politics—a hatred of dictators and Jew haters, a belief in struggle. I think the shul achieved its primary goal: making us identify as Jews and to feel a connection with downtrodden people. It was less successful in teaching us Yiddish.[59]

The heritage of secular Jewishness played a role for Naomi Weisstein as well, though her Yiddish skills remained similarly undeveloped.

My mother was very atheist and her father, my grandfather, who had come from Russia, used to sit on the steps of shul on Yom Kippur, eating a ham-and-cheese sandwich. They had a sort of positive commitment to secular Jewishness, and a rabid anticlericalism. But they did send me to Yiddish school, not Hebrew school, so that I could learn the folkways of my people. I couldn't stand it because I am very bad at languages. Finally Mrs. Lerner called my mother and asked, "Is Naomi retarded?" My mother took me out. Why pay for this?[60]

Also identifying as "secular Jewish," Heather Booth absorbed the Judaic values of social justice during her childhood and adolescence. This tradition became a vital lens with which she interpreted the world.

Many of my mother's family were Orthodox, some Hasidic, and lived in walking distance of each other in Bensonhurst. My mother married someone who was Conservative. When another relative married outside of Orthodoxy, the father sat shiva for the daughter. But my father was going to be a doctor; also [my mother] was sort of a loved child with many loving members of her extended family. My father's family was also very loving and close.

My mother became anti–organized religion. But many, many of the elements of Judaism were consciously part of my upbringing, so I couldn't say where one [part of my identity began and one] ended. Was I who I was because I was in a loving family, because we shared common values, because I was a woman, because I was white, because I was in Brooklyn? They were all part of a common definition. I thought being Jewish meant sharing values—believing in freedom and justice and the struggle for freedom itself. The holidays were very important; what is Passover but the struggle for freedom that ends up being successful? This is true for many of our holidays, celebrated in many of our traditions—standing up for what is just and right. Even the Bible says, "Justice, justice shalt thou pursue." Twice it says "justice," because it is that important.[61]

In addition to parental models, the education provided in synagogues and more informally in community centers, camps, and through travel impacted the social values with which the women identified. Rothstein "grew up in the Jewish Center community, which offered an alternative Jewish life. That way, Jewish children could have an identity that was not antireligious but not ritualistic—camps, after-school sports programs, etc. My family was clearly Jewish. We went to synagogue for the High Holidays, but we were not synagogue members. For women, study and confirmation were not very common."

For Rothstein, Labor Zionist camp was especially meaningful.

> I think the place I got my feminism from in terms of the Jewish community was Hashomer Hatzair, the [Zionist labor] camp which I went to for about three years. Hashomer Hazair was very radical and had a Sabra mentality; it did not believe in sex roles. We were not allowed to wear lipstick. Equality between the sexes was valued. They taught us to use rifles (never loaded), and to staff guard towers. We were supposed to go to Israel. Our leader wound up marrying an Arab guy. For this left-wing Zionism at the time, Arab culture was considered very cool.[62]

Heather Booth was deeply influenced by confirmation studies, a trip to Israel, and her progressive rabbi.

> We finally ended up in a synagogue with a very progressive rabbi after some bad experiences. By this point, we moved to the North Shore [of Long Island]. The rabbi played a very important role for me, and I wanted to be a rabbi. Of course I was told women couldn't be rabbis (at that time), couldn't be bat mitzvahed. But I was confirmed, and my confirmation study was the Book of Amos: "Let justice flow like a river and righteousness like a mighty stream" comes from Amos. And we really studied and understood what a prophetic tradition is, in order to live by its precepts. And in '63, to accompany a friend of mine who was going to Israel, I lived on a Hashomer kibbutz in the northern Negev. And supported an Arab who was running for mayor in a nearby city. So the tradition [was] sort of reaffirmed. It was part of who I was and what I believed in. I considered living in Israel, but returned to be part of the civil rights movement in the States.[63]

Visiting Yad Vashem, Israel's Holocaust Museum, had a "transforming effect" on Booth: "I promised myself that in the face of injustice I would struggle for justice." Judaism came to mean that "I valued the struggle for freedom and felt tied to a people who had an obligation to continue that struggle."[64]

Yet the peer culture inhabited and shaped by Jewish men clashed with many of the positive values bequeathed by Jewish family and community. Amy Kesselman explained:

> As I became involved in politics at male-dominated City College, I started resenting Jewish men, who, I told my friends, "had their penises in their

heads." Men asked the five-paragraph questions in the classrooms and dominated the political movements that I was involved in. When women's liberation erupted in my life, I looked back critically on the dynamics in my family
and the way they enshrined my father as the political and intellectual superior whose approval I always sought but never felt that I fully gained.

So my Jewishness bequeathed a mixed legacy—a commitment to social
justice, and anger at the sexism embedded in Jewish culture.[65]

Role models offered by Jewish mothers offered a further source of confusion.
Like the influence of family and community life generally, the impact of Jewish
mothers was profound, yet it pulled in opposite directions. Some women's liberationists, like Rothstein, whose refugee mother raised her as a single parent,
greatly admired and respected their mothers' examples of strength and autonomy. In these women's eyes, Jewish mothers seemed more empowered than
other postwar females. Rothstein's mother offered a different model from the
outset, one definitely not defined by the postwar feminine mystique. "I grew up
with just my mother," Rothstein explained. "She was the head of our family. She
had left my father when I was born. I had great total respect for my mother. I was
completely connected to her. I was totally in love with her." In Rothstein's opinion, most refugee mothers bore, as did her own, much of their families' financial
burden. "Their husbands had been middle-class businessmen in Europe, like my
father, but in postwar America, they were déclassé and couldn't find similar
work. In this community, men were supposed to be the strong ones, but women
ran the finances. It wasn't the feminine mystique model at all."[66]

These women's effectiveness, as well as their nurturing and caring attitudes—
"really loving kindness," as Booth phrased it—shaped their daughters' values and
initiated them into the Jewish tradition of social and community concern. Booth
elaborates:

> I viewed my mother as sort of the mother—the mothering person, which she
> was—and my father as the intellectual who made activity in the world. My
> mother's father believed women shouldn't go to college. And, though she
> had won a scholarship to go to Hunter—she had been valedictorian in her
> high school—he told Hunter not to accept her, that he wouldn't accept the
> scholarship. So she didn't go to college until we were in high school. And
> then got her master's, became a special ed teacher. . . .
>
> It turns out that she also was an activist as a young person. Before World
> War II, part of her valedictory speech was a pro-peace speech. She also at one
> point worked selling gloves in a store, and tried organizing people in the
> store into a union. I didn't get that kind of appreciation of her until there was
> a women's movement.
>
> Seeing women be active in the world in roles other than taking care of
> kids and being the homemaker was really exhilarating. For me, my peers,

as mentors or at least friends, had at least as strong an influence in terms of feminist activism. But in terms of the values which we learn to live by, my mother and my father were very strong influences.[67]

But other of the women felt mainly anger, and sometimes betrayal, at what they viewed as mothers' subordination to fathers and to men generally. Naomi Weisstein vowed that as the daughter of a politically radical mother who gave up her career as a concert pianist to raise her family, she herself "would never get married and that I would never have kids. I was sure it ruined her life." All her life, Weisstein's mother "struggled against my father's male supremacy. At the same time I thought I was never going to be like my mother, because she gave up. [But] she didn't really. She struggled all her life, but she stopped *being*. That was terrible, as far as I was concerned." Weisstein also believed "that she really hated the daughters, me and my sister, because we had destroyed her career."[68]

"I really did not want to be like my mother," Kesselman concurred. "I did not think of her as an empowered person at all. And in my family she was really systematically diminished by my father, who had all the brains and the political expertise; I wanted to be like him and discovered that nobody was going to let me do that." Kesselman admits that she did not understand her mother "until feminism made me think differently about the dynamics of my family. There were strong women in the culture that we lived in, but they were mainly seen as secondary in the life that mattered. The life of the mind."[69]

The women's movement provided the context for understanding mothers whose aspirations had been thwarted by the forces of postwar domesticity, even in left-wing households. Kesselman had not understood the reason for her mother's departure from the Communist Party—"because people weren't nice to each other"—as a substantive political position until feminism enabled her to see that her mother's action had been taken in critique of the party's authoritarianism.[70] Weisstein had a similar experience: "When feminism came along, I moved beyond my crude adolescent take instead to really appreciating [my mother] and thinking, my God, what a hard life, trying to continue her music when my father snored loudly whenever he heard it. What had seemed weakness on the part of mothers now became attributable to the inexorable workings of the patriarchy." Booth agrees: "With the rise of the women's movement, I came to understand the incredible strength and . . . real human beauty that my mother had." Kesselman suggests that the characteristics validated by women's liberation, which included strength, intelligence, toughness, wit, and a kind of brazenness and boldness, might have been especially applicable to the proverbial "sharp-tongued, pushy" urban—read Jewish—woman.[71] This might well have included mothers.

The legacy of the Holocaust exerted a significant, if silent, influence as well in shaping the attitudes and ideals of these radical feminists. Prodded by Weisstein, the "Gang of Four" discussed this issue with me during a second group conversation, in September 2008.

"One of the things that influenced my politics in the 1960s was the lesson I drew from the Holocaust, which was the value of collective resistance," Weisstein declared. "I'd always been a resister. But the idea . . . that you needed collective resistance to change the world and change the way things work, that occurred to me more after I started thinking about the Holocaust."[72]

Rothstein concurred. "I was affected in the way in which I understood the progressive forces, particularly in Germany, could not coalesce against the Nazis." Rothstein found that college friends on the left were in fact hostile to German Jews for not fighting back. It shocked her that such people "had no understanding really of what people went through and what they lost, and really no sympathy." For years she stopped talking to activist colleagues about her parents' experience.[73]

Awareness of the Holocaust was part of Booth's background, as well. She saw the numbers written on the arm of her Uncle Pinkus, and she thought not only about the terrors of the Holocaust but also about resistance. She felt "It was part of a long continuum of what . . . Jewish history was, a struggle for justice in the face of injustice."[74]

Kesselman did not tie the experience of the Holocaust to resistance and struggle, but nonetheless her sense of herself as a Jew of East European heritage included awareness of twenty family members who died in the concentration camps. She grew up with that sobering picture.

In addition to the traditions, experiences, and attitudes of Jewish family and community, then, beliefs about the Holocaust played a role in shaping these women's notions about protest and collective action. This influence, as well as a consciousness of oppression, the pull of social justice ideals derived from Jewish values, and a sense of themselves as outsiders, often alienated from the general culture, provided the "Gang of Four" with the ability to view inequitable conditions critically, and helped to galvanize their commitment to work for radical change. The women's movement provided added, crucial insights.[75] In so doing, it helped the women move beyond the lessons of postwar female subordination to create new identities as empowered women.

During our conversations, several of the "Gang of Four" noted their impression that Jewish women were highly represented among radical feminists. "If you compare NOW and women's liberation," Rothstein observed, "you will see a much greater percentage of Jewish women in women's lib. This is probably because they came out of the left and from large urban centers. They also drew on a legacy of immigrant culture, where, as outsiders, it was easy to be critical. Criticism was encouraged in Jewish culture. My mother used to say that there was no Jewish pope—no authority to dictate—and therefore everyone has her own relationship to God. Judaism encourages independent thinking. To be critical is not blasphemous but the basis of the religion."[76] Booth believes that Jews were even more disproportionately represented in the early radical women's movement than in liberal feminism. For Booth, strong "moral, often religiously based values"—"Jewish, Catholic, and other"—may have explained the significant presence of Jewish women in both branches of feminism.

Nevertheless, as Weisstein points out, "the obvious Jewishness, both on the left and in women's liberation, was suppressed. We didn't talk about it. . . . It was so embarrassing to have so many Jews around, since Jews weren't the workers who built the garrisons." But, she adds, "of course they were. . . . It was sort of a whiff of anti-Semitism. There was even a silent agreement that we didn't bring it up because it was counter the universalist vision of that time."[77] This defensiveness about Jewish origins was, she believes, a product of the ideology of universalism characteristic of many New Left groups at the time, not only of women's liberation.

The Jewish presence in the feminist movement was noticed by others, in ways often destructive. As Heather Booth recalls: "Amy and I were teaching in a high school with another friend, Robin Kaufman. Robin and Booth were not Jewish-sounding names, but Kesselman and Kaufman were. The principal, who we think had been in the Lithuanian army for the Nazis, always got us confused and treated us the same way. We all looked different, but we were all Jewish. Finally we were all fired in different ways."[78]

The Problem of Jews in the Feminist and Left Movements

In addition to the ethos of universalism, the problem of self-silencing, and overt discrimination, the difficult political climate for American Jews in the late 1960s played a part in minimizing radical activists' self-conscious identification as Jews. Coinciding with the birth of women's liberation in 1967 came the Arab-Israeli War. For most American Jews, Israel's military victory signified a source of deep pride, even among young Jews strongly identified with the antiwar and civil rights movements. But other progressive Jews condemned Israeli military actions.[79] For many radical feminists and activists whose primary political identity was not as Jews, the tensions created by the Six Day War provided an added layer of ambivalence about Jewish identity.

Further complications came the following year, with the Ocean Hill–Brownsville school dispute that pitted African Americans and Jewish teachers against each other over the issue of community control. Reopening the wounds of the Six Day War, Ocean Hill–Brownsville fragmented the black–Jewish alliance, helping to sow seeds not only for the black consciousness movement of the 1970s but for a "Jewish consciousness revival" as well.[80] Internal differences among Jews escalated, with progressives, liberals, and conservatives disagreeing about affirmative action. The universalistic values of the civil rights movement, once commonly held, now seemed under threat. For women's liberationists whose feminism stemmed from civil rights activism, the tense alliances of the late 1960s further challenged their identifications and values as Jews.

As much as radical feminists felt compelled by the Jewish tradition of *tikkun olam*, moreover, they also chafed under Judaism's patriarchal rigidities. Rejecting the subordination of women in Jewish religious life, they focused their activism outside Jewish organizations and culture. The start of a new impetus for equal rights within Jewish life in 1972 followed the close of the first phase of radical feminism. One of the earliest thrusts of the nascent Jewish feminist movement came in March of that year, when the small group of Jewish feminists known as Ezrat Nashim ("women's help," or "women's court") presented a "call for change" to the Rabbinical Assembly of the Conservative movement, demanding that the movement include women in the minyan, synagogue services, and rabbinical and cantorial schools, and drastically overhaul the male-dominated power structure of Conservative Jewish religious and communal life. Like the women's liberationists of the New Left, Ezrat Nashim women had been galvanized into action by feminist consciousness-raising groups and political action projects, as well as by anger at the sexism of colleagues in the Jewish student movement.[81] According to Paula Hyman, a professor of Modern Jewish History at Yale University and one of the group's leaders, the women "were all well-educated, in both Jewish and secular terms, and had been deeply affected by the nascent American feminist movement. . . . Within several months we determined that if any Jewish issue required political action, it was this one, the status of women."[82]

In February 1973, with the help of Ezrat Nashim and a committed group of secular Jewish feminists, the first National Jewish Women's Conference took place in New York City. Much as many American women had been shocked into awareness by Friedan's exposé a decade before, participants at the Jewish Women's Conference were transformed by collective acknowledgment of what until then had seemed private misery. Suddenly, "We all knew ourselves to be oppressed within our Jewishness," recalled one delegate; this knowledge came not only through the formal program but in the stirring of "long-buried emotions" felt by the five hundred women gathered together.[83]

A second Jewish feminist conference, in 1974, triggered the formation of the Jewish Feminist Organization, a loose coalition of Jewish women committed to the dual agenda of developing women's full potential through their equal participation in all aspects of Jewish culture and promoting the survival and enhancement of Jewish life. Although the organization would last for only a few years, its significance lay in moving Jewish women "out of isolation into sisterhood," as its statement of purpose proclaimed, bringing together secular leftists and committed religious Jews.[84]

By the end of the 1970s, many of these Jewish feminists had a new issue of concern.[85] At the 1975 U.N. Conference on Women in Mexico City, the anti-Zionist rhetoric of conference delegates left many confused and outraged. Jewish women who were once regarded as sisters in the plight against gender oppression were suddenly named as outsiders and enemies. The 1975 conference included a "Zionism is racism" plank in its final declaration, which Congresswoman Bella Abzug, among others, believed to have "set the stage" for the U.N. General Assembly Resolution 3379 the following year.[86] For some Jewish women, the 1975 international conference served as a call to arms; this was the click, Letty Cottin Pogrebin recalled, that initiated her life as a *"Jewish*-feminist."[87]

At the next International Women's Conference, in Copenhagen in 1980, anti-Zionism and anti-Semitism resurfaced, with non-Israeli Jewish women the subject of openly anti-Semitic attacks from delegates from every part of the world, and with passage of a resolution calling for the elimination of Israel. Two years later, after interviewing scores of women all over the United States, Pogrebin wrote a startling eleven-page article on anti-Semitism in the women's movement for *Ms.* Citing "anti-Semitism and sexism" as "twin oppressions" of women, the article described the prevalence of anti-Semitism on the radical left as well as on the political right, within the black community, and among Christian feminists who blamed Jewish monotheism for the extinction of Goddess cults and the death of Jesus.[88]

The assumption that there was a single, common women's experience came under growing scrutiny as feminist groups increasingly organized according to discrete racial and ethnic lines. The well-publicized 1977 statement of the African American Combahee River Collective named a new kind of "identity politics," articulating the need of all women, especially women of color, to organize around the particularities of race, religion, or ethnicity. Even while proclaiming the convergence of women's multiple and overlapping oppressions, the statement provided an alternative to "universalistic visions of an identity of sisterhood."[89]

To many women's liberation activists, the growth of identity politics called forth a resurgence of the particularism they had rejected. One letter from ten Jewish academic feminists in response to Letty Pogrebin's *Ms.* article was a case in point. "We are distressed that within the Women's Movement, a politics of *identity* (Jewish, black, lesbian, disabled, fat, and so on) appears to be superseding a politics of issues," the group wrote. In their view, "An assertion of Jewish identity and a focus on anti-Semitism" allowed many Jewish feminists "to participate in the politics of the oppressed"; they believed that the attention to anti-Semitism was "disproportionate."[90] To Pogrebin, though, the letter's charge itself signaled a "lack of ethnic pride" and the failure to engage against the dangerous scapegoating Jewish women.[91] This charged conflict around the converging issues of anti-Semitism in the women's movement and Jewish "tribalism" made it increasingly difficult for Jewish women to find a common feminist voice in the early 1980s.[92]

At about this time, a group of radical Jewish lesbian feminists came together around another form of identity politics within Jewish feminism; they, too, identified anti-Semitism as a primary issue. For Evelyn Torton Beck, who edited the landmark anthology *Nice Jewish Girls: A Lesbian Anthology* in 1982, anti-Semitism had not been taken seriously in either the straight feminist or lesbian feminist movement. Poet/activist Irena Klepfisz concurred: "Jewish lesbian/feminists have internalized much of the subtle anti-Semitism of this society," she wrote in a letter to a feminist newspaper in 1981. "For these women, the number of Jews active in the movement is not a source of pride, but rather a source of embarrassment, something to be played down, something to be minimized."[93] Beck, Klepfisz, and five other women (Adrienne Rich, Melanie Kaye/Kantrowitz, Bernice Mennis, Gloria Greenfield, and Nancy Bereano) formed a new group, *di wilde chayes* (wild beasts), with the goal of preventing an intensification of anti-Semitism in society at large and within the women's movement. Yet within a year, the group had dissolved, a consequence of geographical distance and political differences around the Israeli/Palestinian conflict and Israel's invasion of Lebanon in 1982. The rifts in this small group mirrored others in the secular women's liberation movement and Jewish feminism.

Convergences and a New Plural History

Although an interpretation of the fissures created by the events of this period must await a fuller discussion, it is salient that over time, the fault lines between group allegiances and the universality of sisterhood have become less deep. Through new theoretical understandings offered by feminist scholars, as well as by effective political praxis grounded in grassroots feminist activism, the "particularity of identity," in Martha Ackelsberg's words, allowed both for greater diversity and the common ground "on which we act together."[94] In addition to these breakthroughs, new organizations for progressive Jewish activism have enabled Jewish men and women on the left to commit to social justice agendas from the perspective of a specifically Jewish ethics.[95] The role of the growing, robust Jewish feminist movement has also encouraged exploration of braided identities as Jews and as feminists.[96]

New understandings that come from feminist scholarship and activism can help radical feminists and other Jewish women claim aspects of their heritage that have yet to emerge as distinct and salient. Despite confounding issues of politics and religious and cultural differences, radical feminists, Jewishly identified Jewish feminists, other women's rights feminists, and Jewish women of all kinds share legacies still to be recognized and scrutinized. "Identity-based politics has been a source of strength, community, and intellectual development," Kimberlé Crenshaw reaffirms. The problem with such politics, she notes, "is not that it fails to transcend difference, as some critics charge, but rather the opposite—that it frequently conflates or ignores intragroup differences."[97]

To acknowledge a distinctiveness based on difference does not contradict the goals of radical feminism. As Heather Booth notes, the key point is to recognize the multiple and varied aspects of Jewish and feminist identity that influenced and shaped women's liberation activism, and to acknowledge the strengths and weaknesses of each aspect, and their interrelations. "The forces that contribute to Jewish identity and to feminism are varied," Booth observes, "and so they interconnect in varied ways. And what they mean is varied—by [each] person and even within each person. And [each separate identity has its] strengths and limitations. . . . It is that sense of living with intertwining and challenging legacies— not all black or white, and all part of who we are—that [provides] the history that shaped us and that we helped to shape . . . and are still shaping."[98]

To acknowledge that Jewish heritage has been a potent force in motivating radical feminists will empower Jewish women, as well as others who have benefited from their social actions. "Ready to turn the world upside down," in Naomi Weisstein's prophetic words, radical women have made good on their promise. A full chronicle of this engagement, and of its Jewish roots and influences, must become part of the ongoing effort to tell the story of feminism in our time.

The openness of the Chicago "Gang of Four" to issues of Jewish identity provides one model of a nuanced and positive encounter with the past that can enrich our accounts of an extraordinary moment in time. Other collectives—for example, Bread and Roses in Boston and New York Radical Women and Redstockings in New York—had significant numbers of Jewish members whose stories also help to illuminate our understanding of the development of a radical consciousness out of the shoals of the postwar feminine mystique.[99] A generation younger than the Jewish wives and mothers who challenged the reigning ideas of domesticity during the 1950s and early 1960s, the pioneer women's liberationists took the lessons of their postwar coming of age onto a new and revolutionary stage. In so doing, they complicate our notions of the postwar *Jewish* feminine mystique and offer a crucial link in the chain of Jewish women's activism across the century.

NOTES

1. The title phrase is taken from Naomi Weisstein, as cited by Susan Brownmiller, *In Our Own Time: Memoir of a Revolution* (New York: Dial Press, 1999), 18. Weisstein notes that she picked up the phrase from Christopher Hill's *The World Turned Upside Down: Radical Ideas during the English Revolution* (New York: Viking, 1972). The text citation is from Amy Kesselman, with Heather Booth, Vivian Rothstein, and Naomi Weisstein, "Our Gang of Four: Friendship and Women's Liberation," in *The Feminist Memoir Project: Voices from Women's Liberation*, ed. Rachel Blau Duplessis and Ann Snitow (New Brunswick, NJ: Rutgers University Press, 2007; original edition Three Rivers Press, Crown Publishing, 1998), 25.

2. See Joyce Antler, *The Journey Home: How Jewish Women Shaped Modern America* (New York: Schocken Books, 1998), 259–267; Kirsten Fermaglich, *American Dreams and Nazi Nightmares, 1957–1965* (Hanover, NH: University Press of New England, 2006), chap. 2, and Daniel Horowitz, *Betty Friedan and the Making of the Feminine Mystique: The American Left, the Cold War, and Modern Feminism* (Amherst: University of Massachusetts Press, 1998). Also see Joyce Antler, "Betty Friedan, 1921–2006," in *We Remember*, Jewish Women's Archive, http:jwa.org/discover/weremember.

3. On Jewish women and radical feminism, see Antler, *The Journey Home*, 279–294. The recent on-line exhibition of the Jewish Women's Archive, "Jewish Women and the Feminist

Revolution," curated by Judith Rosenbaum, provides a wealth of information about Jewish women's role in each aspect of feminism, including artifacts from seventy feminists, a time-line, and material on common themes. See "Jewish Women and the Feminist Revolution," Jewish Women's Archive, http://jwa.org/feminism/. Also see Judith Rosenbaum, "Jewish Women as Feminist Pioneers: What Drove Jewish Women into the Feminist Movement," *MyJewishLearning.com*, accessed September 2, 2008.

4. Studies of second-wave feminism are plentiful. See, for example, Kathleen C. Berkeley, ed., *The Women's Liberation Movement in America* (Westport, CT: Greenwood Press, 1999); Susan Brownmiller, *In Our Time: Memoir of a Revolution* (New York: Dial Press, 1999); Barbara A. Crow, ed., *Radical Feminism: A Documentary Reader* (New York: New York University Press, 2000); Alice Echols, *Daring to Be Bad: Radical Feminism in America, 1967–1975* (Minneapolis: University of Minnesota Press, 1989); Sara M. Evans, *Personal Politics: The Roots of Women's Liberation in the Civil Rights Movement and the New Left* (New York: Vintage Books, 1980); Stephanie Gilmore, ed., *Feminist Coalitions: Historical Perspectives on Second-Wave Feminism in the United States* (Urbana: University of Illinois Press, 2008); Ruth Rosen, *The World Split Open: How the Modern Women's Movement Changed America* (New York: Viking Penguin, 2000); and Barbara Ryan, *Feminism and the Women's Movement: Dynamics of Change in Social Movement, Ideology, and Activism* (New York: Routledge, 1992). Also see Blanche Linden-Ward and Carol Hurd Green, *Changing the Future: American Women in the 1960s* (New York: Dwayne Publishers, 1993).

5. Crow writes that radical feminists first called themselves radical women, fearing that the left would not take their issues seriously. She dates the shift to the term *radical feminists* as occurring on October 17, 1968, when a group designated themselves *feminists*. (*Radical Feminism*, 2). Disagreements within women's liberation over whether the primary cause of oppression was capitalism or male supremacy led some groups to prefer the term *socialist feminist*, and others *radical feminist*. In an e-mail to the author, August 7, 2008, Meredith Tax, a prominent theorist of women's liberation, writes that: "In B&R [Bread & Roses] and CWLU [Chicago Women's Liberation Union] we called ourselves socialist feminists and thought of ourselves as autonomous but still related to the broader left. I would not call myself a radical feminist even now. Radical yes, feminist yes, but not together, because that implies a Robin Morgan 'goodbye to all that.'" Amy Kesselman prefers *women's liberation activists*, a term that she believes corresponded to actual usage at the time. For purposes of clarity of expression within this article, I will use *radical feminism* to stand for the entire spectrum within women's liberation. To further complicate matters, Betty Friedan also spoke of herself as a *radical feminist*. (See Ryan, *Feminism and the Women's Movement*, 61.)

6. On the distinction between these groups, and on the blurring of lines of thinking and organizing, see Susan Brownmiller, *In Our Time*, 7–10. Also see Benita Roth, *Separate Roads to Feminism: Black, Chicana, and White Feminist Movements in America's Second Wave* (Cambridge: Cambridge University Press, 2004), 1–3; Berkeley, *The Women's Liberation Movement*, 52–54; and many of the articles in DuPlessis and Snitow, *The Feminist Memoir Project*.

7. Roth, *Separate Roads to Feminism*, 1.

8. Winifred Breines, *The Trouble between Us: An Uneasy History of White and Black Women in the Feminist Movement* (New York: Oxford University Press, 2006).

9. See, for example, Evans, *Personal Politics*; Echols, *Daring to Be Bad*; Rosen, *The World Split Open*; and Brownmiller, *In Our Time*.

10. Paula E. Hyman, "Jewish Feminism Faces the American Women's Movement: Convergence and Divergence," in *American Jewish Identity Politics*, ed. Deborah Dash Moore (Ann Arbor: University of Michigan Press, 2008), 223.

11. For an exploration of Jews in the civil rights movement, see Melanie Kaye/Kantrowitz, "Stayed on Freedom: Jew in the Civil Rights Movement and After," in *The Narrow Bridge: Jewish Views on Multiculturalism*, ed. Marla Brettschneider (New Brunswick, NJ: Rutgers

University Press, 1996), 105–122; and Debra L. Shultz, *Going South: Jewish Women in the Civil Rights Movement* (New York: New York University Press, 2001).

12. Sara M. Evans, "Foreword," in Gilmore, *Feminist Coalitions*, viii, 5.

13. Kesselman, "Our Gang of Four: Friendship and Women's Liberation," 25–53; telephone conversations August 9 and September 13, 2008.

14. See Stephen J. Whitfield, "Between Memory and Messianism: A Brief History of American Jewish Identity," in *The New Authentics: Artists of the Post-Jewish Generation* (Chicago: Spertus Museum: Spertus Institute of Jewish Studies, 2008), 51–52.

15. Rosenbaum, "Jewish Women as Feminist Pioneers."

16. See, for example, the account of Vivian Rothstein's participation in the civil rights movement, in Shultz, *Going South*, 85–87. On Jews and radicalism generally, see Stephen J. Whitfield, "Famished for Justice: The Jew as Radical," in *Jews in American Politics: Essays*, ed. L. Sandy Maisel and Ira N. Forman (Lanham, MD: Rowman and Littlefield, 2004), 214–230. Sara Evans notes that "left-wing Zionists" were among the Old Left groups whose daughters became involved in the 1960s women's movement. (*Personal Politics*, 119).

17. Echols, *Daring to Be Bad*, 101.

18. Brownmiller, *In Our Time*, 16. Among accounts of the break from the New Left, see Ellen Willis, "Women and the Left," in Crow, *Radical Feminism*, 513–515; Echols, *Daring to Be Bad*, 103–137.

19. Brownmiller, *In Our Time*, 17. Jo Freeman wrote several articles under her movement name, "Joreen," a contraction of her two names, but later dropped that name. http://www.jofreeman.com/joreen/joreen.htm, accessed November 17, 2008.

20. Jo Freeman, aka Joreen, *On the Origins of the Women's Liberation Movement from a Strictly Personal Perspective, http://www.uic.edu/orgs/cwluherstory/jofreeman.com/aboutjo/persorg.htm*. A condensed version is in DuPlessis and Snitow, *The Feminist Memoir*, 171–196.

21. Brownmiller, *In Our Time*, 17. In just a few years, Firestone would publish one of radical feminism's most influential treatises, *The Dialectic of Sex*, which shocked many in her community, and certainly her observant parents, with its call to free women from the "tyranny of their biology," allowing childbearing to be replaced by technology, and the nuclear family by nontraditional, and in her view more humane, households. Rejecting her Orthodox upbringing, which she found rigid and confining, Firestone became a key theorist, as well as organizer, of the women's liberation movement. See Joyce Antler, *You Never Call! You Never Write! A History of the Jewish Mother* (New York: Oxford University Press, 2007), 153–155.

22. Naomi Weisstein observes that the style on the left at the time was to imitate the notion of national liberation, as in the Vietnamese National Liberation Front Conference Telephone Call, August 9, 2008.

23. Cited in Brownmiller, *In Our Time*, 18.

24. Ibid. Echols writes that radical feminists in New York were connected to the New Left more marginally than elsewhere, and as a consequence were "far less constrained by new left orthodoxy than radical women in Chicago." Echols, *Daring to Be Bad*, 73.

25. New York Radical Women was founded in 1967; in 1969, Firestone, with Ellen Willis, founded Redstockings, also in New York City. Firestone gave the group its name (Brownmiller, *In Our Time*, 140).

26. The other Boston group was the Female Liberation Front, later known as Cell 16/Female Liberation. On Bread and Roses, see Breines, *The Trouble between Us*, and Ann Hunter Popkin, "Bread and Roses: An Early Moment in the Development of Socialist-Feminism" (Ph.D. diss., Brandeis University, 1978).

27. Rosen, *The World Split Open*, 129.

28. Naomi Weisstein and Vivian Rothstein, "A detailed report on the CWLU's organizing strategy," *Journal of Liberation,* http://www.cwluherstory.org/chicago-womens-liberation-union-2.html.

29. Kesselman, "Our Gang of Four," 46.

30. Ibid., 30.

31. Ibid., 42.

32. Booth turned Jane over to the collective in 1968. See "Jewish Women and the Feminist Revolution," Jewish Women's Archive, http://jwa.org/feminism/.

33. Kesselman et al., "Our Gang of Four," 38.

34. See Naomi Weisstein, in "Jewish Women and the Feminist Revolution," Jewish Women's Archive, http://jwa.org/feminism/.

35. CWLU Herstory Website Editorial Committee, "The Chicago Women's Liberation Rock Band," http://www.cwluherstory.com/CWLUAbout/rock.html; Naomi Weisstein, "Days of Celebration and Resistance: The Chicago Women's Liberation Rock Band, 1970–1973," in *The Feminist Memoir Project,* 354–355, 361.

36. This account comes from Kesselman, "Our Gang of Four," 25–53.

37. Ibid., 28.

38. Ibid., 32.

39. Ibid.

40. Ibid., 26.

41. Ibid., 35.

42. Ibid., 28–29.

43. Ibid., 30–31.

44. Ibid., 33–34. (Weisstein received a Ph.D. in Social Relations from Harvard University in 1964. She was active in the Congress of Racial Equality, Students for a Democratic Society, and Chicago SNCC later in the decade.)

45. Ibid., 27–28.

46. Ibid., 35.

47. Ibid., 36.

48. Ibid., 38.

49. Ibid.

50. Ibid., 32.

51. Ibid., 33.

52. Thanks to Naomi Weisstein for the title of this section.

53. Conference call, August 9, 2008.

54. E-mail from Naomi Weisstein to author, August 18, 2008.

55. E-mail from Amy Kesselman to author, August 20, 2008.

56. Ibid.

57. E-mail from Vivian Rothstein to author, August 31, 2008.

58. E-mail from Vivian Rothstein to author, August 1, 2008.

59. E-mail from Amy Kesselman to author, July 31, 2008.

60. Conference call, August 9, 2008.

61. Ibid.

62. Ibid.

63. Ibid.

64. E-mail from Heather Booth to author, August 20, 2008.

65. E-mail from Amy Kesselman to author, July 31, 2008.

66. Conference call, August 9, 2008.

67. Ibid.

68. Ibid.

69. Ibid.

70. Ibid.; and e-mail from Amy Kesselman to author, August 20, 2008.

71. Cited in Kaye/Kantrowitz, "Stayed on Freedom," 115.

72. Conference call, September 13, 2008.

73. Ibid.

74. Ibid.

75. See Antler, *You Never Call! You Never Write!* chap. 6, "The Mother and the Movement: Feminism Constructs the Jewish Mother," 149–167.

76. Conference call, August 9, 2008.

77. Ibid.

78. Ibid.

79. See Michael E. Staub, *Torn At the Roots: The Crisis of Jewish Liberalism in Postwar America* (New York: Columbia University Press, 2002), 129–130, 132; Clayborn Carson, "Black-Jewish Universalism in the Era of Identity Politics," in *Struggles in the Promised Land: Toward A History of Black-Jewish Relations in the United States*, ed. Jack Salzman and Cornell West (New York: Oxford University Press, 1997), 188–189.

80. Carson, "Black-Jewish Universalism," 192.

81. See Antler, *The Journey Home*, chap. 10. On the origins of the Jewish feminist movement, see Paula Hyman, "Ezrat Nashim and the Emergence of a New Jewish Feminism," in *The Americanization of the Jews*, ed. Robert M. Seltzer and Norman Cohen (New York: New York University Press, 1991), 284–295; Hyman, "Jewish Feminism Faces the American Women's Movement," 222–240; Alan Silverstein, "The Evolution of Ezrat Nashim," *Conservative Judaism* (Fall 1975): 41–51; Anne Lapidus Lerner, " 'Who Has Not Made Me A Man': The Movement for Equal Rights for Women in American Jewry," *American Jewish Yearbook*, 1977, 3–38; Steven Martin Cohen, "American Jewish Feminism: A Study in Conflict and Compromise," *American Behavioral Scientist* 23, no. 4 (March/April 1981): 519–588; Reena Sigman Friedman, "The Jewish Feminist Movement," in *Jewish American Voluntary Organizations*, ed. Michael N. Dobkowski (New York: Greenwood Press, 1986), 575–601; and Deborah E. Lipstadt, "Feminism and American Judaism: Looking Back at the Turn of the Century," in *Women and American Judaism*, ed. Pamela S. Nadell and Jonathan D. Sarna (Hanover, NH: Brandeis University Press, 2001), 291–308. For an analysis of the impact of feminism on Jewish religious practice and communal organization, also see Sylvia Barack Fishman, *A Breath of Life: Feminism in the American Jewish Community* (New York: Free Press, 1993).

82. Paula Hyman, "Statement," Jewish Women and the Feminist Revolution, Jewish Women's Archive. http://jwa.org/feminism/. Also see Pamela S. Nadell, "On Their Own Terms: America's Jewish Women, 1954–2004," *American Jewish History* 91, no. 3–4 (2003): 389–404.

83. Friedman, "The Jewish Feminist Movement," 581–582.

84. Antler, *The Journey Home*, 293.

85. Ibid., 226. Hyman writes that Judith Plaskow, especially, "brought to American feminists an analysis of anti-Semitism as 'the unacknowledged racism' of the women's movement," 228.

86. Cited in Antler, *The Journey Home*, 275.

87. Ibid., 274 (quoted from Pogrebin, *Deborah, Golda, and Me*, 154.)

88. See, for example, Judith Plaskow, "Blaming the Jews for the Birth of Patriarchy," *Lilith* 7, no. 1 (1980): 11–12.

89. The Combahee River Collective, *The Combahee River Collective Statement: Black Feminist Organizing in the Seventies and Eighties* (New York: Kitchen Table: Women of Color Press, 1985); Roth, *Separate Roads to Feminism*, 123–124.

90. Letter to the editor, from Deborah Rosenfelt, Judith Stacey, et al., *Ms.*, February 1983, 13, cited in Martha Ackelsberg, "Toward a Multicultural Politics: A Jewish Feminist Perspective," in *Jewish Views on Multiculturalism*, ed. Marla Brettschneider (New Brunswick, NJ: Rutgers University Press, 1996), 90–91.

91. Pogrebin, *Deborah, Golda and Me*, 228–2231; *Ms.* editors wrote that the "overwhelming majority" of letters supported Pogrebin, yet it published only three, which challenged her critique. For other explorations of anti-Semitism in the women's movement at this time, see, for example, Irena Klepfisz, "Anti-Semitism in the Lesbian/Feminist Movement," in *Nice Jewish Girls: A Lesbian Anthology*, ed. Evelyn Torton Beck (Boston: Beacon Press, 1989), 51–57; and Elly Bulkin's extended essay, "Hard Ground: Jewish Identity, Racism, and Anti-Semitism," in Elly Bulkin, Minnie Bruce Pratt, and Barbara Smith, *Yours in Struggle: Three Feminist Perspectives on Anti-Semitism and Racism* (Ithaca, NY: Firebrand Books, 1984), 91–228. In their study, *Controversy and Coalition: The New Feminist Movement* (Boston: Twayne Publishers, 1985), Myra Marx Ferree and Beth B. Hess note (p. 111) that anti-Semitism among feminists was a problem not only on the international scene, but within the New Feminist Movement at home, where it created a "potentially destructive situation" for the movement.

92. For an example of the conflict around these issues, see Ellen Cantarow, "Zionism, Anti-Semitism, and Jewish Identity in the Women's Movement," *Middle East Report*, no. 154 (September–October 1988): 38–43 and 50; Evelyn Torton Beck, "The Politics of Jewish Invisibility," *NWSA Journal* 1, no. 1 (1988): 93–102; Jenny Bourne, "Homelands of the Mind: Jewish Feminism and Identity Politics," *Race & Culture* 29 (Summer 1987): 1–24; and Francesca Klug, "Jewish Feminists Answer Back," *Jewish Socialist* 12 (Winter/Spring 1988): 12–14.

93. See Evelyn Torton Beck, "Why Is This Book Different from All Other Books?" and Irena Klepfisz, "Anti-Semitism in the Lesbian/Feminist Movement," in *Nice Jewish Girls*, ed. Beck, xv–xxxviii, 53; Gloria Greenfield, "Jewish Women and the Feminist Revolution," http://jwa.org; Greenfield, "The Tools of Guilt and Intimidation," *Sojourner* (July 1983). Interviews with Evelyn Torton Beck, December 22, 2008, Gloria Greenfield, February 2, 16, 2009, and Irena Klepfisz, March 11, 2009. Also see Melanie Kaye/Kantrowitz, "Anti-Semitism, Homophobia, and the Good White Knight," *off our backs* 12 (May 1982): 30–31.

94. Ackelsberg, "Toward A Multicultural Politics," 91–92.

95. See, for example, the mission statement of the New York City–based group, Jews for Racial and Economic Justice, http://www.jfrej.org/history.html, accessed September 3, 2008.

96. Adrienne Rich, "If Not with Others, How?" in *Identity Politics in the Women's Movement*, ed. Ryan, 334. Also see Rosenbaum, "Jewish Women as Feminist Pioneers."

97. Kimberlé Crenshaw, "Mapping the Margins: Intersectionality, Identity Politics, and Violence against Women of Color," *Stanford Law Review* 43, no. 6 (July 1991): 1242.

98. E-mail from Heather Booth to author, August 20, 2008.

99. In addition to published works and doctoral dissertations, archival collections at Duke University, the Schlesinger Library at Radcliffe College, and Smith College, and on Web sites devoted to women's liberation are major resources for the study of women's liberation. See, for example, Documents from the Women's Liberation Movement: Duke Special Collections, (http://scriptorium.lib.duke.edu/wlm/); CWLU Herstory project (http://www.cwluherstory.com); Redstockings (www.redstockings.org), and "Jewish Women and the Feminist Revolution, Jewish Women's Archive (http://jwa.org/feminism/).

Jewish Women Remaking American Feminism / Women Remaking American Judaism

REFLECTIONS ON THE LIFE OF BETTY FRIEDAN

DANIEL HOROWITZ

This essay begins with the life of Betty Friedan and moves out to explore a series of issues central to the ways historians think about the history of Jewish women in the United States since 1945. I concentrate on four key topics that both illuminate Friedan's life and connect her life to larger concerns animating this volume. First, to what extent did the "feminine mystique," to use the phrase Friedan connected to motherhood, generations, and careers, shape her own life and the lives of Jewish American women? Second, how do we understand suburbanization as a force that influenced Friedan's life and the lives of Jewish American women in the postwar period? Third, how did many of the major public issues that Jewish women distinctively faced in the postwar period, particularly anti-Semitism, the Holocaust, and Israel, shape both Friedan's life and the lives of her peers? Fourth, how does a consideration of Friedan's life help us ponder questions surrounding the definition of Jewish women's history as a field, especially the relationship between post-1963, presumably secular, feminism, on the one hand, and post-1972, more religiously connected Jewish feminism, on the other?

To begin with, the concept of a feminine mystique has fundamentally shaped how scholars understand the history of American women in the postwar world. Although it had precedents before 1940 (as we see in discussing Friedan's own life), it was to a considerable extent a postwar phenomenon, a way of marking a cultural formation that differed somewhat from what had come before. In her transforming 1963 book, *The Feminine Mystique*, and in her life, Friedan connected this key notion of the feminine mystique to issues of motherhood, generations, careers, and suburban captivity.

In her life and in the lives of other Jewish American women, the feminine mystique tied into issues of motherhood, both Friedan's relationship to her mother and her own role as a mother of three children.[1] Friedan was profoundly shaped by her own mother's frustrated aspirations, as well as by her mother's efforts to frustrate her daughter's ambitions. The father of Miriam Horwitz Goldstein blocked his daughter from going to Smith College, and Harry Goldstein, Betty's father, forced his wife to give up her career as a writer and stay at home to raise their children, Betty and her two younger siblings. This suggests that, for Friedan, the notion of a feminine mystique drew on her family's experience in the 1930s, as well as on what she herself confronted in the 1950s. With Betty's arrival in 1921, Miriam Goldstein had begun an active life as a volunteer woman in the Jewish community and in non-Jewish Peoria, yet she never overcame her anger at having given up so much—and in turned passed that sense of loss and anger on to her daughter Betty.

In the scholarship on the history of Jewish women in America, the relationships of women to their mothers loom large.[2] Yet Friedan's life offers several cautionary notes. First, it is problematic to focus primarily on the mother/daughter dyad without giving full attention to the mother/daughter/father triad. For instance, in Friedan's life it was precisely the fights between her parents, as well as her mother's frustrations and her father's high ambitions for her, the daughter, that so shaped her. Moreover, no single type of Jewish mother produced second-wave feminists. The differences in the lives of Friedan and Bella Abzug, born one year apart, can be instructive: Friedan reacted to the ways her mother frustrated her ambition, while Abzug achieved with the encouragement of her mother.[3]

Friedan's portrayal of motherhood was a commentary on the stereotypical Jewish mother seen in postwar portrayals such as Herman Wouk's novel *Marjorie Morningstar* (1955). Many historians have suggested that one phenomenon that proved distinctive about the experience of Jewish American women was the depth of their commitment to domesticity and family. How then do we read the trajectory of Friedan's writings?[4] For Betty, her own mother's example of Jewish-inflected domesticity or community service was negative.[5] Perhaps, in *The Feminine Mystique,* Friedan thus was offering a critique of the domesticity of the traditional Jewish woman or, more likely, the particular aspirations of middle-class Jewish upwardly mobile mothers, without labeling these aspirations as such. From this viewpoint, we can look at her *The Second Stage* (1981), with its embrace of family, nurturance, and ambition, as an especially Jewish response to radical feminism.[6]

Friedan's life also reminds us of the complicated impact of the feminine mystique on a woman's career decisions. From the moment she left Smith College in 1942, Friedan was never without a career, but what she pursued constantly shifted. This would indicate that, when we think of Jewish women and careers, we have to avoid the admittedly problematic male model of a unitary line. In addition, Friedan's life complicates the understanding of her situation that we might glean from her book. There, she emphasized the force of the feminine mystique; yet in early drafts, she set out to demonstrate that a liberal arts education in a women's college had provided her and her classmates with what she called "the key to the trap," the ability to use an educated intelligence to challenge the power of the feminine mystique.[7]

We must ask what, if anything, is distinct about Jewish American women's experience with the feminine mystique.[8] Given the unusually high level of education attained by generations of Jewish women, including Friedan, when compared to education levels among non-Jewish women, perhaps they were bound, as Friedan suggested, to be more frustrated in the 1950s by the confinement in the suburbs that she depicted.[9] Or perhaps the outsider identity Jewish women had long experienced made them less vulnerable to "the problem" that had "no name." There is also the question whether the extensive involvement of Jewish women in radical politics in the 1930s and 1940s (and 1960s) was a factor that shaped their experience with, or resistance to, the feminine mystique. We have also to ask about the daughters and granddaughters of the women whom Friedan described, and to focus on the extraordinary professional achievements of succeeding generations.

Suburbanization is the second issue that connects the life of Friedan with the lives of other American Jewish women. Was there something distinctive about the urban orientation of Jewish women that made their shift to suburbs especially problematic? In *The Feminine Mystique*, Friedan used for feminist purposes the critique of postwar suburbs that widely read male social critics had already offered. In books by such authors as David Riesman, William Whyte, and Vance Packard, women, to the extent that they appeared at all, were portrayed as neurotic, lonely matriarchs who controlled the lives of their husbands and children.[10] In the vast scholarship on suburbia in the 1950s, some written by Jewish men, some texts do explicitly explore the distinctive experience of Jews, but these rarely use a gendered analysis.[11] One important book was by Albert Gordon, who, in *Jews in Suburbia* (1959), asserted that the Jewish woman "has become the modern matriarch of Jewish suburbia. Her ideas, opinions, and values clearly dominate."[12] In contrast, Friedan used the same emphasis on the ways American suburbs stifled the inhabitants, to reveal that, far from being matriarchs, suburban women were hemmed in by a frustrating restraints.

Friedan's book is actually complicated on issues of the experience of Jewish women in suburbs. Within *The Feminine Mystique*, the author offered several alternatives to what she saw as suburban captivity. She talked about the many women who remained in cities and pursued professional opportunities. She also highlighted types of suburban women who avoided the feminine mystique. First there were some, many of whom had benefited from psychotherapy, whose commitment to professional achievement made it possible to confine housework to a limited sphere. Then there was the first group of women to move to suburbs, those who had completed their college education before 1950, who were like adventuresome pioneers on the American frontier.[13] In contrast, members of the groups who moved later "were perfectly willing to fill their days with the trivia of housewifery."[14] When she sketched these alternatives, Friedan was relying on her own life history as a woman with sustained professional commitments, who had benefited from psychotherapy, who lived in distinctively unconventional suburbs, for whom city life remained a beacon, who graduated college before 1950, and whose suburban volunteer work was transformative.[15]

In thinking about the locale of American Jewish women, we can go far beyond the terms Friedan established. Here, the work of new suburban historians is helpful.[16] The dominant narrative of Jewish American suburban history focuses on the Jews who came to the United States from Eastern Europe after 1880, moved in the interwar period from the Lower East Side to the boroughs of New York City, and then after 1945 to suburbs where they lived in mostly Jewish neighborhoods or side-by-side with others who migrated from city to suburb. This narrative is problematic in several respects. Its focus on New York, though understandable, is now being challenged by studies of other locations, notably Deborah Dash Moore's work on the Jewish migration to Florida and California.[17] In some cases, Jews moved to suburbs that contained a mix of peoples of various ethnicities. Moreover, as Rosalyn Baxandall and Elizabeth Ewen remind us in *Picture Windows*, even around New York some suburbanites sustained the patterns of activism that we usually identify with urban living.[18] More generally, aside from narrowly focused communal histories, there are relatively few studies of the lives of Jewish suburban women in other regions—scholarship that would enable us to test the relationship between new environments and new experiences. Clearly, to understand the lives of Jewish women who lived in Kansas City or Shreveport or New Haven, to take three possible examples, we need to rethink the dominant narrative. Moreover, as the new suburban historians suggest, the definition of a *suburb* is itself problematic, raising questions about what exactly were the varieties of experiences of Jewish suburban women.[19] Several key feminists of the postwar period came from neighborhoods that were not typically suburban, or not suburban at all. I am thinking here of Carolyn Heilbrun and Bella Abzug. As Abzug noted in 1995, Mount Vernon was "not the usual hoi-polloi suburban bullshit."[20] Her geographical movement from city to suburb to city underscores, as does Friedan's, an important pattern that undercuts the usual narrative.[21]

There are other dimensions to the social and political location of postwar American Jews in the suburbs—but also outside them—that need exploration. With our emphasis on the 1950s and Friedan's generation, we risk missing other, more varied stories of historical importance. What of the working-class Jewish women who remained in cities or lived in the first, inmost ring of suburbs? What of the Orthodox Jewish women, many of whom ended up in such suburbs, close to major cities?[22] And we must regard the relationship of Jewish women to their African American counterparts, both as employers and as coworkers on interracial projects.[23] We must consider lesbians, whether closeted or open.[24] Again, if we shift away from Friedan's cohort, we must look at the meaning of a more complex tapestry of Jewish women: émigrés from Nazism (like Gerda Lerner, and the women discussed by Rebecca Kobrin in this volume); Hungarians who arrived after 1956; Egyptians fleeing in the mid- and late 1950s (discussed by Audrey Nasar in this volume); Cuban Jews who left before and after Castro came to power; and—as a result of the 1965 immigration law—the numerous Israeli, Iranian, North African, and Russian women who immigrated to the United States. And there were also the politically conservative Jewish women, perhaps counterparts to the suburban warriors whom Lisa McGirr found in Orange County, California, or those prominent as writers—for example, Lucy Dawidowicz (discussed by Nancy Sinkoff in this volume), Ayn Rand, Midge Decter, and Gertrude Himmelfarb.[25] What I am suggesting is a variety of perspectives to complicate our usual picture of Jewish women in the postwar period, in suburbs and elsewhere.

The third topic under consideration involves the intersections of the issues of anti-Semitism, the Holocaust, acculturation, and Israel. The general outline of Friedan's relationship to Jews, Judaism, and Jewishness is familiar. She was born to Jewish parents, an acculturated mother from Peoria and an immigrant father from near Kiev who spoke with an accent that embarrassed both his wife and young Betty. The young future author grew up as an agnostic and socially marginal girl in Peoria, celebrating Christmas and Passover, getting confirmed at the local Reform temple, and keenly aware of anti-Semitism in Peoria and in Nazi Germany. From an early age, issues of Jewish identity were fraught with anxiety, as she struggled with the tension between acculturation and marginality.[26] She later spoke of her early experiences as having intensified her sense of the connection between commitment to social justice and an outsider status.[27]

Friedan's experiences as an undergraduate at Smith College from 1938 to 1942, precisely the years when anti-Semitic fascism swept across Europe, intensified her sense of herself as a Jew. Smith was an institution with a significant proportion of Jews on the faculty, both native-born and émigrés; with a non-Jewish president intent on rescuing Jews from Nazi Germany, and on speaking out against fascism; and with a student body in which a brainy but socially awkward Jew from the provinces was an outsider.[28] Soon after graduating, she returned to Peoria and spoke at her synagogue on "Affirming One's Jewishness."[29]

After a year in graduate school in Berkeley, Friedan wrote, from 1943 to 1952, for left-wing publications, including articles on anti-Semitism and the ways it was linked to attacks both on African Americans and on radicals. In February 1945, she denounced the Nazis' "systematic mass murder of more than five million Jews."[30] In 1953, she wrote articles in a Jewish periodical supported by the Communist Party.[31] In 1947, she married a Jew from a more observant background, Carl Friedan, born Friedman, and moved through a series of suburbs until she returned to Manhattan in 1964, divorcing Carl Friedan in 1969. During her years in

the suburbs, she lived the life of a secular and unaffiliated Jew. In ethnically integrated neighborhoods where many of her Jewish friends were Unitarians, she celebrated Passover every year as a story of liberation, organized what she called
her sons' "atheistic bar mitzvahs," and was keenly aware of anti-Semitic attacks
on Jewish radicals.[32] Some might see her actions as strategies for denying one's
Jewishness, but it may be more fruitful to consider them as ways of redefining
her situation as a Jew.

In *The Feminine Mystique*, Friedan's explored the suburb as a "comfortable
concentration camp" but never specifically mentioned Jews.[33] But at Smith and
later, Friedan had pondered the meaning of marginality, anti-Semitism, and
Jewish self-hatred. These were issues, as Kirsten Fermgalich has shown, that led
Friedan to understand "the oppression of Jews and women." In drafts but not in
the published version of *The Feminine Mystique*, Friedan addressed these issues, as
she had continuously during the 1940s and 1950s.[34] As Fermgalich has written,
"Her personal background as a Jewish woman and several key intellectual influences . . . clearly shaped her portrait of self-destructive women and Nazi concentration camp inmates as victims who colluded in their own oppression."[35]

Only later, years after the publication of her book, did Friedan talk extensively, openly, and publicly about being Jewish.[36] Several key moments mark this
trajectory. In the 1970s, the curiosity of her children about their Jewish roots
sparked Friedan's interest in her own. In 1970, when she spoke at a march in
Manhattan marking the fiftieth anniversary of the women's suffrage amendment,
"I found myself harking back," as she remembered, "to the religion of my ancestors, and giving voice to a variation on the prayer that religious Jewish men recite
each morning 'I thank Thee Lord I was not born a woman' . . . I hope from this
day forward in all religions, women will wake up in the morning and be able to
pray 'I thank Thee Lord that I was born a woman.'"[37] She made her first trip to
Israel in 1972 or 1973.[38] It was a disillusioning experience: she saw the separation
of women and men at the Wall, had her beliefs in the egalitarian nature of the
Israeli army and kibbutzim overturned, and was angered by the refusal of Prime
Minister Golda Meir to meet with her.[39] In 1974, when Yasser Arafat spoke before
the United Nations, she protested both the U.N.'s welcoming of him and his anti-
Zionist and anti-Semitic language. A dozen years later, she made a second and
more successful trip to Israel, returning to the United States with the satisfaction
that she had helped to build a women's movement in the Jewish homeland. As
happened with other Jewish feminists, her concern grew, at two international
women's conferences—Mexico City in 1975 and Copenhagen in 1980—that feminists abroad were anti-Semitic.[40] She also feared the emergence of anti-Semitism
within the U.S. women's movement, especially in the argument that Jewish
patriarchs killed a flourishing matriarchal emphasis on the power of Goddesses.[41]
And so, in the 1970s and 1980s she turned her considerable energies to exploring
the links between Judaism and feminism. She spoke out against the negative

WHAT KIND OF WOMAN ARE YOU?

FRANTIC COOK?

Chauffeur?

Smothered Mother?

TOO INVOLVED?

Restless?

Interesting?

Informed?

Responsible
Parent?

Motivated?

Satisfied?

BETTY FRIEDAN
author, "THE FEMININE MYSTIQUE"

Betty Friedan will help you decide when she speaks on

 "A NEW IMAGE OF WOMAN"

Attend Temple Emanu-El Sisterhood

DONOR LUNCHEON

Tuesday, October 29, 1963

Sherry - 11:30 a.m.   Luncheon - 12:15 p.m.

Figure 13.1 Announcement of a talk by Betty Friedan at a Sisterhood lunch at Temple Emanu-El, Dallas, Texas, 1963.
Photograph by Pellegrini, reproduced courtesy of Schlesinger Library, Radcliffe Institute, Harvard Library.

stereotypes of the Jewish mother and "Jewish princess." She participated actively in Jewish consciousness-raising and discussion groups, longed to explore Jewish texts and spirituality, and assumed leadership positions in mainline Jewish organizations as they turned their attention to the position of women in the Jewish community. Events in the 1980s may also have spurred in her a new appreciation for the Jewish family: "The next stage for everyone's survival has got to be the articulation of the values of family and life and community," she noted in an interview printed in *Tikkun* in 1988.[42]

Thus, as historians such as Paula Hyman, Joyce Antler, and Matthew Frye Jacobson have noted, Friedan came (or returned), like others of her generation, to her Jewish identity after having reformulated her identity as a woman.[43] There is, however, a tendency to make a sharp break at 1970, when historians tell the story of the return of Friedan and others to Judaism and Jewishness.[44] This is true in the discussion of Friedan's rejection of the Orthodox prayer, a rejection often treated as appearing out of nowhere.[45] To speculate for a moment, I have to ask where Friedan may have earlier encountered a discussion of the gratitude of Orthodox men that they were not born women. Perhaps she heard it from a Reform rabbi in Peoria who was commenting on how his tradition differed from that of Orthodox Jews. But more surely she heard this idea in discussions among Popular Front Jewish feminists: for example, in a 1950 issue of *Jewish Life*, a Communist Party publication to which Friedan soon contributed, she may have read an article by Irene Epstein, "Woman under the Double Standard," in which its author emphasized Orthodox Judaism's relegation of women to subordinate positions.[46] (Irene Epstein was a pseudonym for Eleanor Flexner, the feminist historian whose prominent father was a Jew and who herself changed her religious affiliation many times.)[47]

My own judgment is that there never was a time when Friedan did not think of herself as a Jew and did not ponder issues of anti-Semitism, her very commitment to social justice inspired by being a Jew and an outsider. In her memoir, she reports that in the middle of the 1970s, in response to attacks on what was seen variously as her atheism or agnosticism, she said "I have lived my whole life in religious terms. In my religion, the Jewish religion, it is your duty to *use* your life to make life better for those who come after."[48] What changed around 1970 were largely things external to her life: the receptivity of audiences; the reemergence of anti-Semitism in the women's movement, at home and, especially, abroad; the feelings of many Jews when Israel went into battle; the maturation of her own children; the spreading national interest in exploring roots; her organizational marginalization after 1970; and the flowering of American Jewish feminism. In *Roots Too: White Ethnic Revival in Post–Civil Rights America* (2006), Matthew Frye Jacobson portrays Friedan's speaking out about her Jewishness as a part of the impact caused by rediscovery of roots among American feminists, Jews and non-Jews alike.

Historians of Jewish women would do well to think in comparative terms in other ways, too: across national borders, across ethnic groups, and among social movements. After all, what affected and paralleled Betty Friedan's emphasis on her Jewish identity were major changes in the women's movement, including the recognition that there was not one feminist movement but many.[49]

In suggesting that there was not, around 1970, a sharp division in Friedan's life, but only in her discussions of her life, I am making a more general point. Historians of American Jewish women differ in how they see the relationship between a secular feminism of the 1960s, in which Jews played a significant role, and a Jewish feminist movement that began in 1972 with the insurgency of Ezrat Nashim at the annual meeting of the Rabbinical Assembly, followed, a year later, by the First National Conference on Jewish Women.[50] Some Jewish women's historians—I think of Joyce Antler and Paula Hyman—understand the reciprocal relationship between these two movements.[51] Yet central to the outlook of some historians of Jewish women is a distinction made by Deborah Lipstadt. For her, Jewish feminism had by definition to involve Jewish women who used a combination of feminism and Judaism to challenge Jewish customs and traditions within the Jewish community. Analyzing the feminism of Jewish women who participated in the movement before 1970 seems to her out of the question, in good measure because of their universalism, their lack of obvious Jewish organizational and religious attachment, and the presence of anti-Semitism among some of the secular feminists they worked with. Thus Lipstadt speaks of "some Jewish women, particularly those already active in the broad-based feminist movement, who often lacked strong Jewish communal and religious attachments, [and who] attacked the cultural and social norms that they believed had shaped them."[52]

Obviously these discussions about who is a Jewish feminist raise larger questions of who is a Jew—what combination of blood, belief, self-identification, or identification by others makes a person a Jew. As historians, our task is to explore how debates over such issues have changed, a task in which Susan Glenn, Laurence Silberstein, Deborah Schultz, and Riv-Ellen Prell have led the way.[53] The next step is to connect such considerations to issues concerning the history of Jewish women. We certainly need more research on those Jewish women active in the women's movement before 1970—something Antler's essay in this volume suggestively provides, in her exploration of the Jewish experiences of some key second-wave feminists. We have to ask whether Jews who were feminists were rebelling against or fulfilling Jewish tradition; we must ask what we know of their Jewish education, identity, and organizational affiliations.

Ample evidence prompts us to interrogate the notion of a sharp division at 1970, the division that many historians make. On the one hand, historians of second-wave feminism generally ignore post-1972 Jewish feminism; on the other, more openly religious scholars largely minimize the importance of the Jewish dimension of this second wave. The general feminist movement of the 1960s raised the consciousness of tens of thousands of women who, in the next decade, participated in the creation and development of modern Jewish feminism. (A case in point: my sister, Judith Horowitz Katz, celebrated her bat mitzvah, in the late 1940s, in a Conservative synagogue with a Reconstructionist rabbi and with her own father as the shul's president—and then, inspired by feminism, she took a major leadership role in creating an egalitarian havurah in suburban Buffalo.) In the first issue of Lilith, in the fall of 1976, the editors remarked, "As women, we are attracted to much of the ideology of the general women's movement."[54] Indeed, Friedan never considered herself a non-Jew. At least some of the young, secular women activists had a strong sense of Jewish identity, which surely changed in intensity over the course of their lives.[55] In Bella Abzug's life, too, we see more continuity than discontinuity, with no sharp break around 1970. And Judith Plaskow, the preeminent feminist Jewish theologian, came to her politics through reading about the Holocaust as a young girl, then at age ten through an intense interest in the civil rights movement, and in 1969 through consciousness raising over the women's issues faced by female graduate students at Yale. In her classic essay of 1973, "The Jewish Feminist, Conflict in Identities," delivered at the first National Jewish Women's Conference, Plaskow said, "We are here because a secular movement for the liberation of women has made it imperative that we raise certain Jewish issues now."[56] Blu Greenberg, perhaps the most important Orthodox feminist, acknowledged that reading The Feminine Mystique provided her initial inspiration,[57] yet in 1976 she stated that "the possibility of a positive relationship between" feminism and those holding "traditional Jewish values" seemed "improbable."[58]

As historians, we may well follow the path of Joyce Antler and see the two movements, the general feminist one in which Jewish women participated in the 1960s, and the Jewish feminist struggle of the 1970s, as reciprocal rather than distinct.[59] As Plaskow noted, in the introduction to Standing Again at Sinai, she moved, over time, from being "overwhelmed by the contradictions between the two identities" (of woman and Jew) to gradually coming to reject "the split between a Jewish and a feminist self."[60] Most recently, Riv-Ellen Prell notes in the introduction to an edited book, Women Remaking American Judaism, that "Jewish feminism . . . grew from . . . Second Wave feminism," yet the essays in the volume generally pay little attention to the continuities between Jewish identity and second-wave feminism.[61] One wonders what it would be like to write a book titled "Jewish Women Remaking American Feminism / Women Remaking American Judaism" that complicated the notion of a sharp divide in the early 1970s.[62]

Of course, what I am getting at here, the fourth topic, is the larger question of the nature and extent of the field of history of Jewish women in America. At one end of this field is a focused definition that concentrates on women-identified dimensions of Jewish theology, spirituality, rituals, and organizations. At the other end (a position with which I associate myself) is a capacious, all-encompassing (some might say problematic) definition of who is a Jew and of what are the boundaries of American Jewish women's history. This latter perspective, or definition, fosters attention to the experiences of any woman in the United States who is or was in some sense a Jew.

If we focus on these definitional issues, two related questions arise. First, why is there so little scholarly work on the Jewishness of the 1960s Jewish women who were feminists? Second, how do we explain the disproportionate percentage of women who were feminist writers and activists in the 1960s and who were, perhaps not coincidentally, Jews?[63] To an exceptional extent, American Jewish women in the postwar period engaged in struggles for social justice. One must note, in this regard, the important work of community-based organizations such as Hadassah, the Emma Lazarus Federation of Jewish Women's Clubs, and the National Council of Jewish Women.[64] Among Popular Front feminists who reemerged in the 1960s, Jewish women were represented to an extraordinary degree.[65] Within second-wave feminism generally, a significant number of Jewish women were prominent as leaders and writers. Such a list raises questions of just what makes a person a Jew, but, using the broadest definition, the list is impressive; it includes, among others, Friedan and Abzug, of course, and also Esther Broner, Esther Brown (of *Brown v. Topeka Board of Education*), Susan Brownmiller, Judith Butler, Phyllis Chesler, Judy Chicago, Nancy Chodorow, Nancy Cott, Ellen DuBois, Andrea Dworkin, Susan Faludi, Shulamith Firestone, Carol Gilligan, Vivian Gornick, Susan Gubar, Carolyn Heilbrun, Florence Howe, Gerda Lerner, Robin Morgan, Grace Paley, Marge Piercy, Letty Cottin Pogrebin, Adrienne Rich, Joan Wallach Scott, Alix Kate Shulman, Gloria Steinem, Meredith Tax, Ellen Willis, and Naomi Weisstein. There are other ways of measuring the extent of participation by Jewish women in second-wave feminism: scholars have noted the high percentage of Jews among the founders of *Ms.* and the Boston Women's Health Collective, to say nothing of those active in the civil rights and antiwar movements.[66]

Focusing on the Jewish roots of second-wave feminism, to be sure, goes against the complex picture now emerging of the varied sources of this movement. Yet some historians correctly recognize and have begun to explain the extensive participation of Jewish women in the post-1963 women's movement. Antler, Diner, Jacobson, Sylvie Murray, Pamela Nadell, and others have pointed out that even the secular Jewish feminists of the 1960s drew, at some level, on Jewish traditions.[67] These scholars point to family and cultural heritage (radicalism, liberalism, and education); knowledge of the Holocaust; negative and positive role models experienced; religious traditions, especially tzedekah and tikkun olam; the influence of the Torah and Talmud; and the women's reaction to stereotypes of Jewish women, their outsider or marginal status, and their experiences with anti-Semitism.[68]

In contrast, some historians—those not affiliated with Jewish studies programs, perhaps those not in some ways self-identifying as Jews, and/or those whose ideological commitments prompt a certain cosmopolitan, gender, or class analysis—offer neither acknowledgment of nor explanation for the significant participation of Jewish women in 1960s feminism. With notable exceptions, many feminist historians, Jews and non-Jews alike, write about women who were Jewish but do not acknowledge them as Jewish women (perhaps out of a fear of fostering anti-Semitism). For example, in what is now the most authoritative history of the women's movement from the 1960s on, Ruth Rosen, herself a Jew, discusses the contribution of many Jewish women to modern American feminism, but neither mentions them as Jews nor explains how their backgrounds may have shaped their participation.[69] My guess is that historians like Rosen rely on a universalist commitment to womanhood and, when narrowing focus, concentrate on women considered oppressed.[70] In some measure, the nonacknowledgment of Jews is part of a waning sense, whatever the reality, of Jews as an oppressed minority, and results in the focus on "workers," African Americans, lesbians, Latinas, and others as members of oppressed groups.[71] In other ways, this nonacknowledgment, or avoidance, reflects the more general tendency among American historians to neglect religion as a topic. So what we have in these cases are both Jewish and non-Jewish women writing feminist history that, though it may pay attention to the role of Jewish women in the shaping of American feminism, does not take Jewishness as a category to be recognized or analyzed. I should also acknowledge improvement: in the two leading readers and a leading textbook for American women's history, each having one Jewish editor or author, recent editions have included more articles on Jews than did earlier ones.[72]

Thus, two groups of Jewish women's historians, those supposedly secular and those Jewishly identified, seldom talk about what it means that so many 1960s feminists were in some sense Jewish: the first because they are universalists, and the second because they are particularists.[73] Moreover, many women's historians who are Jewish have not paid much attention to the emergence of American Jewish feminism in the 1970s.

What we need more of is sustained exploration of the causal links between being Jewish women and having a commitment to work for social justice. To a considerable extent, we have such exploration in the historical writing about Jewish women active between 1880 and 1920. In this literature—for example the writings of Gerald Sorin, Annelise Orleck, Alice Kessler-Harris, and Susan Glenn—a generally accepted explanation of why so many Jewish women participated in radical, reform, and women's movements has emerged.[74]

In explaining why so many feminists were Jews, we can draw on what others have written, often in different contexts. Scholars trying to understand the high levels of achievement Jews have attained, as well as the disproportionate participation of Jews in radical movements, point to a series of nongenetic factors: the nature of the experience of Jews in Europe, including participation in activism;

anti-Semitism; a commitment to literacy and textual analysis; marginalization; worldliness; a receptivity to modernization; a commitment to education; the social capital of communal networks and institutions; and Jewish traditions of social justice.[75] Sometimes these explanations are gender specific: what spurred Jewish women on were their history of entrepreneurship, their commitment to education, their relationship to their mothers, their traditions of activism, and specific elements of their family structure and dynamics.[76] Of course, what might explain the achievement and politics of Jewish women for the period 1880–1920 might not apply to a later period. And to develop a more comprehensive and suggestive answer to the question of the disproportionate role of Jewish women in second-wave feminism, we may ask about the prominence of Jews, women and men, in business, intellectual life, and social movements.

For explanatory models, we might turn to a number of places, including the recent and controversial work of the Russian historian Yuri Slezkine, whose 2004 book *The Jewish Century* provocatively suggests how to think of Jewish history in historical and comparative ways.[77] Slezkine sees Jews, but also migrants from Lebanon to Latin America, from China to the Philippines, from Armenia to many parts of the world, as "service nomads" or Mercurians. These groups were entrepreneurs whose ways of life stood in opposition to the Apollonians, or food-producing majorities. Jews, like other Mercurians, Slezkin argues, were in a position to take advantage of, and play a significant role in, the modernization that characterized the twentieth century. Outsiders, they were urban, literate, mobile. They had the skills to succeed—they were flexible when it came to occupation, and agile when it came to ideas. They balanced a particularism that provided social networks, and a universalism that made them hold host societies to a high standard. These were elements of Jewish cultural capital that both enabled them to succeed and impelled many into radical movements. Slezkine pays little attention to gender—but I do wonder how his insights, applied to the history of Jewish women in America, might influence the field. For example, why did Jewish women play such a prominent role in radical movements when Armenian ones presumably did not? How did access to media in New York make the experience of Jewish women distinct? Would seeing Jewish women as "service nomads" or as embracing modernity to an exceptional degree help us explain their engagement with feminism and their entry into the professions?

What I am trying to puzzle out is how to think of the dynamics of the participation of Jewish women in 1960s secular feminism. For, from what I can see, except for Debora Schultz's work on civil rights and, more recently Antler's work, there is remarkably little primary source–based, sustained, and analytic exploration of the issue of disproportionate participation of Jewish women in social movements since 1960. Ironically, we have more of this focus in synthetic work—I think here of books by Diner, Antler, and Jacobson—than in journal articles or scholarly monographs.

What I have tried, in this essay, to show is how the contribution of Betty Friedan complicates and illuminates how we think about issues key to understanding the history of Jewish women in America since 1945. The ways in which the feminine mystique did and did not trap Friedan (and many of her peers) prompts us to understand the complex hold that it had—and did not have—on American Jewish women. Friedan's relationship to suburban living, along with the relationship of others to urban and suburban life, suggests that we think more carefully about the interaction between social location and identity. How Friedan and others engaged with anti-Semitism, Israel, the Holocaust, and acculturation forces us to return again and again to these issues. The story of the lives of Friedan and others as Jews should prompt us to reconsider issues of identity and chronology. The essays in this volume advance considerably the richness of the field of American Jewish women's history for the post-1945 period. I hope they will inspire a new generation of historians of Jewish women.

ACKNOWLEDGMENTS

I am grateful to Rachel Gelfand, Kimberly Prolobus, and Caitlin Gleason, students at Smith College, for their research assistance and reading skills. Among the others who have helped me with this essay are Hasia Diner, Susan Glenn, David Hollinger, Helen Lefkowitz Horowitz, Daniel Rivers, Judy Smith, Rachel Kranson, and Lynn Dumenil.

NOTES

1. Throughout this essay, I am relying, for biographical information on Friedan, upon Daniel Horowitz, *Betty Friedan and the Making of the Feminine Mystique: The American Left, the Cold War, Modern Feminism* (Amherst: University of Massachusetts Press, 1998).

2. Most recently, see Joyce Antler, *You Never Call! You Never Write! A History of the Jewish Mother* (New York: Oxford University Press, 2007); Janet Burstein, *Writing Mothers, Writing Daughters: Tracing the Maternal in Stories by American Jewish Women* (Urbana: University of Illinois Press, 1996).

3. On Abzug, see Antler, *You Never Call! You Never Write!* 151, and the work of Leandra Zarnow, who is writing on Abzug for her doctoral dissertation at the University of California at Santa Barbara.

4. Sydney Stahl Weinberg, *The World of Our Mothers: The Lives of Jewish Immigrant Women* (Chapel Hill: University of North Carolina Press, 1988).

5. Hasia R. Diner and Beryl Lieff Benderly, *Her Works Praise Her: A History of Jewish Women in America from Colonial Times to the Present* (New York: Basic Books, 2002), 384 and 386, note that Friedan's situation as a child denied her the opportunity to understand the importance to Jewish women of motherhood, domesticity, and community work.

6. Betty Friedan, *The Second Stage* (New York: Summit Books, 1981).

7. Horowitz, *Betty Friedan*, 210.

8. Jessica Weiss has made us aware that our emphasis on women's captivity in the 1950s overlooks the life cycle of these very women, including how they pursued alternatives to the feminine mystique at later points in their lives once the responsibility of caring for children waned: Jessica Weiss, *To Have and to Hold: Marriage, the Baby Boom, and Social Change* (Chicago: University of Chicago Press, 2000).

9. Betty Friedan, "Jewish Roots: An Interview with Betty Friedan," *Tikkun* 3 (January/February 1988): 26.

10. David Riesman, *The Lonely Crowd: A Study of the Changing American Character* (New Haven, CT: Yale University Press, 1950); William H. Whyte Jr., *The Organization Man* (New York: Simon and Schuster, 1956); Vance Packard, *The Status Seekers: An Exploration of Class Behavior in America and the Hidden Barriers That Affect You, Your Community, and Your Future* (New York: David McKay, 1959).

11. Whyte, *Organization Man*, 374–376, discussed the Jewish community of Park Forest, Illinois, but said little of the role of Jewish women in it. Riesman, *Lonely Crowd*, 334–346, briefly discussed Jews but paid no attention to Jewish women. When Herbert Gans paid attention to women, he focused mostly on their roles as mothers and community organizers. On the former, see Herbert J. Gans, "The Future of American Jewry: Part II," *Commentary* 21 (1956): 556. Gans wrote an article on the Jews of Park Forest, in which he discussed participation of Jewish women in organizational life and child rearing; see Herbert Gans, "The Origin and Growth of a Jewish Community in the Suburbs: A Study of the Jews in Park Forest," in *The Jews: Social Patterns of an American Group*, ed. Marshall Sklare (Glencoe, IL: Free Press, 1958), 205–248. The following influential and widely read volume contained one article that focused specifically on women, through a psychoanalytic discussion of two mothers, one European-born and one American-born: Martha Wolfenstein, in *Jews: Social Patterns of an American Group*, 520–534. William M. Dobriner, *Class in Suburbia* (Englewood Cliffs, NJ: Prentice-Hall, 1963), 94–95, noted that the percentage of Jews in Levittown grew from 15 in 1950 to more than 17 ten years later; on pp. 97–99, when discussing "occupational characteristics," he made no mention of women's labor; he only mentioned in passing Jewish women and gender lines (66, 100, and 107). For a perceptive article that focuses on the experience of Jews in suburbia but has almost nothing to say of the experience of women, see Harry Gersh, "The New Suburbanites of the 50s," *Commentary* 17 (1954): 209–221. Among the most important works on the topic of Jews in the suburbs is the series of essays by Evelyn Rosman, published in *Commentary* during the 1950s about her life in "Northrup," (actually Sharon, Massachusetts). Among the possible exceptions to the rule of minimal attention to Jewish women in suburbia is *Crestwood Heights* (1956), a study of a Canadian suburb that had a considerable number of Jewish residents, presumably including those whom the authors described as "many a Crestwood mother, while 'accepting' the culturally approved maternal role, reveals an underlying resentment. The demands made upon her as a wife and mother she may often find irksome in contrast to the communal, more lively world, of university, profession, or office": John R. Seeley, R. Alexander Sim, and Elizabeth W. Loosley, *Crestwood Heights: A Study of the Culture of Suburban Life* (New York: Basic Books, 1956), 179; see also 139–142 and 278. In his introduction to the book, Riesman noted the complications arising from the triangle, in suburban studies, of "male experts and researchers, their female clients, and the latter's husbands," who, unlike the researchers, were absent on weekdays; see David Riesman, introduction, *Crestwood Heights*, v–vi.

12. Albert I. Gordon, *Jews in Suburbia* (Boston: Beacon Press, 1959), 59. See also Marshall Sklare and Joseph Greenblum, *Jewish Identity on the Suburban Frontier: A Study of Group Survival in the Open Society* (New York: Basic Books, 1967), 258; Judith R. Kramer and Seymour Leventman, *Children of the Gilded Ghetto: Conflict Resolutions of Three Generations of American Jews* (New Haven, CT: Yale University Press, 1961).

13. Betty Friedan, *The Feminine Mystique* (New York: W. W. Norton, 1963), 244. This analysis echoed that of Stanley Elkins and Eric McKitrick, "A Meaning for Turner's Frontier," *Political Science Quarterly* 69 (September/December 1954): 321–353 and 565–602; it is possible that Friedan knew of the work of Elkins, a professor at Smith College, her alma mater.

14. Friedan, *Feminine Mystique*, 245.

15. Already in the early 1950s, writers were questioning the stereotypical assumptions about suburban life: See, for example, Phyllis McGinley, "Suburbia: Of Thee I Sing," *30th Anniversary Reader's Digest Reader* (Pleasantville, NY: Reader's Digest, 1952), 227–230. However, the major source of skepticism came in the 1960s, including in Herbert J. Gans, *The Levittowners: Ways of Life and Politics in a New Suburban Community* (New York: Pantheon, 1967). Gans neither mentioned Friedan's book nor explored the situation Jewish women faced, in any explicit or extensive manner. But Gans cast a skeptical eye on the notion of suburbs, in general, having "a suburban matriarchy"; instead, he noted, suburban life had fostered "family cohesion," "the reduction in boredom," and a "trend toward greater equality between the sexes." At one point, he said suburban loneliness was rare and then remarked that Jewish women, feeling stuck and facing the monotony of housework, had "considerably higher increases" in boredom than had their Gentile counterparts (quotations, 220, 224, and 229). Appearing four years after the publication of Friedan's book and one year after the founding of the National Organization for Women, Gans's book paid remarkably little attention to "the problem that had no name" or to professional careers and political activism for women. See, for example, his recommendation for solving the loneliness of women: Gans, *Levittowners*, 241–244. Gans did mention the objections of Orthodox Jews in Levittown to "the prominence of women" in discussions about the organization of Jewish religious and communal life (74). For an earlier discussion, see Herbert Gans, "Urbanism and Suburbanism as Ways of Life: A Re-Evaluation of Definitions," in *Human Behavior and Social Processes*, ed. Arnold M. Rose (Boston: Houghton Mifflin, 1962), 625–648. Carol A. O'Connor, *A Sort of Utopia: Scarsdale, 1891–1981* (Albany: State University of New York Press, 1983), one of the best histories of a suburb—and of a suburb whose Jewish population grew dramatically in the postwar period—did not focus on issues, such as the experience of Jewish women or of their relationship to others, that are of concern in this essay. Lizabeth Cohen, *Consumers' Republic: The Politics of Mass Consumption in Postwar America* (New York: Alfred A. Knopf, 2003) does discuss the experience of Jews. Generally speaking, however, recent books on suburban history do not focus on Jews: see, notably, Kevin M. Kruse and Thomas Sugrue, ed., *The New Suburban History* (Chicago: University of Chicago Press, 2006).

16. Kruse and Sugrue, *New Suburban History*. Also suggestive is Gerald Gamm's comparative study, *Urban Exodus: Why the Jews Left Boston and the Catholics Stayed* (Cambridge, MA: Harvard University Press, 1999).

17. Deborah Dash Moore, *To the Golden Cities: Pursuing the American Dream in Miami and L.A.* (Cambridge, MA: Harvard University Press, 1994). Moore pays considerable attention to the role of mothers in the family and community. Moore also offers an admirable focus on the disruptive and transformative power of World War II, a subject to which historians of American Jewish women in the postwar period could pay more attention.

18. Rosalyn Baxandall and Elizabeth Ewen, *Picture Windows: How the Suburbs Happened* (New York: Basic Books, 2000), 152–157.

19. Deborah Dash Moore, *At Home in America: Second Generation New York Jews* (New York: Columbia University Press, 1981), which focuses on the 1920s and 1930s, raises the question of in what ways areas within the city limits of New York were suburban: 26, 33, 43, and 78.

20. Bella Abzug, interview, November 11, 1995, 96, Oral History Research Office, Columbia University, New York City.

21. For another example of a leading Jewish feminist who remained oriented to the city, consider the life of Gerda Lerner, who moved with her family in the late 1940s from Hollywood to Manhattan (briefly); to Astoria, Queens; to Peekskill, New York, where the family was "too far removed from struggle, too comfortable, too isolated" (315); in 1952, unable to afford Manhattan prices, they moved to a free-standing house in a racially integrated neighborhood of St. Albans, Queens. Around 1958, still resident in Queens, Lerner, whose political life until then divided between local campaigns in Queens and national/international ones in the city,

entered the New School in Manhattan. See Gerda Lerner, *Fireweed: A Political Autobiography* (Philadelphia: Temple University Press, 2002), 303–373.

22. Etan Diamond, *And I Will Dwell in Their Midst: Orthodox Jews in Suburbia* (Chapel Hill: University of North Carolina Press, 2000), which focuses on a suburb of Toronto, pays some attention to women's role in the kitchen and in associational life, but sheds little light on questions that animate discussions of women's historians.

23. See Cheryl Greenberg, "Negotiating Coalition: Black and Jewish Civil Rights Agencies in the Twentieth Century," in *Struggles in the Promised Land: Toward a History of Black-Jewish Relations in the United States,* ed. Jack Salzman and Cornel West (New York: Oxford University Press, 1997), 153–176.

24. See Evelyn Torton Beck, ed., *Nice Jewish Girls: A Lesbian Anthology* (Trumansburg, NY: Crossing Press, 1982); Rebecca Alpert, *Like Bread on a Seder Plate: Jewish Lesbians and the Transformation of Tradition* (New York: Columbia University Press, 1997).

25. In 1961, Midge Decter published in *Commentary,* which her husband Norman Podhoretz edited, an article on women (neither specifically Jewish nor suburban) that spoke of young, married, college-educated women as "plagued with choices . . . that breeds restlessness," prefiguring in some ways what Friedan would say two years later. Where Decter differed from Friedan was also obvious. Although admitting that women faced unjust discrimination in the job market, in the end she reminded them, and her readers, that they did so because of "their one revocable privilege: they always have a place of retreat when failure threatens—that is not what they really are, what they really do": Midge Decter, "Women at Work," *Commentary* 31 (March 1961): 249–250. On Rand, see Jennifer Burns, *Goddess of the Market: Ayn Rand and the American Right* (New York: Oxford University Press, 2009). On activism by conservatives, see Lisa McGirr, *Suburban Warriors: The Origins of the New American Right* (Princeton, NJ: Princeton University Press, 2001).

26. "She could not help avoid internalizing some of Peoria's anti-Semitism," Joyce Antler has written of Friedan: Joyce Antler, *Journey Home: Jewish Women and the American Century* (New York: Free Press, 1997), 263.

27. "Ever since I was a little girl," Friedan remarked in 1976, "I remember my father telling me that I had a passion for justice. But I think it was really a passion against injustice which originated from my feelings of the injustice of anti-Semitism": Betty Friedan, quoted in "Friedan at 55: From Feminism to Judaism," *Lilith* 1 (Fall 1976): 11. On this connection, see Friedan, "Jewish Roots," 25, "So being Jewish made me an observer, a marginal person."

28. In the summer of 1940, Friedan studied at the University of Iowa with Kurt Lewin, a psychologist whose work in these years focused on the dynamics of both anti-Semitism and Jewish self-hatred. Adopting a Popular Front position, she remained in opposition to America's entry into World War II until Pearl Harbor, a decision that reveals how ideology trumped a determination to fight anti-Semitism. Kirsten Fermgalich, *American Dreams and Nazi Nightmares: Early Holocaust Consciousness and Liberal America, 1957–1965* (Waltham, MA: Brandeis University Press, 2006), 63–66, explores the Friedan/Lewin connection.

29. Friedan, in Stone, "Friedan at 55," 12.

30. Betty Goldstein, February 1945 article in *Federated Press,* quoted in Horowitz, *Betty Friedan,* 115.

31. Horowitz, *Betty Friedan,* 151.

32. Friedan, in Stone, "Friedan at 55," 40. She was, she later declared, part of a tradition of "agnostic, atheistic, scientific, and humanist" Jews: Friedan, "Jewish Roots," 25.

33. Fermgalich, *American Dreams,* 59; for her extended consideration, see 58–82. "The women who 'adjust' as housewives, who grow up wanting to be 'just a housewife,' are in as much danger as the millions who walked to their own death in the concentration camps": Friedan, *Feminine Mystique,* 294.

34. Fermgalich, *American Dreams*, 65.

35. Ibid., 82.

36. Diner and Benderly, *Her Works Praise Her*, 382–385; Paula E. Hyman, "Jewish Feminism Faces the American Women's Movement: Convergence and Divergence," 299 and 308, in *American Jewish Women's History: A Reader*, ed. Pamela S. Nadell (New York: New York University Press, 2003); Antler, *Journey Home*, 259, 261–267, and 276–279. For Friedan's perspective on her reemergence as a Jew, see Stone, "Friedan at 55," 11–12 and 40–41; Betty Friedan, "Women and Jews: The Quest for Selfhood," *Congress Monthly* (February/March 1985): 7–11; Friedan, in "Jewish Roots," 25–29; Jennifer Moses, "She's Changed Our Lives: A Profile of Betty Friedan," *Present Tense* 15 (May/June 1988): 26–31.

37. Friedan, "Women and Jews," 7. In reflecting, in the mid-1970s, on her life, Friedan speculated that her "passion against injustice . . . may have stemmed from my own experience of injustice as the daughter of an immigrant Jew in Peoria": Betty Friedan, introduction to 1976 edition of '*It Changed My Life*,' *Writings on the Women's Movement* (New York: W. W. Norton, 1976), 6. In Betty Friedan, *Life So Far: A Memoir* (New York: Simon and Schuster, 2000), she discusses being a Jew, at several points, most notably 24, 28, 35, 36, 39, 53, 56, 71, 277, 308–309, and 330–331.

38. Most sources give 1973 as the date, but in an article in *Congress Monthly*, Friedan used 1972.

39. "I was told, she commented soon after, 'Go back to America and take the Israeli women's libbers with you'": Friedan, in Stone, "Friedan at 55," 40.

40. Friedan, in Stone, "Friedan at 55," 11.

41. "I don't like feminism to be used in any way to justify anti-Semitism": Friedan, "Jewish Roots," 27.

42. Friedan, "Jewish Roots," 29; see also Friedan, "Women and Jews," 9–10.

43. Hyman, "Jewish Feminism," 308; Antler, *Journey Home*, especially 266–267; Matthew Frye Jacobson, *Roots Too: White Ethnic Revival in Post–Civil Rights America* (Cambridge, MA: Harvard University Press, 2006), 246–311; on Friedan, see 257–259 and 267–268. For a compelling exploration of issues of dual identity, as a Jew and as a woman, see Letty Cottin Pogrebin, *Deborah, Golda, and Me: Being Female and Jewish in America* (New York: Crown, 1991).

44. To be sure, some recognize continuity; see Antler, *Journey Home*, 261: "Her family history provides evidence" that oppression of Jews and women had long "been joined in her experience."

45. One scholar writes that Friedan's articulation of the Orthodox view of women's role "emerged from the recesses of her memory" (Antler, *Journey Home*, 259). In an article on Friedan in the first issue of *Lilith*, Amy Stone remarked that in 1970 Friedan was "suddenly out in front as a Jew," recalling an interview in which Friedan had explained "what had suddenly made her aware of herself as a Jew": Stone, "Friedan at 55," 11. In 1985, Friedan herself, reflecting back on that moment, referred to her response as occurring "for some strange reason—strange because my own background was not religious and I cannot remember ever having heard the familiar prayer before": Friedan, "Women and Jews," 7.

46. Irene Epstein, "Woman under the Double Standard," *Jewish Life* 4 (October 1950): 8–12.

47. On Flexner, see Daniel Horowitz, "Feminism, Women's History, and American Social Thought at Midcentury," in *American Capitalism: Social Thought and Political Economy in the Twentieth Century*, ed. Nelson Lichtenstein (Philadelphia: University of Pennsylvania Press, 2006), 191–209.

48. Friedan, *Life So Far*, 308–309.

49. For earlier models of comparative work, see Linda Gordon Kuzmack, *Woman's Cause: The Jewish Woman's Movement in England and the United States, 1881–1933* (Columbus: Ohio

State University Press, 1990), and Judith E. Smith, *Family Connections: A History of Italian and Jewish Immigrant Lives in Providence, Rhode Island, 1900–1940* (Albany: State University of New York Press, 1985).

50. There are many important works on Jewish feminism. See, for example, Joyce Antler, "Feminism, American," in *Jewish Women in America: An Historical Encyclopedia*, ed. Paula E. Hyman and Deborah Dash Moore (New York: Routledge, 1997), 1: 408–415, and note that Antler says, of Jewish women active in civil rights in 1960s, "While most of these women were not Jewishly identified, they acknowledged that their sense of 'otherness' as Jew, along with progressive family values, stimulated their involvement in the movement" (413). See also Martha Acklesberg, "Introduction," in *The Jewish Woman: A Reader*, ed. Elizabeth Koltun (New York: Schocken, 1976), xiii–xx; Deborah E. Lipstadt, "Feminism and Judaism: Looking Back at the Turn of the Century," in *Women and American Judaism: Historical Perspectives*, ed. Pamela S. Nadell and Jonathan Sarna (Hanover, NH: Brandeis University Press, 2001), 291–308; Sylvia Barack Fishman, *A Breath of Life: Feminism in the American Jewish Community* (New York: Free Press, 1993), especially pp. 1–15; Judith Plaskow, *Standing Again at Sinai: Judaism from a Feminist Perspective* (San Francisco: Harper and Row, 1990); Pamela S. Nadell, "On Their Own Terms: American Jewish Women, 1954–2004," *American Jewish History* 91 (September/December 2003): 389–404; Paula E. Hyman, "Jewish Feminism Faces the American Women's Movement: Convergence and Divergence," in *American Jewish Women's History*, 297–312; Antler, *Journey Home*, chap. 10. Jacobson, *Roots Too*, 286–311, where he places the story in the larger context of discovery of feminist spirituality.

51. Antler, *Journey Home*, 259–327, and essay in this volume; Hyman, "Jewish Feminism," 297–312. Yet even in Hyman's work there is a distinction. She might well have seen American feminism of the 1960s as in many ways inflected, influenced by Jews. She probably does not go down that road because, to her and to others, there is a distinction, as Hyman wrote of Robin Morgan, Friedan, and Shalumith Firestone, between women feminists "of Jewish origin" who, because of their commitment to a gendered analysis, did not deal "specifically with Judaism or with the Jewish community," and those who asserted "a Jewish dimension to their feminism" and brought "the issue of gender equality to the Jewish community": Hyman, "Jewish Feminism," 299.

52. Lipstadt, 291–304, quotation on 292. See also Fishman, *Breath of Life*, 2 and 5–12. For another statement of the division between the secular feminism of Jewish women and American Jewish feminism, see Riv-Ellen Prell, *Fighting to Become Americans: Jews, Gender, and the Anxiety of Assimilation* (Boston: Beacon Press, 1990), 196.

53. Susan Glenn, "In the Blood? Consent, Descent, and the Ironies of Jewish Identity," *Jewish Social Studies* 8 (Winter/Spring 2002): 139–152; Prell, *Fighting to Become Americans*; Laurence J. Silberstein, ed., *Mapping Jewish Identities* (New York: New York University Press, 2000). Deborah L. Schultz provides a nuanced discussion of issues surrounding Jewish identity in the civil rights movement; see Deborah L. Schultz, *Going South: Jewish Women in the Civil Right Movement* (New York: New York University Press, 2001), especially in chaps. 3–5. See also Daniel Boyarin and Jonathan Boyarin, ed., *Jews and Other Differences: The New Jewish Cultural Studies* (Minneapolis: University of Minnesota Press, 1998).

54. "From the Editors," *Lilith* 1 (Fall 1976): 3.

55. Schultz, *Going South*, 129–192.

56. Judith Plaskow, "The Jewish Feminist: Conflict in Identities," originally delivered and published in 1973, reprinted in Judith Plaskow, *The Coming of Lilith: Essays on Feminism, Judaism, and Sexual Ethics, 1972–2003* (Boston: Beacon Press, 2005), 35. For biographical information, see Judith Plaskow, "Intersections: An Introduction," in *Coming of Lilith*, especially 6–9.

57. See Antler, *Journey Home*, 292.

58. Blu Greenberg, "Judaism and Feminism," in *Jewish Woman*, 179; originally published in *Hadassah Magazine* (April 1976).

59. For a useful anthology, see Susannah Heschel, ed., *On Being a Jewish Feminist: A Reader* (New York: Schocken Books, 1983).

60. Plaskow, *Standing Again at Sinai*, vii and ix.

61. Riv-Ellen Prell, "Introduction: Feminism and the Remaking of American Judaism," in *Women Remaking American Judaism*, ed. Riv-Ellen Prell (Detroit: Wayne State University Press, 2007), 1. In stating that second-wave feminism "began at the very end of the 1960s," Prell offers a later birth date than would many other historians; see Prell, "Introduction," 1.

62. Thus when Rochelle L. Millen says "it is important to place Plaskow in historical context," she is referring to post-1970 events involving Jewish feminists, not Plaskow's own earlier engagement with the Holocaust, civil rights, or consciousness raising: Rochelle L. Millen, "'Her Mouth Is Full of Wisdom': Reflections on Jewish Feminist Theology," in Prell, *Women Remaking American Judaism*, 28.

63. In 1955, Seymour Lipset asked "why there are so many Jewish sociologists and so few sociologists of the Jews": Seymour Lipset, "Jewish Sociologists and Sociologists of the Jews," *Jewish Social Studies* 17 (July 1955): 177–178.

64. Antler, *Journey Home*, 244–253; Faith Rogow, *Gone to Another Meeting: The National Council of Jewish Women, 1893–1993* (Tuscaloosa: University of Alabama Press, 1993); Joyce Antler, "Between Culture and Politics: The Emma Lazarus Federation of Jewish Women's Clubs and the Promulgation of Women's History, 1944–1989," in *Women's America: Refocusing the Past*, ed. Linda K. Kerber and Jane Sherron DeHart (New York: Oxford University Press, 2000), 519–541.

65. The list is quite compelling: Betty Friedan, Gerda Lerner, Eleanor Flexner, Helen M. Hacker, Mim Kelber, Bella Abzug, to name only a few. On the more rank-and-file level, one need only look at the people whom Kate Weigand and Sylvie Murray describe in their histories of Red Feminism and community activism in Queens. See Kate Weigand, *Red Feminism: American Communism and the Making of Women's Liberation* (Baltimore: Johns Hopkins University Press, 2001); Sylvie Murray, *The Progressive Housewife: Community Activism in Suburban Queens, 1945–1965* (Philadelphia: University of Pennsylvania Press, 2003).

66. Diner and Benderly, *Her Works Praise Her*, 382 and 389; Schultz, *Going South*, 19. For a brief discussion of the role of Jewish women in post-1963 feminism, see June Sochen, "Happy Endings: Individualism and Feminism in American Jewish Life," *American Jewish History* 81(Spring/Summer 1984): 343–344. For other perspectives on Jews in the civil rights movement, see Melanie Kaye/Kantrowitz, "Stayed on Freedom: Jews in the Civil Rights Movement and After," in *The Narrow Bridge: Jewish Views on Multiculturalism*, ed. Marla Brettschneider (New Brunswick, NJ: Rutgers University Press, 1996), 105–122.

67. See, for example, Nadell, "On Their Own Terms," 389–404.

68. Antler, *Journey Home*, 285–308; Jacobson, *Roots Too*, 252–257; Diner and Benderly, *Her Works Praise Her*, 389, 392, and 394. Debra L. Schultz , "Going South: Jewish Women in the Civil Rights Movement," in *American Jewish Women's History*, 281–296, emphasizes the importance of family traditions, of the Holocaust, of exposure "to a liberal Jewish moral framework of social justice," and "of a universalist concern with justice that has roots in Jewish history, ethics, and political radicalism" (283 and 284).

69. Ruth Rosen, *The World Split Open: How the Modern Women's Movement Changed America* (New York: Viking Penguin, 2000). Neither Alice Echols, *Daring to Be Bad: Radical Feminism in America, 1967–1975* (Minneapolis: University of Minnesota Press, 1989), nor Cynthia Harrison, *On Account of Sex: The Politics of Women's Issues, 1945–1968* (Berkeley and Los Angeles: University of California Press, 1988), contains any reference in the index to Jews or Judaism. Sara M. Evans, *Born for Liberty: A History of Women in America* (New York: Free Press,

1989), has a few references to Jewish women, but no analysis of their disproportionate participation in early twentieth-century union and radical movements or in second-wave feminism. In her widely used textbook on the history of American women, Nancy Woloch explicitly notes the presence of many Jewish women in the social movements of the Progressive period, but does not in regard to second-wave feminism; see Nancy Woloch, *Women and the American Experience*, 2nd ed. (New York: McGraw-Hill, 1994), 204, 206, 211, 212, 214, 215, 231, 243, 260, and 298.We need more local studies, including those that move away from New York City and explore the nature and extent of the participation of Jewish women in feminism elsewhere; for a preliminary study, see Marj Jackson Levin, "Jewish Women for Social Justice," *Michigan Jewish History* 45 (Fall 2005): 32–40. The following books contain no explicit references to Jews or Judaism: Joanne Meyerowitz, ed., *Not June Cleaver: Women and Gender in Postwar America, 1945–1960* (Philadelphia: Temple University Press, 1994); Wini Breines, *Young, White, and Miserable: Growing Up Female in the Fifties* (Boston: Beacon Press, 1992); Richard Flacks, *Making History: The American Left and the American Mind* (New York: Columbia University Press, 1988); Eugenia Kaledin, *Mothers and More: American Women in the 1950s* (Boston: Twayne, 1984). In *Homeward Bound: American Families in the Cold War Era*, rev. ed. (New York: Basic Books, 1999), Elaine Tyler May has one reference to the importance to Jewish parents of having children to make up for those lost in the Holocaust (17) and another referring to the approval of birth control devices by Jewish organizations (134).

70. Weigand, *Red Feminism*, points to the role of immigrants and ethnics in the Communist Party, but does not mention Jews, despite their statistically disproportionate number in the party. The same can be said for Amy Swerdlow's story of the peace activists of the 1960s: Amy Swerdlow, *Women Strike for Peace: Traditional Motherhood and Radical Politics in the 1960s* (Chicago: University of Chicago Press, 1993). For a fuller acknowledgment of the role of Jews in progressive postwar politics, see Murray, *Progressive Housewife*. Murray acknowledges the importance of anti-Semitism, Jews, and Jewish organizations (for example, 67, 76, and 77); she ascribes the participation of Jews in left politics to "the strong tradition of radical activism in the New York Jewish community" and to the "concern for social justice that had long characterized Jewish communities" (61).

71. For a clear statement concerning the absence of discussion about the lives of Jewish women, and about anti-Semitism in feminist discussions even when the discussion focuses on ethnicity and prejudice, see Evelyn Torton Beck, "The Politics of Jewish Invisibility," *NWSA Journal* 1 (Autumn 1988): 93–102.

72. See Vicki L. Ruiz and Ellen Carol DuBois, ed., *Unequal Sisters: A Multicultural Reader in U.S. Women's History* (New York: Routledge, 2000), 379–389, 492–511, and 519–538; Kerber and DeHart, ed., *Women's America*, 294–309; Ellen Carol DuBois and Lynn Dumenil, *Through Women's Eyes: An American History* (Boston: Bedford/St. Martin's, 2009).

73. Schultz, *Going South*, 20, notes "many civil rights scholars have had trouble seeing secular Jews as Jews."

74. Kathie Friedman-Kasaba's *Memories of Migration: Gender, Ethnicity, and Work in the Lives of Jewish and Italian Women in New York, 1870–1924* (Albany: State University of New York Press, 1996) is by a Jewish scholar interested in the experience of these two groups on each side of the Atlantic; as a sociologist, she has interests to a considerable extent secular and theoretical and pays relatively little attention to the religious aspects of immigrant life. Other comparative books are Smith, *Family Connections*, and Kuzmack, *Woman's Cause*.

75. For a review, see Paul Burstein, "Jewish Educational and Economic Success in the United States: A Search for Explanations," paper in possession of author. For an important and perceptive series of essays on the role of Jewish intellectuals in American life, see David A. Hollinger, *Science, Jews, and Secular Culture: Studies in Mid-Twentieth-Century American Intellectual History* (Princeton, NJ: Princeton University Press, 1996). Kevin MacDonald's *The Culture of Critique: An Evolutionary Analysis of Jewish Involvement in Twentieth-Century*

Intellectual and Political Movements (Westport, CT: Praeger, 1998) is useful for its citations to the literature on Jewish achievements, and highly problematic for its arguments.

76. Diner and Benderly, *Her Works Praise Her*, xvi; Gerald Sorin, *The Prophetic Minority: American Jewish Immigrant Radicals, 1880–1920* (Bloomington: Indiana University Press, 1985), ix and 124–141; Charlotte Baum, Paula Hyman, and Sonya Michel, *The Jewish Women in America* (New York: New American Library, 1977), 55–56, 85–86, and 99. Nancy Dye's *As Equals and as Sisters* directly addresses the questions of why so many Jewish women were politically engaged on the left. Not only were they familiar with trade unions, she notes, but, "in traditional Jewish culture, the qualities of assertiveness, toughness, and practicality were valued in a woman. Although formally assigned a subordinate social status," she concludes, "in actuality, women were accustomed not only to having a central economic role, but also to making decisions": Nancy Schrom Dye, *As Equals and As Sisters: Feminism, the Labor Movement, and the Women's Trade Union League of New York* (Columbia: University of Missouri Press, 1980), 65–66; Annelise Orleck, *Common Sense and A Little Fire: Women and Working-Class Politics in the United States, 1900–1965* (Chapel Hill: University of North Carolina Press, 1995), 19–20. One of the richest explorations of these issues, with an emphasis on the openness of Jewish women to modernity and experimentation, is Susan A. Glenn, *Daughters of the Shtetl: Life and Labor in the Immigrant Generation* (Ithaca, NY: Cornell University Press, 1990), especially pp. 1–7. See also, Antler, *Journey Home*, 73–97 and 283. In "Housewives, Socialists, and the Politics of Food: The 1917 New York Cost-of-Living Protests," *Feminist Studies* 11 (Summer 1985): 264, Dana Frank speaks of "a Jewish tradition of women's activism, and consumer activism in particular, transplanted from Europe." Alice Kessler-Harris talks of "a well-developed ethic of social justice" that "played its part in producing perhaps the most politically aware of all immigrant groups"; see Alice Kessler-Harris, "Organizing the Unorganizable: Three Jewish Women and Their Union," *Labor History* 17 (Winter 1976): 8. See Paula Hyman, "Immigrant Women and Consumer Protest: The New York City Kosher Meat Boycott of 1902," *American Jewish History* 70 (September 1980), 91–105, especially 103 where she discusses "the relative freedom of political activity accorded women within the Jewish community." In contrast, Elizabeth Ewen, *Immigrant Women in the Land of Dollars: Life and Culture on the Lower East Side, 1890–1925* (New York: Monthly Review Press, 1985), which focuses on Jewish and Italian women and emphasizes class more than ethnicity and religion, asserts that both groups of women "grew up in patriarchal European societies that narrowly defined the boundaries of female possibility" (15), and does not stress the uniqueness of the Jewish experience. For example, in her chapter "Sweatshops and Picket Lines," Ewen does not raise the question of whether the two groups of working-class women drew on different cultural and political traditions (241–262). Weinberg's *World of Our Mothers*, although it pays remarkably little attention to the political engagement of its subjects, points to three characteristics of Jewish immigrant women: "a reverence for education"; "an acceptance of married women's working to support their families"; and "the strong position of women within the family" (xix).

77. Yuri Slezkine, *The Jewish Century* (Princeton, NJ: Princeton University Press, 2004). Historians of women, such as Kitty Sklar and Ellen DuBois, are now turning their attention to comparative studies. For an earlier example, see Kuzmack, *Woman's Cause*.

Biographies of Contributors

JOYCE ANTLER is the Samuel Lane Professor of American Jewish History and Culture and a professor of Women's and Gender Studies at Brandeis University. The author of many books on women's history, including *The Journey Home: How Jewish Women Shaped Modern America* and *You Never Call! You Never Write! A History of the Jewish Mother*, she is at work on a book about second-wave feminism and Jewish women.

REBECCA BOIM WOLF is a doctoral candidate in the Hebrew and Judaic Studies Department at New York University. Her dissertation, "Selling Hadassah: The Shifting Images, Icons, and Impressions of the Women's Zionist Organization of America," examines the growth of Hadassah within the context of twentieth-century American Jewish history.

GIOVANNA P. DEL NEGRO is an associate professor of English at Texas A&M University and coeditor of the *Journal of American Folklore*. Her current research focuses on issues of gender, whiteness, assimilation, and class in women's stand-up comedy.

HASIA R. DINER, one of the editors of this volume, is the Paul and Sylvia Steinberg Professor of American Jewish History at New York University and the director of the Goldstein-Goren Center for American Jewish History. The author of numerous books, she wrote, with Beryl Lieff Benderly, *Her Works Praise Her: A History of Jewish Women in America from Colonial Times to the Present*.

DANIEL HOROWITZ, Mary Huggins Gamble Professor of American Studies at Smith College, is author of *Betty Friedan and the Making of "The Feminine Mystique": The American Left, the Cold War, Modern Feminism*.

REBECCA KOBRIN is an assistant professor of American Jewish history at Columbia University. Her forthcoming book, *Jewish Bialystok and Its Diaspora: Between Exile and Empire*, was awarded a Cahnman Award from the Association for Jewish Studies. She was recently awarded a Milstein Family Research Fellowship to continue her research.

SHIRA KOHN, one of the editors of this volume, is a doctoral candidate at New York University in the Departments of History and of Hebrew and Judaic Studies. Her dissertation examines Jewish sororities and their encounters with American postwar social and political movements.

RACHEL KRANSON, one of the editors of this volume, is a doctoral candidate in the Departments of History and of Hebrew and Judaic Studies at New York University. Her dissertation focuses on Jewish anxieties over affluence in postwar America.

KATHLEEN A. LAUGHLIN is professor of history at Metropolitan State University in St. Paul, Minnesota. She specializes in women's public activism in postwar America and is the coeditor of the forthcoming anthology *Breaking the Wave: Women, Their Organizations, and Feminism, 1945–1985*.

RAYMOND A. MOHL teaches at the University of Alabama at Birmingham and writes on modern American urban and social history. He is the author most recently of *South of the South: Jewish Activists and the Civil Rights Movement in Miami, 1945–1960*.

AUDREY NASAR is currently a graduate student at the Bernard Revel Graduate School of Jewish Studies at Yeshiva University, studying modern Jewish history. She is also the chair of the Jewish History Department at Magen David Yeshivah High School in Brooklyn, New York.

BARBARA SICHERMAN is Kenan Professor Emerita, Trinity College, Hartford, Connecticut. She is coeditor of *Notable American Women: The Modern Period* and author of *Alice Hamilton: A Life in Letters* and of a book, tentatively titled *Reading and Imagination: American Women, Books, and Identity, 1860–1920*, to be published in 2010.

NANCY SINKOFF is an associate professor of Jewish Studies and History at Rutgers University and the author of *Out of the Shtetl: Making Jews Modern in the Polish Borderlands*. She is at work on a political biography of Lucy S. Dawidowicz.

JUDITH SMITH is a professor of American Studies and the director of the American Studies master's program at University of Massachusetts—Boston, where she teaches courses in women's history, American culture since 1945, and the cultural history of U.S. media and film. She has written on immigration and ethnicity, on urban and family history, and most recently on postwar film, drama, and television in *Visions of Belonging: Family Stories, Popular Culture, and Postwar Democracy, 1940–1960*.

DEBORAH WAXMAN is a doctoral candidate in American Jewish history at Temple University. Her dissertation, "Ethnicity and Faith in American Judaism: Reconstructionism as Ideology and Institution, 1935–1959," focuses on constructions of American Jewish identity in the years around World War II. Waxman graduated as a rabbi from the Reconstructionist Rabbinical College in 1999.

Index

Page numbers in *italics* refer to illustrations.

militarism. *See* cold war
Mississippi Freedom Summer Project, 217
Mizrachi Women of America, 82
Mizrahi, 140–141n6
Moir, Heather C., 24
Moore, Deborah Dash, 40, 72, 238
Moorling, William H., 166–167
Morgan, Robin, 211, 245
mother-daughter relationships, 236
motherhood, 235–236. *See also* domestic
  feminism
Motion Picture Association of America
  (MPAA), 167
MPAA. *See* Motion Picture Association of
  America
Ms. magazine, 227, 234n91, 245
Munaker, Sue, 213
Murray, Sylvie, 54, 245
Muslims, 129
Muste, A. J., 25
Myerson, Bess, 195

NAACP. *See* National Association for the
  Advancement of Colored People
Nadell, Pamela, 104n69, 245
Naditch, Judah, 186–187
"nameless problem," 154
Naomi Says "Yes" (film), 79
Nasser, Gamal Abdel, 130
National Association for the Advancement
  of Colored People (NAACP), 18, 20
National Clearinghouse on Civil Liberties,
  58, 59
National Committee for a Sane Nuclear
  Policy, 18
"The National Committee of the
  Communist Party of the U.S.A. on Work
  among the Jews" (Dawidowicz), 39
National Committee to Secure Justice, 40,
  41
National Community Advisory Relations
  Council, 52
National Conference for New Politics in
  Chicago, 212–213
National Council of Catholic Women, 56,
  58
National Council of Jewish Women
  (NCJW): contribution to communal
  politics, 9–10; founding of, 51;
  implications of suburban growth on,
  54–55; leaders in, 6; local civic projects,
  54, 245; meeting with Kennedy and
  Johnson, 53; membership, 49, 51, 55–56,
  77; organizational reform, 51–52; politics

after World War II, 48–67; resolutions to
  national issues, 56–57; Zoloth's
  engagement in, 22
National Council of Negro Women, 56, 58,
  60
National Federation of Jewish
  Philanthropies, 186
National Federation of Temple
  Sisterhoods, 98
National Jewish Women's Conference,
  226
"The National Jewish Youth Conference
  (NJYC): Example of Communist
  United-Front Policy in Action"
  (Dawidowicz), 39
National Leadership Conference on Civil
  Rights, 60
National Organization of Women (NOW),
  26, 211, 224
National Organization on Civil Liberties
  (NOCL), 58
national security issues, 53, 56–58
National Women's Committee on Civil
  Rights, 60
Nazism, 38
NCJW. *See* National Council of Jewish
  Women
New Deal, 48, 162, 164, 166
The New Leader, 31, 40, 197
New Left, 212, 213–214, 217, 218, 231n24
*New Lives: Survivors of the Holocaust Living
  in America* (Rabinowitz), 121n3
New York Association for New Americans
  (NYANA), 105, 106–125
New York City, New York, 105–125
"New York intellectuals," 5, 31
"The New York Intellectuals: A Chronicle
  and a Critique" (Howe), 31
New York Radical Women, 214, 229, 231n25
New York Times, 164, 169, 172, 177, 185, 187,
  198
Nice Jewish Girls: A Lesbian Anthology (ed.
  Beck), 228
NOCL. *See* National Organization on Civil
  Liberties
North Africa, 239
Not June Cleaver (Meyerowitz), 9
Notes from the First Year (New York Radical
  Women), 214
NOW. *See* National Organization of
  Women
nuclear bomb testing, 5, 14, 23, 25–26, 68
NYANA. *See* New York Association for
  New Americans

Riesman, David, 237
Rifkin, Simon, 169
Robeson, Paul, 164
Robinson, Jackie, 179, 181
Robinson, James, 20
Robson, Mark, 171
Rockefeller, Nelson, 186
rock music, 215
Roe v. Wade, 215
Rominski, Fran, 213
Roosevelt, Eleanor, 179, 189
Roosevelt, Franklin D., 36, 152
Roosevelt, James, 60
Rosen, Marjorie, 161
Rosen, Ruth, 211, 246
Rosenbaum, Judith, 212
Rosenberg, Al, 20
Rosenberg, Ethel, 40, *41,* 42, 166
Rosenberg, Julius, 40, *41,* 42, 166
Rosenfeld, Isaac, 197
Roth, Benita, 211
Roth, Philip, 178
Rothschild Hadassah University Hospital
   (Ein Kerem, Israel), 71
Rothstein, Vivian, 211, 212, 213, 214, 215–219,
   221–222, 224
RSNS. *See* Reconstructionist Synagogue of
   the North Shore
Russia. *See* Soviet Union

SAJ. *See* Society for the Advancement of
   Judaism
Salk, Jonas, 179
Salpeter, Bernice, 81
Salzman, Annabelle. *See* Barth, Belle
Samuel, Maurice, 196
SANE, 22, 23–26, 27
Sarachild, Kathie, 214
SAYG. *See* Sholem Aleichem Gezelshaft
Schappes, Morris, 39
Schildkret, Lucy. *See* Dawidowicz, Lucy S.
school segregation/desegregation:
   connection to second-wave feminism,
   212; efforts by Graff, Zoloth, Stern, 5,
   15–16, 19, 20, 22, 23, 25, 26; efforts by
   Hadassah, 68; efforts by Jewish women,
   13; efforts by National Council of Jewish
   Women, 60; efforts in Miami, 14
Schwartz, Goldie. *See* Abbott, Patsy
SDS. *See* Students for a Democratic Society
Seagrave, Kerry, 145
The Second Stage (Friedan), 236
Second Trip around the World (Williams),
   148, 149

second wave feminism, 9, 92, 99, 210, 211
Sephardim, 127, 140n 6
The Seven Year Itch (film), 171
"Sex Equality in the Synagogue"
   (Eisenstein), 95
Shatzky, Jacob, 33
Sholem Aleichem Folk Institute schools, 31
Sholem Aleichem Gezelshaft (SAYG), 32–33
Shore, Irene, 75–76
Shore, Josselyn, 75
Shulamith Finds Tomorrow (film), 79
Shulman, Alix Kate, 245
Silberstein, Laurence, 243
Simchat Torah, 92, 102n29
Six-Day War, 130, 225
Sklare, Marshall, 69
Slansky, Rudolf, 40, 42
Smith College, 236–237, 239, 240
Smothers Brothers Show (television variety
   show), 154
SNCC. *See* Student Non-Violent
   Coordinating Committee
Snitow, Ann, 212, 215
Sobel, Ross, 188
social issues, Jewish women as activists in,
   4, 5, 22
social mobility, and education, 109, 122n20,
   212
Social Services Employees Union (SSEU),
   38, 117–118
social work agencies, 107, 116–118
Society for the Advancement of Judaism
   (SAJ), 87, 92–100
The Solid Gold Cadillac (film), 171–172
Soller, Fannie, 19
Sommerstein, Emil, 33
Soviet Union, 5, 25, 33–37, 40, 41, 239
Spellman, Francis Joseph, 24, 186
SSEU. *See* Social Services Employees
   Union
Stalin, Joseph, 34, 36–38
Standing Again at Sinai (Plaskow), 244
"The Status of the Jewish Woman"
   (Kaplan), 89, 93
St. Cyr, Lili, 145
Steinem, Gloria, 245
Stern, Philip, 22, 23, 26
Stern, Thalia, 5, 15–16, 20, 21, 22–26, 27
Stettinius, Edward, 50
"Stoop Down to Your Wife" (Mehlman),
   91
Storm Center (film), 59
Student Non-Violent Coordinating
   Committee (SNCC), 212, 217

Breinigsville, PA USA
07 September 2010
244900BV00002B/2/P